The British at War

Cinema and Society Series
General Editor: Jeffrey Richards

Published and forthcoming:

THE BRITISH AT WAR
Cinema, State and Propaganda, 1939–1945

James Chapman

I.B. Tauris Publishers
LONDON · NEW YORK

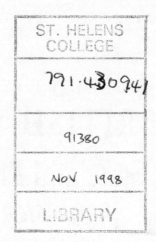
For my parents

Published in 1998 by I.B.Tauris & Co Ltd,
Victoria House, Bloomsbury Square, London WC1B 4DZ
175 Fifth Avenue, New York NY 10010

In the United States of America and in Canada distributed by
St Martin's Press, 175 Fifth Avenue, New York NY 10010

A full CIP record for this book is available from the British Library
A full CIP record for this book is available from the Library of Congress

ISBN 1 86064 158 X

Library of Congress catalog card number: available

Printed and bound in Great Britain by WBC Ltd, Bridgend

Contents

General Editor's Introduction

Few periods of British film history are as encrusted with myth and misconception as the Second World War. The received view of the period has been heavily coloured by the opinions and reminiscences of the participants, often recalled years afterwards in memoirs which sometimes embellished the facts for the sake of a good story and sometimes sought to settle old scores. In this wide-ranging and vigorously argued study, James Chapman dispels the misconceptions and sets the record straight by the judicious use of contemporary sources, particularly government records, the trade press, newspaper reviews, Mass-Observation surveys and, where appropriate, private letters, memoranda and committee minutes. He reassesses with the aid of such materials the film policy of the Ministry of Information, its structures, policies and personnel. He uncovers its policy battles with Michael Balcon of Ealing Studios, its marginalisation of potential rivals such as the British Film Institute, and its recovery from initial criticism and setbacks to become a confident and successful agency of propaganda. He charts the histories of the Crown Film Unit and of the service film units, who between them produced some of the most moving and memorable wartime documentaries. He also analyses the films themselves, both long and short, fictional and factual, to assess how key themes of the war effort were dramatised. Throughout he seeks to establish audience response and always to question received wisdom on such subjects as the success level of documentary shorts. In this multi-layered, sophisticated and thoroughly researched study,

James Chapman shows how a democratic state created a workable and efficient propaganda organisation almost from scratch and one which played its full part in achieving eventual victory.

Jeffrey Richards

List of Illustrations

Acknowledgements

This book started life as a doctoral thesis undertaken in the History Department of Lancaster University. My thanks are due in the first place to Professor Jeffrey Richards, who not only supervised my research but also suggested that the thesis should be turned into a book. As both supervisor and editor, his scholarly rigour and friendly advice have been invaluable.

Numerous friends provided assistance in the form of various re-search materials, including Charles Barr, Alan Burton, Ian Conrich, Michael Coyne and Eugene Finn. Dr Richard Taylor kindly provided me with a useful bibliography of works on propaganda. Professor John MacKenzie read the original thesis with a keen eye for any *non sequiturs*. And I owe a particular debt of gratitude to Dr Tony Aldgate of The Open University, who read both the thesis and the draft manuscript of this book, and who has provided a ready source of knowledge and advice.

Like all historians, I am most grateful for the practical and efficient assistance of numerous librarians and archivists: the ever-helpful staff of the Public Record Office, of the British Newspaper Library, and of the British Film Institute Library, particularly Janet Moat of the Special Collections Unit. The Film and Video Archive of the Imperial War Museum has always been most helpful and courteous in assisting my research, and thanks are due in particular to Kay Gladstone and Paul Sargent. I would also like to acknowledge the help of both the Lancaster University Inter-Library Loans Office and the Open University Library for their tenacity in tracking down books and pamphlets that were usually out-of-print and sometimes quite scarce.

A special note of thanks should be recorded for Philippa Brewster, my editor at I.B.Tauris, for her ever friendly and efficient support during the preparation of the manuscript, and without whose timely intervention the finished book would have been even longer than it stands at present.

The illustrations in this book were provided by the Stills, Posters and Designs Division of the British Film Institute. Grateful acknowledgement is extended to the Rank Organisation, the Weintraub Entertainment Group, and Carlton Television, for reproducing stills from films in which they hold the copyright. Stills from all GPO and Crown Film Unit productions are Crown copyright.

Finally, my thanks to my parents, who endured with stoical good humour their front room being turned into a makeshift study while I worked on this book, and to whom the dedication is a small token of my gratitude.

List of Abbreviations

ABCA	Army Bureau of Csurrent Affairs
ABPC	Associated British Picture Corporation
ACT	Association of Cine-Technicians
AFPU	Army Film and Photographic Unit
AFS	Auxiliary Fire Service
AKS	Army Kinematograph Service
ARP	Air Raid Precaution(s)
ATS	Auxiliary Territorial Service
BBC	British Broadcasting Corporation
BBFC	British Board of Film Censors
BFI	British Film Institute
BFPA	British Film Producers' Association
CEA	Cinematograph Exhibitors' Association
COI	Central Office of Information
DAK	Department of Army Kinematography
EMB	Empire Marketing Board
GBPC	Gaumont-British Picture Corporation
GFD	General Film Distributors
GPO	General Post Office
IWM	Imperial War Museum
KRS	Kinematograph Renters' Society
LDV	Local Defence Volunteers
MGM	Metro-Goldwyn-Mayer
MOI	Ministry of Information
NFS	National Fire Service

PRO	Public Record Office
RAF	Royal Air Force
SHAEF	Supreme Headquarters Allied Expeditionary Force
WAAF	Women's Auxiliary Air Force
WRNS	Women's Royal Naval Service ('Wrens')
WVS	Women's Voluntary Service

Introduction

The cinematograph film is today one of the most widely used meansfor the amusement of the public at large. It is also undoubtedly a most important factor in the education of all classes of the community, in the spread of national culture and in presenting ideas and customs to the world. Its potentialities moreover in shaping the ideas of the very large numbers to whom it appeals are almost unlimited. The propaganda value of the film cannot be over-emphasised. *Report of the Committee on Cinematograph Films* (1936)[1]

The potential of the cinema as a medium of national propaganda was widely recognised before the beginning of the Second World War. In the totalitarian regimes of interwar Europe, the cinema had been adopted by the state as an instrument of political indoctrination and social control. Lenin famously declared that 'Of all the arts, the cinema is for us the most important', while Goebbels regarded the cinema as 'one of the most modern and far-reaching media that there is for influencing the masses'.[2] But it was not only in the Soviet Union and Nazi Germany that the possibilities of film propaganda were recognised; in interwar Britain both the major political parties used film for electioneering, realising that in the age of universal suffrage it was a medium which had mass appeal. 'The Conservative Party are now making use of the cinematograph regularly in propaganda work,' *The Times* observed in 1926. 'Political propaganda seems to be the thin end of the wedge, the other end of which may be national propaganda.'[3] Indeed, on a national level the British government had already shown an interest in the role of film in the presentation of British customs and values to a wide constituency at home and abroad. When the ailing British film production industry was threatened by the economic and cultural hegemony of Hollywood in the 1920s, the Cinematograph Films Act, or Quota Act, was brought in as a protective measure. This was intended to assist film production by establishing a minimum quota of British films which cinema exhibitors would be obliged to show. One of the arguments used in favour of the quota legislation was that a healthy domestic film industry was necessary to ensure that favourable images of Britain were put on the screen. The Moyne Committee, appointed in 1936 to investigate the renewal of the Quota Act, also attached great importance to the cinema's role as a medium of national projection. By this time, the prediction of *The Times* that the next step would be national propaganda had also come true in the form of the official film unit which operated first under the Empire Marketing Board and then under the General Post Office. While the state sponsored the documentary film as a form of national publicity, there were others who argued that documentary had a wider social value. John Grierson, generally regarded as the founding father of the British documentary film movement, saw an important role for the medium in the fields of education and mass communication. 'In a world too complex for the educational methods of public speech and public writing, there is a growing need for more imaginative and widespread media of public address,' he wrote in 1935. 'Cinema has begun to serve propaganda and will increasingly do so.'[4]

Why was film considered such a valuable medium of propaganda? As the most popular and universal form of mass entertainment from the 1920s to the 1950s, the cinema had a profound cultural and ideological significance. If ideology is to be defined in a common-sense way as the ideas or beliefs underlying a social or political organism, then the cinema can be seen to fulfil an ideological role: films can reflect or actively seek to promote a particular ideology. The historian Richard Taylor has written that 'the cinema has been, and indeed still is, the only truly mass medium'.[5] Its value for propaganda arises from the unique nature of the filmic medium which distinguishes it from other mass media (principally the press, radio and television).

The first criterion of successful propaganda is that it has to reach as many people as possible. There is no doubt that in its heyday the cinema reached a vast audience. The first comprehensive survey of cinema-going in Britain, undertaken by the statistician Simon Rowson in 1934, found that 18.5 million people visited the cinema every week (out of a total population of 46 million).[6] Cinema attendances were to continue on an upward trend for over a decade and the weekly attendance had reached up to 30 million by the mid-1940s. In 1943 the Wartime Social Survey found that 70 per cent of the adult population said they sometimes went to the cinema and a third said they went at least once a week.[7] Moreover, it was found that cinema-going was a more ingrained social habit than reading either books or newspapers. The Wartime Social Survey concluded that 'it may be said that the larger groups of the population are relatively better represented in the cinema audience than they are in the publics reached by other visual publicity media such as newspapers and books.'[8] The cinema, therefore, met the first criterion of successful propaganda, that it should be disseminated as widely as possible. It also met the second criterion, that in order to be effective, propaganda should be widely and easily understood. Obviously it was no use reaching an audience of millions if those people could not understand the message. Film was not only a popular medium but it was also a universal medium in which no conscious effort was required to understand the meaning. The primacy of the visual image (even after the advent of sound cinema) means that film transcends boundaries of literacy, language and culture in a way that the print media and radio cannot do. Furthermore, the experience of cinema-going, which is done in a public space and where the individual spectator becomes part of a crowd, is fundamentally different from the reception of the other mass media, which is done in a private, domestic space. The individual spectator in a cinema auditorium is affected not only by what he or she sees on the screen but also by the behaviour and reactions of other members of the audience. This provided what contemporary writers on propaganda from the social sciences referred to as the 'stimulus-response' situation: an environment which it was deemed necessary to create in order to influence people on a subliminal level. The cinema was the only medium where the stimulus-response situation came ready-made. 'For the purposes of propaganda, then, the motion picture is an ideal medium,' wrote the American academic Professor Leonard Doob, because 'the people themselves solve the first problem of the propagandist: they make his stimulus-situation outstanding by their enthusiastic patronage.'[9]

Historians of film and propaganda have tended to concentrate on Soviet Russia and Nazi Germany – 'the two best known and best documented examples of highly politicised societies that the world has ever known'.[10] The reason for this is not just that the totalitarian states are intrinsically interesting in themselves; nor is it just that they produced some of the most famous and outstanding propaganda films ever made, notably Sergei Eisenstein's *Battleship Potemkin* (1925) and Leni Riefenstahl's *Triumph of the Will* (1935). It probably also has something to do with the fact that in these closed political systems, where the supply of information and the expression of opinion was so strictly controlled, propaganda can be seen relatively unproblematically as an expression of the official party ideology. State control of the film industry and the rigorous exercise of censorship meant that audiences in the totalitarian countries could see only those films which met with official approval. In the democratic countries, however, the relationship of propaganda to the state is rather more problematic. This point was made by British academic Professor Frederick Bartlett at the beginning of the Second World War:

> In the modern world, political propaganda may be said to have been adopted as a weapon of State, but very nearly everywhere it has been adopted as the tool of a single political party within the State. This is precisely what cannot happen, except in an incomplete way, in a democracy.[11]

The differences in political culture between the democracies and the totalitarian states meant that propaganda operated in a different way. As Bartlett observed, the democratic state, by its very nature, incorporated different political parties with different points of view. This is not to say, of course, that there was no form of censorship in the democracies. The British Board of Film Censors, for example, operated a quite rigorous moral and political censorship which had considerable influence over the content of British films during the 1930s.[12] Even so, the quasi-autonomous BBFC was far removed from the centralised state censorship apparatuses of Nazi Germany or Soviet Russia. And even though democratic governments could increase their powers drastically during wartime, they did not have (or were reluctant to use) the same powers of coercion exercised by the dictatorships. As Richard Taylor points out, in the democracies 'the use of the cinema has been less well developed, less well systematised, and certainly less well centralised'.[13]

This book is a survey of film propaganda in Britain during the Second World War. British cinema of the Second World War has recently begun to receive more critical and scholarly attention, but it is still the case that the history of film propaganda, and particularly the role of the Ministry of Information's Films Division, has hitherto remained largely unwritten. The most glaring gap is the complete absence of the cinema from the standard history of the MOI, Ian McLaine's otherwise splendid and impeccably-researched *Ministry of Morale* (1979).[14] And there are only fleeting references to film in Michael Balfour's useful comparative study of Britain and Germany, *Propaganda in War* (1979).[15] Social historians have paid some heed to the social role of the cinema and to its importance as a medium of entertainment, though even such a classic and authoritative work as Angus Calder's *The People's War* (1969) is prone to the occasional error when discussing the question of popular and critical tastes.[16] The preference of specialist film historians was initially for the German and Soviet cinemas rather than the British, and although this was partly remedied by the emergence of a new film historiography in the 1980s, which saw an increased interest in British cinema, this work is still incomplete. The rationale of this book, therefore, is to fill a gap in the existing historiography.

There are, generally speaking, three broad schools of critical and historical writing on the British cinema of the Second World War. The first group, who might be termed the old film historians, comprises mainly Roger Manvell, Paul Rotha and Basil Wright.[17] Significantly, all three of these men were involved in official film propaganda during the war: Manvell as a Regional Films Officer for the MOI, Rotha and Wright as documentarists who made films on the ministry's behalf. They all wrote histories of the cinema which, despite containing a large degree of personal narrative, are still valuable for what they reveal about the critical preferences of their generation. They are part of the dominant realist discourse which has long been the orthodoxy for most critical writing about British cinema. They share the assumption that realism (by which they mean films which seem authentic and are true to life) was the most perfect aesthetic form of the filmic medium, and they tend to see the history of the cinema in a Whiggish fashion as the progress towards this ultimate goal. Accordingly, they exhibit a strong preference for the films of the documentary movement and for those feature films made in the documentary style. This position was shared by the film critics of the quality press and by progressive film journals such as *Documentary News Letter*. Contemporary critics identified a 'wartime wedding' of the commercial feature film and the documentary which resulted in celebrated films such as *In Which We Serve, Millions Like Us, Fires Were Started, San Demetrio, London, The Way Ahead* and *The Way to the Stars*.[18] These films, and others like them, exemplified the qualities of which the dominant critical discourse approved: realistic treatment, sober narratives, and characterisations based on stoicism and emotional restraint. So dominant was this documentary-realist discourse that it became the accepted orthodoxy for a whole generation of writers. Its long-term significance was to establish a critical pantheon of classic wartime films which has only recently started to be challenged.[19]

The first revisionist work on British wartime cinema came from a group of academic historians who are best described collectively as the empiricist school. Most of the historians in this group – such as Nicholas Pronay, Jeffrey Richards, Anthony Aldgate, Philip Taylor and Sue Harper – have, in addition to their own books, contributed to the *Historical Journal of Film, Radio and Television*, a highly scholarly publication founded by Kenneth Short in 1981 which was one of the most important developments in the emergence of the new film historiography. The origins of this school date back to the 1970s and the release of official documents relating to wartime propaganda in the Public Record Office under the Thirty-Year Rule. Using these and other primary sources, the empiricists reconstruct the production histories of films and the nature of their reception by both critics and audiences. Their approach, as Philip Taylor observed, is 'contextual rather than purely textual'.[20] The rigorous scholarship of these historians has done much to revise some of the critical prejudices and assumptions of the earlier generation of writers about how successful certain films were. A good example is the case of *Ships With Wings*, Ealing's patriotic 1941 film about the Fleet Air Arm. This was dismissed by Roger Manvell because it 'failed to combine actuality with an elaborately romantic drama' and did not fit the tradition of realism associated with other Ealing war films.[21] However, as Jeffrey Richards showed by looking at the contemporary reviews of the film and at an audience survey by Mass-Observation, *Ships With Wings* was in fact well received by the popular press and was very successful with audiences.[22] Outside the

Historical Journal, the joint work of Richards and Aldgate has provided close case studies of a number of important wartime feature films.[23] Although this approach is perhaps most typical of the school, the work of the empiricists is not confined to a micro-level. For example, Margaret Dickinson and Sarah Street have explored the policies of successive British governments towards the film industry from an economic perspective, drawing extensively on official documentation and trade sources.[24] And Sue Harper has provided an impressive study of the British costume film from the dual perspectives of official attitudes towards the depiction of history (including the much derided work of the British Council as well as the MOI) and the particular appeal of this genre for female audiences.[25]

A very different kind of revisionism was forthcoming in the 1980s from a third group of writers who are film theorists rather than historians. In an important essay in *Screen* in 1977 Steve Neale outlined what he saw as 'the theoretical bases for the specification of propaganda in the cinema'.[26] Although he chose German and Hollywood cinema for his examples, Neale's analytical approach to the modes of textual address in film propaganda has since been applied by other writers to British cinema. Annette Kuhn's analysis of *Desert Victory* in the same journal in 1981, for example, used close textual analysis to discuss how the film constructs and addresses the spectator.[27] Other members of the *Screen* school, such as Christine Gledhill, Andy Medhurst and Andrew Higson, all contributed to a volume entitled *National Fictions: World War Two in British Films and Television* (1984). This collection was 'concerned to demonstrate the extent to which the meanings accruing to a specific "event" or "period" (World War II) are *constructed*, hence subject to contestation, struggle, transformation and change'.[28] Some of the essays engage with the textual analysis of selected films, while others attempt in general terms to construct an ideological basis for wartime cinema through the application of Gramsci's notion of hegemony. For these writers the war presents an ideological paradox – the advance of the left on a popular level at a time when the country was led by one of its most totemic right-wing figures, Winston Churchill – and it is how this paradox is addressed in wartime films which interests them. It is surely no accident that this school of criticism emerged during the 1980s, the decade of Thatcherism. However, the constant parallels which these writers draw between Churchill and Thatcher – both, after all, dominant Tory icons who effectively polarised the politics of their respective periods – does raise some doubt about their understanding of the political and social conditions of the war. Their work also employs conceptual models of semiotics and structuralism and exhibits a Marxist perspective of ideology which is far removed from the contextual approach of the empiricist historians.[29]

While these three schools account for the majority of scholarship on the British cinema of the war, there are some writers who cannot be labelled so conveniently. Foremost among these is Charles Barr, whose background was in film criticism and education but who also has a strong affinity with the film historians. His definitive book on *Ealing Studios* (1977) was one of the most important contributions to British film historiography. In a perceptive analysis of Ealing's wartime films, Barr identifies a 'broad congruency' between the history of Ealing and social and political developments in the country as a whole, interpreting films like *San Demetrio, London* as reflecting a national consensus.[30] The mid-war years were the crucial period in the development of a distinctive studio style at Ealing, brought about by several factors, including the influx of documentary personnel to the studio (such as Alberto Cavalcanti and Harry Watt), the forming of a 'team' of directors responsible for most of the studio's output (Charles Frend, Basil Dearden, Charles Crichton and Robert Hamer), and studio head Michael Balcon's own interest in the creation of a truly 'British' national cinema which dramatised the common experiences of ordinary people.[31]

This book seeks to locate British films of the war in the context of official propaganda policy. It adopts for British cinema the approach which has been applied to the propaganda films of Nazi Germany by David Welch and to Hollywood cinema of the war years by Clayton R. Koppes and Gregory D. Black.[32] It is divided into two sections. Part I, 'Organisations and Policies', looks at the institutional organisation of the film propaganda machinery and the development of official policy for film propaganda. It explores the role of the MOI Films Division and discusses the relations between the MOI and the different sectors of the film industry, particularly the commercial feature film producers and the makers of short films and documentaries. The MOI had to deal with two very different modes of film practice and find a place for them both within the official scheme of things. There is also an examination of the work of the government film units during the war, the GPO/Crown Film Unit, which became the MOI's official production agency, and the film units of the services, particularly the Army and Royal Air Force. Part II, 'Subjects and Themes', looks at the content of British propaganda films, both features and shorts, by delineating the main thematic categories. The dramatisation of the British people at war, the representation of the services, the role of women, the images of Britain's allies and enemies, and the frequent invocation of historical parallels, are all discussed with close reference to specific examples. As far as possible, the interpretations and conclusions offered are based on the evidence of primary source materials. Foremost among these is the Public Record Office, an invaluable source for any modern historian concerned with aspects of government policy. The records of the MOI, the Prime Minister, the War Office, the Foreign Office and the Board of Trade all yielded useful information. Official documentation alone, however, rarely tells the whole story, so it has been supplemented where possible by other sources, such as the papers of film-makers deposited with the British Film Institute and the minutes of the British Film Producers' Association. Contemporary journalism – including the national and trade press as well as specialist publications such as *Documentary News Letter* and *Sight and Sound* – reveals much about attitudes towards film propaganda in general as well as opinions of specific films. And the film research of Mass-Observation, the independent social survey organisation founded in 1937, has also been used. Although Mass-Observation's research methods were crude and its sampling techniques small compared with today's rather more sophisticated public opinion research, its work is nevertheless valuable as the only real indication of how audiences responded to certain films. At least it strove to be empirical and objective, even if it did not always manage to be so.[33] From the evidence of these sources (supplemented, where appropriate, by the memoirs of key players in the film industry), it is clear that film propaganda in wartime Britain was not simply the expression of an official ideology or point of view, but rather that it involved a range of different ideologies, discourses and institutions which all had some influence on the cinematic representation of the British at war.

Part I

Organisations and Policies

1

The MOI Films Division

The Ministry of Information was a great success, and its Films Division was one of its triumphs. *Michael Powell*[1]

I

Michael Powell's verdict on the MOI and its Films Division is sufficiently different from the views expressed by most other commentators that it makes a provocative starting point for a survey of British film propaganda during the Second World War. The MOI has been the subject of so much criticism and, often, outright ridicule, that it is refreshing to find a figure like Powell, who had many dealings with it during the war, expressing such a favourable opinion about it. Neither contemporaries nor historians have usually lavished such extravagant praise upon an institution which was dubbed 'the Ministry of Dis-Information' and 'the Ministry of Muddle' shortly after it came into being and which struggled thereafter under the widespread impression of blundering bureaucracy and amateurish incompetence. To quote Ian McLaine: 'It is ironic, and not a little poignant, that the body charged with sustaining public morale and with maintaining confidence in the government should itself have suffered from chronically low morale and been the object of general ridicule.'[2] During its troubled early days in particular, the MOI became a favourite target for wartime satirists. In his novel *Put Out More Flags* (1942), for example, Evelyn Waugh portrayed the ministry as being full of inept intellectuals who joined 'the great press of talent in search of occupation' which flocked there after the outbreak of war.[3] One of the 'gentleman amateurs' recruited to the MOI was Sir Kenneth Clark, the Director of the National Gallery. In his memoirs, Clark was eloquently dismissive of the whole institution:

> For anyone with my background there was an obvious source of employment, the so-called Ministry of Information. This notorious institution had been put together rather hastily when the threat of war could no longer be ignored, and housed in an enormous modern building, fortunately very solid, the Senate House of London University. It was said to contain 999 employees ... Most of the 999 consisted of an uneasy mixture of so-called intellectuals, ex-journalists and advertising men, ex-politicians and discarded *éminences grises*. In this undirected orchestra it was necessary for each man to blow his own trumpet as loudly as he could.[4]

Clark was not the only contemporary to pour scorn on the MOI. Duff Cooper, the third Minister of Information, was a reluctant incumbent in the ministerial chair who did not have a happy time there. 'A monster had been created,' he later wrote, 'so large, so voluminous, so amorphous, that no single man could cope with it.'[5] It was not only in retrospect that the MOI was ridiculed for its bureaucracy and incompetence, for many commentators remarked upon its inefficiency at the time. Lord Halifax, the Foreign Secretary under Neville Chamberlain, described it as 'a body without a head and not very effective limbs either'.[6] The total of 999 employees who worked at the ministry in its first days was purely accidental, but it provided satirists and the press with a figure with which to ridicule the unhappy institution.[7] The journalist Norman Riley, who had first-hand experience of the MOI, published a damning critique entitled *999 And All That* (1940) in which he described the ministry's early history as 'more fantastic than anything Lewis Carroll could have devised for an Alice in Blunderland'.[8] Although the MOI was to function quite efficiently later in the war, and employed far more personnel than the notorious 999, it never completely shook off the negative impression that it had made at the beginning and was stuck thereafter with a reputation for blundering and incompetence.

The general impression of the MOI's Films Division reflects in microcosm the opinions expressed of the ministry as a whole. It was criticised at the time for its lack of direction, for its persistent failure to provide any policy guidelines for the film industry, and for its tendency to obstruct rather than to assist film production. 'A film tended too often to become a file and not a film,' the documentarist Paul Rotha was later to observe.[9] Among the intellectuals who were recruited to the MOI was the poet John Betjeman, who for a while found himself improbably employed as a script-reader for the Films Division. In an unpublished poem, he painted an amusing picture of the division as a den of jovial amateurism and incompetence:

> Take down this letter, dear Miss Broom,
> And send it – to you know whom;
> Say that we've got a peculiar feeling
> There was an idea received from Ealing
> Last month – or was it the month before –
> We've lost it – but couldn't he send some more.
> Say that we're glad to have anything new, Sir
> Make it amusing – write dear Producer.
> There's the letter, now go and compile it
> Get a reply and forget to file it.[10]

Betjeman's whimsical picture of life at the Films Division may sound somewhat far-fetched, but it was no more absurd than an item from the *Evening News* in December 1940 which declared: 'The chief officers of the Films Division spend much of their time in conference discussing the shortcomings of their own films – Gilbertian though such a fact may seem.'[11] Therefore, there is a significant discrepancy between Michael Powell's praise for the Films Division and the views of most other commentators. Was it a 'triumph', as Powell suggests, or were the charges of inefficiency and incompetence justified? The aim of this chapter is to address that question by exploring the institutional history of the Films Division. It will discuss the role and organisation of the division, the nature of the criticisms which were levelled against it, and how the division responded to them.

II

The troubles which beset the MOI at the beginning of the war were due in part to the inadequate nature of its planning and preparation. The origins of the MOI date back to October 1935 when a sub-committee of the Committee of Imperial Defence had been set up to prepare general guidelines for the establishment of an official news and propaganda organisation in the event of war. In July 1936 the committee reported to the Cabinet and recommended that a Ministry of Information should be set up to 'present the national case to the public at home and abroad in time of war'.[12] The Home Office was made responsible for overseeing the planning, while Sir Stephen Tallents, a senior civil servant who had valuable experience of publicity work at the Empire Marketing Board, the General Post Office and the British Broadcasting Corporation, was made Director-General Designate and put in charge of the detailed preparation. It was decided that the MOI should combine five broad functions: the release of official news; the security censorship of the media, including the press, films and radio; responsibility for morale; publicity campaigns for other government departments; and the dissemination of propaganda abroad to enemy, allied and neutral countries. It was therefore assumed that the MOI should be responsible for all official information and propaganda. This was one of the lessons learned from the First World War, when a centralised Ministry of Information had been set up only belatedly in March 1918, under the press baron Lord Beaverbrook, to co-ordinate the various propaganda activities that were being carried out separately by several different departments. The body responsible for official film propaganda for most of the First World War was the Cinema Propaganda Department, which had been set up under Sir William Jury, a leading trade figure, and its policy had been not to produce films itself but rather to commission them from the established commercial producers and to release them through the existing exhibition channels.[13] It was simply taken for granted that the planned Film Publicity Division would work on the same principle as its predecessor.

In fact, very little attention was given to the organisation of the film propaganda machinery, as the planners were preoccupied with other matters which pushed film propaganda down their list of priorities. In particular, they devoted much of their time to the question of film censorship rather than propaganda. It was realised that film (like other media) would have to be subject to security censorship during a war, particularly the newsreels which would be reporting military developments. Lengthy and detailed deliberations finally arrived at the conclusion that the existing censorship apparatus, the British Board of Film Censors, should be used as the means of security censorship. The MOI's Censorship Division was to appoint extra officials to the BBFC to supervise the security censorship of films.[14] However, the amount of time devoted to working out the precise arrangements meant that the question of using film for propaganda purposes was largely overlooked. Another factor which militated against much consideration being given to films was that it had been decided by the Home Office that cinemas (along with other places of public entertainment) would be closed immediately upon the outbreak of war until the dangers posed by air raids could be gauged. The fear that the outbreak of hostilities would be marked by massive air raids against large centres of population had become uppermost in the minds of both strategists and politicians during the 1930s. As Stanley Baldwin had observed in 1932, it was widely believed that 'the bomber will always get through'.[15] Cinemas were seen as potential death-traps where a direct hit might cause untold carnage. This possibility had in fact been vividly illustrated in Alexander Korda's film *Things to Come* (1936), based on the book by H. G. Wells, which had prophesied the outbreak of a European war in 1940 and had included a chillingly effective sequence in which the British city of 'Everytown' is reduced to rubble by aerial bombardment: in one shot a cinema receives a direct hit.[16] The destructive power of the bomber had also been revealed by the newsreels during the Spanish Civil War: Anthony Aldgate has shown how incidents such as the bombing of Guernica in 1937 'forcefully conveyed the full implications of aerial bombing to a British audience'.[17] The planned closure of cinemas was therefore a sensible precautionary move by the government which feared massive civilian casualties. But if the cinemas were closed, even only temporarily, there would be no outlet for propaganda films immediately after the outbreak of war.

The first time that the plans for the shadow MOI were put to the test was during the Munich Crisis of September 1938, which in Nicholas Pronay's words revealed 'a state of dreadful unpreparedness'.[18] Tallents was made the scapegoat and was removed from the planning of the MOI, responsibility for which passed to the Home Secretary, Sir Samuel Hoare. The preparation for propaganda films was, by all accounts, piecemeal. Norman Riley intimated that in July 1939 representatives of other government departments had been asked for their ideas and 'were invited to note that the Ministry of Information had planned three films – three whole films which, with their co-operation, could be made quickly in an emergency. This was going to be our reply to

Goebbels!'[19] It was only very shortly before the war that Sir Joseph Ball was 'invited by Sir Samuel Hoare to become Director of the Films Division of the Ministry of Information should war break out'.[20] When war came, the shadow MOI was only half ready. A. J. P. Taylor eloquently described the British government at the outbreak of war thus: 'The war machine resembled an expensive motor car, beautifully polished, complete in every detail, except there was no petrol in the tank.'[21] The simile would apply very well to the MOI itself.

The half-hearted preparations made before the outbreak of war are one of the reasons why the MOI got off to the poor start that it did in 1939. The ministry's early days were to be marred by a catalogue of errors and misjudgements which meant that it was soon riding a storm of both press and parliamentary criticism. While it might only be expected that any new ministry was bound to experience some teething troubles, in the case of the MOI it was all the more serious because its mistakes were made in the public domain. But just what was wrong with the MOI? In the first place, the appointment of a minister who sat in the House of Lords and who was thus unable to answer criticisms made of his department in the House of Commons was not an auspicious start. Lord Macmillan, a Tory peer and a distinguished judge, was completely ineffectual. The only apparent explanation for his appointment is that no one else was available; Sir John Reith, who had been considered a likely candidate for the job during the planning stages, was unavailable at the outbreak of war.[22] But the initial failure of the MOI was due to more than just the inadequacy of its first minister. Its initial attempts at propaganda misfired badly. While the MOI itself cannot be blamed for the government's refusal to make a declaration of war aims, its attempts to mobilise popular support for the war effort were ill-conceived to say the least. The most notorious example was the MOI's first poster, an appeal for National Savings which declared: '*Your* Courage, *Your* Cheerfulness, *Your* Resolution, Will Bring *Us* Victory'. This slogan was widely criticised, and in hindsight it could almost have been calculated to sow the seeds of discontent in that it seemed to imply the efforts of the people would be made for the benefit of the ruling elite.

The MOI was found wanting not only in the field of propaganda for the home front, but also in the supply of news and information to the media. The system for the release of news broke down because there had been no co-ordination between the planning of the MOI and the regulations enforced by the service departments; the MOI was then blamed for the lack of official news. This was to be a major source of frustration for the news media, including the newsreel film companies who at first were prohibited from filming any military subjects. As the Director of the Films Division told the minister in October 1939:

> It is quite true that, for a month after the outbreak of war, it was impossible for Newsreel Companies to photograph any news items dealing with military activity, but this was due entirely to the rigid nature of the Defence Notices and to the Control of Photography Order dated the 10th September issued by the Secretary of State for War.
>
> The Films Division of the Ministry has made strong and repeated protests on this point, but has not yet succeeded in obtaining what is required, viz., drastic modification of the Defence Notices and of the Order.[23]

The mishandling of news and information was such that the MOI quickly alienated both press and public. An unofficial report by Mass-Observation in October 1939 remarked that 'the source of all Government publicity, the Ministry of Information, is almost universally discredited in the eyes of the masses', and painted a damning picture of the lack of co-ordination between the ministry, the services and the press. 'The position of under-information and lack of a steady instructional flow in which the masses place confidence', it concluded, 'is therefore exceedingly serious.'[24] That this situation should have arisen so quickly after the outbreak of war is testimony to the inadequate planning of the MOI. So inept did the ministry prove to be that some of its original functions were removed. A separate Press and Censorship Bureau was set up temporarily to oversee the release of official news, while responsibility for propaganda to enemy countries was transferred to the Foreign Office for the rest of the war. Meanwhile, a political storm was brewing around the MOI which focused in particular on the Films Division and the choice of its first director.

III

The trials and tribulations of the Films Division during its first few months illustrate in microcosm the problems which beset the ministry as a whole. Just as the MOI was to lose its first minister by the New

Year, so the Films Division was to lose its first director. To what extent were the problems of the Films Division due to the appointment of Sir Joseph Ball? Nicholas Pronay has described Ball as an 'unfortunate choice' and 'supremely tactless'.[25] On another occasion, however, the same historian referred to Ball as 'the carefully and intelligently chosen Head of the Films Division [who] came to be one of the sacrificial victims when, for no fault of his own or even his staff, the initial film coverage of the war proved to have left much to be desired'.[26] The truth perhaps lies somewhere between these two views. In Ball's defence, it can at least be said that he was not one of the dilettantes to be found elsewhere in the MOI, but a hard-nosed professional who had experience of film propaganda work from before the war. As the Director of the Conservative Party Research Department and Deputy Director of the National Publicity Bureau, Ball was largely responsible for the Conservative Party's successful use of film during the 1935 general election. T. J. Hollins has shown how the Conservatives used a fleet of mobile projector vans and some well-made films to present a modern image of the party to the electorate. He suggests that the Conservative and Unionist Film Association was 'one of the most effective disseminators of political views then available'.[27] However, Ball was so closely associated with the Conservative Party that suspicions about his political affiliation inevitably arose on the left. This was exacerbated by Ball's well-known antipathy towards the documentary movement, the progressive left-wing sector of the British film industry. Some of their work, notably Paul Rotha's *Peace Film* (1936) which had criticised the rearmament programme, exhibited an overtly political dimension. Edgar Anstey was in no doubt that the documentarists were excluded from the MOI for this reason. 'The documentary people, all of us, were left in the wilderness,' he said. 'We weren't used because the Chamberlain government was very much opposed to everything we stood for, and they had their own film people, who moved into the Ministry of Information and were powerful in other quarters.'[28] Ball was not the only member of the Films Division to have some connection with the Conservative Party: D. K. Clarke had been General Secretary of the Conservative Research Department and Oliver Bell, on loan from the British Film Institute, had once been a press officer at Conservative Central Office.[29]

If Ball was a suspect choice in the opinion of the left, however, his appointment was welcomed warmly by the commercial trade interests.

The columnist 'Tatler' of the *Daily Film Renter* remarked that Ball's appointment 'has given great satisfaction to the trade' because they found him to be 'a Government official who definitely knows what he is talking about – is entirely willing to co-operate with the industry – and, more important still, is definitely out to do so with a minimum of fuss'.[30] Ball had met the 'leaders' of the British film industry – by which he meant the commercial feature film producers and the newsreel companies – at a luncheon shortly before the outbreak of war, where they had 'expressed unanimously their warm approval of the proposed appointment and promised me their full support'.[31] The meeting resulted in the setting up of a Trade Advisory Committee which Ball met once more after the outbreak of war 'for the purpose of helping them formulate and present their case for the re-opening of the kinemas'.[32] Ball's close relations with commercial producers and newsreel companies were in line with the token plans made for film propaganda whereby it was envisaged that the Films Division would work through co-operation with the trade rather than producing films itself. Ball himself believed that working with commercial producers was the best policy, because then 'we shall be reaching ready-made world-wide audiences with films produced by the trade for commercial purposes ... and which will, therefore, not be suspected of being propaganda films at all'.[33]

What did the Films Division actually achieve under Ball? Paul Rotha described Ball's tenure as 'a four-month period distinguished by inertia'.[34] The feeling of the documentary movement that they had been excluded from the MOI was reflected in the post-war Arts Enquiry Survey, written by, among others, Rotha and Basil Wright, and published as *The Factual Film* (1947). This report suggested that at first the activities of the Films Division 'were largely without purpose and effect. It relied mainly on the newsreel companies and on the initiative of the film industry in general to do its work, but gave no adequate lead.'[35] It was not only the documentarists who were unhappy; the Films Division was soon drawing criticism from the trade press for its failure to provide any guidelines for commercial producers. The one propaganda feature film to have been made, Alexander Korda's *The Lion Has Wings* (1939), was made at the producer's own initiative. When Lord Macmillan said that 'the Ministry of Information is fully alive to the value of film as a medium of propaganda', the columnist 'Onlooker' of *Today's Cinema* retorted in his characteristic clipped style:

> Lord Macmillan had plenty to say about films in course of debate
> on Ministry of Information, but can't say I'm impressed with
> amount of work done so far by the Ministry to utilise a medium
> which he considers 'very, very important'. So far net result to date
> seems to be, one feature made, and British production industry
> reduced to desperate straits.
>
> One cannot expect the Government to think of everything, but
> in laying plans for the Ministry of Information in anticipation of
> hostilities, one would have expected some scheme would have been
> worked out to use British studios and the world's cinemas im-
> mediately. Position, after nearly two months of war, is not good
> enough.[36]

The criticism was directed at the failure of the government to prepare
the MOI adequately, not at Ball personally, but it was hardly a good
omen that the section of the industry with whom Ball most wanted
to work was already feeling disaffected.

There were some mitigating circumstances for the Films Division's
lacklustre start. Contrary to the opinions of some commentators, Ball
was not inactive during his time in office. The problem, however, was
that his time was spent mostly on administration rather than on
formulating policy. 'There is no doubt that he is badly in need of extra
help,' said the MOI's Deputy Director-General A. P. Waterfield. 'At
present his work is much in arrears, and he does not find it possible
to comply with all the requests that the Publicity-user Divisions are
making to him for the preparation of films for publicity purposes.'[37] In
particular, he spent much time working out the staff structure of his
department. The organisation of the Films Division under Ball assumed
a division of labour based on expert knowledge. He created posts for
two specialists: Sir Edward Villiers, a former Korda employee, was
appointed to deal with commercial producers, while A. G. Highet, a
civil servant from the General Post Office, was appointed to deal with
shorts and documentaries. Another experienced Post Office publicist,
G. E. G. Forbes, became Deputy Director of the Films Division, while
the trade interest was also represented by Colonel A. C. Bromhead, a
veteran exhibitor who had been a member of the Cinema Propaganda
Department during the First World War, who was made honorary
adviser to the Films Division. Ball's scheme also envisaged a role for
the Government Cinematograph Adviser. This post, presently occupied

by one J. G. Hughes-Roberts, had been created at the end of the First World War to supervise the preservation of actuality footage acquired by the government. The recruitment of Alderman Joseph Reeves, formerly Secretary of the Workers' Film Association, the film education body set up jointly by the Labour Party and the Trades Union Congress, went some way towards countering the Tory dominance within the Films Division. His role was to oversee 'the selection and distribution of instructional and educational films by non-theatrical means, largely to self-educating societies of the working classes'.[38] It was also under Ball that a process began whereby the British Film Institute was gradually excluded from the official film propaganda machinery. Oliver Bell, the Director of the BFI, had joined the Films Division to liaise with film societies and the like, but he did not fit in and was soon to return to the BFI. Ball said:

> I have some *prima facie* reason to believe that the Film Institute would welcome Mr Bell's resumption of his normal duty and that Mr Bell also would prefer this. Much as I appreciate the work which he has done in the period just ended, I have come to the conclusion that with his special experience he will be able to render better service to the national interest at the Film Institute than in this Division.[39]

The implication seems to be that Oliver Bell had been something of a nuisance; Sir Kenneth Clark was later to say so in no uncertain terms.

The fact that Ball had to devote so much time to organising the Films Division was a legacy of the inadequate pre-war planning of the film propaganda machinery. However, the failure to formulate any specific policies meant that the division was perceived as having achieved nothing during its first months. It even came under fire from within the government, and by November 1939 there was a move afoot to demote its place in the MOI's divisional hierarchy. 'The Films Section of the Ministry of Information has now been in existence for over two months, and so far as can be seen astonishingly little has been achieved,' said a memorandum by Charles Peake, the Head of the News Department of the Foreign Office.[40] He placed particular emphasis on film propaganda abroad, suggesting that some countries would be more receptive to British films than others, and recommending that the MOI's

Foreign Publicity Division should 'survey the entire world from this point of view and then tell the Films Division the order of importance of the various countries'. He therefore envisaged the Films Division working as an adjunct to the Foreign Publicity Division:

> If the view stated above is correct then it follows that the Film Section should work as the 'servant' of the Foreign Publicity Division *so far as policy is concerned*, and its chief function should be, by virtue of the specialised knowledge which it should possess and of its contacts with the film industry, to put into effect the policy laid down by the Foreign Office, [and] the Colonial and Dominions Offices.

There was almost certainly some inter-departmental rivalry behind Peake's memorandum in that the Foreign Office was also involved in publicity work abroad and wanted to guard its own sphere of influence against the upstart new ministry. In the event, however, the proposals were not acted upon. Indeed, they would have been impractical in so far as they ignored the Films Division's work in domestic film propaganda. While it is true that much importance was attached to presenting a favourable image of Britain abroad, home propaganda was a matter of equal if not greater concern.

IV

Given the amount of flak that the Films Division had drawn, it was inevitable that there would be a change at the top. In the event, Sir Joseph Ball resigned in December 1939. He was replaced by Sir Kenneth Clark, a young, urbane, cultured aesthete who had built up a good reputation in artistic circles through his role as Director of the National Gallery and Surveyor of the King's Pictures. 'It was an inexplicable choice,' Clark later admitted, 'and was commonly attributed to the fact that in those days films were spoken of as "pictures", and I was believed to be an authority on pictures.'[41] Whereas Ball had been an expert publicist with first-hand knowledge of the film trade, Clark was a talented amateur with no knowledge of films but much personal charm and enthusiasm. Pronay has suggested that Clark's appointment, far from being inexplicable, was due to a 'belated recognition of the importance of good relations with the *literati*'.[42] Ball had been *persona non grata* with the intelligentsia because of his preference for the commercial cinema, tainted in their eyes by vulgar populism, whereas Clark had a favourable reputation with the intellectual community (from whose ranks the art and film critics of the quality press were drawn). Clark's appointment was certainly welcomed by the documentary movement, who had much in common with the *literati* in their dislike of the low-brow, commercial nature of popular cinema. The journal *Documentary News Letter* was the successor to *Cinema Quarterly* and *World Film News* as the voice of the independent documentary movement. Its first issue in January 1940 declared:

> Sir Kenneth Clark's appointment as film chief at the Ministry of Information, in the place of Sir Joseph Ball (who has resigned), will be welcomed by everyone except the less imaginative of Wardour Street ... There is every hope that he will take immediate steps to end the inertia which has till now more or less im- mobilised the personnel of (among other branches of cinema) documentary ... What is needed from the Ministry is approval, goodwill, cooperation and initiative – especially initiative. Sir Kenneth is likely to supply them.[43]

Documentary News Letter was right in that Clark's appointment did not meet with the approval of 'the less imaginative of Wardour Street'. The trade journalists were critical because Clark had no knowledge of the film industry. When Clark left the Films Division three months later, 'Tatler' of the *Daily Film Renter* was happy to see him go:

> I'm certainly not going to weep any salt tears over Sir Kenneth's going. I'll pay tribute to him as a well-meaning, courteous, and earnest young man who, I should say, has an excellent drawing- room manner, but who, as far as I could discern, had no especial flair for the job to which he was appointed. If he had I'm afraid I never noticed it.[44]

'Tatler' concluded that Clark 'has definitely not imbued Wardour Street with any enthusiasm' and that 'he has definitely made a lamentable number of blunders in his handling of members of the trade'. The reaction to Clark among the different groups of the film industry was therefore the opposite of that accorded Sir Joseph Ball: the docu- mentarists were happy with his appointment whereas the trade interests were not.

What did Clark accomplish during his brief tenure of office? The first point that should be made is that his time there coincided with a considerable upheaval: the reorganisation of the MOI due to the arrival of a new minister. Lord Macmillan was asked by Chamberlain to resign 'with a view to facilitating other rearrangements in the Government and to remove the embarrassment which has been experienced owing to the fact that you have not yourself been able to speak for your office in the House of Commons'.[45] He was replaced by Sir John Reith, the former Director-General of the BBC. 'Sir John Reith is a man whose services should emphatically not be wasted in times like these,' declared *The Times*. 'He is a proved organiser, something of an autocrat (both of them qualities essential at his new post) and steeped in the business of disseminating information.'[46] Reith immediately set about the task of reorganising and streamlining the structure of the MOI. It is against this background of institutional upheaval that Clark's time at the Films Division should therefore be judged.

Clark was responsible for two very significant developments while in charge of the Films Division. The first of these was to take a major step towards the definition of official policy for film propaganda. On 29 January 1940 he presented a paper entitled 'Programme for Film Propaganda' to the Co-Ordinating Committee of the MOI. This document, which began by stating that it 'assumes the importance of films as a medium of propaganda', marked the first attempt to formulate specific ideas for the use of films by the MOI.[47] The themes outlined by Clark – 'What Britain is fighting for', 'How Britain fights' and 'The need for sacrifice if the fight is to be won' – were based on a Policy Committee paper written in December 1939 by Lord Macmillan.[48] This suggests that Clark recognised the need to co-ordinate the specific work of the Films Division within the broader work of the MOI as a whole. The Programme envisaged a role for all three main types of film – feature films, newsreels and documentaries – and suggested how each was best suited to putting British propaganda on the screen.

The other development for which Clark was responsible was the effective marginalisation of the British Film Institute for the rest of the war. In this he was continuing a process begun by his predecessor, but it was due mainly to Clark that the BFI came to be excluded completely from the official film propaganda machinery. Early in 1940 the BFI made approaches to the MOI and other government departments, in effect putting itself forward as an important authority which should (in its own estimation) be consulted on all matters relating to film and its use in the war effort. For example, Oliver Bell wrote to the President of the Board of Trade:

> The Governors of the British Film Institute have given long and anxious consideration to the effect of the war upon the British Film Industry, and in particular to the assistance that the industry may be able to afford to the National interest. They have already indicated that the Institute is prepared to place its full services at the disposal of the Government in an advisory capacity, and feel that, as an independent body in touch with both public and trade interests, their experience and connections should not be without value.[49]

The BFI, which was funded partly by public money, had been set up in 1933 to 'encourage the use and development of the cinematograph as a means of entertainment and education'.[50] It was, however, widely regarded as a conservative, sectional body whose Board of Governors was controlled by trade interests. Its offer of service was given short shrift by the Films Division, which obviously wanted to keep the BFI at arm's length. Sir Edward Villiers suggested that they should keep 'in touch' with the BFI but that 'the "in touch" should be a very tentative one from which we can always break away'.[51] Sir William Brass, the Chairman of the Institute and a Conservative MP, presented Clark with a set of notes outlining the services which the BFI might render to the MOI. These included advising on the propaganda value of scripts submitted by producers, collecting press clippings and supervising the non-theatrical distribution scheme; moreover, the BFI expected to be paid for these services.[52] Clark replied that there was 'a fundamental difficulty in that all the services which you propose are those which the Films Division is bound to have organised within itself'.[53] Clearly, he did not envisage any role for the BFI within official film propaganda policy. In private he scorned the BFI's unsolicited offer and declared that 'the Film Institute is incompetent and Mr Oliver Bell a muddle-headed busybody'.[54] Bell continued to lobby on behalf of the BFI throughout the war, but he was ignored by the MOI and the Institute became increasingly marginalised.

However, both these developments – the Programme for Film Propaganda and the exclusion of the BFI – were internal matters which had no effect on the perception of the Films Division by either the trade or the public at large. From the outside, the division would be judged by results – the number and quality of films produced – and here it was found wanting. Pronay writes: 'Two-thirds of all films produced by the Ministry of Information during the first six months of the war were either withdrawn immediately or never released; those which were shown ran the gauntlet of pungent and increasingly hostile criticism in the press, and produced constant complaints in and out of Parliament.'[55] The main problem was that the Films Division was not equipped to produce its own films; it was not until April 1940 that the GPO Film Unit was formally taken over by the MOI as an official production agency. The films made during this period had to be commissioned from outside producers, which meant that the MOI exercised less effective control over their form and content. It was yet another occasion when the British found that the system which had worked for them during the First World War (to use the existing trade channels for film propaganda) was unsuitable for the Second World War.

In the event, Clark was not destined to last much longer at the Films Division than his predecessor had done. A further administrative reorganisation when the MOI reacquired the Press and Censorship Bureau in April 1940 brought Clark promotion to a more senior position as the Controller of Home Publicity. 'My new post, although it gave me more prestige, was shapeless and indeterminate,' he recalled. 'Various departments, including the Films Division, were nominally "under" me, but, except on points of principle, their directors had to run them in their own way.'[56] His departure from the Films Division was welcomed not only by the trade press but also by William Connor, alias the columnist 'Cassandra' of the *Daily Mirror*, who made a scorching attack on Clark and the whole ethos which he personified:

Three months ago the Assyrian rug experts who control the Ministry of Information decided to improve their film section.

Dropping their weaving for a moment, they started a search for somebody who knew nothing about films and had not the taint of Wardour-street, Denham, Elstree or the show business.

Having searched through the directories (or so the story goes) and found no interesting entries under 'films', they had a bright idea and looked up 'pictures'.

It was there that they stumbled upon Sir Kenneth Clark, the director of the National Gallery.

Sir Kenneth was young, rich, and knew the best people.

The fact that he knew nothing at all about films was probably glossed over, and he got the job.

His only qualification that I can find was 'that he was a keen cinemagoer and a star fan'.

In spite of this professional ignorance he had the suave impertinence to take the job.

Armed with his knowledge of the Gothic Revival, the Drawings of Leonardo da Vinci, the Paintings of English Landscape and the Last Lectures of Roger Fry, this Keeper of Fine Art Museums blandly assumed control of what can be – but isn't – one of the most powerful weapons of propaganda.[57]

Clark's work at the Films Division was dismissed as 'the dilettante dabblings of this brash amateur' and it was urged that 'this expert picture-hanger should stick to his frames'. It was an attack as much upon the ethos of the Chamberlain government as a whole as upon Clark personally, and as such it was an example of the *Daily Mirror*'s political agenda in attacking the way in which the country was being governed during the 'phoney war'. To the *Mirror*, Clark's appointment typified everything that was wrong with the British war effort: the faith in well-connected 'gentleman amateurs' at the expense of genuine experts, and the apparent failure to realise that the country was engaged in a fight for survival. It was a damning verdict indeed on Clark's time at the Films Division.

V

The third Director of the Films Division was Jack Beddington – 'one of the most unjustly forgotten men of the war', according to Michael Powell.[58] Beddington had experience of industrial public relations work in that he had previously been Director of Publicity for the Shell Group; and, significantly, he was acquainted with the documentary movement through the work of the Shell Film Unit, which had acquired a good reputation during the 1930s for its output of predominantly informational films with only a discreet company symbol advertising their commercial sponsor. Beddington was to remain in the job until the MOI was wound up in 1946, thus outlasting three ministers, and this fact alone would seem to suggest that he was more successful than either of his predecessors. But at the time his appointment did not satisfy everybody and there were murmurings of discontent within the trade. The road towards the recovery of the Films Division was to be a long and tortuous one.

Beddington's appointment, like that of his predecessor, was initially welcomed by *Documentary News Letter*, which suggested that his practical experience of publicity work combined with his positive attitude towards the arts were just what the job required: 'He will bring to his new post both taste and a sense of public need – two qualities only too rarely associated with commercial ability.'[59] But Wardour Street was again critical of the new appointment, on the grounds that Beddington had no experience of the film trade. 'It's an absolute scandal, to my way of thinking, that we should have foistered [*sic*] on us somebody whose knowledge of the film trade is practically nil,' opined 'Tatler'; 'he may be a very brilliant publicity man – but you need more than a publicity man to get propaganda pictures made and into the neutrals.'[60] The criticism was not of Beddington personally but rather of the MOI for having appointed him. The same journalist urged the trade to take a less conciliatory line than it had done hitherto:

> As a plain matter of fact, the Ministry have no policy at all, and, until somebody is appointed with serious trade knowledge, then they will flounder and make more of a laughing stock of themselves than they have to date. The trade ought to present a strong case to the Government for a film man to direct film propaganda. Up to the moment they have been far too easy-going ... Now it's time for them to say they won't stand for publicity managers to come in and tell them what they have got to do. The position is really too stupid, and, I think, it is most undignified that this industry should have to put up with such well-meaning but totally inefficient measures.[61]

Beddington was fortunate in that he won a victory in the summer of 1940 which deflected some of the criticism. He was instrumental in negotiating with the Cinematograph Exhibitors' Association the scheme to show an official 'five-minute film' in every programme. 'Commentator', another trade journalist, detected evidence of a new driving force at the Films Division:

It also appears to be a feather in the cap of Jack Beddington that this scheme should make such a swift advance during his administration. The trade has been very critical of this gentleman since he took over, but I am assured by those who should know that, with this official in control, we can at last expect some rapid action, because he's starting to push things around in no uncertain fashion.[62]

Beddington would eventually win the confidence of the trade, though it would be an uphill struggle most of the way.[63]

Beddington's arrival once again coincided with a period of upheaval at the ministry. The fall of Neville Chamberlain and the subsequent formation of the Churchill coalition in May 1940 had an immediate effect on the MOI in that it brought about the removal of Sir John Reith. The turn-over of ministers at the MOI was now so frequent that *Kinematograph Weekly* remarked that 'there was a deep indentation in the pavement outside Senate House where successive holders of the office have come out on their ear'.[64] Reith's departure was due to the personal animosity between him and Churchill, which dated back to the General Strike of 1926 when Churchill, as a member of Baldwin's government, had allegedly wanted to take over the BBC and which was exacerbated in the 1930s when Churchill blamed Reith for keeping him off the air during his years in the wilderness. The new incumbent, Duff Cooper, was an able parliamentarian, but he ran foul of the press over the 'Cooper's Snoopers' affair – an investigation into public morale in the summer of 1940 which caused much discontent. The advent of another new minister brought more changes and yet another wave of reorganisation.

In addition to the changes within the MOI, the course of the war in 1940 – the fall of France and the evacuation from Dunkirk, the fear of invasion, the Battle of Britain and the Blitz – meant that official propaganda and information were constantly having to take account of a changing situation. The MOI had to adapt quickly from the tedium of the 'phoney war' to a national emergency which threatened Britain's very survival. It is against this background of continuous upheaval that the first months of Beddington's regime at the Films Division must be judged.

Despite the many problems which the Films Division faced, there was no abating in the criticisms which it attracted. *Documentary News Letter* set itself up as the chief critic, constantly attacking the MOI for its vacillation and urging it to do more to make use of film for propaganda purposes. In July 1940, for example, the journal's editorial condemned 'the inefficiency, muddleheadedness and bureaucratic stupidity of the Films Division'. It went on:

> In ten months this Division has achieved a mere fraction of what it should have achieved. Its lack of imagination, no less than its abysmal failure to be even competent at its job, have been the despair of all persons in the film trade who sincerely want to place their expert abilities at the disposal of the national effort.[65]

There are some qualifications that should be made regarding the attitude of *Documentary News Letter*. First, it may have been that the documentarists were less hostile in practice than they were in print, particularly as Beddington had demonstrated his willingness to work with them. And second, it should be considered that *Documentary News Letter* was a specialist journal with a limited distribution reaching a relatively small readership. The extent of its influence is therefore difficult to determine.[66] When similar criticisms appeared in the national press, however, the MOI would have had to take notice. In June 1940, in his capacity as film critic of the *Spectator*, Basil Wright penned a damning attack which might have been lifted from the pages of *Documentary News Letter*:

> A few sporadic and often ill-chosen films, a great deal of muddle and inefficiency, and a total lack of imagination have been its own contribution to the national war effort ... That, alas, is still the situation! After ten months of total war the Films Division is still largely a waste of the public's money.[67]

It was therefore against a background of publicly expressed criticism that Beddington had to work.

The difficult task which Beddington faced was to find a policy for the Films Division that would appease the critics. He did this mainly by bringing the documentary movement into the official fold while at the same time maintaining the contacts with the commercial producers and newsreel companies established by his predecessors. It is possible to draw a parallel between the reorganisation of the Films Division under Beddington and the reconstitution of the government as a whole. When Churchill became Prime Minister he immediately brought the Labour Party into his coalition government, exemplified by seats in the War Cabinet for Clement Attlee, Arthur Greenwood and later Ernest Bevin. Similarly, Beddington turned to the left, and specifically to Film Centre, a 'film consultancy' body set up by John Grierson in 1937 to act as a liaison between documentary producers and sponsors. This body had been excluded from the pre-war discussions about film propaganda due to the great distaste in which Grierson was held by senior civil servants. But with Grierson now at the National Film Board of Canada for the duration of the war, Film Centre, which published *Documentary News Letter*, was headed by Arthur Elton, a liberal intellectual who, in Pronay's words, 'appeared to be the least associated with the more extreme and dogmatic political activities of the documentary group'.[68] According to *The Factual Film*, 'at the request of the new Director a memorandum on the use of film for propaganda (which came to form the basis of much of the Division's subsequent work) was submitted by Film Centre'.[69] Furthermore, a number of the documentarists were recruited into the Films Division itself. Thomas Baird, pioneer of the documentary movement's experiments in non-theatrical distribution during the 1930s, was brought in to organise the MOI's non-theatrical programme. And early in 1941, Arthur Elton was appointed to a senior position as Supervisor of Production, replacing Dallas Bower, a producer-writer from the commercial cinema who had performed that role since May 1940. In addition to the new appointments, reshuffling had by the end of 1940 brought about substantial changes in the personnel of the Films Division. In particular, Forbes and Highet – both sceptics regarding the value of documentary – had by then moved to other departments.

To what extent did the changes made under Beddington constitute a documentary 'take-over' of the Films Division? Some contemporary commentators believed that the documentarists had infiltrated the division. For example, Neville Kearney of the British Council's Film Department complained that 'the Film Centre attitude and atmosphere pervades the whole outfit'.[70] On the other hand, Harry Watt, a director with the GPO Film Unit, later complained that Beddington 'wanted to be in with the newsreels' and always put their interests before those of documentary.[71] While the documentarists had certainly been incorporated by the Films Division, they did not control it. The policy which Beddington followed was to find a balance between the trade interests and the documentary movement. This was exemplified by the recruitment of Sidney Bernstein as the second honorary adviser to the

Films Division. Bernstein was a commercial exhibitor, an entrepreneur who had built up the Granada cinema chain and who was well known and respected in the trade. At the same time he was also acceptable to the documentarists: as a member of the Labour Party he shared their general political outlook; he had an interest in the minority film culture of which documentary was a part, having been a leading member of the Film Society in London in the late 1920s; and he had provided financial support for Grierson's *World Film News* during the 1930s. He personified the approach that was to become the hallmark of Beddington's administration: to secure the support of the entire film industry by balancing the different interest groups within it.[72]

Before all these changes had been implemented, however, the Films Division had to stave off a threat from Parliament in the form of the Select Committee on National Expenditure. The Select Committee had been set up to investigate the war expenditure of certain government departments and to make recommendations for economies. A sub-committee had investigated the MOI Films Division during the spring and summer of 1940, and its report reached the verdict that 'the work of the Films Division in the Home field has been largely ineffective through the lack of clearly defined objectives on the part of the Ministry'.[73] The recommendations put forward undermined much of the work that had been done under Clark and Beddington. The Select Committee criticised 'the pre-occupation of the Films Division with the feature film and the full length documentary film as the principal modes of propaganda by film'. It suggested that in future the division 'should be given clear policies to carry out and should not embark upon the production of any film without receiving clear directions either from the Ministry or from another Department of the Government' – a recommendation which, had it been acted upon, would effectively have removed the Films Division's executive responsibility. Among the specific recommendations made by the report were no more official subsidy for feature films, reduction in the amount of documentary production, winding up the non-theatrical programme, consulting the Government Cinematograph Adviser over production, and closer ties with the BFI.

How far was the Select Committee's report acted upon? Beddington was not impressed by many of the recommendations. He dismissed the suggestion that the Films Division should not carry out any production without directions from the MOI or other departments, a recommendation which he said 'has not been taken to mean that Films Division is to be reduced to a secondary level of existence without any power of initiative'.[74] He accepted that the MOI should not subsidise feature films, while as far as non-theatrical distribution and documentaries were concerned a compromise was reached whereby they were continued on a reduced scale. There were, however, two points on which Beddington refused to compromise. He gave short shrift to the recommendation that the Government Cinematograph Adviser should be consulted about production because 'neither his experience, qualifications, knowledge of the trade nor technical equipment fits him in the smallest degree to advise the Films Division upon its programme of work, with the possible exception of questions concerning copyright and the storage of film, upon which his advice has been, and will continue to be, taken'. Nor was Beddington prepared to countenance an official role for the BFI:

> The offers of service made by the British Film Institute have meant, in the last analysis, that Government should subsidise the British Film Institute to employ relatively less competent persons to perform the work undertaken by relatively more competent persons in the Films Division. The British Film Institute fulfils a valuable function in certain restricted spheres, such for instance as the compilation of a library, or museum, of extinct but interesting films. It was not designed, nor in the opinion of Films Division is it competent, to undertake national film propaganda.
>
> Films Division cannot altogether dismiss a feeling of scepticism concerning the claim of the British Film Institute, quoted by the Committee, and no doubt made in entire good faith, to be the best centre of information on the Cinema in Europe, if not in the world.

It is clear that under no circumstances was the Films Division going to allow the BFI into its confidence. On this point at least, its policy had been consistent. The BFI itself, no doubt smarting from repeated snubs at the hands of the MOI, used its quarterly journal *Sight and Sound* to launch an attack on the ministry for not paying sufficient heed to the report:

> Our new despots in the Ministry of Information are showing callous disregard of Parliamentary wishes as expressed in the

Thirteenth Report of the Select Committee on National Expenditure. So far as can be seen few, if any, of the 13 recommendations
are being implemented ... It is a disturbing thought that a Select
Committee's suggestions can be set aside by those fledgling Civil
Servants of Malet Street whose little brief spell of authority seems
to have gone to their heads.[75]

This seems to have annoyed Beddington, as he complained that the
BFI 'should be discouraged from attacking in public the film policy of
H.M. Government departments'.[76] But he was told by Deputy Director-
General Eric St John Bamford that he was taking the matter too
seriously: 'I do not like ... laying too much stress on the attack on us
in *Sight and Sound*, which, after all, is a publication of no great importance.'[77] Thus it was that the senior hierarchy of the MOI scorned
the BFI, and the deliberate exclusion of the Institute from the film
propaganda machinery continued for the rest of the war.

VI

The compromise reached after the Select Committee's report proved
to be the last major upheaval for the Films Division. There were no
more major changes in policy or administration, while the personnel
and staff structure remained stable. Beddington gradually won the
respect of both the trade interests and the documentary movement.
This change in fortune can be related in part to a general turn-around
for the MOI as a whole. Just as in the first year of the war the
division had been adversely affected by the overall instability of the
MOI, so after 1941 it benefited from a new-found institutional stability.
Most commentators agree that the appointment of Brendan Bracken,
who became the fourth Minister of Information in July 1941, led to
an improvement in the MOI's fortunes. Bracken was a close friend
and confidant of Churchill's, so he had access to the Prime Minister;
he was a former journalist who was able to win the confidence of the
press; and he was a confident and often combative parliamentarian
who was able to defend the MOI very effectively in the House of
Commons. In combination with Cyril Radcliffe, who became the sixth
and final Director-General in December 1941, Bracken purged the
MOI of the 'gentleman amateurs' who had attracted so much op-
probrium. 'They were an ideal combination and at last succeeded in

giving the Ministry some point,' recalled Sir Kenneth Clark, himself one of those to go. 'I belonged to the old, amateurish, ineffective, music-hall-joke Ministry, and had long been an unnecessary member of even that ramshackle body. Cyril was a friend of mine, for whom I had a great admiration. He told me to leave in the kindest possible terms.'[78] Thus it was that under the Bracken–Radcliffe administration many of the grounds for criticism were removed, and as a result the attacks from both press and Parliament lessened. 'On the domestic side of the department the criticism, which amounted to a hubbub in the early days, is now by comparison a subdued murmur,' *The Times* observed in July 1942.[79] Indeed, the critics had become so quiet that during a Commons debate in August 1943 Bracken positively welcomed discussion of the MOI, albeit with a touch of sarcasm:

> I am encouraged by the opportunity of talking to the House about anything concerned with the Ministry of Information because the House has ceased to have any interest in our Department. We are now less exciting than the British Museum. The House has not even taken the trouble to discuss our estimates. Of all the dull jobs in the Government the Ministry of Information is becoming the dullest so that any discussion in Parliament gives us some encouragement because we feel that the House is still in a mild way interested in its old favourite, at any rate its old whipping boy.[80]

Such was the extent of the MOI's rehabilitation that in 1944 an official report detected 'a thoroughness and solidity, combined with flexibility and enterprise, which are the hall-marks of administrative efficiency'.[81]

The Films Division naturally benefited from the ministry's new-found stability. That is not to say that all the criticisms ceased immediately. For example, in November 1941 Lord Kemsley, the proprietor of the *Daily Sketch*, launched a broadside against the film propaganda effort. While he acknowledged the progress made by the MOI under Bracken, he thought the Films Division was still thoroughly inadequate:

> Under the energetic and able direction of its latest supervisor, Mr Brendan Bracken, it [the MOI] has recently shown much better results, a keener disposition to treat the Press as its ally and not as its enemy, and to live up to the implications of its title.
>
> There is, however, one department of its activities that makes a clamant call for drastic reform. That is its films section.

Whether the inefficiency and weakness shown by the officials who are responsible for the MOI films are due to lack of generosity by the Treasury or whether they are due to insufficient imagination and deficient enterprise on the part of the War Cabinet in its general attitude towards films I am not in a position to know.

But the deplorable fact remains that British news and propaganda as conveyed through our official films demand immediate and thorough overhauling and improving.[82]

Kemsley's attack was inspired by what he perceived as the superior quality of Soviet propaganda films. He was supported by two leading members of the film industry, Michael Balcon and Leslie Howard, who placed the blame on the government's failure to provide any policy guidelines. Balcon complained that commercial producers 'have been left high and dry, with no one to advise us on policy', while Howard wrote that 'the official film propaganda industry is limited in scope and gets very little encouragement'.[83] A feeling still existed, therefore, that the MOI was not doing enough to help the film industry.

The rehabilitation of the Films Division in the eyes of its critics was a long and hard-earned one. The chief critic was still *Documentary News Letter*, which continued to act as an unofficial watchdog of the division's work. Its editorials provide a useful indicator of the gradual reappraisal of the Films Division during the middle years of the war. Certainly the journal could no longer complain that nothing was being done on the film propaganda front, but it still criticised the lack of an overall plan or policy. The main complaint now was that the Films Division's work was geared towards the specific needs of the moment, that it was essentially *ad hoc* and merely responded to events in the short-term rather than adhering to any long-term objectives. Although the division was making films, it was 'still in the anomalous position of planning its production programmes in a tentative and piecemeal manner, lacking any hint of that directive policy without which the use of film as an expressive weapon is severely hampered'.[84] The journal argued in the same vein consistently throughout 1942 and 1943, repeating the same sort of criticisms in almost every issue. However, blame for this lack of policy was laid not solely at the door of the MOI, but also on the government as a whole. The journal was widening the scope of its attack and, like Lord Kemsley had done, was hinting that a lack of direction at the top of government was largely responsible for the poor state of affairs. This situation affected not only film, but also other forms of propaganda, including the radio. 'We sympathise with the officials at the MOI and the BBC,' the journal said in August 1942. 'They have no direct instructions on policy nor have they permission to institute a policy of their own. They are fighting in a fog.'[85]

For much of the war, therefore, the official film propaganda machinery continued to attract criticism from the left. Once again, it must be noted that *Documentary News Letter* had its own agenda to pursue and that its views were not necessarily shared across the film industry as a whole. The trade columnist 'Onlooker', for example, disliked the journal's attitude. 'The most curious and interesting fact about the writers of *Documentary News Letter* is their supreme assurance,' he wrote. 'They are obviously convinced that the light on all human (and other) affairs have been specially given to them.'[86] Indeed, there does seem to have been an assumption on the part of *Documentary News Letter* that it always knew best on anything relating to film propaganda. Nevertheless, the fact that it went on challenging the MOI in print illustrates that criticism did continue throughout the war, even if it was now confined to a specialist sheet of limited distribution. It was not until 1944 that the journal accepted that the MOI was performing adequately. It reviewed its own position, and declared that it was no longer attacking the MOI for its general inadequacy, but was merely criticising it on specific points of detail:

> *DNL* has never hesitated at any time to criticise the MOI when criticism seemed necessary; and we believe much of our criticism has been useful and constructive. But one thing is clear. To begin with, criticism could only be directed at the MOI's failure to do anything at all. Later, criticism fell on its doing things the wrong way. But finally and recently, the criticisms have been aimed only at what seemed to be errors or mishandlings of schemes and plans which are essentially good and practical. The MOI today is no more and no less open to criticism than any other Government department.[87]

In August 1945, at the very end of the war and with a Labour government now in power, the journal even praised the Films Division, declaring that 'the planning of the division's work is greatly superior today to what it was only two years ago, when the subjects seemed to be chosen at random out of Harrod's catalogue'.[88] Thus it was that after five years, and close to the end of the war, the MOI and its Films Division had finally won over their most trenchant critic.

The rehabilitation of the MOI had been a long process, but it was deserved. Given the hostile criticism it had attracted, especially at the beginning of the war, it is hard to accept Michael Powell's verdict that the MOI was a 'great success' and its Films Division was a 'triumph', but nor were they the total failures that most other commentators have suggested. The blunders which were made at the beginning of the war determined the popular perception of the 'Ministry of Dis-Information', but this reputation has overshadowed the improvements which were made after 1940. While historians have concentrated on the mistakes, they should also recognise the achievements that were made later in the war. The problems regarding the supply of news and information, for instance, had been largely overcome by the middle of 1940, after which the system worked smoothly. Posterity has judged Jack Beddington as having brought about improvement at the Films Division and, while it must be considered that neither of his two predecessors really had time to prove themselves, it is also evident that Beddington had a clearer idea of policy – a policy which he implemented with considerable success. Beddington's strength was that he realised the Films Division needed to work with both poles of the film industry, the commercial trade on the one hand and the documentary movement on the other hand. The need to balance and reconcile these two different interests became the guiding principle of his administration.

2

A Policy for Film Propaganda

The film being a popular medium must be good entertainment if
it is to be good propaganda. *Programme for Film Propaganda* (1940)[1]

I

Quite apart from the piecemeal nature of its planning and the weaknesses of its initial organisation, one of the main problems which
beset the MOI at the beginning of the war was that in devising plans
for national propaganda and information it was starting from scratch.
The fact that Britain had neither an organisation nor a policy for
propaganda when the war broke out meant that Germany was able to
steal a march in the propaganda war. A number of commentators were
soon drawing unfavourable comparisons between the British and
German film propaganda efforts. In November 1939 Charles Peake of
the Foreign Office News Department lamented 'Germany's tremendous
start over this country in respect of film propaganda'.[2] This was a
matter of particular concern to the Foreign Office and the diplomatic
service, who were anxious about the way in which the British war
effort was perceived abroad, particularly in the United States where the
first British efforts at propaganda had made little impression. As Lord
Lothian, the British ambassador in Washington, informed the Foreign
Secretary Lord Halifax on 28 September 1939, 'there is no doubt that
after three weeks of war the general impression is that the Germans
have handled their propaganda better. They have done so because they

have studied the art more clearly and are more efficient at it.'[3] In Germany, the Ministry of Popular Enlightenment and Propaganda had been established under Goebbels shortly after the Nazi takeover in 1933 and therefore had a head start over the British at the beginning of the war.

One reason why the MOI at first had no clear idea of propaganda policy was the distaste for the very idea of propaganda felt by the western democracies. In 1935, the American academic Professor Leonard Doob observed: 'the word propaganda has a bad odor. It is associated with war and other evil practices.'[4] Among these 'evil practices' were totalitarian regimes where propaganda was widely used, in conjunction with censorship, as a means of social control and political indoctrination. Given the way in which propaganda was employed in states like Nazi Germany and Soviet Russia, there was an assumption in the democratic political cultures that propaganda itself was 'undemocratic': it sought to secure unquestioning support for and loyalty to the party and the state. Particularly in Britain, there was a deep antipathy towards the idea of propaganda, which was widely considered an 'unBritish' practice. This attitude was evident both on the part of the public and in official circles. Commenting upon Korda's propaganda feature *The Lion Has Wings*, for example, one respondent in a Mass-Observation survey said: 'I think it un-British to shove propaganda down your throat like that.'[5] And Duff Cooper remarked in his memoirs: 'I believe the truth of the matter to be that there is no place in the British scheme of government for a Ministry of Information.'[6] There is a sense in which this attitude was a piece of self-denial by the British, who were widely perceived at home and abroad to have acquitted themselves well as propagandists during the First World War.[7] However, this fact sat uncomfortably with the popular view in Britain that propaganda was alien to its liberal, democratic political culture. This view can be seen to influence not only the criticisms of the MOI – as Charles Barr suggests, the 'eloquent rubbishing' of the MOI by contemporaries such as Clark, Waugh and Betjeman was due partly to 'an embarrassed guilt at the existence of this "unBritish" propaganda institution'[8] – but also the contemporary arts and literature. It has been suggested, for example, that tensions about the role of propaganda and censorship are at the heart of George Orwell's novel *Nineteen Eighty-Four* (1948), which some commentators have interpreted as an allegory of Orwell's own unhappy experiences of working for the

MOI.[9] The antipathy towards the idea of propaganda and the work of propaganda organisations was therefore deep-rooted in the British psyche, and it was widely expressed before, during and after the Second World War. It was a psychological hurdle that Britain's wartime propagandists had to overcome. With hindsight, it was clearly one of the factors which handicapped the MOI following the outbreak of war.

II

The MOI started the war, therefore, with no propaganda policy and no theoretical grasp of what propaganda itself really was. The main preoccupation during the planning stages had been with constructing the appropriate machinery and, accordingly, little thought had been given to the techniques of propaganda. Various papers had been written by supposed experts during the late 1930s, but they tended to be vague and often confused about the theory of propaganda. One of the problems was that the most successful official propaganda organisation of the time was the German model. A paper prepared by the Royal Institute of International Affairs in June 1939, which laid down eighty-six ground-rules for propaganda, illustrates the confused state of thinking. It was influenced not only by the experience of the First World War ('during the Great War it was found that one good poster would do the work of twenty public meetings') but also by Hitler's views on propaganda in *Mein Kampf* ('According to Hitler, propaganda should use basic ideas and should address itself solely to the masses'). The influence of the totalitarian method of propaganda is evident in the belief that it should appeal to people's emotions ('As regards the masses of people, appeal to their instincts and not to their reason'). The assessment of film as a medium of propaganda was restricted to such general statements as 'the cinema provides the great mass audience'.[10] Such vague ideas were hardly very useful for the propagandists of the MOI.

The MOI did make an attempt, albeit somewhat half-heartedly, to get to grips with the theory of propaganda. The 1930s had seen a proliferation of academic books and monographs on propaganda arising from the political and social sciences in both Britain and America. The context for this body of work was the extensive use of propaganda by the totalitarian states in Europe; many of the writers were concerned with how propaganda could be used in democracies to counter totalitarian ideologies. Contemporary discourses were based largely on the role of propaganda and communication in the age of the mass society: how the dissemination of news, ideas and opinions was vital for mass participation in the processes of democratic government.[11] The writing on propaganda in Britain on the eve of the Second World War was dominated by what might be termed the liberal academic discourse. A representative example of this school of writing was Frederick Bartlett, a Cambridge Professor of Psychology who wrote a monograph entitled *Political Propaganda* (1940) at the behest of the MOI following the outbreak of war. Bartlett was very much concerned with the differences between dictatorship and democracy, and his argument was based on the assumption that the different character of democracy meant that a fundamentally different approach to propaganda was required. Bartlett described the ways in which democratic propaganda was different from the propaganda of dictatorship thus:

> It does not despise the intelligence of those whom it addresses, as the dictator propaganda does. It does not go all out to short-circuit reason, as the dictator propaganda does. It recognises that men act where their affections, sentiments and emotions are concerned, but that these must and can be led by intelligence without losing their strength. It knows that the stability of a social order does not depend upon everybody's saying the same thing, holding the same opinions, feeling the same feelings, but upon a freely achieved unity which, with many sectional and individual differences, is nevertheless able to maintain an expanding and consistent pattern of life.[12]

Bartlett therefore identified two essential differences between the propaganda of dictatorship and the propaganda of democracy. First, whereas the technique of dictator propaganda was aimed towards arousing the emotions of the masses, democratic propaganda was based as much on reasoned argument as it was on emotion (a view in which Bartlett differed from the Royal Institute of International Affairs). And second, propaganda in a democracy could and should acknowledge the existence of different shades of opinion, which of course would never be allowed in the dictator states.

To what extent was the MOI influenced by the liberal academic discourse on propaganda which Bartlett exemplified? Sue Harper writes that the MOI 'rebuffed him savagely' and that in rejecting his ideas 'the Ministry effectively banished subjectivity, gender and psychoanalysis from its repertoire'.[13] However, this assertion is rather misleading and requires some qualification. While it is true that the MOI did not engage with the psychological implications of Bartlett's work, it did come to share the same basic ideas about the nature of propaganda for democracy. Two examples illustrate this. First, Bartlett's view on the importance of news and information was identical to the policy adopted by the MOI. 'The basis of all effective propaganda in a democracy is an effective news service,' Bartlett wrote, adding that 'news alone can give to propaganda necessarily concrete character; news alone can provide intelligence with its needed factual material'.[14] This view is very similar to Sir John Reith's oft-quoted dictum that 'news is the shocktroops of propaganda'; one of the cornerstones of the MOI's policy was that accurate and, in so far as was possible complete, news and information should be provided for the public.[15] And second, Bartlett's view that democratic propaganda should be based on reason rather than on emotion also came to be accepted by the MOI, albeit not immediately. The MOI's early propaganda campaigns, which adopted the exhortational style, did not prove to be very effective. There was a gradual change of policy to propaganda based more on reasoned argument and factual information than on emotional exhortation. As Harold Nicolson, the Parliamentary Secretary to the MOI, noted in his diary in 1941:

> From the propaganda point of view all that the country really wants is some assurance of how victory is to be achieved. They are bored by talks about the righteousness of our cause and our eventual triumph. What they want are facts regarding how we are to beat the Germans.[16]

The same view was expressed by Dr Stephen Taylor, the Director of Home Intelligence. 'The British public as a whole shows a very high degree of common-sense,' he wrote in October 1941. 'Given the relevant facts, they will listen to and accept explanations when they will not accept exhortations.'[17] This was one of the fundamental differences between British and German propaganda, according to the liberal academic discourse, and it came to be accepted by the MOI after some of its initial attempts at exhortation had failed.

How did the cinema fit into this discourse on propaganda? Bartlett did not have much to say specifically about films beyond the assertion that 'What is photographed is usually accepted as "real", and the part played by modern propaganda in developing the documentary film, especially for foreign display, is considerable'.[18] However, other commentators of a similar persuasion agreed that film propaganda should also be based on information rather than exhortation. Mass-Observation's research into the reactions of cinema audiences to official films found that they were turned off by strongly exhortational messages. A report from one London cinema on the response to a five-minute film entitled *Seaman Frank Goes Back to Sea* (1942), which concluded with an appeal for National Savings, suggested that people disliked the constant appeals to keep on saving:

> People *do not* like to be reminded of Savings all the time, and after a spell of very intense savings propaganda, were rather tired of hearing more about it ... There is a feeling that when you go to the cinema, you expect to be amused and distracted from everyday life, and you leave worries behind for two or three hours. If, while you are in that mood, someone on the screen lectures at you, you are inclined to resent it.[19]

The point that people went to the cinema for escapism – one of the factors which enhanced its popular appeal during the war – was an important one in assessing its value for propaganda purposes. Given that the cinema was a place of entertainment, was it an appropriate environment for propaganda? 'The ordinary picture house is not a suitable place for direct propaganda,' the theorist R. S. Lambert had written in 1938. 'For each time the film-goer enters he pays for a ticket entitling himself to be entertained ... anyone who has paid for his entertainment, and then finds himself subject to propaganda, has reasonable grounds for complaint.'[20] Indeed, the question of 'entertainment' versus 'propaganda' was to become the central issue in a debate over the nature of film propaganda which raged throughout the war between the two opposite poles of the British film industry.

III

Although there was general agreement both inside and outside the government that Britain should make use of film propaganda, there was no consensus on which was the best type of film for propaganda purposes. The debate soon divided into two main points of view: those who favoured the commercial feature film and those who favoured the documentary film. The British government's initial reaction was to favour the commercial film industry. The Foreign Office, for instance, was concerned about the way in which the British war effort was projected overseas. In October 1939 Lord Halifax complained about the lack of propaganda feature films, and in a long memorandum went on to explain why he thought them more important than documentaries:

> I am rather disturbed at our total failure to use the film weapon effectively. It is in fact the most effective of the lot. So far, although the war has been in progress for nearly two months, we have only made one film, other than documentaries, and that is the Korda film that has been on private view this week. This film was made entirely on Mr Korda's own initiative and at his own expense. We ought of course to have had a number of these by now. Documentaries are all very well in their way, but they appeal at best to a public that can be counted in tens of thousands. But a big film is a dead loss unless it is seen by a rock bottom minimum of sixty million people, and success consists in being seen by a minimum of something nearer two hundred million people. Moreover, the real effect of films only comes by getting at the emotions. Documentaries of course can never do that. There are plenty of people in Hollywood who would be delighted to make films which would work our way, if they were provided with the material. Many of the leading actors would give their services for nothing or practically nothing.
>
> So far, I would report, we have made no real use whatever of the most potent of all means of propaganda.[21]

Halifax's memorandum raises a number of significant points. In the first instance, it shows that one member of the Chamberlain government did take an interest in film propaganda, though none of Halifax's colleagues in the War Cabinet appear to have shared his interest. Halifax's reasons for preferring feature films to documentaries were that features reached a much larger audience and that, unlike documentaries, they appealed to the emotions of the spectator. He was clearly of the view that the most effective propaganda would be directed at the audience's emotions (through the feature film) rather

than based on fact (through documentary) and in this sense he differed
from the views of the British liberal academic discourse. He was
broadly in line with the views of the MOI at the time, which had
shown an initial preference for feature films over documentaries and
which had not yet fully embraced the policy that propaganda should
be based on fact and an appeal to reason rather than to emotion.
However, his complaint that Britain had produced only one propaganda
feature film, Korda's *The Lion Has Wings*, and that several other such
films should have been made, was rather unfair in that it took no
account of the length of time needed to make a feature film. *The Lion
Has Wings* was a special case which had been rushed into production
and completed in a hurry, and it was unrealistic to expect that several
films of the same type could have been made within so short a time.
Finally, he also seems to have thought that Hollywood could play a
part in the projection of Britain on the screen. The suggestion that
Hollywood could make propaganda films on Britain's behalf was probably based in part on the ban placed by the British government on
propaganda in America at the beginning of the war lest it should
offend American neutrality. There was a large contingent of British
actors and directors in Hollywood, and some Hollywood studios had
made films during the late 1930s with an anti-fascist and often pro-
British theme.[22] However, Hollywood was to be left largely to its own
devices in making pro-British films, both before and after America's
entry into the war. This was illustrated in 1940 by the case of a
proposed film of C. S. Forester's *Captain Horatio Hornblower*, the script
for which was written by Forester himself for Warner Bros, who wanted
to withdraw from Britain any revenue that it might accrue (Hollywood's
profits having been 'frozen' in Britain by the Treasury) in return for
a strongly pro-British slant in the film. The suggestion was supported
by the Foreign Office but was turned down by the MOI and the
project was shelved.[23]

The Foreign Office was by no means the only party to consider
that commercial feature films were the most useful vehicles for propaganda. The same view was quite naturally taken by the feature producers
themselves and it was expressed many times in the trade press. There
were two broad arguments. The first was that feature films in general
(whether British or American) were such a popular form of entertainment that they would play a valuable role in maintaining morale. An
editorial in *Kinematograph Weekly* in the first week of the war suggested

that it was the trade's duty 'to present in pleasant, harmless form a relief from the very ugly world in which we are living today' and asked, 'Can one think of a safer anodyne to the disturbed public mind than the screen play?'[24] Of course, the trade had its own interests to consider – the editorial was arguing for the reopening of cinemas following their closure upon the outbreak of war – but the value of the cinema in helping to uphold morale was quite generally accepted. For example, the first wartime report of the Cinematograph Films Council, which had been set up in 1927 to review the state of the film industry for the Board of Trade, declared: 'The only favourable factor contributed by the war was the enhanced value of the film as a medium for conveying information and for strengthening morale.'[25]

The second broad view put forward by the trade concerned the question of entertainment and propaganda. It was consistently argued that films, even those with a propaganda content, should first and foremost be good entertainment. This was to be one of the main issues affecting British film propaganda during the war. The trade's position was outlined by the journalist P. L. Mannock in September 1939:

> Which brings me to that difficult and much-abused word 'propaganda'. We must be preserved from the bland jingoism that still prevails in some official circles, but which does not correspond to to-day's national temper in the least. Nor do we want dreary documentaries of what the Ministry of Information sees fit to allow about the fighting Services.
>
> If the history of screen propaganda tells us anything at all, it tells us that the less blatant it is, the more effective the result. The one guide, of course, is that of genuine entertainment, in which almost anything can be put over.[26]

This effectively summarises the position which the trade was to maintain throughout the war: that feature films rather than documentaries were most useful for propaganda, but that in order to be effective they must first be good entertainment. There is evidence that the MOI Films Division agreed to some extent with this view. In a lecture to the Royal Society of Arts in February 1940, for example, Sir Kenneth Clark remarked that in the cinema 'there is a saturation point – a point where people who pay their sixpence to be entertained will object if they hear one more gun going off'.[27]

There was also a belief on the part of the trade that film propaganda should be uncomplicated and presented in a form easily understood by the audience. A *Kinematograph Weekly* editorial entitled 'Propaganda – For The People' declared:

> One lesson which must be driven in upon both the M of I and the British Council in this matter of propaganda pictures is that the message to be delivered must be direct and not obscured by 'arty' fussiness. A well-edited newsreel is much better propaganda than any amount of 'cinema' – a mirage which distorts the message and confuses the beholder.
>
> It is no use playing Honegger and Stravinsky to a people whose musical appreciation does not go beyond 'The Lambeth Walk', in the hope that they will eventually prefer these composers. Propaganda must be disseminated in the language most widely understood, and this applies to the films destined for foreign audiences too.
>
> Symbolism may make its appeal to a few cultured minds, but propaganda, to have its widest and strongest appeal, must speak what a former generation called 'the vulgar tongue'.[28]

The editorial was, according to historian Paul Swann, 'an accurate representation of the attitude of commercial exhibitors and their clientele'.[29] It exhibits a patronising attitude towards the ordinary cinema-goer, and is not dissimilar to the views of Nazi propagandists that the intelligence and comprehensive powers of the masses were limited. This does not mean that *Kinematograph Weekly* despised the masses in the same way that Hitler did, but it does show that the trade inclined towards the view that audiences were used to straightforward film language which was uncomplicated by 'arty' touches.

The views of the British documentary movement towards film propaganda were very different from those of the commercial trade. The documentary movement represented the nearest thing to a propagandist tradition in the British cinema in that it saw its role as one of publicity and education. It sometimes compared itself to the Soviet school of film-making which had emerged in the 1920s, including directors like Eisenstein and Pudovkin who combined theory and practice to use cinema as a propagandist tool. There is a comparison to be made in so far as the documentarists were influenced to some extent by Soviet montage theory but, although the documentary movement enjoyed some state support (through the EMB and later GPO Film Units), it was only ever a marginal mode of film practice whose films appealed to a minority audience. However, the documentary group can be identified with the use of film towards specific ends, and if their popular appeal was limited they did nevertheless receive considerable critical acclaim from the intelligentsia. *The Times* recognised documentary's role as a realistic medium of national projection when it said in 1938: 'It is the short film of the documentary kind, and not the popular feature film, that presents the most authentic picture of our national life.'[30] Given their experience in the field of publicity and disseminating information, documentarists naturally expected that they would be at the heart of the official film propaganda effort during the war and were annoyed when they were initially left out in the cold by the MOI. They also felt that for most of the war they were fighting a rearguard action against a government which did not place sufficient value on their skills and expertise. For instance, in defending document-ary film-makers against call-up by the Ministry of Labour and National Service in 1941, *Documentary News Letter* argued that documentary personnel were more valuable to the war effort in their present capacity:

> The documentary movement represents a special expertness in the use of films for propaganda and informational purposes. For eleven years its members have been working to a thesis of public enlightenment which now fits closely to official needs ... Documentary, whether anyone likes it or not, is by its very nature the right medium for a continuous flow of films such as envisaged and practised by organisations like the Ministry of Information Films Division.[31]

Thus it was that the documentarists saw themselves as the film-makers best suited to propaganda work.

The difference of opinion between the documentary movement and the commercial industry over the nature of propaganda becomes very apparent when the views of *Documentary News Letter* are compared to those of the trade press. For instance, whereas the trade press thought that the use of documentary was limited due to its small audience, the documentarists argued that the feature film was limited because commercial necessity always came before the needs of propaganda: 'Propaganda by feature films is strictly limited by considerations of box-office.'[32] In particular, *Documentary News Letter* did not agree with the distinction made between propaganda and entertainment by the trade press, which it considered to be artificial. In May 1942 the journal complained that 'there still exists a tendency to believe that entertainment value and propaganda value must be separate considerations' and criticised the nature of many feature films, where an obvious propaganda message was tagged on almost as an afterthought to a conventional storyline:

> On this line of reasoning we generally finish up with an old-fashioned thriller incorporating odd irrelevant lines of dialogue about freedom, persecution, fascism; or one of the characters will hold up the action while he makes a wordy and self-conscious speech about democracy ... The obvious weakness of this type of film is the clear division between what is regarded by producers as entertainment and what has been added as propaganda. The audience is over-aware of the distinction.[33]

Films such as Leslie Howard's *Pimpernel Smith* and Ealing's *Ships With Wings* were criticised 'because they present the war in absurdly romantic terms'. By contrast, *49th Parallel* was praised because 'propaganda and entertainment were fused – it was the propaganda itself that was entertaining'.

The documentary movement also had its own particular agenda for the content of film propaganda. *Documentary News Letter* inherited from the Griersonian tradition of the 1930s the view that one of the purposes of documentary was to further the cause of social reform. This was evident in the first issue of the journal, which declared: 'The documentary idea (the dramatisation of fact) ... has become a practical weapon in the drive towards social progress.'[34] It was documentary which during the 1930s had paid most heed to social problems in films such as *Housing Problems* (1935) and *Enough to Eat* (1936) which had highlighted the problems of slum housing and poor nutrition among the British working classes. In this area the documentarists again differed markedly from the commercial cinema, which had generally avoided addressing controversial issues. The documentarists argued that during the war official propaganda could not avoid examining social problems. 'Our policy of national publicity is yet to be determined, and in drafting it we begin with the advantage of a clean slate,' *Documentary News Letter* said in March 1940. 'But a policy must be written, and it must be a policy which provides for the screen ex-

amination of social issues, whether controversial or not.'[35] The documentarists' concern with promoting the cause of social improvement
reflected the views of the British left more generally. For example, in
a book entitled *The New Propaganda* (1939), written for the Left Book
Club, the Marxist writer Amber Blanco White had argued that left-
wing propaganda in a democracy should be based on promoting social
change: 'We want the electorate to feel, and to feel passionately, that
they deserve a better order than the present social system and are
prepared to make sacrifices in order to get it.'[36] Although this radical
agenda never became official MOI policy, it was nevertheless to influence a good number of the wartime films made on its behalf by
the documentary movement.

IV

Thus it was that there were two very different and indeed diametrically
opposed schools of thought within the British film industry on the
subject of propaganda. A wide gulf existed between the commercial
trade interests on the one hand and the documentary movement on the
other. In formulating a film propaganda policy the MOI Films Division
therefore had to deal with two different interest groups which each had
its own particular agenda to pursue. The approach which was adopted
was to try to incorporate both groups within official policy so that
both were harnessed to the national propaganda effort. This approach
is evident as early as January 1940 with the Programme for Film
Propaganda drawn up by Sir Kenneth Clark. This document marked
the first considered attempt to define official policy for film propaganda.
Clark was evidently concerned with how film specifically could be used
to implement the more general principles of British propaganda: 'It
follows the principles outlined by Lord Macmillan's memorandum to
the War Cabinet with such changes as are made necessary by adapting
abstract ideas to the concrete, dramatic and popular medium of film.'[37]
It adopted the three themes of British propaganda suggested by
Macmillan – 'What Britain is fighting for', 'How Britain fights' and
'The need for sacrifice if the fight is to be won' – and applied them
to the different modes of film practice. It outlined specific roles for
both feature films and documentaries by indicating the areas in which
each would be most useful. It considered that feature films were the
best medium for the presentation of 'What Britain is fighting for':

British ideas and institutions. Ideals such as freedom, and institutions such as parliamentary government can be made the main subject of a drama or treated historically. It might be possible to do a great film on the history of British Liberty and its repercussions in the world (Holland in the 17th, France in the 18th centuries).

As this was the kind of subject that was best presented in the form of a dramatic narrative, the feature film was seen as the ideal medium for it. The suggested use of historical parallels actually foreshadowed a number of prestigious British feature films, such as Carol Reed's *The Young Mr Pitt* and Laurence Olivier's *Henry V.* Documentaries, by contrast, were not considered very useful for this sort of propaganda:

> The treatment of British life and institutions has been the subject of a number of films in the last few years, and it should not be necessary to add greatly to their number. Moreover the projection abroad of British culture is primarily the work of the British Council who have a considerable grant for films.

Documentary, as an essentially factual mode of film practice, was therefore not regarded as a good form for dramatising stories of British institutions and ideas of liberty. Clark was presumably thinking of the work of the GPO Film Unit with films such as *Night Mail* (1936) and *The Islanders* (1938) in his reference to documentaries in recent years which had portrayed British life and institutions. However, the factual nature of documentary made it more appropriate for the presentation of 'How Britain fights'. Clark envisaged an extensive series of documentaries covering all aspects of the war effort:

> A long series should be undertaken to show this country, France and the neutrals the extent of our war effort. There should be, in the first place, full and carefully worked out films of each of the fighting services; then shorter films of all the immediately subsidiary services, i.e. merchant navy, munitions, shipbuilding, coastal command, fishermen, etc. Most of these subjects are susceptible to detailed treatment from different angles, e.g. one-reel films on the Bren gun, the training of an anti-aircraft gunner, etc.

Again, the Programme anticipated, in the general idea at least, the series of official documentaries, both feature-length and shorts, made about all aspects of the British war effort, principally by the Crown Film Unit.

The Programme for Film Propaganda therefore identified specific roles for both the feature film and the documentary. It recognised that each had a propaganda value depending on the subject matter which it treated. 'It was for the most part a reasonable and rational film programme, though it was noticeably lacking in suggestions for comedy and good humour,' comments Anthony Aldgate.[38] This was indeed a rather curious omission, for humour was an important aspect of the contemporary discourses on propaganda. 'In England, it is safe to say,' Bartlett had written, 'two types of appeal must always be prominent: to humour and to sport.'[39] In most other respects, however, the Programme was broadly in line with the liberal academic discourse. It placed a great deal of emphasis on the difference between democracy and dictatorship, and it followed the argument that propaganda in a democracy should be based on news and information with its declaration: 'The selection and proper presentation of news reel material is one of the most vital factors in propaganda.' Two of its other general recommendations are worth commenting upon. First, it stressed the importance of the general entertainment value of films:

> The film being a popular medium must be good entertainment if it is to be good propaganda. A film which induces boredom antagonises the audience to the cause which it advocates. For this reason, an amusing American film with a few hits at the Nazi regime is probably better propaganda than any number of documentaries showing the making of bullets, etc.

In this particular instance, the Programme was more inclined to the viewpoint of the trade press than the documentary movement. It also led to another suggestion regarding the nature of official involvement in film propaganda:

> This leads to the further consideration that film propaganda will be most effective when it is least recognisable as such. Only in a few rare prestige films and documentaries should the Government's participation be announced. The influence brought to bear by the Ministry on the producers of feature films, and encouragement given to foreign distributors, must be kept secret. This is particularly true of any films which it is hoped to distribute in America and other neutral countries, which should in some instances actually be made in America and distributed as American films.

The last suggestion was rather naive, as it would have violated American law: the McKellar Act decreed that the origin of all films released in the United States had to be made known. However, the suggestion that the MOI's influence on producers should be kept hidden came to form the basis of the ministry's relationship with the commercial film industry. After its much-publicised backing of *49th Parallel*, the MOI preferred to work behind the scenes in suggesting film projects to producers. Unfortunately, this has led some historians to construct elaborate theories about official involvement in film propaganda, where the MOI's covert influence is detected even in the most unlikely cases.[40]

While the Programme for Film Propaganda outlined several of the general principles which were to inform British propaganda films during the war, its terms were not set in stone. Like all forms of propaganda, film had to be flexible and able to adjust to changing circumstances. For example, the suggestion that 'an important feature film could deal with the good relations of French and British troops in France' became redundant after the fall of France in the summer of 1940. Nor did the Programme include every subject that would be covered in propaganda films during the war. It had nothing to say specifically about the contribution of women to the war effort, or about how the British Empire and Commonwealth should be presented on the screen: both were subjects on which the MOI had yet to decide where it stood. For example, it was not until its 'Empire Campaign' in the autumn of 1940 that the MOI made a concerted attempt to provide a rationale of Britain's status as an imperial power. A Policy Committee paper of October 1940 emphasised the role of the Commonwealth as a democratic alternative to Hitler's 'New World Order':

> The Nazis are proclaiming loud and long that they are creating 'a new world order'. In fact, they are merely resurrecting the old vicious idea of a slave Empire in which the subjugated races are held down by force and exploited for the benefit of the *herrenvolk* – 'the master folk'. It is not the Nazis and the Gestapo who have the goods to deliver, but the British Commonwealth. This is true because the Empire has been gradually transformed from being a political organisation owing obedience to central authority in London to an association of free and equal partners. It is in itself a League of Nations.[41]

These ideas were translated on to celluloid by the two-reeler *From the*

Four Corners (1941), an official film in which Leslie Howard discussed with a Canadian, an Australian and a New Zealander their reasons for participation in the war, emphasising that the self-governing dominions entered of their own accord and that the Commonwealth was an alliance of free nations.[42] This was an example of film being used as part of a wider propaganda campaign, which also covered posters, press, radio and public meetings. The campaign, moreover, had arisen out of specific circumstances: when Britain was threatened with invasion it was important to remind the public that she was not alone but had the might of the Commonwealth behind her; and, at a time when Britain needed American support, it was important also to present the British Empire in a positive light. Thus, film propaganda could be made to fit the needs of the moment. For the most part, however, the general principles laid down by Clark in January 1940 provided the basis for British film propaganda policy during the war. In particular, his broad definition of the different roles of feature films and documentaries was to be followed through to a large degree in British wartime cinema. It was by identifying particular roles for both these different modes of film practice that the MOI was able to reconcile and incorporate the views of both groups within its film propaganda policy.

3

The MOI and Feature Film Propaganda

The wide distribution secured by commercial feature films gives excellent opportunities for disseminating, if not direct propaganda, an impression of the British attitude both to the issues of war and to war-time conditions. *Thirteenth Report from the Select Committee on National Expenditure* (1940)[1]

I

The feature film has usually been considered the most important vehicle for film propaganda. In their article on *The Way Ahead*, for example, Porter and Litewski state: 'During the Second World War, the feature film played a key role in the British government's propaganda campaign.'[2] This is the view widely held among film historians, and it is reflected in the concentration on feature films which characterises most of the new film historiography. The feature film now attracts the most attention because it is seen as the most representative example of the cultural and ideological values of any national cinema; it is the feature film which draws people into the cinemas and which appeals to the widest audiences. Porter and Litewski's article on *The Way Ahead* was the first application of empiricist methodology to a British propaganda film, using material from the Public Record Office to reconstruct the details of the film's production and contemporary reviews and

audience surveys to analyse its reception. A similar methodology under-
lies the work of Aldgate and Richards, who have undertaken close
case studies of a number of key wartime features.[3] A body of work
exists, therefore, which has put certain films on the historiographical
map. The emphasis, however, has been on case studies of individual
films rather than on the development of official policy towards feature
film propaganda in a more general context. The main line of inquiry
in this chapter, therefore, will be to discuss the MOI's policy for feature
film propaganda. This will of course involve discussion of specific
films, in particular two features which were made under unique circumstances and with a large degree of official involvement (*The Lion Has
Wings* and *49th Parallel*), but the main emphasis will be to draw some
general conclusions about the relationship between the MOI and the
feature film industry.

II

Although the feature film came to play a key role in British propaganda
policy, the first feature-length propaganda film of the war was produced
at the initiative of a commercial producer in the absence of any official
guidelines on film propaganda. The production of Alexander Korda's
The Lion Has Wings (1939) illustrates the *ad hoc* nature of official
involvement with the film industry at the beginning of the war. This
film was a hastily concocted hodge-podge of newsreel material, clips
from old documentary films and newly filmed studio scenes, which
was intended to show how and why Britain was fighting against Germany. In particular, it illustrated the work of the RAF in both its
offensive capacity (a reconstruction of the Kiel Canal raid) and its
defensive role (repelling a fictitious German air attack on England).
Both these aspects of the film were as much fiction as they were
documentary: the success of the Kiel raid was greatly exaggerated,
while one scene suggested that German pilots were ignorant of barrage
balloons and would flee in terror upon seeing them. A montage of
newsreel footage comparing the British and German systems of
government was put together for an opening sequence providing the
background to Britain's declaration of war; dramatised scenes featuring
Ralph Richardson and Merle Oberon as a supposedly 'typical' English
couple were filmed at Denham Studios to provide a linking narrative;
and an extract from Korda's earlier historical epic *Fire Over England*

(1937), with Flora Robson as Elizabeth I, was inserted to draw an allegorical parallel with the Spanish Armada of 1588. Three directors were involved (Michael Powell, Adrian Brunel and Brian Desmond Hurst), Ian Dalrymple was put in overall charge of the production, and well-known newsreel commentators were used for the narration (E. V. H. Emmett of Gaumont-British News for the domestic version and Lowell Thomas of Movietone for the American version). Dalrymple said at the time that the film was meant to show 'that there was a British ideology arising from our national character; that it was valuable to the world; and that it should not be lost'.[4] Most commentators, however, now agree that the film is propaganda of an old-fashioned, overtly patriotic sort. The commentary begins with the portentous phrase 'This is Britain where we believe in freedom', but there is no real suggestion of how this idea relates to ordinary people. The casting of Richardson and Oberon as the personification of a British couple now seems to present a very narrow picture of class and nation, for their elocution and demeanour is suggestive only of the English Home Counties. Moreover, the film's idea of what the war was being fought for (Oberon says at the end that is for 'truth and beauty and fair play and kindliness') is extremely vague and did not satisfy those critics who wanted to hear about something more than just British decency and fair play. 'As a statement of war aims, one feels, this leaves the world beyond Roedean still expectant,' wrote Graham Greene in the *Spectator*.[5] Most film historians dislike the film because of its heavily class-ridden attitudes which now seem more redolent of the British cinema of the 1930s than the new democratic realism which was to emerge during the war years. Clive Coultass, for example, writes: 'It was meant to be a justification, in crude propaganda terms, of Britain's intervention in Europe, and it was expressed through a text clearly conditioned by traditional concepts of Tory paternalism.'[6] In retrospect, it belongs to the same tradition of propaganda as the MOI's notorious slogan '*Your* Courage, *Your* Cheerfulness, *Your* Resolution, Will Bring *Us* Victory' in that it implies that the war was being fought to preserve the establishment and the class system. At the time, however, it was well received by many critics and was very popular at the box-office in the last months of 1939.[7]

The initiative behind *The Lion Has Wings* came from Korda, who had apparently planned it in some way before the outbreak of war. Ian Dalrymple recalled a studio meeting at Denham:

A few days before 3 September, some of us working at the Denham Studios — a fortuitous gaggle of directors and writers of various ages and origins, all of sadly unbellicose aspect — were summoned to Alex's office. He told us that we were to make a film to reassure the public of the power of the Royal Air Force, and that a liaison officer from the Air Ministry was on his way to assist us ...

Those among us geared to undertake the film promptly set to work: though with little conviction that we would complete it before the Germans blew us to bits.[8]

Michael Korda denied that any official help was provided for the film, writing that his uncle 'cashed in his life insurance policies to finance it, and completed it in less than two months without any assistance from the government, which was as helpless in the field of propaganda movies as it was in the supply of rifles'.[9] This account is in fact only partially correct, due perhaps to a tendency on Michael Korda's part to perpetuate a myth of his uncle as carrying out his patriotic work in the face of official apathy. While there was no government subsidy for the film, the newly established MOI was nevertheless very interested in the production. When the nature of official involvement was raised by the Labour MP Reginald Sorensen, Sir Edward Grigg, the Parliamentary Secretary to the MOI, wrote in reply:

This film is to be produced at the company's expense without any subsidy, under terms which give the Government very full control over its production and distribution. The statement of cost will be subject to Government audit and, therefore, the Government will have the option to purchase all rights in the film at an agreed figure, or to share equally in any profits without liability for losses, or to disclaim all financial concern in the film.

The hon. Member will no doubt agree that these terms represent a particularly generous expression on the part of the company and of their willingness to co-operate with the Ministry in the national interest at this juncture.[10]

Grigg added, somewhat over-optimistically as it turned out, that the MOI 'will be only too happy to consider offers from other companies to produce films on terms similar to those which I have described'. It is evident, therefore, that the production was carried out to a large degree under official auspices. Korda personally praised the assistance received from the Director of the Films Division. He told the trade press:

> Sir Joseph Ball backed our ideas from the very beginning on. He helped us with our ideas. He believed in what our unit intended to do, and encouraged us step by step from the first moment on, through the various stages of making the film, story conferences, first rough cutting – and he alone was in a position to secure us the wonderful help we had from the Air Ministry.[11]

Not only was an RAF liaison officer provided, but the Air Ministry also allowed Michael Powell's unit to undertake location shooting at Mildenhall air base in Norfolk.

In return for the facilities which were provided, the MOI secured a deal entitling the government to a share of the film's profits. This provoked a great deal of criticism in the trade press. 'Onlooker' of *Today's Cinema* was incredulous:

> Alexander Korda tells me the Government are going to get 50 per cent of the profit on this picture. Why?
>
> You can search me for the answer. I don't know it. Korda says it's because of facilities placed at his disposal by the Government. Tells me the Government didn't put up a shilling. Is this how they are going to help the film industry put the British idea on the screens? Every bean of the Government's share ought to go back to Korda to make more films of the same calibre. As to these precious 'facilities', they should be free anyway.[12]

In the event, the government made a considerable profit from the deal: by May 1944, the Exchequer had received a total of £25,140 from the commercial distribution of the film.[13]

The Lion Has Wings was completed in remarkably quick time. Trade shown on 17 October, it was released on 3 November. Its distribution was handled by United Artists, who offered it to exhibitors at a generous rate 'on condition that the exhibitors, on their side, waive their usual barring clauses'.[14] This was unusual because it meant the film would not be restricted to only one cinema in any given locality but would be shown instead 'without bars'. The arrangement was apparently carried through at the behest of the MOI, illustrating the interest which it took in the film. E. J. Hinge of the Cinematograph

Exhibitors' Association said that 'it was the desire of the Ministry that the film be shown in as many kinemas as early as possible'.[15] It was shown by all but one of the major cinema circuits (including Gaumont, Odeon, Granada and County; the ABC chain was the exception). A further sign of its privileged status is that it was the first film seen by King George VI and Queen Elizabeth after the outbreak of war.[16]

As the first propaganda feature film of the war, *The Lion Has Wings* attracted much attention. The most enthusiastic reviews came from the trade press, which is not surprising given their desire to sell the film to exhibitors. The *Daily Film Renter* described it as 'a magnificent job of work, remarkable for the unerring manner in which it has woven into a piece of compelling film entertainment an inspiring national message'.[17] The film also found its admirers among the national press. *The Times*, in its usual considered manner, offered a reasoned analysis of the film's propaganda content, and in particular praised the opening sequence contrasting life in Britain and Germany:

> This film at the Leicester Square theatre is emphatically a weapon of war, and it is skilfully aimed at a variety of targets. First, the English appear as an almost incredibly harmless people, entirely devoted to games and amusements, and so impeccably dedicated to the pursuit of happiness that they even play cricket for pleasure. Then, in the distance, there is the ominous thunder of marching feet, regimented herds of Nazis are contrasted with the happy observations of a Derby Day crowd, and the shrill exclamations of their leader with the hoarse clamour of English bookies and tipsters. The simpler acts of derision are used, but most effectively used, and the preliminaries will certainly put any audience in a happy temper.[18]

The Times did detect 'some awkward moments, as when Miss Merle Oberon is put forward to speak about goodness, truth and beauty', and suggested that 'it does not need the interlude of the Spanish Armada', but it concluded that 'on the whole it is stirring and good-humoured propaganda'.

The critical reception of the film was therefore on the whole favourable. It was only from the left that it attracted negative reviews, though it is on such reviews that its reputation is now based. The most hostile reaction came from *Documentary News Letter*, which ridiculed the unrealistic combat scenes and disliked the conclusion:

Puerile it is that all the successes should be on our side, that the Nazi pilots are cowardly morons (remember *Kaiser – The Beast of Berlin?*), that the Nazi air command is ignorant of the balloon barrage. Finally, Merle Oberon speaks for the women of England. She starts talking to Ralph Richardson beneath a Denham tree. The camera moves in until, as she gulps 'and – kindliness', she is in full close-up. Sadly she turns from the audience to Richardson – her audience: he is asleep, a smile of forbearance on his face. This may be 'realism', but it is a poor understanding of the psychology of film propaganda.[19]

Documentary News Letter's attitude towards the film may have been coloured by an audience survey carried out in December 1939 by Mass-Observation. Tom Harrisson, who wrote a precis of the survey for the journal's second issue, concluded that although the film was widely seen, it had not necessarily had the effect intended:

Many of those who said they liked it apparently only did so because they thought it the right thing to say, and those who did not like it time and time again objected to both propaganda and story. It seems likely that famous actors confuse matters if they are dragged into a picture only because of the box-office value of their names, and that the propaganda of the film needs to be much more subtle.[20]

Harrisson's article was a reasonably accurate summary of the results of the Mass-Observation survey, though he did perhaps exaggerate some of the criticisms which the respondents made.[21]

The MOI evidently attached much importance to securing a wide release for the film abroad. A sum of £3000 was provided to make dubbed or subtitled prints for Portugal, Spain, Italy and Turkey.[22] By far the most important overseas market, however, was the neutral United States, and it was here that the film was to expose differences between the MOI and the Foreign Office. When Korda went to America to promote the film his expenses were deferred from the MOI's share in the profits, which effectively amounted to an acknowledgement by the ministry that the film had its seal of approval. However, as F. R. Cowell of the Foreign Office News Department told the MOI's American Division:

As you know, His Majesty's Government is on record in the House of Commons and elsewhere to the effect that it is not going to undertake propaganda in the United States. This film, *The Lion Has Wings*, seems to be the first definite breach in this guarantee to the Americans, and I think it will be extremely difficult to defend it if it gets challenged.[23]

The incident was one factor in the institutional rift which was emerging between the Foreign Office and the MOI. There is also evidence of some disagreement within the MOI itself, for when Korda's visit to America to promote the film was announced to the press, Sir Frederick Whyte, Director of the MOI's American Division, complained that 'the Films Division went ahead without stopping to consider what they were doing'.[24] The Foreign Office was of the opinion that the incident 'reveals a disastrous lack of liaison within the Ministry'.[25] The whole episode illustrates the confusion which beset the official propaganda machinery at the beginning of the war.

III

The Lion Has Wings has been discussed at some length because it illustrates the unique circumstances surrounding the production of the first propaganda feature film of the war. The arrangement had been an *ad hoc* one to facilitate a speedy production which obviously had the MOI's approval. However, both the ministry and the film industry soon realised that they could not proceed in the same way with every film likely to be of some propaganda value; a policy was required from the government if the resources of the commercial producers were to be harnessed to the war effort. The period between the autumn of 1939 and the Thirteenth Report of the Select Committee on National Expenditure in August 1940 saw an on-going discussion in both trade and official circles about the nature of the government's involvement with feature film propaganda.

The first issue to arise between the industry and the MOI in respect of film propaganda was the question of whether the government would provide any money to subsidise the production of propaganda films. The terms under which Korda had produced *The Lion Has Wings* had been very advantageous for the MOI in that it exercised substantial control over the film and accrued a financial benefit without having subsidised it. Although Sir Edward Grigg had said that the ministry would consider offers from other producers to work on similar terms, there do not appear to have been any others willing to do so. The feeling of the trade was that, while they were quite ready to make films of a propagandist nature, they should not be put in the position of effectively making films for the government at their own expense. This point was made by Ealing's Michael Balcon, who praised Korda's action but questioned the terms under which producers were expected to work:

> Mr Korda has come forward with an offer which, at the present time, can only be described as public-spirited in the highest degree … But is the Government's reaction to his public-spiritedness equally generous? What I should like to know is for how long – under present conditions – can the British film production industry as a whole continue to afford to work for the Government on a similar basis?[26]

Balcon wanted 'encouragement of a more material kind', which would seem to imply some kind of subsidy, but on this question the MOI was equivocal. Lord Macmillan said:

> The idea that we have is that we should put up a proposition to the film industry and get anyone who is willing to take it up. So far as subsidy is concerned we would be willing to subsidise a film that had propaganda value, but some of them may be, and I think this one [The Lion Has Wings] has been, so good that it is going to be a commercial success.[27]

Macmillan certainly suggested that a subsidy might be possible, but it was far from the unambiguous statement that the trade wanted. The fact was that the MOI had not yet determined its policy and was keeping its options open.

A subject that was widely discussed both by the trade press and within the government was the possibility of setting up a Film Bank to assist the production of British films. This question arose in the autumn of 1939 due to the uncertainty which the outbreak of war had caused for the film industry. It was feared that a shortage of finance, which had become acute in the late 1930s following an economic slump, would be aggravated by the war situation. There was some support for the idea of a central finance organisation within the MOI Films Division, where Sir Edward Villiers argued that such a body was necessary if the needs of film propaganda were to be met:

In the case of the film industry, the setting up of a sound financing organisation will not only secure for the country what it needs for the film industry during wartime, but will establish once and for all an industry which is vital to the needs of the Empire in peace as in war, and that, too, at a, comparatively speaking, small cost to the Government; for the essence of good film propaganda is that it should be good film entertainment, and this in a large measure should pay for itself.[28]

Villiers therefore supported the trade interests in coupling the need for a sound financial base to the need for propaganda films. In January 1940 a report by the Cinematograph Films Council of the Board of Trade recommended that the government should set up a Film Finance Corporation with a minimum capital of £1.8 million to subsidise British film production. Lengthy and detailed discussions followed between the Board of Trade, the Treasury, the Bank of England and the film industry, but although there was considerable support for the idea in official circles nothing was to come of it.[29]

While the main concern of the feature producers following the outbreak of war was the subsidy question, they were also concerned about the propaganda content of feature films. What sort of subjects and themes should they be using for propaganda films? Despite Macmillan's suggestion that the MOI would put forward ideas to commercial producers, none of these seem to have been taken up. The trade was soon complaining about the lack of policy guidelines from the MOI. Indeed, producers themselves began drafting papers and submitting them to the ministry. Ian Dalrymple recalled that, during production of *The Lion Has Wings*, 'I had become interested in the whole use of film for war ends; and with naive enthusiasm I composed an exhaustive paper which I submitted to the Ministry through a friend in the Films Division. This evoked no response whatever.'[30] Several other trade figures had also submitted papers to the MOI but had received no reply. George Elvin, the General Secretary of the Association of Cine-Technicians, told *Kinematograph Weekly*:

Within five days of the outbreak of war a memorandum was submitted to the Ministry of Information signed by leading producers, film directors and other technicians. In those days it was anticipated that the powers-that-be were alive to the importance of films in war, and the memorandum outlined how best, in the signatories' opinion, that medium could be used.

The document has been read, so we understand, and filed. It has not been acted on. I am not unduly blaming the department to whom it was addressed. I believe it realises the importance of films, and strove hard to get things going. But by now it appears to have got tired of trying, and the ghost has been given up.[31]

The MOI's main problem, Elvin considered, was that it was 'obstructed by the Maginot Line of Whitehall bureaucracy'.

The initiatives for propaganda films during the first months of the war came from the industry rather than from the MOI. Ealing's *Convoy* (1940) is a case in point. This film was announced in November 1939, and according to the reports in the trade press, it was Michael Balcon's own idea that the convoys would provide 'a film subject not only of engrossing entertainment but one that will also act as powerful propaganda here and among friendly nations'.[32] When *Convoy* became the biggest British box-office hit of 1940, trade journalists were quick to point out that the credit belonged to Ealing rather than the MOI. 'Onlooker' criticised the government's attitude:

Sitting back, intensely interested in *Convoy* at this week's trade show, I again marvelled at the complacency of a nation that leaves the display of its amazing maritime genius and power to the enterprise of some individuals. Had not Michael Balcon and his Ealing lieutenants gone to the Admiralty and asked for co-operation in shooting and countless other details the wonders of *Convoy* would never have been shown to the world.[33]

The *Sunday Express* reported that when representatives of the MOI saw the film they were 'dubious of its propaganda value'. When the film became a huge popular success, however, the lesson to be learned was that 'the MOI must recognise that experienced commercial producers like Balcon, [John] Corfield and [Edward] Black understand films as a medium of propaganda, *plus* entertainment, better than they do'.[34]

No guidelines for film propaganda were forthcoming from the MOI because the Films Division was having to evolve its policy in the light of experience during the course of 1939–40. Sir Kenneth Clark was evidently concerned to ensure that he was in a position to advise film-makers when they asked for guidance, for at a meeting of the MOI's

Co-Ordinating Committee in April 1940 he 'reported that film producers were asking for fresh subjects, and asked for suggestions to be given to him for books etc. capable of being turned into suitable films'.[35] The most significant outcome of the Clark administration, however, was that the Films Division started to consider seriously subsidising feature film propaganda. Shortly after taking office he hinted to one journalist that 'if a production which looked to be really excellent from his point of view needed a thousand or two, it might be forthcoming'.[36] Soon, the possibility had become more definite, and Clark was saying that rather than just helping out here and there the MOI was ready to sponsor a major feature film. 'So far, the Ministry has not paid for the production of a long feature film, but we shall probably do so in the near future,' he wrote in a circular to Regional Information Officers early in 1940.[37] What was the reason for this shift in official policy? The most likely explanation seems to be that Clark was dissatisfied with the propaganda films which had been made hitherto. He held a low opinion of *The Lion Has Wings*, which he described as 'three documentaries strung together to attain feature length'.[38] In his memoirs, Clark recalled that several feature projects were planned but for various reasons never got off the ground:

> We prepared a long film on minesweepers and Graham Greene wrote an excellent script for a film on the Gestapo in England. I also planned to do a film on Anglo-French collaboration, with Leslie Howard and Danièle [*sic*] Darrieux in the leading parts, to be produced by René Clair. Everything was arranged, and I went to Paris with Leslie to see our brilliant producer. It was about a fortnight before the German advance.[39]

A film on minesweepers was mentioned in the Programme for Film Propaganda as being 'in preparation', though no such film was ever made. And the trade press reported that a film entitled *Flight to Victory*, involving Leslie Howard, David Niven and Danielle Darrieux, which was to have been 'tentatively sponsored by the M of I', was abandoned 'due to unforeseen difficulties brought about by war conditions'.[40] There is some anecdotal evidence to suggest that Clark's willingness to sponsor propaganda films was soon known on Wardour Street. Michael Powell suggested that the word was out that the Films Division was ready to take a more active role in feature film propaganda. 'About February, John Sutro, who was a great friend of Korda's and one of his directors on the board, came to me and said the Government definitely wants to back films, they will even put Government money into it if we can't raise the money elsewhere,' Powell said. 'I went with him to see Kenneth Clark.'[41] The result of Powell's meeting with Clark was that the MOI agreed to back *49th Parallel*. As this was the only feature film for which the MOI provided direct financial support during the war, it is worth investigating in detail.

IV

Anthony Aldgate describes *49th Parallel* as 'nothing if not a thoroughly schematic and heavily programmed attempt to fulfil all the criteria of excellence for film propaganda laid down by the Films Division of the MoI'.[42] It exhibits many of the principles outlined in Clark's Programme for Film Propaganda: it dramatises the ideological differences between democracy and Nazism; it addresses the theme of why the British Commonwealth was fighting the war; and it provides the good entertainment value which was considered desirable for film propaganda.

There are conflicting sources of evidence regarding the origins of this film. As early as January 1940, an MOI Policy Committee paper entitled 'Publicity about the British Empire' had recommended making 'a first-class feature film developing as an exciting story the history of the growth of freedom, referring to the American parallel and stimulus in order to give it an appeal to United States audiences'.[43] The idea was very similar to the final form which *49th Parallel* was to take; it certainly shows that the MOI had identified a need to address questions about democracy and freedom in the British Empire before it embarked on the production of this specific film. And Clark recalled that early in 1940 the then Director-General of the MOI, Sir Kenneth Lee, had suggested 'that we should make a full-length feature film which would indirectly describe the reasons why we are fighting this war'.[44] There is evidence, therefore, that the initial idea for the film originated within the MOI, unlike the case of *The Lion Has Wings*. However, the press notes for the film's premiere state that Powell had got the idea for the film from a Canadian newspaper late in 1939 and 'talked over his ideas with scenarist Emeric Pressburger, so that he would have something concrete to show Sir Kenneth Clark when the two met some weeks later'.[45] Wherever the idea originated, it is clear that *49th Parallel* was made possible by the friendly relations with commercial film-makers fostered by Clark. The outcome of the meeting was that Powell and Pressburger went on a location trip to Canada with £5000 'development money' in the spring of 1940 to work out a story, and then returned to London to secure the production money.

Powell's story of how he got money for the film from the Treasury is a heroic tale of triumph over Whitehall officialdom. He suggests, moreover, that it was secured only through the personal intervention of the Minister of Information:

> The Treasury, of course, were madly against this and hated the film. Imagine at the time when we came back – France was falling, the battle of Britain was looming, and here's some bastard who wants £80,000 or £50,000 to go and make a film in Canada. I told Duff Cooper what the scope of the film was ... and in the end Duff Cooper stood up and said to the Treasury, 'Finance must not stand in the way of this project,' and walked out, and so the Treasury very sourly folded up their briefcases, and we were off.[46]

However, it may have been that the Treasury was not as averse to backing the film as Powell suggests. During Clark's regime the Films Division had accepted the idea of backing at least one major feature film, and it seems unlikely that it would have adopted this policy if it did not have financial approval to do so. Moreover, at this time the Treasury was involved in the on-going discussion about the Film Bank, which involved a far greater sum than the amount provided for this one film. Further evidence of official willingness to provide financial assistance for feature films arose in the case of Gabriel Pascal's production of *Major Barbara* (1941). This film ran out of money in the summer of 1940 and there was a possibility that it might be lost to Hollywood; the Board of Trade was asked to find £25,000 completion money, though in the event the sum was provided by the National Provincial Bank.[47] Therefore, at the time of *49th Parallel*'s production there was considerable support within the government for the principle of providing financial assistance for British films. In any case, *49th Parallel* was not financed solely by the MOI, as over half the budget was provided by J. Arthur Rank. The precise nature of the financial terms was at first a closely guarded secret, and it was not until a question was asked in Parliament in December 1940 that Duff Cooper announced the MOI had by then advanced a total of £22,086 13s. 7d. for the film, adding that 'the Ministry's contribution is expected to be substantially less than half the total cost'.[48] The final amount advanced by the MOI by the end of production was slightly less than £60,000.

The production of *49th Parallel* did not proceed without some controversy. It came under attack from both Wardour Street and Parliament. The trade press, having been clamouring for so long for the MOI to provide a subsidy for propaganda films, now turned on it for backing this particular project. The main bone of contention was that a film unit was being sent overseas at official expense while other film-makers were being urged to stay at home. *Today's Cinema* declared:

> This being so the Ministry of Information should have stayed at home, set the example and not roused the feeling that this exodus to Canada has caused right through the business.
>
> The example is terrible to all those people who have been told it is their duty to stay around and make pictures. Sure we want the MOI to make pictures, but this attitude which upsets everybody and achieves but the same result as could have been done at home is obviously a step off on the wrong foot.[49]

Even more serious opposition came from the Select Committee on National Expenditure, which was investigating the MOI Films Division at the same time that the location shooting for the film was under way in Canada. The Select Committee doubted the wisdom of investing in feature films:

> There are two principal difficulties. One is the great length of time necessarily required for the production of a full length feature film. The other and more serious consideration is the highly speculative character of feature film production. Effort and experience, art and imagination, genius itself, none nor all of these have power to command infallible success. Only one thing is certain in feature film production – the uncertainty of success.[50]

The Select Committee expressed 'the gravest misgiving' about *49th Parallel* and recommended that 'no more feature films should be undertaken even if the film now being made should be as successful as it is hoped it will be'. Thus it was that the Select Committee scotched any further plans which the MOI may have had for sponsoring feature films.

49th Parallel was the foremost example of direct collaboration between the MOI and the film industry during the war. It was different from *The Lion Has Wings* in that it was not a hodge-podge but rather a fully worked-out dramatic linear narrative. It encapsulates most of the themes of British film propaganda: the ideological differences between Nazism and democracy, the rights of free people against bullies and aggressors, the nature of the political culture of the British Commonwealth, and the shared bonds of democracy and freedom between the Commonwealth and the United States. The narrative is structured around a series of set pieces which put these themes into dramatic form. A voice-over commentary refers to the forty-ninth parallel as 'the only undefended frontier in the world', while aerial photography of mountain ranges, accompanied by the evocative music of Ralph Vaughan Williams, creates an impression of the vastness of that frontier.

The story begins with a German U-boat sinking a merchant ship off the Labrador coast ('So the curtain rises on Canada!' declares the captain). Attempting to evade detection, the U-boat seeks refuge in Hudson Bay, but is found and sunk by the Royal Canadian Air Force. A reconnaissance party of six men, put ashore before the U-boat was bombed, are the only survivors. They are led by the fanatical Lieutenant Hirth (Eric Portman). Their various misadventures, as they try to make their way home (or at least to internment in the neutral United States), then provides the main line of narrative. They encounter all manner of Canadians, who represent different aspects of the country's liberal and democratic culture. First they come across an isolated trading post on Hudson Bay where they encounter a French-Canadian trapper (Laurence Olivier), just returned from a hunting expedition, who is unaware of the war. His Eskimo assistant is clubbed to death and the trapper, Johnny, is shot and left for dead when he tries to call for help on the radio. One of the Nazis is shot by an Eskimo as they escape by plane, and another is killed when the plane runs out of fuel and crashes. The four survivors come across a Hutterite religious community of Germanic origin where they are welcomed by Peter (Anton Walbrook). One of the Germans, Vogel (Niall MacGinnis), is attracted by the Hutterite way of life and becomes friendly with Anna (Glynis Johns); he decides to stay, whereupon he is summarily court martialled and shot by Hirth. The remaining three Nazis are hunted across Canada. One is captured at the Indian Day festival in Banff. Hirth and Lohrmann (John Chandos) flee into the mountains where they encounter Philip Armstong-Scott (Leslie Howard), an intellectual who scorns war and prefers to lead a life of peaceful solitude researching Indian customs. To the Nazis he is the embodiment of soft, decadent democracy, but he proves to have nerves of steel when he corners and captures Lohrmann ('Well, he had a fair chance. One armed superman against one unarmed decadent democrat!'). Hirth tries to escape to America by hiding on a freight train, but the intervention of Andy Brock (Raymond Massey), an ordinary Canadian soldier, and the US Customs at Niagara Falls, leads to his capture.

49th Parallel was not released until October 1941, some eighteen months after the initial meeting between Powell and Clark. Although it had been a long time in the making and its costs had escalated, it nevertheless vindicated the MOI's faith in the project by becoming a major critical and financial success. The critics expressed approval of the story, acting and the authentic locations. *The Times*, for example, thought that it was an exciting and well-made thriller:

> This film has been an incredibly long time in the making, passing through almost as many vicissitudes as the German naval fugitives whose adventures in Canada it chronicles, but it reaches us at last without any obvious signs of travail. It offers the same kind of pleasure that we get from a John Buchan novel. The incidents are sufficiently exciting to carry the patriotic theme, there are agreeable touches of humour and the big backgrounds of mountains and spruce forests to lift the spirit of the tale.[51]

The American trade paper *Variety* described it as 'an important and effective propaganda film' and suggested that 'there is every indication that it will realize a handsome profit, in addition to its propaganda value throughout the democracies'.[52] The film was retitled *The Invaders* for America, where it was released early in 1942 and won an Academy Award for Best Original Screenplay. The box-office takings of the film more than repaid the MOI's investment: by September 1944 some £132,331 in receipts had been passed to the Exchequer.[53] In a letter to *The Times*, Powell declared that it had 'earned its entire production cost in the first three months of its exhibition', which was 'a most re-markable achievement for a feature film, and one that justifies the faith that the then Minister of Information placed in our venture.'[54]

V

By the time *49th Parallel* was released, the Select Committee on National Expenditure had caused the MOI to rethink its policy of investing directly in feature films. Its report was highly critical of the Films Division's failure to work with the film industry and it expressed concern that none of the projects suggested to producers by the division had been taken up. Therefore the report urged that in future 'the Films Division should not waste time in trying to devise subjects that would usually be rejected, but should ask the producers of feature films to allocate a definite proportion of their production to films of a distinct national value'.[55] It was also suggested that 'producers should choose their own themes and carry them out in their own way', a suggestion which, if it had been enacted, would effectively have put film propaganda in the hands of the trade. Jack Beddington was strongly opposed to the committee's recommendation. He dismissed the suggestion that producers should be asked to allocate a 'definite proportion' of their production to propaganda films on the grounds that it implied a 'mathematical fraction' which would be difficult to suggest and impossible to measure. And he was adamant that the Films Division should 'reserve the right to suggest subjects to producers, or to pass forward to them suggestions made to the Division; in other words, to act as a critical clearing house for ideas'.[56] It is clear that Beddington was not prepared to allow responsibility for film propaganda to be passed to the trade. In this, he was supported by the documentary interests who, of course, did not share the trade's view that commercial producers were the best arbiters of good propaganda. An article in *Documentary News Letter* suggested that the trade's wish to have control of film propaganda had a covert intention:

> The Trade Press in general has repeatedly shown that it does not want propaganda (even of the most disguised sort) in cinemas at all, so its call to have propaganda turned over to the commercial film trade springs simply from the desire to see it disappear altogether, or see it limited to warlike backgrounds and the usual love story, which is all the film trade has contributed so far.[57]

Ealing's *Convoy* and *Ships With Wings* were cited as typical examples of the commercial trade's ideas of propaganda because of their reliance on traditional melodramatic conventions.

The conflicting views about who should have responsibility for film propaganda – the MOI or the trade – came to the fore in the rift which developed between the ministry and Ealing Studios during the latter half of 1940. This was due largely to an abortive attempt by

Balcon to take over the GPO Film Unit, but it was also undoubtedly influenced by Balcon's very public criticisms of the MOI in both the national and the trade press. The first evidence of official opposition to an Ealing film was over *The Big Blockade* (1941), a feature-length semi-documentary made to illustrate the economic blockade of Germany. 'Mr Beddington reported that Mr Balcon refused to make this film for the Ministry, and declared that he was making it for the Ministry of Economic Warfare,' recorded the minutes of the MOI's Planning Committee on 16 December 1940. '[It was] Agreed that Mr Beddington should take action to prevent this.'[58] The MOI apparently did not approve of other government departments becoming involved in film production, particularly with a producer who had made frequent public criticisms of its policy. The fact that the MOI evidently tried (albeit unsuccessfully) at this moment to stop that particular film from going ahead was almost certainly influenced by Balcon's announcement in December 1940 that Ealing was splitting from the ministry and would henceforth go its own way in terms of propaganda. The *Evening News* reported the rift thus:

> Mr Michael Balcon's decision to produce no more propaganda pictures for the Films Division of the Ministry of Information must be one more blow for a department that has led anything but a comfortable life since its inception.
>
> The point made by Mr Balcon is that as a commercial producer – he made *Convoy* – he is tired of trying to get Films Division cooperation for subjects which he, as a showman with patriotic instincts, thinks would make good entertainment and impressive propaganda.
>
> 'The Films Division has shown no signs of having a planned or coherent programme of production,' he said to me last night.[59]

Balcon's complaint was that the MOI did not offer enough support to commercial producers. Yet the rift also illustrates a difference of opinion over the nature of propaganda, for Balcon's ideas of what constituted good propaganda were not the same as those of the Films Division. Beddington explained why support was not always given to producers who asked for it:

> Actually, as commercial producers, in asking for facilities, often submit the briefest synopses on which to form a judgement, it

happens that extensive facilities are granted for productions which do not deserve them. Efforts are being made to prevent this happening, but a good example is one of Mr Balcon's own productions, namely *Ships With Wings*, which received every facility from the Admiralty in the making and yet is so bad that the Prime Minister attempted to have its distribution stopped.[60]

Ships With Wings, directed by Sergei Nolbandov, had been allowed location shooting facilities on board HMS *Ark Royal*. According to Balcon's memoirs, when Churchill saw the film at Chequers he disliked it so much that he 'was insisting that release should be held up, if not cancelled altogether, on the grounds that it would cause "alarm and despondency", as the climax of the film was something of a disaster for the Fleet Air Arm'. In retrospect Balcon admitted that the film was not good propaganda because it was 'too heavily fictionalised', though he recalled that at the time Churchill's opposition 'was not only a terrible blow to our pride but also to our pockets, as the film represented a substantial investment'.[61] The film was released and in the event was a popular success. However, given that the trade was making films which did not always meet with official approval, it is easy to appreciate why Beddington was so strenuous in resisting the Select Committee's suggestion that decisions on the subjects and treatment of propaganda films should be left to the commercial producers themselves.

The gulf between the MOI and the trade over what made good propaganda was bridged by the Films Division finally finding a formula for the 'friendly and mutually acceptable working arrangements' that the Select Committee had said should be established with the film industry. This was done first of all by the setting up of an Ideas Committee at the end of 1941 to provide a forum for discussion and the exchange of ideas. Described as the 'MOI Brains Trust' by the trade press, the Ideas Committee consisted of leading members of the film industry who met to discuss projects informally. Its membership varied over time, including such people as Leslie Howard, Anthony Asquith, Michael Powell and Sidney Gilliat. Commercial film-makers seem to have been prevalent, though documentary was also represented. Paul Rotha recalled that the committee 'met round a table over beer and rather lousy sandwiches once every fortnight' but considered that it worked well: 'We would talk backwards and forwards across the table for about a couple of hours, and then we'd go down to the theatre and see some films, and this was a very healthy and excellent thing ... a lot came out of this committee.'[62] Rotha's verdict is supported by the trade press, which reported in March 1942 that Beddington 'feels the constructive suggestions which have emerged have more than justified the new committee'.[63] The Ideas Committee was an informal set-up, but it seems to have worked effectively as a channel of communication between the Films Division and the industry. It allowed for the discussion of films before production and, importantly, it meant that commercial producers were kept aware of what the MOI considered was good propaganda. Porter and Litewski even go so far as to describe the Ideas Committee as 'the fount of feature film production ideology'.[64]

The Ideas Committee was not the only channel of communication between the MOI and the film industry. The British Film Producers' Association had been set up by the commercial producers themselves to represent their interests to various government departments, particularly the Board of Trade and the Ministry of Labour. Shortly after Beddington's arrival at the MOI Films Division, the BFPA took the initiative in writing to him 'in regard to an appointment ... for the purpose of discussing any proposals the Ministry had for the making of propaganda films'.[65] However, it was not until the middle years of the war that closer relations were established between the BFPA and the MOI. Early in 1942 the BFPA had discussed 'the possibility of the Association keeping in closer touch with the Ministry of Information'.[66] The BFPA was perturbed when it was not invited to be represented on the Ideas Committee (even though several individual members were common to both) and the approach which it made to the MOI for closer links was probably due to a fear on the association's part that it was being excluded from easy access to the official ear. This time Beddington responded rather more enthusiastically to the BFPA's overtures: he 'agreed to co-operate fully with the Association and ... expressed his willingness to attend any of its meetings at which his presence was desired'.[67] Beddington was then able to use the BFPA as another channel for keeping the trade informed of official propaganda requirements. He attended some of the association's meetings and used it as another forum for suggesting possible projects to the commercial producers. In March 1942 'it was agreed that Mr Beddington should submit to the Association stories brought to his attention which, in the opinion of the Ministry, would be good propaganda if made into films'.[68] However, although Beddington put forward several suggestions, none of them were taken up by producers.[69]

It was through the channel of the BFPA that Beddington defined the MOI's policy towards feature film propaganda in the middle of the war. In March 1942 he 'stated that it was the policy of the Ministry of Information to give all possible aid to British Film Production and the Ministry held the opinion that any good British production could be regarded as "propaganda" even though the subject matter of the film could not in some cases be so described'.[70] This marked a gradual shift in official thinking towards the view that quality films, even those not directly concerned with war subjects, could be valuable in presenting images of Britain. In this matter, Beddington seems to have been influenced by the views of some of the leading members of the trade. For example, C. M. Woolf, the President of the BFPA, said at its annual general meeting in June 1942 'that he thought there was a tendency on the part of producers to concentrate entirely on war or purely war subjects' but that cinema-goers were 'already getting tired of this type of picture and were asking for films which took their minds off the tragedy now taking place'. He suggested that the concentration on war subjects was due to official policy:

> The Ministry of Information had been extremely helpful in assisting to obtain the temporary release of artistes, but they were apt to couple their recommendations for such release with the stipulation that the film must definitely be of a war propaganda kind. This had the effect of limiting producers to this class of film and helped to perpetuate the tendency he referred to.[71]

Beddington appears to have accepted Woolf's point, for a month later the BFPA was informed 'that the Ministry was prepared to support all types of pictures – both war and non-war – provided they were of the highest quality'.[72]

This modification of policy towards feature films was indicative of a wider change going on across the British cinema as a whole. War films had been popular with audiences in the first years of the war – *Convoy, 49th Parallel, The First of the Few* and *In Which We Serve* were the most successful British films at the box-office in successive years from 1940 to 1943 – but the popular trend thereafter was towards more escapist fare such as the Gainsborough melodramas. In suggesting that war films were no longer automatically considered to be of propaganda value, the MOI was responding to popular audience tastes. Films about the war continued to be made, of course, but the MOI stressed the importance of quality and realism. In a policy statement of March 1943, the Films Division declared that it wanted 'first class war subjects realistically treated; realistic films of everyday life; high quality entertainment films', but that it disapproved of 'war subjects exploited for cheap sensationalism; the morbid and the maudlin; entertainment stories which are stereotyped or hackneyed and unlikely because of their theme or general character to reflect well upon this country at home and abroad'.[73] This trend in the nature of war films is best exemplified by the production policy at Ealing Studios, which abandoned the false heroics of films like *Ships With Wings* for the more sober realism of *The Foreman Went to France* and *San Demetrio, London*. In his autobiography Balcon described his production ideology thus:

> The aim in making films during the war was easy enough to state but more difficult to achieve. It was, first and foremost, to make a good film, a film that people would want to see, and at the same time to make it honest and truthful and to carry a message, or an example, which would be good propaganda for morale and the war effort. I think *San Demetrio, London* was an outstanding example of a film that amply fulfilled all those requirements. The story came from the news. *San Demetrio* was an oil tanker which was practically cut in half in mid-Atlantic and heroically brought home by its stricken crew.
>
> This story so caught the popular imagination that the Ministry of Information issued a special pamphlet, written by Tennyson Jesse, and we decided to make a film of it.[74]

Although *San Demetrio, London* is now generally regarded as the quintessential Ealing war film – Charles Barr, for example, describes it as 'the culmination of Ealing's war programme, the ideal fulfilment of Balcon's policy'[75] – it should be borne in mind that it was based on an official pamphlet and was also very much in line with the MOI's requirements that war films should be treated realistically and without sensationalism. Much has been made, not least by Balcon himself, of Ealing's decision to concentrate on realism from the middle of the war, but there is a strong case to argue that, following its schism with the MOI in 1940, the studio's production policy in fact marked a belated acceptance of the ministry's requirements.

VI

From about 1942–43 it is possible to identify a broad consensus between the MOI and the commercial film-makers over the nature of film propaganda. The rift between Balcon and the MOI appears to have been healed, with Ealing fully incorporated into the national propaganda effort. Through the Ideas Committee and the BFPA, the MOI had effective channels of communication with the main producers. The control which it exercised was informal and, for the film-makers, voluntary, but as Aldgate points out, it was 'sufficient to ensure that British film production in general, and not just "official" films, followed precisely the line that the Ministry wished it to follow in mobilising support for the war effort and in constructing the essential wartime ideology of popular national unity'.[76] In one sense the views of the Select Committee on National Expenditure were taken on board in that feature films were used not for direct or immediate propaganda but rather for presenting more general images of the British at war. The feature film was obviously more suited to long-term propaganda because of the length of time which it took to produce. As Michael Powell remarked: 'we were guessing a year ahead what the general position of the war would be and what would be the propaganda message.'[77]

How did the relationship between the Films Division and the commercial producers developed under Beddington actually work? Through the channels of communication which he had opened up, a dialogue was possible with producers which allowed for informal discussion and unofficial vetting of projects beforehand. Sidney Bernstein described the procedure thus:

> The Ministry both advised the producers on the suitability of subjects which they had suggested, and proposed subjects which we thought would do good overseas. Whenever the Ministry had approved a subject we gave every help to the producer in obtaining facilities to make the film. For instance, we helped them get artists out of the services, we aided them to secure raw-stock, travel priorities and so on.[78]

Michael Powell recalled the relationship from the film-maker's point of view:

It must be understood that the way the Ministry of Information worked with commercial film-makers was that Beddington would send for one of the well-known film-makers to discuss an idea that the Ministry wanted dramatised, or else we would come to Beddington with ideas of our own. We would discuss with him and the idea would either be approved or not. In our case, because of the unique nature of our creative partnership, it usually was. The point was that these films were financed commercially after having obtained the Ministry's approval of the themes and the general content.[79]

A working relationship was therefore achieved between the MOI and the film industry. It was a two-way process in which ideas could be suggested by both sides. Although the MOI would not put up any money for features, it would assist films of which it approved by providing 'facilities' (which would then be charged to the producers at cost price). For war films, this often involved providing troops as extras. It has been suggested that the control of raw film stock amounted to an indirect form of censorship. 'The films division was given control of all negative film which was made available to producers only after approval of each script,' wrote Thorold Dickinson.[80] The shortage of film stock, which was caused by shipping losses in the Atlantic, became acute in 1942 and was rationed under the Cinematograph Film Control Order of March 1943. Distributors had to reduce their consumption by 20 per cent, while producers were allocated stock for individual films. However, stock was controlled by the Board of Trade, not the MOI, and there is no direct evidence of stock having been withheld to stop a particular film from being made.[81]

Although the MOI was no longer in the business of financing feature films, there are numerous cases where it apparently prompted certain projects and was quite closely involved in the production. According to official records, the script of Launder and Gilliat's *Millions Like Us* (1943) 'was first commissioned by the Films Division and then sold at cost price to a feature production company'.[82] And Laurence Olivier recalled that he was once 'summoned to the Ministry of Information to see Jack Beddington' who 'asked me to undertake two pictures intended to enhance the British cause'.[83] As a result Olivier starred in Anthony Asquith's *The Demi-Paradise* (1943) and directed and starred in *Henry V* (1944). The MOI arranged for Olivier to be released from his service in the Fleet Air Arm in order to make these films. There are other cases of films where, even if there is no direct evidence (either documented or anecdotal) of official involvement, there is nevertheless good reason to believe that the MOI was in some way behind the production. Ealing's *Went the Day Well?* (1942), directed by Alberto Cavalcanti, depicts a fictitious German invasion of a sleepy English village and the subsequent defeat of the invaders through a combination of civilian and military effort. Aldgate has shown that the film was made at a time during the spring of 1942 when the MOI was anxious about the effects of an invasion scare on public morale and confidence. He writes that 'it is difficult to escape the conclusion that it was, in effect, an "official" film and that it carried the MoI stamp of approval'.[84] For example, the film was based on a short story originally written for the MOI in 1940 by Graham Greene, and it made use of troops of the Gloucestershire Regiment provided 'by kind permission of the War Office'.

However, in identifying this consensus between the MOI and commercial film-makers from the middle of the war, it should not be assumed that the relationship was without problems. There were occasional points of friction. The most notorious of these was *The Life and Death of Colonel Blimp* (1943), a film which Powell and Pressburger made in the face of intense official hostility. The controversy which the film provoked shows that in this instance there was a serious ideological difference between the film-makers and the government over the nature of propaganda. In making a major Technicolor film based on the character of 'Colonel Blimp' – a political diehard and military lunatic created by cartoonist David Low – Powell and Pressburger had set out to show 'that Colonel Blimp was a symbol of British procrastination and British regard for tradition and all the things which we knew and which were losing the war'.[85] On this occasion, the informal vetting of projects by the MOI before production failed to deter Powell and Pressburger, who went ahead despite the rumblings which the project had caused in Whitehall. The government's objection to the film was due to the apparent implication that the British Army was full of 'Blimps' whose old-fashioned attitudes and reactionary ideas were hindering the effective prosecution of the war. 'I find myself in complete disagreement with the basic idea underlying *The Life and Death of Colonel Blimp*,' the Secretary of State for War, Sir James Grigg, told Powell after hearing about the proposed film.[86] The War Office's attitude rubbed off on the MOI who, after reading the script, told Powell: 'we cannot bring ourselves to feel that the public interest would be served by the production of the film as it stands, nor do we see how it could be rendered of positive value from the point of view of national propaganda, by alterations in the dialogue or in the treatment of individual sequences.'[87] In this case, the MOI refused to facilitate Laurence Olivier's release from the Fleet Air Arm to star in the film. Powell and Pressburger went ahead nevertheless, casting Roger Livesey as 'Blimp' and making the film without any official facilities being made available to them.

What made the *Colonel Blimp* affair unique was the personal inter-vention of the Prime Minister. When Churchill heard about the film (then in the course of production at Denham Studios) from the War Office in September 1942, he immediately decided that it must be suppressed. 'Pray propose to me the measures necessary to stop this foolish production before it gets any further,' he instructed Brendan Bracken. 'I am not prepared to allow propaganda detrimental to the morale of the Army, and I am sure the Cabinet will take all necessary action.'[88] Churchill's intervention was a cause of some irritation for his Minister of Information, who does not appear to have been as violently opposed to the film as the Prime Minister himself. Bracken replied that the MOI 'has no power to suppress the film' and explained why it was inadvisable to try to do so:

> I am advised that in order to stop it the Government would need to assume powers of a very far-reaching kind. These could hardly be less than powers to suppress all films, even those based on imaginary stories, on the grounds not of their revealing informa-tion to the enemy but of their expressing harmful or misguided opinions. Moreover it would be illogical for the Government to insist on a degree of control over films which it does not exercise over other means of expression, such as books or newspaper articles. Nothing less, therefore, than the imposition of a com-pulsory censorship of opinion upon all means of expression would meet the case, and I am certain that this could not be done without provoking infinite protest.[89]

Bracken realised that to suppress the film would have been a politically insensitive move in a democracy at war. It would have involved adopting an extensive censorship apparatus on a par with that exercised by the

Nazi state, which was the last thing that Bracken wanted given that so much of the MOI's work was concerned to show how Britain was different from Nazi Germany. In the event Churchill was persuaded to let the matter rest, though the film's overseas distribution was delayed.

The *Colonel Blimp* affair is significant in several respects. It shows that the Prime Minister took a personal interest in some aspects of film propaganda; it suggests that the government's powers to stop films of which it disapproved had certain practical and political limitations; and it illustrates that there was sometimes a degree of friction in the relationship between the MOI and commercial film-makers. As *Colonel Blimp* was the most severe of these points of friction, it has inevitably attracted much attention from historians.[90] Yet for all the controversy surrounding the film, it was an isolated example which is not typical of the relations between the MOI and the film industry. Although Powell recalled that he had numerous 'rows' with Jack Beddington over the film, they did not sour his relations with the MOI in the long term. Indeed, any animosity that was incurred was quickly overcome, for Powell and Pressburger continued working with the ministry throughout the war. For example, shortly after *Colonel Blimp* they made *The Volunteer* (1943), a training and recruitment film for the Admiralty which was produced by the MOI. And one of Powell and Pressburger's later films, *A Matter of Life and Death* (1946), apparently started with a suggestion from Beddington to make a film about Anglo-American relations as the war drew to a close.[91] Thus it was that even the film-makers who had done most to rock the boat during the war were still closely involved in the MOI's propaganda effort.

4

The MOI and Short Film Propaganda

Upon the shoulders of a comparative handful of people rests the responsibility of projecting national publicity, not only at home, but overseas. The short has re-entered the cinema from which it was ousted, but now in an official capacity, and in carrying out its important work, it has made the public more 'short-conscious' than ever before. *Sight and Sound* (1942)[1]

I

During the Second World War, some 1400 official short films were 'presented' to the British public by the MOI. Most of them were commissioned by the ministry from one of several sources: the Crown Film Unit, the independent documentary producers, the commercial studios or the newsreel companies. Some were released in the cinemas, while others were made for exhibition through the MOI's non-theatrical programme. The large number of short films produced would seem to suggest a comprehensive propaganda campaign by the MOI. There was certainly a greater degree of exposure to shorts and documentaries for audiences, particularly in comparison to pre-war days, which may have led to some cinema-goers becoming more 'short-conscious'. However, many commentators and historians have been sceptical of the value of official short films and documentaries for propaganda purposes. It has usually been assumed that, unlike feature film propaganda, short film propaganda was largely unsuccessful. This assumption, which is to be found in most of the historiography, seems to have started with the complaints made by cinema exhibitors during the war about the unpopularity of official films with their audiences. In 1942, for example, one exhibitor remarked: 'As a result of the cheaply and badly made MOI films, even in those cinemas where the presentation is properly done, that section of the public who occupy the cheaper seats give vent to an audible groan when MOI appears on the credit titles.'[2] Similar testimony was provided by some cinema-goers themselves, such as one of the respondents to Mass-Observation's 1943 questionnaire on favourite films, who declared: 'At practically every occasion on which I visit a cinema I have to digest some miserable propaganda film about the war.'[3] While it will be shown here that such views were not necessarily representative, most historians have hitherto accepted uncritically the views of commentators such as these. Although Paul Swann notes the success of some individual films (he cites *Britain at Bay* as being 'extremely popular'), he still considers that 'judging by the extent to which Ministry of Information films were excluded from regular cinema programmes, they were not generally well received by audiences'.[4] And Nicholas Pronay is even more extreme in dismissing the MOI's entire non-theatrical programme (and by implication all other official documentaries too) as completely ineffective: 'As far as the war effort was concerned, the country could have dispensed with the whole lot without an iota of difference. The real propaganda *war* was carried out in the commercial cinemas and by the newsreels, not in any significant way by the documentary film.'[5]

In order to assess the role of shorts and documentaries to the film propaganda effort, it is necessary to consider three questions. First, what was the MOI's policy towards shorts and documentaries, and how was it carried out? Second, were MOI shorts accepted by audiences or were they, as Swann and others suggest, generally not very well received? And third, how far did official shorts actually influence people's attitudes and behaviour, in so far as this can be determined? By asking these questions it is possible to provide a critical overview of the MOI's short film propaganda effort.

II

Despite Sir Joseph Ball's antipathy towards the documentary movement, it is evident that he did see some role for documentaries in official propaganda. Although he attached more importance to feature films and newsreels, he did indicate that he also saw a place for documentary. 'We can, in addition, finance or help to finance some of the best British documentary film producers for the production of short documentary films approved by us,' he said in September 1939. 'Provided such films are of first-class quality, I have already obtained an undertaking from the three big British circuits and the Cinematograph Exhibitors' Association that they will be shown throughout the cinemas of the United Kingdom.'[6] Ball was clearly not averse to making use of documentaries, and had even discussed the matter with exhibitors, but whether he had a definite idea of what to do with them is quite another matter.

Although numerous shorts and documentaries were commissioned during Ball's regime, there is a somewhat *ad hoc* air about them and certainly no sign of an overall programme or policy. Twelve 'themes for documentary films' were submitted to the MOI's Co-Ordination Committee on 7 December 1939 by the Films Division's Deputy-Director G. E. G. Forbes. Among the ideas which he proposed were several which were turned into films under the same or another title: *The New Britain* (Strand, 1940) was about the social services; *Civilian Front* (GB Instructional, 1940) illustrated the war work of ordinary citizens; a film referred to as 'Sentinels of the Sky (Balloon Barrage)' was clearly *Squadron 992* (GPO Film Unit, 1940); 'The Men Behind the Guns' was renamed simply *Behind the Guns* (Merton Park, 1940); while 'Don't Gossip' and 'Keep Your Mouth Shut' could have been the working titles for any of the anti-gossip films made in 1940. Much importance was attached to this subject by the committee, where A. P. Waterfield 'emphasised the particular desirability of making progress with the anti-gossip film, in view of the wish of the Cabinet for publicity in this matter'.[7]

The rationalisation of short film propaganda really began during Sir Kenneth Clark's administration. A memorandum of March 1940 suggested that shorts and documentaries could be accommodated usefully in cinema programmes alongside features:

In the big theatres the owner looks naturally on the feature film as his main draw and the 'short' or Documentary (with which one includes such things as Travel films, Educational, such as the growth of a bean or a fish, etc.) he looks upon more as padding than anything else, and for them he pays very little. At the same time a good 'short' or Documentary or instructional film will definitely hold an audience and in themselves such as these 'shorts' [*sic*] made of such topical subjects as the building of tanks or the mass production of Bren guns, etc., can be made sufficiently interesting to hold the audience's attention and to impress them with something of the power of the country concerned.[8]

Some thought had clearly been given to the different types of cinema, as the paper also distinguished between the ordinary commercial cinemas and newsreel theatres, where there was more of a ready-made market for shorts. Clark himself had evidently given some attention to the role of short documentaries, for in a circular to Regional Information Officers he categorised the different films which had been commissioned hitherto. Some of them he described as 'purely informational, e.g. films of Britain's war effort in munitions, the Navy, etc.', some he said were 'designed both to reassure and encourage, e.g. a dramatic reconstruction of the German raid on the Firth of Forth', while others were 'designed to wake people from apathy, e.g. a film on the German machine-gunning of lightships'.[9] Clark appreciated, therefore, that shorts could be used for various different propaganda objectives. Whether those objectives were met is another matter. Two of the films to which he alluded – *Squadron 992* and *Men of the Lightship* – were delayed for several months after production due to negotiations with distributors. Both films were reconstructions of incidents which had occurred during the 'phoney war' winter of 1939–40, but by the time they reached the cinemas in the summer of 1940 the war situation had changed. *Documentary News Letter* said of *Squadron 992*: 'though the fine qualities of [Harry] Watt's direction retain their vitality and the film remains a splendid description of the life and work of the balloon barrage men, it has lost the gripping topicality which it derived from being based on the Forth Bridge raid.'[10]

There were, broadly speaking, two approaches to short film propaganda, which might be described as the 'documentary' and the 'story' modes of film practice. The documentary mode – exemplified by *Squadron 992* and *Men of the Lightship* – was used mainly for reconstructions of real events. The documentary school was considered best for this type of propaganda, and both films benefited from the GPO Film Unit's traditional emphasis on realism and authenticity. Alberto Cavalcanti, then the Supervising Producer at the Film Unit, was particularly concerned with achieving realism in *Men of the Lightship*. After seeing the first rushes he sent a telegram to the director David Macdonald (a recruit from the commercial film industry) stating: 'Your sailors totally unconvincing, suggest you sack entire cast and use real people.'[11] It was an unwritten rule at the Film Unit that non-professional actors were preferable because they denoted 'real' people rather than fictional characters. Cavalcanti also used the principle of authenticity to defend the film against the Air Ministry, who wanted to make alterations to the script. Although the actual German raid on the East Dudgeon lightship had not been intercepted, the Air Ministry objected to the film on the grounds that 'it was considered undesirable that the impression should be created abroad that raids on lightships could be made, with impunity, by German aircraft, without any apparent effort to counter them'.[12] It wanted a scene inserted which showed the raiders being caught and shot down by the RAF. The Film Unit refused to countenance this because 'to introduce a dog-fight into the picture really meant, from the propaganda angle, a recasting of the whole story and therefore a departure from the original intention of authentically reconstructing what happened and substituting a picture which an audience would be inclined to regard as introducing the usual element of "movie fiction".'[13] In the event Cavalcanti got his way and the film was completed without the additional sequence wanted by the Air Ministry.

The other approach to short film propaganda was the 'story' mode which was characteristic of the commercial studios rather than the documentary movement. For example, when the MOI wanted a series of shorts for its anti-gossip campaign early in 1940 it turned to a commercial studio, in this case Ealing, to produce them. The three films were part of the MOI's 'Careless Talk Costs Lives' campaign, which also included the famous posters of the artist Fougasse, and which represented one of the first attempts to incorporate film within the wider scope of the MOI's work. The trade press saw the films as evidence that the MOI was starting to get its act together:

Film, as a means of public propaganda, is more prominently

before the Ministry of Information than is recognised by the public. A comprehensive scheme has already been prepared, and the first shots in the campaign have already been fired.

The nation-wide anti-gossip warnings by poster are only part of the campaign that is being undertaken by the Ministry of Information. Sir Kenneth Clark, Director of the Films Division of the Ministry, has commissioned a series of short films dealing with the same subject.[14]

It was also reported that Clark 'has obtained the co-operation of the Presidents of the KRS and the CEA who are arranging the distribution and exhibition throughout the country immediately the films leave the studios'. The fact that these particular three films were released much quicker than *Squadron 992* and *Men of the Lightship* suggests that the trade was more favourably inclined towards taking conventional 'story' films from a commercial studio than the documentaries of the GPO Film Unit. The three anti-gossip films were all directed by John Paddy Carstairs and took the form of short dramatic thrillers. *All Hands* features a German spy ring including a café proprietress and a butterfly collector: the former overhears a sailor mentioning that a warship will be sailing from Plymouth and passes the information on to the latter, who then signals to a U-boat which sinks the ship with the loss of 'all hands'. *Dangerous Comment* features a German spy in the guise of a barman who overhears RAF personnel discussing a raid on the Bender Dam and passes the information on to his superiors, though in this case the spies are discovered and the raid is recalled. And *Now You're Talking* features German agents planting a bomb in a factory where a scientist is studying secret equipment from a crashed German aircraft, the information having been leaked through the careless chatter of factory workers in a pub. The critical reaction to the films was mixed, and in particular it was asked whether the melodramatic plots were the best vehicle for putting across the message of careless talk. *The Times*, for example, said:

The films hold the attention and are most skilfully made; the only question that has to be asked is whether their obviously sensational quality will in some instances provoke incredulity. But perhaps, after all, this does not matter; if attention is attracted to the idea that there is a connection between indiscretion and disaster, that is all that is wanted, and these films will certainly do this.[15]

Other critics, however, were sceptical. *Documentary News Letter* complained of a lack of authenticity in the settings: 'The whole effect in films of this kind may be spoilt if they seem to take place, not in real pubs, or cocktail bars, but on conventional studio sets with the old familiar faces playing the old familiar parts.'[16] It is hard to judge the impact of the films on audiences, but a clue is provided by a Mass-Observation report which suggested that the representation of class in official films was of considerable importance:

> There has generally been a much higher degree of popularity and response from middle-class people than from working-class people (sex differences are very slight). This seems to derive *largely from the essentially upper- and middle-class attitudes* of many of the films; this started with the original 'Careless Talk' films, in each of which the spy was a worker (barman, cafe proprietress, pub crawler), while in two of them the gossipers were working class, though in only one was the cast as a whole working class. The hero of one of these films, a factory scientist with a beautiful large house, is killed by the idiocy of a factory worker. The hero of another is a rich young airman; his fiancee lives in a luxury flat.[17]

Thus the films were seen to imply that working-class people were more prone to careless talk than middle-class people. This kind of class distinction was reminiscent of the MOI's earliest efforts at propaganda and was hardly likely to be popular with working-class audiences who might resent the suggestion that they were the most dangerous chatterboxes.

It can be seen that during the first six months of the war the MOI's use of short film propaganda was *ad hoc* and somewhat erratic. There was no overall policy to guide the production of shorts, nor was there any definite idea within the Films Division of how best to make use of this type of propaganda. However, one issue which did emerge, and which was to remain of considerable importance throughout the war, was the distinction between 'documentary' and 'story' shorts. Documentaries, and in particular those of the GPO Film Unit, were considered more realistic (and therefore better propaganda) by some critics than story-type films such as Ealing's 'Careless Talk' trilogy. This distinction was also to influence the five-minute film scheme which was introduced in the summer of 1940 and which represented the first systematic use of shorts for propaganda.

III

On 3 July 1940, *The Times* announced:

> Five-minute films covering food rationing, home defence, air-raid
> precautions, and similar subjects will soon be a feature at all the
> 4,000 cinemas in the country. Members of the Cinematograph
> Exhibitors' Association have offered to show such official films
> free of charge. Leading producers and directors have put their
> services at the disposal of the films division of the Ministry of
> Information for the expert and rapid production of official films.[18]

The five-minute film scheme had been inaugurated in order to meet
the MOI's immediate propaganda and instructional needs. It is not
entirely clear where the idea for the scheme originated. 'It was [Alex-
ander] Korda who suggested the plan which was to become the chief
activity of the Films Division, the making of films so short (two
minutes) that the exhibitors would admit them into their programmes,'
Sir Kenneth Clark later recalled, though this is uncorroborated by any
other sources.[19] In fact, Clark himself had suggested using shorts in
this way in the Programme for Film Propaganda:

> Apart from this general scheme of film propaganda, the Govern-
> ment will often wish to use the film as an immediate means of
> communication with the people, e.g. to prevent gossip, to induce
> greater caution in pedestrians, to explain the shortage of food,
> etc. These urgent needs are best served by short dramatic films
> on the model of the American *Crime Does Not Pay* series. They
> can be quickly made and have a wide appeal.[20]

The minutes of the MOI's Policy Committee show that discussions
had been entered into with the CEA by June 1940. When the possibility
of enforcing the compulsory exhibition of MOI films was raised, Clark,
now in the job of Director of Home Publicity, said that 'an alternative
suggestion was now being pursued with the CEA by which they would
agree to set apart 10 minutes in each programme to such films as we
required'. A voluntary arrangement, he thought, would 'be much more
satisfactory than bringing into force some regulations which they would
generally attempt to evade'.[21] When asked whether ten minutes 'gave
as much time as we ought to have', Clark replied that 'he thought that
the 10 minutes for propaganda films were as much as people could

stand'.[22] Finally it became a five-minute slot for official films in every cinema programme, though in practice most of the films in the scheme were to run slightly longer. The details were worked out in discussions between the MOI and the General Council of the CEA. 'W. R. Fuller [President of the CEA] told me this scheme has been under discussion between them and the Ministry for a considerable time,' one trade journalist reported on 27 June. 'By this decision the CEA appears to be a jump ahead of the Ministry, and Fuller assures me an enormous amount has already been accomplished towards getting the fullest possible co-operation between the MoI and the kinemas.'[23] The films were given free to exhibitors through the shorts distributor National Screen Services. The nature of the arrangement was explained in a divisional circular by Jack Beddington, who described it as 'an entirely friendly and, as it were, unofficial arrangement: it retains the goodwill of the cinema trade and ensures that screen time is available to the MOI without the exercise of any official powers'.[24] Clearly it was important to the MOI that the exhibitors' co-operation should be voluntary. To have compelled the exhibition of official films may have backfired in that it would not only have created resistance within the trade but it would also have looked as if the MOI was trying to force its films on to cinema patrons.

The five-minute film scheme came into operation in July 1940. Dallas Bower was put in charge of the production programme, and he was assisted for a while by John Betjeman as a script reader. The scheme was welcomed as a sign that the Films Division was at last getting its act together. 'This policy of an intimate message week by week to the cinema goers of Great Britain is the most important step in British film propaganda since the beginning of the war,' declared *Documentary News Letter*.[25] However, there was criticism of the scheme from Michael Balcon, who resented the fact that the five-minute films were given away free and attacked the MOI's policy as a waste of money. Ealing's press release announcing its split from the ministry in December 1940 stated:

> We disapproved of the free distribution of films to kinemas, be-lieving that propaganda films of merit could still be sold in the ordinary way in the open market and get wide distribution.
>
> We believed that public money was being ill-spent by this body [the MOI] in several ways – for instance, we understand that as

many as a thousand copies have been printed of a five-minute film on more than one occasion. (It may be of interest to add here that an average George Formby comedy which has over 2,300 bookings on its general release uses no more than 75 copies.)[26]

Balcon's criticisms do seem rather misplaced. The MOI was anxious that the five-minute films should be shown as widely as possible, and exhibitors could hardly be expected to pay for them having agreed voluntarily to show them in all programmes. Moreover, Balcon completely failed to appreciate that the MOI needed a large number of prints to secure the quick and wide release that was necessary for films intended for short-term and immediate purposes which would quickly become out of date. The comparison between the five-minute films and Ealing's George Formby features is therefore entirely inappropriate.

The aim of the five-minute films, according to Clark, was 'to help people remember government messages by putting them in dramatic form'.[27] The wide range of subjects covered by the series is illustrated by the first batch of six weekly films. The first film in the series was *Westward Ho! 1940* (Denham & Pinewood), written and directed by Thorold Dickinson, which was part of the government's appeal for controlled evacuation. It shows the journey of evacuee children from London to Torquay, where they are shown to be happy and safe from bombing. The idea for a film explaining the evacuation policy was apparently Dickinson's own after he had read a letter in a newspaper from a mother complaining about the evacuation of her children.[28] *Britain at Bay* (GPO Film Unit) was a compilation film narrated by J. B. Priestley which was intended as a morale-raising film for the British people, illustrating their determination to fight on after the fall of France. A visual equivalent of the famous 'Postscripts' which he gave on the wireless on Sunday evenings, the film was very popular and was widely regarded as having caught the mood of the moment. The film critic William Whitebait described it as 'a striking piece of work which captures the eye and the imagination at the same time. It is propaganda, but only in the sense that a poem by Auden or McLeish is propaganda.'[29] *A Call to Arms* (Denham & Pinewood), directed by Brian Desmond Hurst, dramatised the contribution to the war effort of women working in a munitions factory, telling the story of a girl who worked at the machines until she collapsed from exhaustion. *Salvage with a Smile* (Ealing), directed by Adrian Brunel and produced by

Cavalcanti, was an appeal to housewives to save scrap paper, metal and bones. *Food for Thought* (Ealing), also directed by Brunel, was an instructional film about the nutritional value of different foodstuffs. And finally, *Miss Grant Goes to the Door* (Denham & Pinewood), based on an idea by Dickinson and directed by Hurst, was part of the MOI's instructional campaign about what to do in the event of an invasion – a campaign which also included the widespread distribution of a leaflet entitled *If the Invader Comes* and which, like *Westward Ho!*, shows how the five-minute films were related to the wider work of the MOI. It was a short dramatic thriller about two spinster sisters who find a dead German parachutist in their garden and then uncover and outwit a spy disguised as a British officer. In this case the film-makers had to tread a careful line between preparing people for the possibility of an invasion (telling them to stay put, to lock away maps, disable motor vehicles, and so on) without scaring them by dwelling on the personal danger. Scriptwriter Rodney Ackland recalled that when the film was shown to representatives of the War Office it 'was pronounced too frightening to be shown' and that it had to 'be shot again as a comedy'.[30] *Documentary News Letter* complained that it was unrealistic:

> A film on how to deal with a parachutist has drawn wide public comment – as any cinema-goer with ears will notice – because it provides the person meeting the German parachutist with a revolver taken from a dead German; most of us have no revolvers and not all of us can expect to find dead Germans available.[31]

Even in the first batch of films, critics detected a difference between the 'studio' and 'documentary' methods. Basil Wright, for example, clearly preferred the latter:

> They vary in style according to the *personnel* employed in their production. From the studio world come dramatised sketches, from the documentary side dramatised messages. On the one hand, therefore, we find Brian Desmond Hurst's *A Call to Arms* and *Miss Grant Goes to the Door*, which dramatise – even over-dramatise – the urgency of female labour in munition factories or the active service of a country lady who is called on by a Nazi parachutist. On the other hand comes the GPO Film Unit's *Britain at Bay*, an illustrated talk by J. B. Priestley, which plays up the visual and concrete determination of British citizens to resist invasion ...

Between the two come films like Thorold Dickinson's *Westward Ho!*, which combines a documentary description of recent evacuation with an appeal to parents to co-operate in getting children out of danger zones.[32]

For documentarist critics such as Wright, there was a natural inclination towards the work of the GPO Film Unit rather than the commercial studios. The differences between the two modes of film practice which had become apparent earlier in 1940 were therefore carried over into the five-minute series.

The ideas for individual films in the series came from a wide range of sources: from within the MOI, from other government departments, from various outside agencies, and not least from film-makers themselves. Official records show that the Films Division was inundated with proposals from the film industry, though they were often considered unsuitable. For example, two shorts about the Local Defence Volunteers (the original name of the Home Guard) were discussed in the summer of 1940, one from a treatment by Leslie Howard, the other entitled *Yeomen of the Guard* by the writer 'Bartimeus'. In the event neither came to fruition.[33] And although Sydney Box of Verity Films told John Betjeman that the company 'is anxious to make short propaganda films for the Ministry of Information', his idea for a cookery demonstration film using the comedian Jack Warner was rejected by the Films Division.[34] The fact that so many ideas were being turned down soon became a cause of concern for short film producers, who were worried that official films were stealing their market. 'Onlooker' of *Today's Cinema* reported:

> Spot of deputation brewing in association with the Ministry of Information shorts. Number of shorts producers have called on me lately, to complain of the difficulty of 'getting in' at the MoI. One of the producers showed me a letter he had just received in which the Ministry admit having been impressed with a number of his productions, but add 'we have nothing we can suggest to you'.
>
> Lot of short film producers are far from satisfied at having their market occupied by MoI produced shorts, while they are finding it practically impossible to get a look in and contribute some of these shorts themselves.[35]

The film industry was not the only external source of ideas for the five-minute films. Proposals were sometimes put to the MOI by agencies which thought their own activities would make good subjects for propaganda. *Citizens' Advice Bureau* (GB Screen Services, 1941) resulted from an approach made in August 1940 to Dr Stephen Taylor, Director of Home Intelligence, by a representative of the organisation who suggested that a film on its work would 'provide an opportunity for nation-wide publicity in order to make the Bureaux known just at this time when the need for them is likely to be greater than ever'.[36] However, a request from the Salvation Army in September 1940 'to make a film on the work of the Army in air-raids' was turned down on the grounds of 'the danger of producing a film on one religious organisation of this kind, when others were doing similar work'.[37]

The most successful film in the five-minute series, with both critics and audiences, was the famous *Britain Can Take It!* (GPO Film Unit, 1940), which illustrated the stoicism of the people of London at the height of the Blitz in the autumn of 1940. It followed in the style of *Britain at Bay* by combining actuality footage with an evocative commentary, this time provided by the American journalist Quentin Reynolds, London correspondent of the magazine *Collier's Weekly*. Ironically, this most successful of all the five-minute films was not originally intended for the series at all but rather for exhibition in the neutral United States. Originally to have been called *London Front*, it was renamed *London Can Take It!* and took the form of a 'film despatch' sent by Reynolds to America. It had been commissioned from a newsreel company, Gaumont-British News, on 20 September, but then it was 'removed' and placed with the GPO Film Unit.[38] The reason, according to co-director Harry Watt, was that the footage shot by the newsreel cameramen showed too much damage and destruction to be considered good propaganda by the MOI.[39] A slightly shorter version, entitled *Britain Can Take It!*, was made for domestic release through the five-minute series, with an on-camera introduction by Reynolds. The MOI was keen to emphasise that 'the film is representative of what is happening in every other British city and town, where resistance to intense aerial attack and powers of endurance are every bit as heroic'.[40] Nevertheless it is as a record of London during the Blitz that the film is remembered. The title is projected over a low-angle shot of the undamaged St Paul's Cathedral, an instantly recognisable image of London which recurs several times throughout the film. The film chronicles one day during the Blitz: it shows people going home from their work, the mass exodus to the shelters, the work of the emergency services during the raids and the cleaning-up operation come the dawn. The images are striking – the city silhouette lighted by the flashes of anti-aircraft guns – while the commentary is quietly inspirational. Reynolds asserts his objectivity ('I am a neutral reporter') and stresses the actuality ('I am speaking from London'; 'These are not Hollywood sound effects'). He pays tribute to 'the people's army of volunteers', the civilians who are in the front line of the war, and emphasises their stoicism and courage ('I can assure you that there is no panic, no fear, no despair in London town; there is nothing but determination, confidence and high courage among the people of Churchill's Island'). The idea of the people's war was to become the most important theme of British wartime propaganda, and it was welcomed by critics like Basil Wright:

> And in all truth this message about our civilian army dominates the film ... For this is a film of the people who, in the end and on their own terms, will win the war for freedom and democracy.
>
> It is the first film clearly to state this important fact. In its pellucid and brilliant camerawork, its leisurely and emphatic cutting and its economy of emphasis, it clears the whole air of dunderhead and paralysing verbiage about the war. It states facts, but with the addition of true drama and true poetry.[41]

The film was also very well received by cinema audiences. Mass-Observation reported that it was 'the most frequently commented on film, and received nothing but praise'.[42] And a report from an MOI projectionist when the film was later shown as part of a non-theatrical programme in a Scottish mining village bore witness to the film's continued success: '*Britain Can Take It!* was by far the most successful film. The reasons, I think, were because of the neutral reporter, the emphasis on the common people and the fact that it showed what the war was like.'[43]

Watt and Reynolds followed the film with *Christmas Under Fire* (Crown, 1941) which used the same techniques – striking visuals accompanied by the dry, restrained commentary of Reynolds – to show how the British people celebrated Christmas under Blitz conditions. Production notes by Watt suggest that the film was again intended 'especially for the super-sentimentalists of the United States. With them Christmas becomes positively orgiastic in its slush, and a film timed to be released right after Christmas, showing Britain carrying on the tradition in its dugouts and outposts is an obvious tear-jerker.'[44] The film's tone is set from the beginning where a man is cutting a fir tree and Reynolds intones: 'It's not a very large Christmas tree. There's no demand in England for large trees this year. They wouldn't fit into the shelters or into the basements and cellars with their low ceilings. This year England celebrates Christmas underground.' It ends with a famous tracking shot along a crowded underground platform to the tune of 'O Come All Ye Faithful' sung by the choir of King's College, Cambridge. It was moving enough to prompt Christian Barman, the Director of the London Passenger Transport Board, to write to Clark:

> I was lucky enough yesterday to see your film *Christmas Under Fire*. I hate superlatives, but I could swear that never in my life have I seen a short film that can be compared with it for imagination and sensitiveness and the sheer deftness of its technique. The finale is truly astounding ... With people who do propaganda as good as this, there is no need to worry.[45]

Together with *Britain at Bay* and *Britain Can Take It!*, *Christmas Under Fire* forms a loose trilogy of morale-raising films which marked the highpoint of the five-minute series.

By the end of 1940, however, the MOI was reconsidering the 'Britain Can Take It' theme of propaganda, fearing that it had been over-used and could appear negative. It was decided after 1940 that propaganda should concentrate less on the defensive aspects of the war and should instead show Britain taking the offensive. It was soon realised that the five-minute films would not be an effective vehicle for this sort of propaganda. Short films about military operations would be rather too similar to newsreel items, and indeed would probably be compiled from the same footage. This problem arose in the case of *Lofoten* (Army and Crown Film Units, 1941), an entry in the five-minute series which took the form of an eye-witness account by Lieutenant-Commander Anthony Kimmins (a director who had made George Formby comedies at Ealing in the late 1930s) of a Commando raid on the Lofoten Islands off the coast of Norway. *Documentary News Letter* said that some exhibitors had not wanted to take the film: 'The Odeon, ABC and GB Circuits may have had some sort of case in refusing to show the Ministry's 5-minute version on the grounds that their audiences had seen the material in the Newsreels.'[46]

What direction did the five-minute series take after 1940? There was a body of opinion, both inside and outside the MOI, that people were beginning to expect more than just the morale-raising type of film which had proved most successful in the first six months of the scheme. This view was expressed, for example, in a reasoned letter to the *Manchester Guardian* from a Liverpool University academic:

> One feels that the Ministry of Information in its films allows its concerns for public morale to obscure its duty to give the information from which a thinking public can draw its own conclusions. A film like Priestley's *Britain at Bay*, the continued popularity of which is proved by its enthusiastic reception at the last MOI film show in Manchester, can scarcely be called a film of information.
>
> But these five-minute films might well be used to give direct information on matters of topical interest. The indirect method which documentary producers have built up has proved its worth, but it should not rule out the direct method ... If the films are well made with good commentary and deal with topical matters they can be as successful as the more dramatic and 'human' films.[47]

There was a slight trend towards more purely informational and factual films. A good example is *A Few Ounces a Day* (Paul Rotha Productions, 1941), which used animated diagrams to show the importance of salvage in offsetting shortages of raw materials caused by shipping losses. *Documentary News Letter* praised it highly: 'Possibly the most effective short film the MOI has commissioned. It has information and instruction on a vital issue, and is an effective call to us all to take action.'[48]

One of the more unusual entries in the five-minute series was *The Dawn Guard* (Charter Films, 1941), made by the twin brothers John and Roy Boulting before they joined the service film units. It takes the form of a dialogue between two members of the Home Guard, standing on sentry duty on a rural hillside, as to what the war was really all about. The older of the two men, Bert (Percy Walsh), sees it in terms of defending the traditional ways of life. He complains about the Nazis 'upsetting the ways and wrecking the lives of millions of people' and believes that 'it's the liberty we had and never thought about we got to fight for, to get our lives back to where they was'. But that is not enough for his younger companion (Bernard Miles), who is progressive in that he looks to the future rather than to the past. He expresses the view that the sense of solidarity brought about by the war should be carried over into rebuilding the world when the war was over. 'We've made a fine big war effort, well when it's all over we've got to see to it we make a fine big peace effort,' he remarks. In particular, he wants to see a world where the blights of unemployment and poverty no longer exist. 'We can't go back to the old ways of living, least ways not all of it,' he says. 'That's gone forever, and the sooner we make up our minds about that the better.' The film was more philosophical than others in the five-minute series, and its progressive theme was welcomed as a positive sign by *Documentary News Letter*:

> The Films Division of the MOI are heartily to be congratulated upon one of their recent five-minute films, *Dawn Guard*. It is a film which is pitched in a quiet key and made with the utmost simplicity; and it comes very near to expressing the feeling of ordinary people as regards what sort of future is to come out of the war ... We have had several reports of an extremely warm audience reaction to this film, and it is to be hoped that the Films Division will note that the more progressive attitude indicated by *Dawn Guard* is good propaganda not merely because it is right in policy, but also because it focuses the desires, so often vague and unformulated, of ordinary people.[49]

However, the testimony of the MOI projectionist showing films in a Scottish mining village suggests that the film did not go down well with audiences there. 'A film like *Dawn Guard* leaves them with the idea that someone is trying to put something over on them,' he said. 'I was surprised at the reaction to this film. They immediately place it as insincere propaganda, and feel that someone is trying to fool them.' The reporter went on to suggest that what this particular audience wanted were films about the war rather than lofty speeches about jobs and living conditions in the future. He concluded:

> The general experience of this and other projectionists who show films in rural Scotland is that there is more interest in factual than in vague theoretical themes. Audiences want to see films of real events – *Britain Can Take It, Lofoten*. They are acutely aware of the contrast between the state of affairs visualised in such films as *Dawn Guard* and the hard facts of their actual conditions.[50]

It is hard to generalise about the form and content of the five-minute series because it covered so many different subjects. In total eighty-six films were released between July 1940 and October 1942. Films such as *Dai Jones Lends a Hand* (Verity, 1941) and *Shunter Black's Night Off* (Verity, 1941) dramatised true incidents which focused on individuals. The former told the story of an unemployed Welsh miner who put his expertise to good use by joining an air raid rescue team, while the latter was about a railway worker whose quick thinking saved an ammunition train from being blown up during an air raid. Most of the five-minute films, however, continued to be used for putting over a specific message, often as part of wider propaganda or instructional campaigns. For example, *You're Telling Me* (Paul Rotha Productions, 1941) was part of the MOI's on-going campaign against rumour and gossip-mongering; *Dangers in the Dark* (Public Relations Films, 1941) was part of the Ministry of Transport's campaign for road safety in the blackout; and *The Nose Has It* (Gainsborough, 1942) was based on the Ministry of Health's 'Coughs and Sneezes Spread Diseases' campaign. The latter film was also an example of the way in which popular comedians (in this case Arthur Askey) were used to put over a particular message with a touch of humour. Other examples of this trend included Sydney Howard neglecting the blackout in *Mr Proudfoot Shows a Light* (20th Century-Fox, 1941), Tommy Trinder promoting the Ministry of Food's new British Restaurants in *Eating Out with Tommy Trinder* (Strand, 1941), and Will Hay showing how not to deal with incendiaries in *Go to Blazes* (Ealing, 1942).

IV

Given the different objectives of the five-minute films, it is hard to judge the effectiveness of the scheme taken as a whole. Until 1942, when evidence came to light that the films were sometimes being omitted from cinema programmes, they would appear to have fulfilled the first criterion of effective film propaganda in reaching a wide audience. Regular cinema-goers were likely to have seen a large number of the films in the series. However, the number of people who saw the films is only one factor in assessing their effectiveness. It was one thing for the films to be widely seen, but it was another for them to be widely understood and appreciated. Evidence of audience response is sketchy: the MOI had no machinery of its own for monitoring the reception of its films and relied on the work of Mass-Observation and the reports of some cinema exhibitors. However, it is possible to make some general observations about the reception of the five-minute films.

It seems that cinema-goers did recognise the five-minute films as official propaganda. 'Onlooker' reported in August 1940:

> The public beginning to ask about the films – they want to know when the next one will be seen and refer to them directly as MOI films. Well, that rather suggests that the bogey of propaganda has been dealt with, although I still think the wary and 'clever' minded will react unfavourably to the credit announcement that they are about to see an effort by the Government's propaganda department.[51]

MOI films were identified as such by the legend 'The Ministry of Information presents ... '. Although there was testimony from some exhibitors that their patrons groaned when this appeared on the screen, this was by no means a universal reaction. A Mass-Observation report in April 1941 found that 'all MoI shorts are widely regarded as "propaganda" and looked at by a considerable number of people as kind of exhibition pieces, the pleasant sermon in the feature programme, the Two Minutes silence after which you get back to making the arguments'.[52] Some film-makers even went so far as to acknowledge that the films were propaganda by incorporating it into the plots. *Partners in Crime* (Gainsborough, 1942), written and directed by Frank Launder and Sidney Gilliat, ingeniously incorporates a recognition and critique of official propaganda into its mode of textual address. The film draws a parallel between the theft of jewellery and the black market in meat: a thief passes on stolen goods through a fence; a butcher buys some black market meat; then a housewife (Irene Handl) complains about her meat ration and asks the butcher for 'a bit extra'. The fence is brought up before a judge (Robert Morley) who tells him: 'You create the demand; you offer the market. You are the real criminal.' At this point the film seems to finish, with the music swelling up and 'The End' appearing over the MOI caption; but then the camera pulls back to reveal a cinema screen on which the film has just been shown. It then cuts to the cinema audience, and to a close-up of the same housewife who remarks: 'Oh, it's only another one of those propaganda pictures.' However, the voice of the judge is then heard again and the film cuts to a close-up of him speaking directly at the camera (therefore addressing both the character in the film and, through the direct mode of address, every cinema spectator): 'Yes, Mrs Wilson, you're right, it is one of those propaganda pictures.' He then delivers a lecture on the evils of the black market, concluding: 'If everybody in this country took only a little more than their fair share, we should all be starving in a very short while. Remember that, won't you, ladies and gentlemen?' The film thus acknowledges that some people did not necessarily pay attention to a film when they knew it was propaganda (such as Mrs Wilson), but then makes its point more forcefully through the unexpected ending.

While audiences seem to have recognised the five-minute films as propaganda, to what extent did they actually like the films? The popularity of individual films inevitably varied, but there is evidence that in general terms they were most successful with audiences in the latter months of 1940. An editorial in *Kinematograph Weekly* in October suggested that the initially unfavourable public reaction had been turned around:

> Kinema-goers have had good opportunity during recent weeks to appreciate the entertainment and propaganda qualities of the M of I films, so efficiently distributed on the 'five minutes per programme' basis arranged with the CEA. That there is an improvement in this type of picture is generally proved by their noticeable acceptance on the part of the public.[53]

And *Sight and Sound*, usually no friend of the MOI, nevertheless suggested that it had scored a success with these films:

> The Ministry of Information Films Division in one aspect of its work has, however, displayed a true understanding of our national psychology and has scored a complete success with its Five-Minute Shorts. The Film Trade, the critics and the public alike seem to be pleased with this novel type of propaganda. On the whole the directors have been successful in condensing their message into the allotted time-span and some of the films have considerable dramatic force in the Grand Guignol manner. The way in which they have gone over proves that even in an entertainment programme which the public has paid to see, it will stand for direct propaganda, and especially propaganda to do with the war, if it is served up as such.[54]

Further evidence that the films found popular approval is that in 1942 the Films Division vetoed a proposal to enforce the compulsory exhibition of its films, citing as one reason the desire not to lose public acceptance: 'At present, MOI films have, on the whole, the goodwill of the public. It is felt that this is likely to be impaired as soon as it is known that the films are being forced upon them.'[55]

The research of Mass-Observation provides most evidence of audience response to the five-minute films. One of the most significant points to emerge is that the popular reception of films ran along similar lines to their critical reception in that the distinction between the 'documentary' and 'story' shorts was also noticed by audiences. According to the senior film researcher Len England: 'If we classify these films into "short stories" and "strict documentaries", and compare the observed audience response of the two main types, we find a considerably higher degree of response to the documentary.'[56] As well as observing the popularity of the films with cinema audiences, Mass-Observation was also concerned with discovering whether audiences understood the points being made in the films and how far they were influenced or persuaded by them. The most comprehensive research into this was an extensive survey carried out between December 1941 and March 1942. Four 'reasonably characteristic' five-minute films were selected and the reactions of audiences in cinemas across the country were monitored by questionnaires. The results of the survey are valuable because in this case the sample was a large one and Mass-Observation's research methods were thoroughgoing and systematic. The four films selected were: *War in the East* (Shell Film Unit, 1941), which used maps and diagrams to elucidate aspects of the war against Japan in the Far East; *Seaman Frank Goes Back to Sea* (Concanen, 1942), in which the radio broadcaster Frank Laskier rejoined the merchant navy and made a plea for National Savings; *Newspaper Train* (Realist Film Unit, 1941), which showed how the delivery of newspapers by train was kept going during the Blitz; and *Rush Hour* (20th Century-Fox, 1942), a plea for shoppers to travel between the hours of ten and four in order to avoid the busiest times and thus ease congestion. The summary report of the investigation suggested that while most audiences liked the films, they did not always understand the point a particular film was trying to make:

Broadly, then, MoI films now command an extensive goodwill.

The limitations on them are partly limitations of what can be done in five minutes in the entertainment cinema atmosphere. But there are also undoubtedly limitations within the films themselves, in lack of precise definition as to the purpose of the film, who it is aimed at, and whether or not the people at whom it is aimed can take it in. That is to say, from the point of view of public reaction, there is undoubtedly room for technical simplification, and more precise focus in the films studied.[57]

It is important to recognise that, in the first instance, the films were on the whole popular, but that, even so, popularity did not necessarily equate with effectiveness. The case of *Seaman Frank* provides the best example. 'Most people liked this film,' the report said, though this was qualified in that audiences 'were often puzzled as to what it was about, or not clear about it'. The problem with this particular film was found to be that the subject of National Savings was introduced only at the end, and then almost incidentally, in a film which had hitherto been about the merchant navy. The least successful of the films studied was *Newspaper Train*, which 'failed to register clearly on people, to hold interest or to show good cause for existing either as entertainment or as propaganda or as anything else'. The most positive reaction was reserved for *War in the East*, which was not only the most popular film in the survey but also proved to have made the greatest impression on audiences in terms of understanding what it was about.

The most significant fact to emerge from the survey was that those films which sought to influence people's attitudes or behaviour were conspicuously less effective than films which simply imparted facts, such as *War in the East*. Therefore, the report concluded: 'the strictly informational film has a particular function not yet fully exploited, whereas the film which attempts to influence habits in a straight propagandist way, like *Seaman Frank* and *Shopping* [sic], may have a more limited use than has been supposed.' The reason for this, the report suggested, was that audiences 'are increasingly tired of exhortations and requests and general propaganda, especially along familiar lines' but that they 'are hungry for more information, straight direction, understanding'. The view that propaganda should adopt a more straight-forward factual approach was, in fact, gaining more support in official circles. In its preference for information rather than 'pep', the MOI was coming around to the same line of thinking. For example, in the first of Brendan Bracken's weekly reports on morale and public opinion to the War Cabinet in April 1942, he said:

(i) There must be more explanation: not only about the Armed Forces and the war situation but also about production, labour, war-time restrictions and the big problems that affect the life of everyone to-day. When the public is bewildered by something new a failure to explain means the risk of driving a wedge between Government and public ... .

(ii) We must stop appealing to the public or lecturing at it. One makes it furious, the other resentful. General appeals to the public or particular sections of it to work harder should not be made. There are too many people already working to the limit of their capacity or unable to do so for reasons beyond their control.[58]

This new attitude within the MOI illustrates a break from the appeals to national unity which had characterised its early attempts at propaganda and a belated acceptance of the view that propaganda in a democracy should be based on information and explanation. For the Films Division, this new attitude was one of the reasons in bringing about a change of policy in respect of short film propaganda in 1942.

V

The decision in 1942 to replace the five-minute films with a series of longer documentaries was influenced by a number of factors. One of these was the limitations of the five-minute format. Mass-Observation had advocated a longer running time for the regular MOI films as well as a more factual content:

A further question arises in connection with the length of the films. The research material on many points indicates that people cannot take in much during the five minutes of a film, or rather that they cannot take in much of a serious message. But some of these messages could only with difficulty be made much simpler, and the question therefore arises whether five minutes is the right length of time. We have not been asked to investigate this point, only to report on four five-minute films. But at many points in the enquiry people have spontaneously mentioned this and suggested that the films could and should be longer. For what it is worth, in our opinion, there is much to be said for having quite considerably longer MoI films, if that were possible, especially films of an informational type, dealing with subjects like war economics, news service, the integration of war strategy, war production, and the many other things which are of general interest and which people need to know about.[59]

This appears to be the first suggestion in favour of a longer running time, and while the report alone would not have determined the change in policy, it probably had some bearing on the thinking of the MOI, which after all had commissioned it.

Another influence on the MOI, and perhaps a stronger one, was the attitude of cinema exhibitors. There is much evidence that by 1942 the five-minute films were too often being left out of cinema programmes. 'While the MOI Five Minute Films seem, on the whole, to be achieving a pretty good circulation, we have recently received disturbing reports that some cinemas have taken to omitting them from their last performance,' *Documentary News Letter* reported in May 1942.[60] Reports in the trade press indicate two reasons why some exhibitors were not showing the films: first, that as the films often ran longer than five minutes they were sometimes difficult to fit in, particularly during the last house; and second, that due to the reduction in the number of distribution prints there were not always enough to go around. The number of prints had been reduced from 1000, first to 750 and then to 400, due to the shortage of film stock.[61] This was obviously unsatisfactory, for it meant that some audiences were not getting to see official films. It was in light of this that the suggestion to switch to a longer monthly film was made, apparently by the exhibitors themselves. On 10 June 1942 the General Council of the CEA resolved that while its members should honour the existing agreement with the MOI and while they should discuss complaints about distribution, they 'should also suggest the possibility of the Ministry issuing one 10-minute film each month instead of the weekly 5-minute subject'.[62] A week later a delegation from the CEA went to Malet Street where, according to one trade journalist, they received 'a most sympathetic reception' to their suggestion of a longer monthly film 'because I know the Films Division chief is of very much the same mind as themselves. In fact, I believe such a proposal has been under consideration down at Senate House for quite a while.'[63] An agreement was reached whereby the five-minute films would be replaced by a monthly short 'with a length not exceeding 15 minutes'.[64] The films would again be given away free in return for the exhibitors' voluntary co-operation. The immediate propaganda needs which had been met through the five-minute films were now met by 'trailers'. These films, such as the 'food flashes' made for the Ministry of Food, were very short items which had been appended to newsreels following an agreement with the Newsreel Association in June 1940.

The fifteen-minute film series started in December 1942 with *Lift Your Head, Comrade* (Spectator, 1942), a documentary about the Pioneer Corps. It was written by Arthur Koestler, a Hungarian author who had escaped to Britain, and it showed how anti-fascists from Germany and Austria were now fighting alongside the British. It was thus a documentary account of an aspect of the Allied war effort rather than a pep talk or an exhortation to the public, and in this it set the trend for most other films in the series. Thirty-seven monthly films were made between December 1942 and December 1945. The main advantage of the new format was that it allowed for more substantial content. 'The added length gave opportunities for fuller and more detailed treatment of more complex subjects,' said *The Factual Film*.[65] The subjects of the fifteen-minute films also reflected the changing course of the war. With the threat of German invasion gone and the worst of the air raids finished, there was no longer any need for the 'morale' propaganda of *Britain at Bay* and *Britain Can Take It!* Instead, the new series illustrated the different aspects of the war effort on both the home front and the battle fronts in a more factual manner. Their longer running time differentiated them from newsreel items, and they found favour with the critics because they not only gave vivid glimpses of the combat fronts but also used documentary techniques to examine some of the problems of war. A good example of this was *Stricken Peninsula* (Army Film and Photographic Unit/Seven League Productions, 1944), directed by Paul Fletcher, which illustrated the problems encountered after the liberation of southern Italy. 'Paul Fletcher has examined his subject from a traditional documentary standpoint,' *Documentary News Letter* observed approvingly. 'Here is no newsreel coverage, but an attempt to select and analyse episodes in the story of liberation, and to assemble them into a picture which will give not only the material facts but also the mood and feeling of Italians suddenly fallen between the two stools of Nazism and liberation.'[66]

Where did the ideas for the fifteen-minute films originate? As the nature of the new programme meant that longer-term planning was required, the subject matter seems to have derived more from the Films Division; there were fewer ideas submitted from other agencies or outside contractors. There was, however, one case of a film in the series being made at the suggestion of the Prime Minister himself. Churchill had evidently seen the notorious German propaganda film *Baptism of Fire* (1940) which illustrated the destruction of Warsaw by the *Luftwaffe*. 'This film, considerably shortened and with an English commentary, would in my opinion be very good propaganda,' Churchill told Brendan Bracken in April 1943. 'Pray consider whether it should not be resuscitated with some examples of what they are getting now. A very good title would be *The Biter Bit*.'[67] Accordingly *The Biter Bit* (Coombe Productions, 1943) was made by Alexander Korda. It opens with German officials showing *Baptism of Fire* at their embassy in Oslo to impress upon members of the Norwegian government the power of the German Air Force – a terror tactic designed to frighten neutral countries so that they would be too frightened to resist the forthcoming German invasion. This is followed by reminders of what the Germans did to Rotterdam, Belgrade, London and Coventry, before the film switches to the building of the British heavy bomber force and the RAF's bombing offensive against Germany. The commentary, written by Michael Foot and spoken by Ralph Richardson, points out that the German propaganda machine has now changed its tune. Having previously glorified the destructive power of their air force, the Germans were now pleading to 'humanise warfare ... think of the historical monuments, of the terrible scenes of fire and destruction, think of the sanctity of human life!' 'Now, why this whining tone?' Richardson asks. 'Why this sudden care for the churches from which Hitler planned to expel Christianity anyway? Why this sudden respect for human life after the holocaust of Rotterdam? Because the biter is bit where it hurts him most – in his war machine.' The film uses Arthur Bliss's stirring march from Korda's *Things to Come* to add dramatic emphasis to its shots of British bombs falling on Dusseldorf, Cologne and Hamburg. Churchill's wish for this film to be made is probably best understood through his concern to justify the policy of strategic area bombing now undertaken by Bomber Command. It was a rare example of retributive propaganda, justifying the bombing of German cities by the British on the grounds that the Germans had done it first.

Taken together, the five-minute and fifteen-minute films were central to the MOI's short film propaganda policy and marked its most planned and co-ordinated use of the medium. There were in addition hundreds of other short documentaries made for the MOI's non-theatrical distribution programme, as well as a number of two- or three-reel films produced for theatrical release each year, mainly by the Crown Film Unit. The evidence regarding the effectiveness of the non-theatrical programme is very sketchy and it is hard to draw any firm conclusions even about the size of the non-theatrical audience.[68] But there is no doubt that those films shown in the commercial cinemas reached a wide audience, particularly the five-minute and fifteen-minute films which were included in most cinema programmes. This was the channel which the MOI used for propaganda that it wanted disseminated as widely as possible.

Although most commentators have hitherto dismissed shorts and documentaries as an ineffective means of carrying out propaganda on the basis that they were resisted by audiences who actively disliked them, in fact the weight of evidence suggests that the films were not without some positive effect. Mass-Observation found that they were on the whole quite well liked. 'Our observations of films in general showed that Ministry of Information shorts were liked generally,' Tom Harrisson recalled. 'They were usually treated with respect; they were never automatically put in a bad category; people were ready to love the good ones.'[69] Whether the films had any influence on people's attitudes and behaviour is another matter, and Harrisson's view was that 'official films never really came into it in people's estimate of what affected them in the crunch'. Yet even this does not mean that they should automatically be considered failures, for the value of film propaganda lies not only in whether it influenced people in the way intended but also in what other effects it might have had. For example, although *Seaman Frank Goes Back to Sea* did not induce people to take out more National Savings, it seems that it did nevertheless increase their admiration for the merchant navy in that it 'had a very definite patriotic appeal, and women in particular were moved to admiration for the seamen who bring our food across the seas'.[70] Furthermore, there were several cases of films which proved extremely successful, particularly the 'morale' films of 1940 such as *Britain at Bay* and *Britain Can Take It!* Given the number of official shorts made during the war, and the many different messages which they were meant to convey, it is only to be expected that their success rate would be uneven. Perhaps the most important point to make, however, is that shorts and documentaries fulfilled a highly specific role in the MOI's film propaganda policy. Whereas the feature film was used for propaganda of a general and indirect nature in dramatising why Britain was fighting the war and presenting images of national unity, the short film by contrast was used for putting over the more direct, immediate and urgent messages that were deemed necessary by the government. Those historians who have devalued shorts at the expense of feature films have perhaps failed to appreciate that shorts were serving a very different function. Their essentially short-term objectives made them disposable and quickly out of date, but they none the less had an important role to play. In their way shorts were no less important than commercial feature films; they just served a different purpose.

5

The Crown Film Unit

The Crown Film Unit, which, as the GPO Film Unit, acquired before the war a high reputation for documentary films, has in its wartime form evolved a technique and skill regarded as more suitable for producing the special type of high quality film required than that possessed by outside studios. *Ministry of Information memorandum* (1942)[1]

I

The Crown Film Unit occupied an important place in the official film propaganda machinery during the war. It produced some eighty films for the MOI, an output which consisted mainly of short documentaries but which also included a handful of feature-length films. While these films were conceived in the context of wartime propaganda requirements, some of them achieved great critical and popular success and a few of them have passed into the canon of 'classic' British cinema on the strength of their aesthetic qualities. Certain titles, such as *London Can Take It!*, *Target for Tonight* and *Fires Were Started*, have since become evocative reminders of the British wartime experience. Yet for all the success and prestige which its films achieved, Crown's place within the propaganda machinery was not always secure. It was beset by bureaucracy and Treasury penny-pinching; it underwent several re-organisations during the first year of the war; it was the target of an abortive take-over attempt by a commercial producer; and, although it was often hampered by the scarcity of resources and the tight purse-strings of official finance, it was nevertheless the object of jealousy and hostility from independent documentary producers and commercial studios because of the favourable treatment which they thought it received. Given this background, Crown's success in becoming the linch-pin of official film production is in itself a noteworthy achievement.

It has become part of the historical orthodoxy that the GPO Film Unit was ignored by the planners of the MOI and that as a result it was left high and dry at the beginning of the war. Paul Rotha suggested that the pre-war planners of the ministry 'appeared ignorant of the fact that there had been an official machine for film-making (the GPO Film Unit) in being without interruption since the EMB Film Unit in 1929'.[2] This account, however, is not entirely accurate. The planners were certainly not ignorant of the Film Unit's existence. Sir Stephen Tallents had been one of the architects of the Film Unit, and he was involved in the planning of the MOI until the autumn of 1938. On 13 October 1938 he wrote to H. V. Rhodes at the GPO: 'I am suggesting in a paper which I am drafting on the subject of Home Publicity (of which you have a copy) that the Post Office Film Unit should be invited to take some thought about its probable needs and extended activity in time of war.'[3] Thus Tallents not only saw a role for the Film Unit in wartime, but also apparently envisaged the Unit itself having some input into its adaptation for wartime needs. The removal of Tallents after the Munich Crisis meant that the Film Unit lost its most influential ally in official circles, but even so the Unit was not forgotten. In April 1939 the International Propaganda and Broadcasting Enquiry declared that 'the Post Office Film Unit will constitute a most important factor in the planning of film publicity'.[4] Therefore, the GPO Unit was certainly not ignored during the planning stages of the MOI. Whether it was adequately employed upon the outbreak of war is, however, quite another matter.

II

The outcome of the planning for the wartime role of the GPO Film Unit was the decision, arrived at in August 1939, that 'the Unit would remain under the control of the Post Office so far as pay, discipline etc. is concerned, but the Ministry of Information would have first call on its services for the production of films, photographs etc'.[5] In practice what happened was that upon the outbreak of war G. E. G. Forbes of the Post Office Public Relations Department became Deputy-Director of the MOI Films Division, in which role he assumed responsibility for the 'administrative and executive control of the Unit'.[6] This meant that some continuity was maintained in the control of the Film Unit and allowed the Post Office to keep an eye on the Unit while it was on loan to the MOI. In December 1939 Forbes's responsibility for the Film Unit was passed to A. G. Highet, another GPO civil servant who moved over to the MOI. This transfer of personnel from the Post Office to the MOI had, in the short term, significant implications for the Film Unit's place in the official propaganda machinery.

During the 1930s considerable antipathy had developed in the civil service towards the documentarists, and particularly towards John Grierson. Although Grierson had resigned from the post of GPO Films Officer in 1937 and was no longer formally associated with the Film Unit, his ethos was still considered by some to pervade the outfit. There was at first some dislike of the Film Unit within the Films Division, in particular from Highet who thought it was an expensive luxury that was often more trouble than it was worth. After returning to the Post Office late in 1940, Highet confided to a colleague that, during his time at the Films Division, 'I found myself being drawn, somewhat unwillingly I admit, to the conclusion that a number of commercial producers could produce perfectly good films at prices strictly comparable with GPO Film Unit costs and with very much less trouble and friction'.[7] Some of the problems seem to have been caused by animosity between the personnel of the Film Unit and their civil service overseer. Harry Watt, a senior director with the Unit, later described Highet as 'a pompous Scot' and derided him because 'the whole film effort of Britain at war, both instructional and propaganda, was controlled by someone whose total creative problems had been bounded by whether to paint the Post Office at Nether Wallop white or pink!'[8] Watt had good reason to dislike the man from the Post Office, who in August 1940 had told the MOI Establishments Division: 'I cannot justify the retention of highly paid film directors' and had recommended the sacking of Watt, Humphrey Jennings and Alberto Cavalcanti, the supervising producer of the Film Unit.[9] In the event, Jack Beddington blocked the removal of these key personnel and

1. ABOVE. **Feature Film Propaganda (I):** *The Lion Has Wings* (Alexander Korda, 1939) was the first propaganda feature film of the war, an overblown tribute to the fighting power of the Royal Air Force.

2. RIGHT. **Feature Film Propaganda (II):** *49th Parallel* (Michael Powell, 1941), sponsored by the MOI, was set in Canada and dramatised the differences between thuggish Nazis (John Chandos, *left,* Eric Portman, *right)* and peace-loving democrats, here represented by Leslie Howard.

3. LEFT. **Short Film Propaganda (I):** In *The First Days* (GPO Film Unit, 1939) the filling of sandbags became a metaphor for class levelling.

4. BELOW. **Short Film Propaganda (II):** *Squadron 992* (GPO Film Unit, 1940) illustrated the work of the Balloon Barrage in defending the Forth Bridge.

5. ABOVE. **Short Film Propaganda (III):** *Men of the Lightship* (GPO Film Unit, 1940) was a dramatic reconstruction of the bombing of the East Dudgeon lightship, using 'real' people.

6. RIGHT. **Short Film Propaganda (IV):** *London Can Take It!* (GPO Film Unit, 1940) was a documentary account of how the 'people's army' withstood the Blitz.

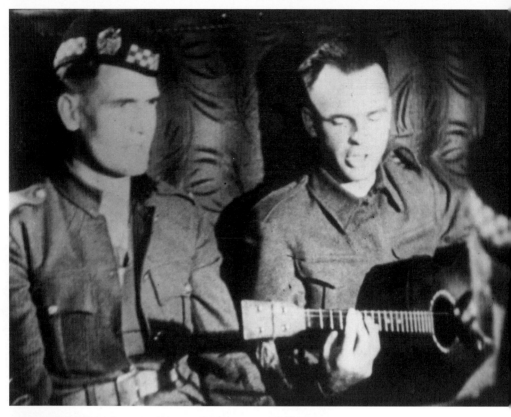

7. ABOVE. Short Film Propaganda (V): Canadian soldiers remember their 'Home on the Range' in Humphrey Jennings's *Listen to Britain* (Crown Film Unit, 1942), a poetic meditation on the sights and sounds of Britain at war.

8. LEFT. Short Film Propaganda (VI): *Night Shift* (Paul Rotha Productions, 1942) was a documentary account of women working in an ordnance factory.

9. RIGHT. **The Crown Film Unit (I):** *Target for Tonight* (Crown, 1941) was the first film to show Britain hitting back, and its success spawned a series of similar feature-length narrative documentaries.

10. BELOW. **The Crown Film Unit (II):** *Coastal Command* (Crown, 1942), the follow-up to *Target,* included dramatic aerial footage of convoy protection work.

11. LEFT. **The Crown Film Unit (III):** The last of the big narrative documentaries was *Western Approaches* (Crown, 1944), which effectively brought home the hazards faced by the merchant navy in the Battle of the Atlantic.

12. BELOW. **The Service Film Units (I):** *Journey Together* (RAF Film Unit, 1945) used professional actors (Jack Watling, Richard Attenborough) to dramatise the training of a bomber crew.

13. RIGHT. **The Service Film Units (II):** The Battle of El Alamein was vividly brought to the screen in *Desert Victory* (Army Film and Photographic Unit, 1943), a feature-length documentary compiled from actuality footage.

14. BELOW. **The Service Film Units (III):** General Eisenhower talks to his troops in *The True Glory* (British and American Service Film Units, 1945), the joint film record of the Normandy campaign.

15. LEFT. **The People's War (I):** Humphrey Jennings's *Fires Were Started* (Crown, 1943) achieved a level of epic narrative poetry in its presentation of the heroism of London's firemen during the Blitz.

16. BELOW. **The People's War (II):** *The Bells Go Down* (Ealing, 1943) was a studio-produced story of the Blitz using professional actors (Philip Friend, Tommy Trinder, Mervyn Johns, Billy Hartnell).

Highet left the Films Division, but the incident illustrates the Film Unit's uncertain position during the first year of the war.

The early wartime history of the GPO Film Unit is usually described as a period of under-employment. The authors of *The Factual Film* said: 'it was not fully employed nor was its work incorporated within the Ministry of Information's film activities.'[10] It had been commissioned by the Home Office in August 1939 to make a film about air raid precautions. This was originally entitled *If War Should Come*, though it was released after the outbreak of war under the title *Do It Now* with a new introduction explaining that 'the film intended as a warning for the future becomes advice for the present'. It was a simple instructional film to tell civilians what to do (listen to official instructions on the radio, empty their lofts of junk to minimise the risk of fire, construct their Anderson shelters if they had not already done so) and what not to do (such as hoarding food or hogging the telephone). However, its use of Elgar's high-toned *Pomp and Circumstance*, while intended to be stirringly patriotic, does seem somewhat over the top. 'The Government's only propagandist film so far has been treated as a joke, although it was supposed to instruct people about ARP,' said a report by Mass-Observation. 'Its audience response, in terms of laughter, nearly equals an indifferent Disney.'[11]

The first GPO film of the war proper was *The First Days* (1939), a two-reeler showing London adapting to wartime conditions. According to Watt, the Film Unit had received no directions from the MOI and made this film off its own bat:

> It was then that Cavalcanti, magnificent old Cav, the alien, whom some Blimps always suspected, took the law into his own hands, and sent us all into the streets to film anything we saw that was new and different. Cav realized that history was being made all around us, and a tremendous opportunity to record it for posterity was being lost, so six small units went out with all our film stock and filmed the extraordinary scenes of a nation amateurishly preparing its capital for a new kind of war. We filmed the frantic sandbag filling, the new balloons rising up in the oddest places, the endless drilling in the parks, the new auxiliary policemen – I remember I got a chap in plus-fours and a monocle directing traffic at Piccadilly Circus – anything that was different from the normal peacetime way of life ...

Off we went to the Ministry and proudly announced 'We've made a film,' and they really replied 'Good God!' They seemed genuinely shocked that someone had actually done something, and horrified when we asked them to handle it for us. Apparently, a committee was going to be formed to discuss whether Government films should be given away free or distributed normally through the trade. And now these awkward blighters had made one – most inconsiderate! As it would obviously take weeks for them to decide their policy, they hedged their responsibility by telling us – unofficially, of course – to do what we liked with the film. So Cavalcanti and I, with the three tins under our arms, hawked the first British official movie up and down Wardour Street, like a couple of hard-up producers![12]

However, Watt's colourful telling of the tale is somewhat at odds with the official documentation. It is evident that Forbes was aware of the Film Unit's under-employment and had raised the matter with the Director of the Films Division:

On the evening of the 8th September I represented to Sir Joseph Ball that the GPO Film Unit, of which the standing charges fall on public funds, is at present doing practically nothing; and that in order to avoid waste of public money and of the enthusiasm of the personnel it was highly desirable to get the Unit to work at once.[13]

Forbes went on to explain that the Film Unit had come up with an idea for a film about the London front:

The Unit had already sketched out a film showing the calm way in which London had made the transition from peace conditions to those of war: and such a film if well executed would be of value not only for exhibition in this country on the reopening of the cinemas but also for propaganda abroad ... Sir Joseph agreed that in the circumstances the Unit should get to work at once on a film of the kind indicated, not to exceed a length of two reels or a cost of £1500; and Mr Highet orally expressed concurrence on behalf of the Co-Ordination Division.

I have therefore instructed the Film Unit to proceed at once, in order to take advantage of present opportunities and of the splendid light-conditions.

Forbes's memorandum bears out Watt's memoirs only in so far as it is clear that the idea for *The First Days* did come from the Film Unit itself. But the project was given official sanction before shooting began, so Watt's account of the MOI's surprise at being presented with the finished film must be treated with some scepticism.

The First Days is an impressionistic little film which is important in that it was the first wartime documentary to use the idea of the 'people's war' which was to become the main theme of British propaganda. It captures the mood of the people of London in the late summer of 1939 through a combination of memorable images, evocative use of popular songs and a refined, eloquent commentary. Opening on 3 September ('London was at peace on this Sunday morning') it shows people going to church, setting out on bicycle rides and walking in Hyde Park. The outbreak of war comes in an almost dream-like manner: the streets are empty and quiet, while people gather to listen to Chamberlain's announcement on the wireless. The peace is broken by the first wail of air raid sirens, though in the event it is a false alarm. The film then shows how London prepared for war: the filling of sandbags, the construction of earthworks and defences, the tethering of barrage balloons, the evacuation of children by train, and the removal of art treasures from the National Gallery and the British Museum. The film suggests that a process of social levelling is under way. The filling of sandbags becomes a metaphor for solidarity and teamwork: 'The thousand classes of London, some from their damp basements and some from their luxury flats, came together to work for the public good. In those first critical hours they did indispensable work which no leader could have ordered and no money could have bought.' Thus the spirit of the people's war is inscribed: people from different class backgrounds are shown working together for the common good. In hindsight, of course, the degree of social cohesion depicted in the film is exaggerated, but at the time it was regarded as a sincere and honest little film. Miss C. A. Lejeune, for example, wrote:

> *The First Days* is a very simple little film, admirable in its understatement, moving in its material. There is no flag-waving in it, and no shouting. It is not propaganda in any serious sense, except in its reflection of a quiet spirit in a great city prepared. A brilliant little corollary to *The Lion Has Wings*. Highly recommended.[14]

The comparison to *The Lion Has Wings* is interesting, as the two films had presented very different images of British society in the early days of the war.

Most of the Film Unit's early projects, however, were not completed.[15] There was much confusion due to the complicated arrangement whereby the Film Unit had been placed at the disposal of the MOI while still nominally belonging to the Post Office. This control mechanism was not working satisfactorily, and by the early months of 1940 a change was on the cards. Eric St John Bamford, a former Treasury civil servant who had been moved to the MOI, told Sir Kenneth Clark that 'I have spoken to Mr Forbes and I understand him to agree that the Unit should now come under the complete control of the Ministry and that we should cut out the extraordinary complexities involved by the present arrangement'.[16] At a meeting between representatives of the GPO and the MOI on 27 February the transfer of the Film Unit to the MOI for the duration of the war was agreed by both parties:

> Agreed in principle GPO Film Unit to be taken over by MOI as from 1st April, 1940, on the understanding that the Unit would be kept together and without prejudice to the question of control of the Unit after the war. Treasury have already agreed semi-officially; the Ministry to write to Treasury for the necessary authority.[17]

The necessary sanction was granted by the Treasury, and accordingly the MOI assumed direct control of the Film Unit. But even after this transfer, the Film Unit continued to experience numerous political and administrative difficulties. Several developments in the summer of 1940 were of long-term importance in defining the Unit's role for the rest of the war.

III

The first important development was that Alberto Cavalcanti left the Film Unit to work for Michael Balcon at Ealing Studios. Cavalcanti, a Brazilian film-maker with a commercial background, had become the supervising producer of the Film Unit after John Grierson's departure. Towards the end of April 1940 it was announced in the trade press that Cavalcanti was to leave the Unit for Ealing, though it was another three months before he made the move.[18] It has often been assumed that the reason for Cavalcanti's departure was his nationality, in that it seemed anomalous to have a foreign national running the official film unit during wartime.[19] This was not necessarily the case, however, for there is evidence that both the MOI and the Film Unit were keen to retain him. Eric St John Bamford said the ministry 'was anxious ... that Mr Cavalcanti should be retained'.[20] And the office manager of the Film Unit, Stanley Fletcher, was of the opinion that 'Mr Cavalcanti is without doubt the best Producer in the country and it is vital that the Film Unit should continue to have use of his services'.[21] Given the support for Cavalcanti in official circles, therefore, it is necessary to find another explanation for his departure.

It seems that Cavalcanti's move to Ealing was connected to an abortive attempt by Michael Balcon to take over the Film Unit in the summer of 1940. A memorandum on the reorganisation of the Film Unit by Stanley Fletcher, dated 26 July, suggested there had been a move afoot for the Film Unit to make a feature film in association with Ealing:

> It is understood that there has been discussion on the possibility of the Film Unit undertaking the production of a feature subject. Mr Balcon is apparently interested in the idea and production would in some way be associated with Ealing Studios. With Mr Cavalcanti in charge, there is little doubt that the Film Unit could make an extremely creditable feature, but before the Ministry embarks on feature production either by its own Film Unit or by an outside company, it should consider carefully possible Trade repercussions. Admittedly the Ministry is sponsoring the Canadian Michael Powell film and it would probably be a good idea to sponsor more.[22]

Further details emerge from a correspondence between Balcon and Beddington early in August 1940. On 1 August, Balcon wrote:

> As you know, I have had a preliminary conversation with Fletcher with regard to the GPO Unit. The decision about this matter is, of course, in your hands, but assuming that we shall be called upon to do something about it, Cavalcanti and I have been discussing a programme.
>
> The programme divides itself into several headings:
> (a) the feature films produced for the standard Ealing programme,

(b) any films we may be called upon to make for the Ministry
of Information,
(c) the GPO films.[23]

Balcon apparently envisaged the Film Unit working at Ealing under
the supervision of Cavalcanti. He suggested that such a move would
be in the national interest.

> In conclusion, you will appreciate that this studio has already
> done valuable work, and if we are fortunate enough to be able
> to add to it an organised programme for the GPO Unit, the
> Films Division will have at their disposal and supplementing their
> own work a first class programme of films harnessed to the
> national war effort.

What he did not say, though it would probably also have influenced
him, was that taking on the Film Unit would also be a way of securing
facilities for his studio and safeguarding his personnel from National
Service.

However, Balcon's plans for the Film Unit were not to be realised.
Beddington poured cold water on the idea:

> Am I right in understanding that your suggestion in regard to the
> GPO Film Unit is that you wish to take it over completely? If
> this is so, I am afraid we have no alternative but to carry on as we
> are, or make some other arrangement. We are, as it were, trustees
> of this unit for the GPO and have undertaken to hand it back to
> them at the end of the war.[24]

This did not satisfy Balcon, who still wanted to effect some form of
tie-up with the Film Unit. His correspondence with Beddington became
increasingly strained. A letter of 6 August adopted a more critical tone:

> If the Ministry of Information had proceeded on the broad lines
> discussed some time ago (and you will remember no doubt that it
> was your suggestion I should take over the GPO Unit and not
> mine) the problem could, in my opinion, have been easily solved
> and here you will not mind my reminding you that I placed myself
> unreservedly at your disposal, being willing to make very large
> personal sacrifices to do so. These proposals were not proceeded
> with and you will remember that it was not until later, when I
> myself made enquiries, that I found you had other ideas.[25]

There had clearly been a misunderstanding between Beddington and Balcon: it seems unlikely that Beddington would have suggested Balcon taking over the Unit (as Balcon intimates) given that Beddington had then said that such a move would be impossible. The tone of Balcon's letter also illustrates his rather arrogant self-importance, particularly the way in which he considered himself more of an expert on propaganda than the Films Division. The combination of Balcon's attitude and what he saw as the Films Division's lacklustre response is an indication of the friction that was developing between them. Balcon's letter of 6 August concludes:

I have written to you at length because my relationship with your Division should not be confused. In the first place, as you know, we hold strong views on the value of film in propaganda and information. Results however can only be obtained by using the best personnel and facilities. Secondly, might I point out that everything that we have done so far for you we have done without remuneration or without profit. Viewing it quite dispassionately, I think that if any major difficulty arose between us, it was my view that the primary function of the Films Division is to get films made and not to make them.

By the way, I should like you to show this letter to the Director General, or better still to allow me to send him a copy.

Beddington cannot have been very happy with the implication in the last sentence that Balcon wanted to go above his head, though in the event Balcon was dissuaded from doing so.

Balcon's attempt to take over the Film Unit therefore came to nothing. For the Film Unit itself, the main consequence of the abortive take-over was the departure of Cavalcanti, though of course that had been on the cards since late April. In terms of Balcon's relationship with the MOI, however, the incident was of much greater significance. It was a major cause of the rift between the two parties which came to a head in December 1940. It is significant that in announcing Ealing's intention to go its own way in terms of film propaganda, Balcon emphasised that the studio was going to produce its own programme of shorts. A front-page article in *Kinematograph Weekly*, entitled 'War Effort Hampered By M of I Films Policy', declared:

The lack of a definite policy of the M of I in the realm of

sponsored production is deplored, and because of the time wasted in fruitless negotiation Ealing Studios has scheduled £35,000 of its own money in planning a schedule of propaganda shorts which will be distributed through the usual commercial channels.[26]

This was a very provocative move by Balcon, who was effectively setting up a rival film propaganda programme to the MOI. The view that Balcon had expressed privately to Beddington – 'that the primary function of the Films Division is to get films made and not to make them' – was now elaborated in public. The Ealing press release declared:

> As commercial producers we resented the competition in produc-
> tion which a Government department was setting up with an
> Industry already faced with many obstacles and difficulties. Instead
> of being distributors of propaganda films and advisers to the
> Industry on policy in propaganda, the Films Division we found
> was setting up as a producing body actively concerning itself in
> the actual technicalities of production.[27]

The rift between Balcon and the MOI was therefore caused to a large degree by Balcon's view that the MOI should not produce its own propaganda films but instead should commission them from com- mercial producers and distribute them through the usual channels (rather like the Cinema Propaganda Department of the First World War). His desire to have control of the GPO Film Unit, the MOI's principal production agency, should therefore be seen in the context of his fears about the competition which it represented for commercial producers. This seems all the more relevant given that later in the war Balcon was to lead the industry's complaints that official film units received favourable treatment in the provision of facilities.

The next important development for the Film Unit in 1940 was the appointment of Ian Dalrymple as Cavalcanti's replacement. Dalrymple came from the commercial side of the film industry, having been a scriptwriter, editor and associate producer for Korda during the 1930s. He later admitted that he had 'little experience of non-fictional produc- tion' and that he thought the members of the Film Unit 'with their art and aims, must have some qualms about accepting a supervisor from the commercial industry'.[28] However, Stanley Fletcher told Beddington that the opinion of the Film Unit was 'that Dalrymple would do as well as anyone and if you have no objections we should like to try him'.[29] Dalrymple was thus appointed, albeit on the understanding 'that the Film Unit is at present under investigation and that the appointment must be subject to any decision which may be reached as a result'.[30]

The fact was that by August 1940 the position of the Film Unit had become rather uncertain. Quite apart from the problems with Ealing, the Unit itself was being reviewed and there was a possibility that it would be disbanded. With its work under review both externally (by the Select Committee on National Expenditure) and internally (by the new Director-General Frank Pick, formerly of the London Passenger Transport Board), the Unit's future was far from certain. 'It may be necessary to reconsider the whole question of keeping the GPO Film Unit in being either as a result of the Director-General's review or in the event of an adverse report by the Select Committee,' Bamford informed Beddington.[31] In the event, both the Select Committee and the Director-General concluded that the Film Unit should be maintained but that it should be reorganised to make economies wherever possible. Harold Boxall, a studio manager at Denham, was commissioned to undertake a thorough investigation of the Film Unit in terms of its personnel, equipment, accounting system and organisation, and 'to recommend how the Unit should be reconstructed in order to cope with a programme of 10–15 films per annum not exceeding 3000 feet in length'.[32] The investigation was sanctioned only 'on the understanding that reliance would be placed by the Ministry on the technical advice of the expert', so the MOI was committed to acting upon Boxall's recommendations.[33]

Fortunately for the Film Unit, Boxall realised that it specialised in films of a particular type which could not be made effectively by anyone else and that if it were disbanded then 'the Films Division would then be forced to rely on other Producers for product over which they would have no control unless the Treasury was prepared to finance such Producers in the production of such subjects as it was deemed desirable to have made'.[34] Boxall also made some specific recommendations to improve the Film Unit. He considered that its existing studio at Blackheath was too old and too small and that it should be moved to newer and better-equipped premises; he identified a need to reduce the staff and restructure the administration; and he recommended that the Unit's stills and photographic work should be transferred to the MOI's Photographs Division. He also suggested that the name of the Film Unit should be changed so that it would 'appear to the general public that here is an ordinary commercial film, and not a Government Propaganda film'. He suggested as a new name 'Victory Pictures' (which would hardly seem to make a film appear less obviously propagandist than maintaining the GPO trademark). Otherwise, however, most of Boxall's recommendations were acted upon – for example, negotiations were promptly undertaken for the Film Unit to move to Denham Studios – and his report served as a guideline for reorganisation.

Ian Dalrymple's response to Boxall's report was to suggest even more sweeping reforms. His own recommendations, if acted upon, would have had the effect of increasing the Film Unit's autonomy from Treasury and civil service control. They included financing the Film Unit's production programme by an annual grant, rather than applying for financial sanction for each film on an individual basis, and removing most of the civil servants involved in clerical and administrative work. It is no surprise that these suggestions were not to the liking of the MOI's bureaucrats. 'Attractive as it may seem, it is really impossible for us to give Mr Dalrymple a block grant of some £70,000 and tell him to get on with the job without Establishment and Financial control from this Ministry,' Bamford remarked.[35] One of Dalrymple's suggestions was to be adopted, however, and that was in regard to the Unit's name:

> The name of the present Production Unit should presumably be changed, but it is desirable to retain the reputation at present inherent in the words GPO Film Unit, with the crown as mark. I would suggest that the Unit be styled the Crown Film Unit and that the crown emblem be retained from the present mark.[36]

Thus it was that the Crown Film Unit officially came into being at the end of 1940.

Following the upheavals of 1940, the renamed and reorganised Crown Film Unit was able to find a more stable and settled place for itself within the official film propaganda machinery. Its future was secured at a meeting in November 1940 which had concluded: 'It is necessary to maintain the GPO Film Unit under the control of the Ministry to meet the increasing demands for direct production of films for the purposes of the Ministry's film propaganda, due to the present difficulties of the film industry.'[37] Under Dalrymple's stewardship, Crown became the most important contributor to the MOI's output of official documentaries, producing some twelve to fifteen films annually, mostly for theatrical distribution. Rather like Jack Beddington at the Films Division, Dalrymple has received a good press from both contemporaries and historians. Michael Powell called him 'the great documentary film-maker of the war'.[38] And Pronay writes: 'Under his patient, highly professional, yet sensitive guidance the Crown Film Unit produced a matchless series of films, the best of which, in the tradition of Renaissance art, elevated good propaganda of the moment into lasting works of art.'[39] The one dissenting voice was that of Harry Watt, who found Dalrymple 'cold, distant and discouraging – to me at any rate'.[40] In 1942 Watt was to follow Cavalcanti in leaving the Film Unit to work at Ealing Studios. It seems that Watt's often volatile temperament had been his undoing, as he left Crown after falling out with Dalrymple. 'I never would have gone to Ealing if we hadn't made the mistake of taking on Ian Dalrymple as producer,' Watt recalled. He went on:

> With Cavalcanti I used to resign about once a week, and Cavalcanti just laughed and said, 'Shut up, you stupid idiot. Get on with the work.' And I went back to work. I did this once too often with Dalrymple, and Dalrymple happily accepted my resignation. I rather regretted it, but Ealing were pressing me to join them, and I thought 'All right, you bugger, I'll go and join Ealing and join Cav.'[41]

Watt apart, however, the other main directors of the Film Unit – Jack Holmes, Humphrey Jennings, Pat Jackson, Stuart Legg and Jack Lee – were to continue working happily with Dalrymple, and under his supervision they did some of their best work.

Dalrymple saw his role as being to create the right working conditions for the Film Unit and to let the documentarists get on with what they did best, which was making films, with the minimum of interference from above. It was this approach, he suggested, which caused his rift with Watt:

> I made up my mind on my function: the Unit could get on with making the films, while I would fight for facilities, conditions and opportunities. This was to lead in time to my difference with Harry Watt, who felt that I should be in the field at the film director's

elbow and not lounging in an office chair; but, with several projects in hand at once, with the need to act as a buffer between the Films Division and the Unit, and with my nocturnal rambles as a Civil Defence warden, my attendance continuously on locations and sets was not practicable.[42]

Dalrymple's energy in fighting for better facilities for the Film Unit was soon to ruffle some feathers within the MOI. 'I think I should call your attention to the fact that, first of all, your new producer, Mr Dalrymple, seems to be taking the bit between his teeth and doing as he likes,' the Director-General complained to Beddington in November 1940. 'This won't do at all; he must do as he is told; the sooner he is brought under control the better.'[43] Beddington, however, defended him. 'I do not agree with you at all about Mr Dalrymple,' he replied. 'I consider him extremely efficient and businesslike and he has improved the Unit enormously.'[44] Thus Dalrymple had the support of the Director of the Films Division as well as the confidence of most members of the Film Unit itself.

IV

Under Dalrymple, the Crown Film Unit adopted a particular production ideology which was to define its unique place in the film propaganda campaign. Crown came to specialise in a certain type of film – the reconstructed narrative-documentary – which distinguished it from both the commercial studios and the other documentary producers. Charles Barr suggests that Dalrymple was a 'crucial figure' in this development 'for the way in which he embodies the crossover between commercial cinema and documentary that was central to the Crown project and to British wartime cinema'.[45] In fact, the narrative-documentary tradition at the Film Unit had its origins in Cavalcanti's time in charge during the late 1930s. For example, Harry Watt's *North Sea* (1938), depicting the rescue of fishermen from a stricken trawler, was an influential film in the development of the narrative-documentary mode of representation. The Home Planning Sub-Committee had singled out this particular film in May 1939: 'Its success has been considerable and warrants serious consideration of the story form in presenting government propaganda.'[46] And early war GPO films such as *Men of the Lightship* (1940), produced by Cavalcanti but with a director (David Macdonald) recruited from commercial cinema, had already shown how the narrative-documentary could be used for wartime needs. So the trend towards narrative films had begun before Dalrymple joined the Film Unit; what he did was to embrace it and develop it to its fullest extent. Crown's work was one example of the 'wartime wedding' of the documentary and narrative modes of film practice. This was illustrated in the production of a series of feature-length narrative-documentaries (*Target for Tonight, Coastal Command, Close Quarters, Fires Were Started* and *Western Approaches*) which made use of studio sets and some of the formal narrative conventions of commercial cinema. These films were an innovation in the documentary field and are widely held to have raised the profile of documentary with the cinema-going public.[47]

Target for Tonight (1941), directed by Harry Watt, was the first of the Crown features and set the style for most of the others. It is a model of the narrative-documentary technique. True to its documentary roots the film gives an illustration of the operational procedures of Bomber Command in a straightforward and realistic manner. The narrative is spare and concise; every scene has a purpose in furthering the story; no shot is superfluous. The film borrows an identification strategy from the mainstream narrative cinema by focusing on the crew of 'F for Freddie', a Wellington bomber involved in a raid on an oil depot at 'Friehausen' in Germany. However, the casting of 'real' people (Watt used serving RAF personnel and even persuaded Sir Richard Pierse, the Commander-in-Chief of Bomber Command, to appear as himself) provides the necessary degree of authenticity for the film to be considered as documentary rather than fiction. A reconstruction of the Bomber Command Operations Room – described by Watt as 'the biggest set ever built by documentary'[48] – was made at Denham, while Mildenhall air base (the same location that had been used for *The Lion Has Wings*) was used as 'Millerton' aerodrome. The film's realism is reinforced through its aesthetic and formal components. Film historian Eric Rhode writes that the film 'now seems as evocative of its period as an ugly, narrow-armed utility chair. The bleakness of its aerodrome setting and the awkwardness of its editing and camera placements capture the austerity of the period with a zeal so puritanical that it begins to assume the conviction of a style.'[49] The unusual editing is evident, for example, in the apparent jump-cuts in the sequence showing the Wellington's flight across the North Sea where the bomber suddenly changes size or position in the frame without any elliptical dissolves.[50] The sequence of the bombing-run in to the target is also marked by unusual camera set-ups (including successive close-ups of the pilot from different angles) which work rather like 'shocks' in the manner of Eisenstein's theory of montage: the uncomfortable angles emphasise the danger as the bomber flies through heavy flak.

The initial suggestion to make a film on RAF Bomber Command came from the Air Ministry in the autumn of 1940. It suggested 'a documentary of about two reels in length' charting the history of Bomber Command from the mid-1930s to the present and justifying the policy of Lord Trenchard in advocating a strong bomber arm. It was critical of 'the long false security of the defensive era' and can thus be seen in the context of Air Chief Marshal Sir Charles Portal's policy in urging a more offensive role for the RAF. The proposed film would show how the RAF found its way around Germany dropping leaflets during 'the dreary winter of 1939' and would end with a reconstruction of a daylight raid over France to 'show our major striking weapon actually on the job'. The Air Ministry was 'anxious for such a film to be made as soon as possible and would co-operate in every way and provide the fullest facilities to the GPO Film Unit'.[51] Harry Watt was chosen to direct the film, planned as a two-reeler entitled *Bomber Command* and formally approved at a cost of £3000 by the MOI Planning Committee on 30 November 1940.[52] Once the project had been adopted by the Film Unit, however, it quickly changed character from a documentary history of strategic bombing to a narrative-based reconstruction of a night raid over Germany. It was to be, in Watt's words, 'a prestige film of Bomber Command, not a factual resume of the long term policy' and for this reason the narrative form was adopted.[53] Crown did not set out intending to make a feature-length film – it was probably first envisaged as being something similar to Watt's *Squadron 992* – but the size of the project grew bit by bit. 'The subject is most important, and Films Division is strongly of the opinion that a three or four reel film is necessary to present it adequately,' the Planning Committee was informed in April 1941.[54] The cost of the film inevitably grew along with its length. When it was completed in July 1941 its length was five reels and its direct cost was £6,406, over twice the original estimate.[55]

Target for Tonight was released in the summer of 1941 to wide critical and popular acclaim. *The Times* exemplified the views of the critics in praising its realism and restraint:

Target for To-Night, without the flourishes and rhetoric of propaganda, records something of the way in which our men go about their duties, and by implication rather than direct statement indicates the spirit that guides them ... All through it realises the emphasis of under-statement, and while other cameras since the war have flung bits and pieces of our war in the air and on sea and land vividly on the screen, here is a record set down in something more than cinematic shorthand, and an inspiring record it is.[56]

The middle-brow critics, therefore, admired the film for its traditional documentary qualities, but it was also favourably received by the popular press. 'Every man, woman and child in this country should see the film,' declared Jonah Barrington of the *Daily Express*. 'It's the first film to earn 100 degrees from me.'[57] It also made a handsome profit at the box-office: by May 1944 the Exchequer had recorded receipts of £73,636, which made it the most successful of Crown's films.[58]

Why was this particular film so successful in a popular cinema that had only rarely, if at all, embraced the documentary? In order to answer this question, it is necessary to look beyond the film's form and style and to consider its historical context. A likely answer is provided by Forsyth Hardy, who wrote that it 'came at the right psychological moment, when we were wearying of the "Britain Can Take It" idea and longing to hear of aggressive action'.[59] It was the first major film to show Britain taking the offensive against Germany rather than just stoically enduring enemy bombardment. In the summer of 1941, strategic bombing was the only means by which Britain could be shown in attack rather than defence. Lord Beaverbrook, the Minister of Aircraft Production, described *Target* as 'a picture which must move and interest audiences wherever it is shown'.[60] It was a considerable success in America, where it was voted the best documentary of 1941 by the National Board of Review of Motion Pictures. The American trade paper *Variety* thought it was both good propaganda and a good box-office prospect:

This is the most realistic picture to come out of the current European war ... It looks like a sure grosser. *Target for Tonight* is propaganda at its peak, a forthright documentary of RAF bombing activities in the present conflict, told in succinct fashion and with thrill packed on thrill.[61]

Some changes were made to make the film more acceptable to American audiences: the voices of the RAF personnel were dubbed by American actors, and it was reported that Alfred Hitchcock re-edited the film for American consumption.[62]

The success of *Target for Tonight* was such that Crown quickly realised the potential of the extended narrative-documentary for reaching a wider audience in the commercial cinema. *Ferry Pilot* (1941), directed by Pat Jackson, was a four-reel 'featurette' which had a production history similar to *Target*'s in that it grew to be a bigger film than originally envisaged, being planned in the first instance as a five-minute film.[63] 'This film does for the pilots of the Air Transport Auxiliary much the same kind of service that *Target for To-night* did for the RAF,' said *The Times*.[64] *Target* had therefore become the critical yardstick against which other Crown films were judged.

Crown's second full-length feature was *Coastal Command* (1942), directed by Jack Holmes, and in this case it was realised from the beginning that it would be a longer and more expensive film than its predecessor. This was due largely to the fact that a unit was sent to Iceland to film some of the aerial sequences. When it started production in August 1941, a budget of £8,738 had been authorised by the MOI, more than the direct cost of *Target*, and the final cost was £16,646.[65] *Coastal Command* is a more polished film than *Target*: its impressive cinematography captures the vast expanses of ocean which the service had to cover, and the action scenes are heightened by a dramatic score from Ralph Vaughan Williams. Like *Target* it focuses on one crew, Sunderland flying-boat 'T for Tommy', involved in convoy escort duty; the parts were once again played by real RAF personnel, including Sir Philip Joubert, the Commander-in-Chief of Coastal Command. The more dramatic work of the service is shown through reconstructions of the sinking of a U-boat and an attack on a German warship. It was another popular and critical success, with receipts of £47,797.[66] *The Times* again compared it to *Target*: 'The Crown Film Unit has done for Coastal Command what, in *Target for To-night*, it did for Bomber Command, and those responsible for interpreting the British war effort to America and Russia now have another strong card in their hands.'[67]

The Crown features all shared certain common characteristics: they were spare, exhibited great narrative economy, and unlike the mainstream feature film and true to their documentary roots they eschewed romantic subplots to concentrate on telling their stories in a straight-forward and uncomplicated manner. Although they were scripted and were in themselves 'fiction', they nevertheless exhibited a documentary approach in that they used 'real' people rather than professional actors and their content was authentic, believable and unsensational. They exhibited all the qualities that were so important for the dominant critical discourse of the time. For example, in reviewing Jack Lee's *Close Quarters* (1943), *The Times* said that it 'was made by the Crown Film Unit, which is another way of saying that it states an heroic case without indulging in heroics and presents the men through the plain, objective mirror of reporting rather than the distorting lens of cinematic fiction'.[68]

However, while they met with critical and popular approval, the Crown feature films did attract complaints from both the independent documentary companies and the commercial producers on the grounds that Crown had facilities not available to them. Paul Rotha later described Crown as 'the luxury unit' because: 'They had cameras. They were moved down to Pinewood Studios. They had unlimited film stock and so on. The independent units, such as my own and such as Realist, had none of these privileges.'[69] Some commercial producers, led by Balcon, were of the opinion that the Crown features were unfair competition and complained about this to the Board of Trade. 'It is understood that Mr Balcon's complaint is against competition from official film units, such as the Crown Film Unit, making short features of the *Target for Tonight* length (six reels) with the assistance of Treasury backing and other facilities not open to commercial producers,' stated an MOI memorandum in response, though it went on to say that 'there are no grounds for the suggestion that such films are produced with facilities which would not be open to commercial producers' and that 'a film like *Target for Tonight* when commercially distributed only displaces commercially made productions on its merits'.[70] The success of the Crown features had evidently caused some waves in the film industry. The concerns of commercial producers such as Balcon are understandable, particularly as several of the Crown features bore a strong similarity to commercial films on a similar theme: *Close Quarters* was similar to Gainsborough's *We Dive at Dawn*, while *Fires Were Started* had the same subject matter as Ealing's *The Bells Go Down*.

While sections of the film industry expressed dissatisfaction at the privileged status enjoyed by Crown, the Film Unit also came under fire from within the government due to its expense. In September 1941 the MOI had to defend the Film Unit against the Treasury. Bamford insisted that Crown was 'a necessary instrument for the production of high-class propaganda films' on the grounds that it was technically superior to other documentary producers and cheaper than commercial studios:

> The essential reason is that for the more important of our films – which means very largely for those designed for commercial distribution both at home and abroad – we need high quality, and we are convinced that films of the required quality are made more economically by the Unit than by contractors. The documentary companies who produce our cheaper films do not reach the same standard. The feature companies are capable of doing so, but only at much greater costs than those of the Unit.[71]

Beddington argued that Crown specialised in a type of film which could not be made by other producers. 'The smaller documentary companies do not do the rather elaborate reconstruction and dialogue work that the Crown Film Unit do,' he told Bamford. 'The big feature producers work almost entirely on fictional stories.'[72] The importance attached by the MOI to Crown thus illustrates the central role which it had come to play in the official film propaganda machinery.

V

Early in 1942 the Crown Film Unit was relocated to Pinewood Studios, one of the newest and best-equipped studio complexes in Britain, which had been requisitioned by the government. The move was part of a rationalisation process whereby Crown and the service film units were brought together under one roof to share facilities. Dalrymple, who now had a general supervisory authority over all the official film units, recalled that the move had ministerial approval: 'Brendan Bracken was by then our minister and showed personal interest in the new development, visiting the studios to inspect the composite set-up and view samples of the product.'[73] However, the move had once again caused ripples of discontent in the film industry because Pinewood was closed to commercial production. Balcon used his position on the Cinematograph Films Council of the Board of Trade to object to the move, arguing that it 'was a menace to commercial producers, for the Pinewood units would be making films (of the *Target for Tonight* type) to compete on the screen with ordinary commercial products, and making them with the advantage of having Treasury financial backing and first call on studios and manpower'.[74] His objections were ignored.

The move to Pinewood marked the zenith of Crown's success and the height of Dalrymple's influence over the Film Unit. He was to continue in the job of Supervising Producer until May 1943, when he resigned. There appear to be a number of reasons for his decision to leave. In his resignation letter he mentioned that he was earning far less than he could in the commercial cinema and also hinted at a degree of fatigue, suggesting that 'a new impetus might be beneficial from the point of view both of the Unit and of the Films Division'.[75] He also disliked the new Board of Management which had been set up at the beginning of 1943 'to control the organisation and work of the Crown Film Unit'.[76] Dalrymple thought that the board was unnecessary and that its role was ill-defined.[77] It also seems that Dalrymple had begun to differ from the MOI over the nature of film propaganda. In his view it was time to turn away from just making films about the war effort and to start addressing the question of reconstruction:

> Another thing was that at that time the Beveridge Report had come out and there was the fact that we should be thinking about what we could do in the difficult period after the war. I made one or two suggestions, but nobody would listen to them at all at the time. They said we must get on with the war.[78]

In short, Dalrymple found that by 1943 his influence was waning and his control of the Film Unit was being eroded by additional civil service bureaucrats.

It would be fair to say that after Dalrymple's departure the Crown Film Unit began to flounder. After 1943 Crown's productivity declined and it lost its sense of direction. The documentarists Alexander Shaw and Basil Wright both turned down overtures to take charge of the Film Unit, with the result that Jack Holmes became the new Senior Producer. Holmes had once before been in temporary charge of the GPO Film Unit, in 1938 between Grierson's departure and Cavalcanti's appointment. Whereas Dalrymple had sometimes annoyed officials with his energetic activity, Holmes was criticised for the opposite reason. Towards the end of the war the MOI's Director-General Cyril Radcliffe told Brendan Bracken he considered 'that 1944 was a poor year for the work of the Crown Film Unit ... We knew at the time that they were inadequately employed and a lack of leadership was getting business into some confusion and holding up production.'[79]

There were several reasons for Crown's decline in the last years of the war. Ralph Nunn May, Deputy-Director of the Films Division, set them out in a memorandum to Beddington. 'The Crown Film Unit was singularly unfortunate in the number of subjects that were suggested during the year as possible films but cancelled after investigation,' he said, listing eleven 'miscarriages' which between them 'occupied much time and attention of the senior members of the Unit and their cancellation is the chief reason why relatively few high-priced major productions were put in hand or photographed during the year.'[80] While projects had been cancelled during Dalrymple's time in charge, for some reason there seem to have been more abortive films after his departure, again suggesting that Crown's production ideology was attributable largely to him.

The series of Crown feature films initiated under Dalrymple's stewardship came to an end with *Western Approaches* (1944). Directed by Pat Jackson, and made in Technicolor, this was the most ambitious and the most expensive of all the Crown films. It started production in 1942 but was beset by numerous difficulties, including location filming in the North Atlantic and delays in processing the film which had to be done by Technicolor's own laboratories.[81] During the course of its production there was a growing feeling that it was so ambitious that it might bring about the end of Crown's feature experiment. 'The Treasury emphasised that we were risking a good deal by putting all our eggs in one basket and that if this film did not come up to expectation, the whole programme of the Unit would have to be reconsidered,' Bamford remarked in September 1942.[82] The escalating cost of the production – its final direct cost was over £86,000 – and the prolonged shooting schedule meant that *Western Approaches* was to be the last film of its kind produced by Crown. It was regarded by some contemporaries as the culmination of Crown's work – Lord Beaverbrook, for example, considered it 'one of the best films of the war, if not the very best'[83] – and this verdict has been echoed by many critics and historians. It tells the story of a group of merchant seamen whose ship is torpedoed and who spend two weeks adrift in a lifeboat until they are rescued. Like the other Crown features it is realistic, spare, austere; even the colour seems subdued. Jack Cardiff's cinematography superbly captures the emptiness of the ocean and the sheer scale of the Battle of the Atlantic. It was one of the films which John Shearman singled out when he coined the phrase 'wartime wedding' in an article for *Documentary News Letter*:

> So the two pre-war worlds of feature and documentary have, during the war, made contact. *Western Approaches* is perhaps the perfect example of the feature-like documentary. It is of feature length; it is made in Technicolor, that spoilt darling of the studios; it uses no commentary. But it was made by a documentary unit under documentary conditions. No professional actor played in it. Synchronised sound, Technicolor camera, cast and technicians went to sea in the real Atlantic, not in a tank or before a back projection screen. Is it feature? Is it documentary? Or is it, like *Journey Together*, some new fusion of both schools?[84]

The comparison with the RAF Film Unit's *Journey Together* (1945) is interesting because that film was a narrative-documentary made on the Crown model. There was a sense in which *Western Approaches* was seen to represent the fulfilment of a trend in wartime cinema to combine the documentary and feature styles. Its long and troubled production, however, had signalled the end of Crown's series of documentary features.

Western Approaches was Crown's last major success. By the end of the war its status as the foremost official film unit had been overtaken by the Army Film and Photographic Unit with its 'Victory' series of actuality-documentaries: *Desert Victory*, for example, had been even more of a box-office success than *Target for Tonight*. Basil Wright, who had turned down Crown's overtures in 1943, became its Supervising Producer in January 1945. The appointment of Wright – co-founder of *Documentary News Letter* and one of the MOI's chief critics during the war – illustrates how far the documentary movement had been absorbed into the official film propaganda effort. Wright's contribution to Crown's work is hard to assess, as he left the Film Unit after only one year. Yet despite its relative decline in the last years of the war, Crown had considerably raised the profile of documentary with the cinema-going public, finding in its wartime films a formula that could accommodate both documentary authenticity and traditional narrative forms. Ian McLaine's remark that 'the work of the Crown Film Unit had little impact' is therefore very wide of the mark.[85]

6

The Service Film Units

What would have happened to documentary if I'd stayed on, I don't quite know, but one very important thing did happen, and that was that suddenly from the service units, which had been gradually forming after they saw the success of the Crown Film Unit, came brilliant and wonderful films like *Desert Victory* and *Burma Victory*. The moment they appeared, the real thing, the front line shot by real army men who were being killed while doing it, the reconstructed documentary, as such, was dead, to my mind. *Harry Watt* [1]

I

The Crown Film Unit was not the only official production agency to be part of the film propaganda machinery during the war. The armed services also had their own film units which produced films about the services for public release. 'These Service Units are independent in manpower and organisation and are part of the armed forces, but look to the Ministry of Information for finance, for guidance on the type of film to be made, and, in so far as their work is directed to publics outside the services themselves, for distribution,' stated an official report into the film propaganda machinery. [2] Therefore, there was a quite complicated control mechanism for the service units whereby they were under military authority as regards manpower and organisation but came under the MOI's influence in terms of policy and the public distribution of their films. From 1942, when Pinewood

Studios became the base for both Crown and the service units, Crown's supervising producer was 'responsible for watching over the production at Pinewood by the Army and RAF Film Units of Army and RAF films intended for public release'.[3] This situation was sometimes to cause a degree of friction between Crown and the service units. After a somewhat shaky start when the quality of their film material was not always thought to be up to scratch, the service units came to rival and, by the end of the war, even to surpass Crown in the production of documentaries which met with wide critical and popular acclaim. In particular, the Army Film and Photographic Unit was involved in the production of a celebrated series of feature-length documentaries (*Desert Victory*, *Tunisian Victory*, *Burma Victory* and *The True Glory*) which used actuality footage taken by front-line cameramen to show the British and Allied campaigns in various theatres of war. They found warm critical approval for their representation of the experience of battle. Roger Manvell, for example, considered that '*Desert Victory*, *Tunisian Victory*, *Burma Victory* and above all *The True Glory* (the latter edited by Garson Kanin of Hollywood and Carol Reed of Great Britain) all were assembled with imagination and rose from the level of mere record into the creative presentation of these great campaigns so that their human significance could be appreciated.'[4]

The service film organisations responsible for these films had expanded rapidly during the war. They involved both front-line cameramen and production units at home to compile films for publicity and training purposes. Millions of feet of actuality footage were shot in various operational theatres by service cameramen, mostly belonging to the Army and the Royal Air Force. The Army's film activities, which were the most extensive of all the services, had increased dramatically since September 1939 when only one War Office cameraman, Harry Rignold, had been attached to the British Expeditionary Force when it was sent to France. The Army Film Unit (AFU) was set up after Dunkirk; in October 1941 it was restyled the Army Film and Photographic Unit (AFPU) when the War Office decided that still photographers should be incorporated in the same service. By 1943 the AFPU had so increased that it comprised some eighty cameramen and eight directors, organised into four sections attached to different sectors. The actuality material which was shot at the front was sent for initial viewing and censorship to the Public Relations Department of the War Office (PR 2). Ronald Tritton, a civilian, was responsible for liaison between the War Office and the MOI and for making footage available to the newsreel companies.

As well as shooting the footage, the AFPU was also responsible for the production of documentaries compiled from it. Most of the personnel recruited to the AFPU (such as David Macdonald, Roy Boulting and Hugh Stewart) came from the commercial film industry. From 1942 the AFPU was housed at Pinewood along with Crown and the RAF Film Production Unit, which had been set up in 1941. The RAF Film Unit was responsible for making navigational training films and records of important operations as well as documentaries for general release. There were also a further two small film units which made training and educational films for use solely within the services. These were the Royal Navy Film Section, based at Plymouth, which made specialised training and instructional films for the Admiralty, and the AKS Production Unit, housed at the requisitioned Fox studio at Wembley, which performed a similar role for the Army. The latter was under the control of the Army Kinematograph Service (AKS), which was responsible for the production and distribution of films within the Army. The AKS commissioned up to 150 films a year during the war, of which about three-quarters were usually made by outside contractors. All the Army's film activities were co-ordinated by the Directorate of Army Kinematography (DAK) which in turn was res-ponsible to the Army Council. The Director of Army Kinematography from August 1941 was a civilian, Paul Kimberley, but when he resigned at the end of 1943 the appointment became a military one and passed to Colonel N. M. Carstairs of the Indian Army, formerly the deputy director. The Army had thus built up an extensive film organisation during the war, but it was to experience all sorts of teething troubles before it made the breakthrough with the successful 'Victory' films.

II

The AFU's first films made for public exhibition did not meet with anything like the critical acclaim later heaped upon *Desert Victory* and the other feature-length documentaries which followed it. For example, *Northern Outpost* (1941), an entry in the MOI's five-minute film pro-gramme which illustrated the establishment of a British garrison in Iceland, was derided by *Documentary News Letter*: 'It looks very much as if the War Office sent someone, and I shouldn't think it was a proper

cameraman, to Iceland, and told him to "get what he could".[5] *Lofoten*
(1941), another five-minute film, illustrated a British Commando raid
on a fish-oil factory on the German-occupied Norwegian islands. The
actuality material shot by the AFU was handed over to Crown for the
compilation work; a commentary was written and spoken by Anthony
Kimmins, the former feature film director who now worked for the
Admiralty's press office. *Documentary News Letter* again complained that
the footage was 'badly shot' and lacked any sense of continuity, problems which 'would have been avoided by a good newsreel man or by
anybody with experience or ideas in this sort of filming'. Furthermore,
the reviewer complained, the raid 'is treated as a daring schoolboy
prank, a pellet flicked at the headmaster while his back is turned –
witness the saucy telegram despatched to Hitler'.[6] The cameraman on
both *Northern Outpost* and *Lofoten* was Walter Tennyson d'Eyncourt,
who would later be captured by the Germans at Tobruk. In noting
Documentary News Letter's poor opinion of the AFU's film material it
should be borne in mind that the journal was the organ of a group of
film-makers who had been largely excluded from the service film units.
However, the documentarists' attitude towards the actuality war films
at this time was shared by others. In November 1941, for example,
Lord Kemsley declared that British war documentaries were, in his
opinion, vastly inferior to those of the Soviet Union. He considered
that the film *Our Russian Allies* (1941) – a feature-length documentary
produced by the Soviet Central Newsreel Studios and released in Britain
by the MOI with an English commentary by J. B. Priestley – 'shows up
our own feeble and ill-nourished efforts in the production of propaganda films for the miserable ineptitudes they are'.[7]

There were mitigating circumstances for the AFU's lacklustre start
to filming British military operations. It was a very new organisation;
many of its personnel were inexperienced at using movie cameras; and
the nature of recording actual fighting is in any case something of a
haphazard affair which depends on a considerable degree of luck.
Some of the practical difficulties involved in filming under combat
conditions were experienced by Harry Watt when he joined another
British Commando raid, this time on the Norwegian coastal town of
Vaagso on Christmas Day, 1941. Watt, at the time still working for
Crown, went as a 'guest director' alongside Roy Boulting and Harry
Rignold of the AFPU and John Ramsden of British Movietone. He
described his experiences in an article for *Documentary News Letter*:

It was really too dark to shoot when we began to go ashore in
Norway, but we got the German warning Verey lights and the
shells exploding on Malloy island ... Our party had agreed not to
make a wet landing, to save the cameras. But the smoke was so
thick that we couldn't see how near we were to the shore. When
I got to the bows of my boat I asked the Navy man in charge if
it was deep as I didn't want to spoil my camera. 'To hell with you
and your camera' was all he said and gave me a push. I leapt wildly
and landed up to my knees. Rignold was more unlucky and got
wet to the waist.[8]

Despite the difficulties which the cameramen experienced, they secured
some impressive and spectacular footage of Commandos fighting in
the snow and of explosions and burning buildings. The MOI did not
in the event make a film about the raid, though some of the footage
was used for newsreels. Watt was critical of the result on the grounds
that 'in every newsreel dramatic moments, specially shot for, were
thrown away', but even so he concluded that 'it's the kind of thing
that should have been done from the start of the war. Whatever its
deficiencies the public loved it, therefore it has helped morale everywhere.' It is perhaps ironic that this better quality film taken by the
AFPU had not been made into a specific film whereas the lesser quality
Lofoten material had been. However, some of the Vaagso footage did
appear later in the documentary *Cameramen at War* (1943), a tribute to
both the newsreel and the service cameramen compiled by Len Lye
for the Realist Film Unit, and in the feature film *The Day Will Dawn*
(1942).

The shooting and compilation of actuality footage was by no means
the only concern of the Army's own film unit. The AFPU also made
films about the work of different branches of the Army which were
not to do with the combat fronts. For example, *ABCA* (1943) illustrated
the work of the Army Bureau of Current Affairs, an organisation set
up in 1941 to further the education of troops by introducing topical
discussion groups into their weekly schedule. The film suggests that
ABCA's work would have a long-term significance. 'We recognise that
the new world is in the building now,' the commentator declares. 'ABCA
is helping to win the war by giving the soldier the weapon of truth and
understanding. It is also laying the foundations of an enlightened society
which will one day enjoy the peace.' *ABCA* was one of the films

shown through the MOI's non-theatrical programme which addressed the issue of post-war reconstruction, and in this particular case a director from a documentary background (Ronald Riley) was employed.

However, it was actuality films of military campaigns which distinguished the AFPU from other documentary film units. The first feature-length actuality documentary of the war was not in fact *Desert Victory* but the lesser-known *Wavell's 30,000* (1942). The travails encountered in the production of this film were to have important consequences for the later development of the AFPU's actuality documentaries. It was an account of the British offensive against the Italian armies in Libya in 1940–41 compiled from both service and newsreel footage. As the AFPU was not yet equipped to undertake a job on this scale, the compilation work was done by the Crown Film Unit. The editing was supervised by the veteran documentarist John Monck and the commentary was spoken by an Australian journalist, Colin Wills. However, Ian Dalrymple recalled that it ran into trouble with Churchill because of certain factual inaccuracies:

> And when the Prime Minister came to the Ministry of Information to inspect it, I heard the Old Man growl sultrily 'Why can't they get their facts right?' The reason was the impossibility of learning them. One or two young officers did come back to enlighten us at home, but they knew nothing outside their immediate sector. But at least the film was the first example of the three fighting services co-operating with each other and with our Ministry on a joint information project, which, in the early days, was an achievement in itself.[9]

As a civilian organisation, Crown was not as closely acquainted with the precise nature of military operations as the AFPU, which was the main reason why the production of campaign films would in future be the responsibility of the services, with Crown providing only technical assistance. *Wavell's 30,000* was unlucky in other respects. First, since it contained a large percentage of newsreel footage, it was not covered by the Quota Act, which meant that exhibitors were reluctant to accept it. As Ralph Nunn May told Jack Beddington:

> M.G.M. say that they are experiencing considerable difficulty in placing the film because it does not rank for British Quota. It seems rather absurd that a film put out by this Ministry because

of its propaganda value should be penalised in this way by the operation of an Act which was drafted when the circumstances of the present time could not possibly have been foreseen.[10]

The quota issue was not resolved and was to resurface over *Desert Victory*. The issue was forgotten because, in the event, *Wavell's 30,000* was quickly overtaken by events. 'The film dated quickly and had to be withdrawn,' stated a laconic official record.[11] What had happened was that the British were forced on to the defensive again by a renewed Axis offensive in North Africa led by Rommel, and General Wavell, who became a scapegoat for British reverses in the Mediterranean, was sent off to be Viceroy of India. It provides an example, therefore, of how the topicality of film propaganda was sometimes affected by the fluctuating fortunes of war.

III

It was *Desert Victory* which, a year after *Wavell's 30,000*, set the style for the feature-length campaign documentaries to follow. It was a documentary record of the war in the Western Desert from the summer of 1942 when Rommel's advance was halted at El Alamein. It shows the strengthening of British forces in preparation for the counter-offensive, the breakthrough of the Eighth Army, now under General Montgomery, and the pursuit of the retreating German and Italian armies across Egypt and Libya. A rolling caption at the beginning establishes the grand theme:

> For the 'desert rats' ... the men of the Eighth Army ... who, on the 23rd October, 1942, left the holes they had scratched for themselves in the rock and sand of the desert, and moved forward to destroy the myth of Rommel's invincibility ... and to complete the liberation of the second Roman Empire overseas.
> For the sister services too ... the RAF and the Navy ... and the workers of Great Britain and the United States ... without whose efforts victory could not have been achieved.[12]

The film therefore makes the link between the armed services and the industrial effort at home; the reference to the United States was probably included because the British are shown in the film using Grant and Sherman tanks. The main focus of the film, however, is on the desert war. The landscape is described in both images and words ('The Western Desert is a place fit only for war,' is the first line of the commentary), while maps are used to explain aspects of strategy and to illustrate the positions and movements of the opposing armies. It was compiled mostly from actuality footage taken at the front by No 1 Army Film and Photographic Section, commanded by Major David Macdonald, though a sequence showing the night advance of British troops at El Alamein was augmented by scenes filmed at Pinewood. The studio scenes were edited into a montage with real shots of the night barrage. Some other shots, although filmed in the desert, would appear to have been staged (judging by the exposed positions of the camera). Nevertheless the film gives a powerful and vivid impression of desert warfare: tanks advancing amidst clouds of sand, soldiers scrambling across the dunes, British field guns thundering and German vehicles burning. The commentary alludes to British military history: the men of the Eighth Army are described as 'fighting as dogged as our infantry at Waterloo', while Montgomery is 'a man who lives as sternly as Cromwell and is as much a part of his modern Ironsides'. The film concludes with Churchill's victory speech to the Eighth Army at Tripoli ('You have altered the face of the war in a most remarkable way ... '). The Lancastrian journalist James Lansdale Hodson wrote the commentary, and a special march was composed by William Alwyn.

Work began on the film at Pinewood immediately after the break-through at El Alamein. 'General Lawson [Head of PR2 at the War Office] has ordered the production to go ahead and the Army Film Unit is working day and night on it,' Ronald Tritton told Beddington on 25 November.[13] The film was planned initially as a two-reel documentary entitled *The Battle of Egypt*. After some to-ings and fro-ings in the early days Major David Macdonald was put in charge of the production, while the editing was supervised by Captain Roy Boulting.[14] Considerable urgency was attached to completing the film and getting it into the cinemas as quickly as possible, but due to the length (it finally came in at six reels) and the optical work which had to be done, it was not completed until the end of February 1943.

The well-documented production of *Desert Victory* illustrates the importance that was attached to this film of Britain's first major military success at the very top of government. Churchill took a personal interest in the project, though as so often the Prime Minister's intervention proved to be just as much a hindrance as a help to the film-makers. Churchill agreed to make a special recording of his Tripoli victory speech to go at the end of the film, but this was not done until after its London premiere. The domestic version of the film therefore had the actor Leo Genn reciting the speech, though Churchill's own voice was used on the version made for American distribution.[15] Then, when he saw the finished film just before its general release in Britain, Churchill made several suggestions for alterations and the MOI had to persuade him against them as it would have involved re-editing and re-recording the film. It is evident, however, that there was great official satisfaction with the finished film. 'What an extraordinarily fine record has been made of the Eighth Army,' Lord Beaverbrook told Sidney Bernstein. 'The photographers merit high praise for their magnificent work.' He predicted that the film 'will have an immense success throughout this country, and I hope it will have wide distribution in the United States'.[16] Jack Beddington wrote to Hodson: 'The film is a first rate one and your commentary does more than anything else to make it so. I hope we shall have many more Victory films and as many more admirable commentaries from you.'[17] Churchill personally was delighted with the film, and even remarked in his war memoirs that it 'excited the greatest admiration and enthusiasm throughout the Allied world and brought us all closer together in our common task'.[18] He had prints of the film sent to Roosevelt, Stalin, the prime ministers of the Dominions and other Allied leaders. To Roosevelt, for example, he wrote: 'I hope you will accept the accompanying copy of the new film *Desert Victory*, which I saw last night and thought very good. It gives a vivid and realistic picture of the battles, and I know that you will be interested in the photographs of the Sherman tanks in action.'[19] It was obviously a matter of great importance to Churchill that the British Army had won a major victory before the Americans were involved in the fighting in North Africa. It was also important to show the Russians that Britain was not leaving all the fighting to the Red Army. This was surely Churchill's desire in sending a personal copy of the film to Stalin, which it was hoped would 'persuade the Soviet authorities to give a good showing of the film in the Russian cinemas'.[20] Stalin's opinion of the British contribution to the war effort is implicit in his carefully-worded reply: 'The film depicts magnificently how Britain is fighting, and stigmatises those scoundrels (there are such people also in our country) who are asserting that Britain is not fighting at all, but is merely an onlooker.'[21]

Desert Victory was an enormous critical and popular success. In Britain it became the most successful of all official films at the box-office: by May 1944 its commercial receipts amounted to £77,250.[22] Critics expressed great admiration for both the subject matter and the treatment. *The Times*, for example, said:

> The desert is not a stretch of country which lends itself to photography nor is modern war with all its eternal emphasis on bombs, explosives, tanks, aeroplanes, and all the monstrous productions of the machine age a particularly suitable subject for the film director, but *Desert Victory*, which is a kind of elongated newsreel, is made with such intelligence and sincerity that it is not only a valuable document but actually succeeds in being good 'cinema'.[23]

It was the authenticity of the film which apparently appealed to cinema audiences. When Mass-Observation conducted an extensive survey of favourite films in November 1943, *Desert Victory* emerged as the third most popular film, and was described by the respondents with phrases such as 'factual stuff', 'pure documentary' and 'the stark reality portrayed'.[24]

Although it was a great success, the distribution of *Desert Victory* did not proceed without some controversy. In Britain it was incorrectly registered under the Quota Act, which caused great concern for Hugh Gaitskell, then a temporary civil servant at the Board of Trade. Long films which comprised over 50 per cent of actuality footage did not count for quota and therefore, as Gaitskell admitted, 'we were wrong in registering *Desert Victory*, and would probably lose the case if the matter were taken to Court'. He recognised that the question needed to be settled, noting that the MOI 'have in mind the production of a number of films similar to *Desert Victory* in the course of the next few months or years'.[25] The MOI urged the Board of Trade to exempt these films from the usual regulations:

> Briefly, our argument is that films which do not count for British quota are inevitably met by substantial sales resistance; that this reduces the extent to which they may be shown by exhibitors, thus making them less attractive to renters; and that such an impediment to the widest possible exhibition of Government propaganda films should not be allowed to be created by legislation not specifically designed to cater for wartime needs.[26]

A situation had arisen, therefore, whereby a pre-war measure to protect the film industry was obstructing the wide distribution of official documentaries. In the event the matter was resolved by an amendment to the Quota Act so that 'long propaganda films consisting "wholly or mainly" of news photographs may be permitted to rank as exhibitors' quota'.[27] The distribution of the film in the United States also did not proceed without some controversy, as the MOI was not happy about its handling by the American distributors. The MOI's George Archibald remarked 'how dissatisfied we were with Twentieth Century-Fox's handling of *Desert Victory*', pointing out that a rival American documentary called *At the Front in North Africa*, which 'was a poor film and much criticised', received more theatrical bookings.[28] Thomas Baird, then with British Information Services in New York, realised that all American distributors were reluctant to promote British films ahead of their own. 'I know that the distribution of films of the *Desert Victory* and *Tunisian Victory* type is going to be increasingly difficult,' he replied, 'and, even if you and I feel that Fox did not do the best job in the world for us, I think it is going to be politic to hold up what they did do (no matter how it was done) as an example and incentive to the other companies whom we might ask to distribute sometimes difficult films.'[29] Given that *Desert Victory* enjoyed not inconsiderable success in America – it was even awarded an Oscar by the Academy of Motion Picture Arts and Sciences as 'the Most Distinctive Documentary of 1943' – then the MOI's reservations about its handling were perhaps a trifle exaggerated. However, the episode does illustrate that by the later years of the war the MOI perceived that Britain was in competition with the Americans over the documentary record of the war. This competition was to come to the surface during the production of the sequel to *Desert Victory*.

IV

The success of *Desert Victory* had several significant effects on the future of official British film propaganda. It spawned a series of feature-length actuality documentaries in a similar vein which also met with critical and popular acclaim. However, the success of the AFPU's documentaries was apparently a cause of some friction with the Crown Film Unit. Ian Dalrymple wanted Crown to have control over the sequel to *Desert Victory*, which would be about the joint Anglo-American campaign in Tunisia. His failure to achieve this was one of the reasons for his resignation. Dalrymple had wanted the film to cover the civilian war effort as well as the military campaign:

> Then, as a record of our invasion of North Africa, I planned a film to show it as the total military and civil effort which it was: and indeed we shot a considerable amount of material covering the industrial and organisational preliminaries which made the landings and campaign possible. This material was handed over to the Army Film Unit who were to undertake the actual film production. But, in the event, they ignored it and confined the film to the Services' operations. I began to feel superfluous.[30]

The rift between the AFPU and Crown, however, was as nothing compared to the rivalry which developed between the British and their American allies over the film which eventually became *Tunisian Victory* (1944).[31] The AFPU had completed a sequel to *Desert Victory*, entitled *Africa Freed*, by the summer of 1943. The Americans had also been working on their own film about the Tunisian campaign, though they had found that their front-line footage was poor in comparison to the British material. After a complicated period of negotiation it was decided that a joint film should be made of the operation, under the supervision of Lieutenant-Colonel Frank Capra of the US Army Signal Corps. The AFPU reluctantly shelved *Africa Freed* and Major Hugh Stewart, who had commanded No 2 Army Film and Photographic Section in Tunisia, worked with Capra on *Tunisian Victory* during the summer and autumn of 1943. The course of the production did not go smoothly. 'I knew the combined film version would deal with sticky high policy decisions involving dual command and national pride and prejudices,' Capra admitted in his autobiography.[32] For their part, the British were concerned that the Americans had taken over the film. 'I have been doing a little fighting to prevent our picture on the Tunisian campaign becoming disbalanced in favour of America,' J. L. Hodson recorded in his diary on 21 September. 'After all, we did most of the dirty work, and had twice as many casualties.'[33]

Tunisian Victory begins with the preparations for 'Operation Acrobat', the Anglo-American landings in French North Africa in November 1942, and from there it charts the course of the war until the surrender of the Axis forces in Tunisia in May 1943, described as 'the greatest mass surrender of fully-equipped troops in modern history'. Much of the British footage in the film was transferred from *Africa Freed*, along with sections of the commentary, written by Hodson and spoken by Leo Genn. The actors Bernard Miles and Burgess Meredith were used to supply the voices of supposedly real ordinary soldiers, a British 'Tommy' called George Metcalfe and an American GI Joe McAdams, who provide a personal perspective which had not been apparent in *Desert Victory*. Like *Desert Victory*, the real combat footage was supplemented by reconstructed scenes where no usable film had been taken of important events. Thus the crossing of the Wadi Zig-Zaou by British troops prior to their offensive against the German Mareth Line was filmed at Pinewood, while the Americans' attack on Hill 609 in western Tunisia was reconstructed in the Mojave Desert in California. The animated maps and diagrams, which given their similarity to those in Capra's famous *Why We Fight* series can probably be attributed to the Americans, are rather more sophisticated than those in *Desert Victory*. In particular, the diagram of a cylinder to explain the strategy for the capture of Tunisia – the Eighth Army is shown as the piston pushing up from the bottom so that the enemy forces are compressed and finally explode when the spark plug is ignited – is an imaginative use of visual technique. *Tunisian Victory* is perhaps more polished but is also certainly more sentimental than *Desert Victory*. The sentimentality is particularly evident in a scene where the soldiers think about their families at Christmas, and again at the end of the film when George and Joe talk about building the new world after the war in order to 'bring the smiles back to the kids' faces all over the world'.

The film was not, on the whole, as well received by the British critics as its predecessor had been. Campbell Dixon of *The Daily Telegraph* thought that the film 'shows signs of having been edited for the American public'.[34] The sentimentality of the ending also drew criticism from *Documentary News Letter*, which remarked that 'the fell hand of Capra's Hollywood is much in evidence'. It also pointed out that in view of the fact that the film had not been released until the spring of 1944, it 'would have been more timely and more valuable last Autumn'.[35]

The problems encountered in making *Tunisian Victory* were also to beset other attempts at Anglo-American co-production. *The True Glory* (1945), the official film record of the liberation of Western Europe, was planned from the beginning as a joint production. Manvell wrote that it 'marked the climax in combined film operations between the

British and Americans'.[36] However, the course of its production had again been anything but smooth.[37] A Joint Anglo-American Film Planning Committee was set up early in 1944 to co-ordinate all aspects of the film from inception to completion, but it soon became a forum for airing the various national rivalries and inter-service jealousies which arose in relation to the film coverage of the European campaign. David Macdonald dropped out of the film at an early stage, after which Britain's Carol Reed and America's Garson Kanin were put in overall charge of the European film on behalf of Supreme Headquarters Allied Expeditionary Force (SHAEF). General Dwight D. Eisenhower, the Supreme Allied Commander, took a personal interest in the film; Kanin is reported to have said that the general 'got to be quite a pain in the neck after a while'.[38] The film was to be compiled from over 5 million feet of actuality material taken during the European campaign by Allied service cameramen, an operation which the British documentarist Donald Bull, then a captain in the Film and Photographic Section of SHAEF, described as 'the most lavishly equipped and planned photographic campaign in history'.[39] The No 5 Army Film and Photographic Section, under Colonel Hugh Stewart, had been newly formed to cover the British role in the campaign, though the British now had fewer cameramen in the field than the Americans. Ian Grant, a British Army cameraman, later complained that *The True Glory* 'gave a convincing demonstration of how the Americans conquered Europe'. He said that 'it did not present a true picture of the involvement of the British, and we of the AFPU wondered why so many of our cameramen had to die without recognition'.[40]

Yet despite all the problems of production, *The True Glory* is a highly impressive documentary. It is introduced by Eisenhower who states that it was 'an account of the really important men in this campaign – I mean the enlisted soldiers, sailors and airmen, that fought through every obstacle to victory'. He also stresses the importance of the 'teamwork among nations, services and men, all the way down the line from the GI and the Tommy to us brass hats' which made the victory possible. The film itself consists entirely of actuality footage (there are no obviously fake or reconstructed sequences), with a few explanatory maps and diagrams, and for this reason it can be considered the most authentic of the campaign documentaries. The tempo is swift, a montage of brief shots and rapid editing, the images matched to the dramatic music of William Alwyn. The film uses two innovative commentary devices. First, a linking commentary in blank verse is spoken by Robert Harris ('American tanks ground on into the east towards Paris and the Upper Seine/Before them the Germans helter-skelter fled away in sore retreat/Or stood with hands upraised by roads all littered with their smouldering gear'). And second, individual commentators describe first-hand some of the incidents in the campaign, incidents which are variously humorous, tragic, poignant, or simply matter-of-fact.[41] This device means that, even more so than either *Desert Victory* or *Tunisian Victory*, *The True Glory* gives an impression of the human side of war as well as the strategic aspects of the campaign. It captures the experiences of men in battle and does not shirk from the hardships suffered by Allied troops and the unpleasant reality of casualties. It also includes some horrific footage of the Belsen concentration camp after it was liberated by British troops. The film ends with Harris reciting Sir Francis Drake's prayer from which the title was taken: 'O Lord God, when thou givest to thy servants to endeavour any great matter, grant us also to know that it is not the beginning, but the continuing of the same, until it be thoroughly finished, which yieldeth the true glory.'

The True Glory was released in Britain in August 1945 and in the United States a month later. It met with high praise from most critics. 'The film is in the finest tradition of *Desert Victory*, and correspondents who saw it agreed that it was better than the Tunisian campaign documentary,' declared the *Evening Standard*.[42] *The Listener* considered that it was more 'human' than previous war documentaries:

> This film tells the whole story of the allied liberation of Western Europe from D-Day to the capitulation of the German armies. But whereas many of the earlier war documentaries composed of actual combat scenes have somehow lacked humanity – have been full of guns and tanks and explosions – *The True Glory* is primarily about people. The other day someone was complaining about being preached at by MOI films. I don't know whether putting history on the screen is preaching, but if it is, then *The True Glory* is a sermon and a half. For here is the first complete official history of Europe's liberation – and it appears not in a book, but on the screen. That's one up to the cinema.[43]

Bosley Crowther of the *New York Times* described it as 'a brilliantly composed screen tribute to the courage and perseverance of our fighting men, as rich in its verbal narration as it is true in its visual images'.[44] Like *Desert Victory*, the film was honoured by the Academy of Motion Picture Arts and Sciences when it was awarded an Oscar for 'the Most Outstanding Documentary Feature of 1945'.

The last of the official campaign documentaries made by the AFPU was *Burma Victory* (1945). Instigated by Admiral Lord Louis Mountbatten, the Supreme Allied Commander South East Asia, this was originally to have been another Anglo-American co-production covering the entire Allied campaign in Burma.[45] 'I am anxious that the film on its presentation to the public be exhibited as a joint British-American effort, somewhat along the lines of the method by which *Tunisian Victory* was handled; and that the proper proportion of scenes of the activities of all who took part be incorporated in it,' Mountbatten told General George C. Marshall, the US Chief of Staff.[46] However, the MOI was by now somewhat jaundiced about the idea of another joint film. Brendan Bracken told South East Asia Command:

> You do not know what trouble you have launched on in projecting a film about the whole Burma campaign with British and American ends. We have had some experience of this with [the] Tunisian campaign and now the Normandy operations and there is no doubt that an overall campaign film which is to suit British and American tastes is slow to produce and that the effectiveness of the film suffers in the process.[47]

The political and military differences between the British and Americans over South East Asia (the Americans were anxious not to be seen to be fighting to support British imperialism) meant that in the end the joint Burma project was abandoned and the Allies went their separate ways. Frank Capra produced a two-reeler entitled *The Stilwell Road* about the American side of the campaign, while David Macdonald and Roy Boulting made the feature-length *Burma Victory* focusing mainly on the role of the British Fourteenth Army. 'Macdonald believes his film will be comparable to *Desert Victory* in quality in which case we are sure that it will secure good showing in America,' Field Marshal Wilson of the Joint Staff Mission in Washington told the MOI.[48] However, it was not released even in Britain until October 1945, after the end of the war, by which time the immediate need for propaganda was gone. Rather, it fulfilled the role of a historical record, which may be the reason why it now seems more contemplative than the other 'Victory' films.

From a British perspective *Burma Victory* is important in that it illustrated a theatre of war which to many people at home seemed distant and secondary to the war in Europe; not without reason is Burma sometimes known as the 'Forgotten War'. The context of the film is significant in that it came in the aftermath of the furore caused in Britain by the fictional Hollywood film *Objective Burma* (1945), which had met with a hostile reception because it showed a handful of Americans led by Errol Flynn winning the war in Burma on their own.[49] Some critics even thought that it was superior to the other campaign films. '*Burma Victory* ... can take its place with *Desert Victory* and *The True Glory* among war documentaries, and I am not sure that it isn't a better record than either,' said William Whitebait, the film critic of *The New Statesman*. 'It realises the jungle, for example, as *Desert Victory* – fine and dramatic though that film was – never realised the desert.'[50]

Burma Victory certainly provides a vivid and powerful picture of the hardships of jungle warfare. The film opens with two British soldiers in a tent (one of the few studio-shot scenes) where one is reading a travel brochure about Burma ('Burma – there is romance in the very word'). The soldier scoffs and throws the brochure out of the tent into the mud and tropical rain. The commentary emphasises the problems caused by the monsoon and disease; dysentery and malaria are described as 'enemies more deadly than the Jap'. The film chronicles the course of the war in Burma from the beginning of 1944. It shows the defence of Imphal on the Indian border, the airborne operations of special forces behind Japanese lines such as Wingate's 'Chindits' and the American 'Merrill's Marauders', the construction of the Ledo Road from China under the American General Stilwell, the long advance of the Fourteenth Army under General Slim through Burma, the crossing of the Irrawady and the battle for Mandalay. There are a few reconstructed scenes of senior British officers discussing strategy and of Japanese soldiers calling out in the night in English to try to make the British troops reveal their positions. The film ends quite symbolically as artillery guns go silent and their barrels are slowly lowered following the Japanese surrender. It is a fitting and symbolic conclusion to the last, and perhaps the best, of the AFPU's 'Victory' films.

V

In comparison to the AFPU, the RAF Film Production Unit made fewer films for public release. This unit had been set up in 1941 mainly to provide a film record of the RAF's role in the war, but also to make training and informational films. It was based at Pinewood from 1942 and it was commanded by, successively, Wing-Commander Derek Twist, Wing-Commander Edward Baird and Squadron-Leader Pat Moyna. The Pinewood unit was the parent unit which co-ordinated the work of overseas detachments in the various theatres of war. Cameras were mounted in aircraft and in this way much operational footage was obtained. Most of the RAF's actuality footage was made available free of charge to the newsreels, who made much use of film of the bombing of German cities. Among the more spectacular film shot by the RAF was the daring raid by Mosquitoes on the Gestapo prison at Amiens in May 1944 in order to breach the walls and assist the escape of members of the French Resistance, and the sinking of the German battleship *Tirpitz* in Tromso Fjord in November 1944 by Lancasters using 12,000-pound bombs. Actuality footage taken by the RAF was also used in several AFPU films, including *Malta, G.C.* (1942) and *Desert Victory*.

The RAF Film Unit made a number of documentaries providing information for both the general public and RAF personnel.[51] The first film initiated by the unit was a four-reeler entitled *Operational Height* (1943), which showed how barrage balloons were moored to drifters at sea in order to protect convoys and minesweepers from aerial attack. With its similarities in subject matter and treatment both to Harry Watt's *Squadron 992* and John Grierson's celebrated *Drifters* (1929), *Operational Height* can be located firmly in the tradition of the British documentary movement. It was directed by Arthur Taylor, who had made documentary films for Bournville during the 1930s. John Shearman made *The Big Pack* (1945), which illustrated the logistical and maintenance work which went on on the ground to organise the supplies needed to keep aircraft operational. A rather pedestrian film, it had been completed in 1943 but its theatrical distribution was delayed for over a year, by which time the public and the critics had lost any interest they might have had in the subject matter. The unit achieved better results with more action-oriented films such as *The Air Plan* (1945), a three-reeler showing the role of the RAF and Commonwealth air forces during the Normandy Campaign.

Towards the end of the war, the RAF Film Unit followed Crown's example by embarking on the production of a feature-length narrative-documentary. This was *Journey Together* (1945), which was in production at Pinewood Studios throughout most of 1944. Subtitled 'A story dedicated to the Few who trained the Many', it was intended originally as a training film but, rather like the case of *The Next of Kin* for the Army, it was also given a commercial release, its distribution being undertaken by RKO. The film's credits state that it was 'Written, Produced, Directed, Photographed and Acted by members of the Royal Air Force'. The service personnel involved in its production included the playwright Terence Rattigan (who had been an air-gunner and wireless operator), the director John Boulting and the principal actors Richard Attenborough and Jack Watling. It therefore differed from the Crown features in one important respect: its cast comprised professional actors. Furthermore, the American star Edward G. Robinson flew over to Britain (on payment of travelling expenses only) to appear in the film at the request of the Air Ministry.[52] Some location shooting was undertaken in Arizona and Canada by a second unit under George Brown, production manager of the RAF Film Unit, but all the studio interiors were done at Pinewood.

The film follows the story of working-class David Wilton (Attenborough) and Cambridge graduate John Aynesworth (Watling) who are sent to a flying school in America where they are taught by instructor Dean McWilliams (Robinson). Aynesworth turns out to be a natural flyer, but Wilton, who has set his heart on becoming a pilot, is unable to judge height and is therefore unsuitable. Resentful, he is posted to another centre in Canada where he trains to become a navigator. When he returns to Britain, Wilton joins Aynesworth's Lancaster crew as a substitute for their usual navigator. A raid on Berlin is successful but on the way home the Lancaster is damaged and has to ditch in the North Sea. It is Wilton's accurate locational fix, transmitted just before the plane ditched, that allows the air–sea rescue launch to find them.

Historian Michael Paris writes that *Journey Together* 'is really concerned to demonstrate the high degree of training given to aircrew and the importance of teamwork in bomber operations'.[53] The title is apt in several ways: a journey is undertaken together by people from different class backgrounds, by the bomber crew all with different but equally essential duties to perform, and not least by the British and Americans. The Anglo-American context of the film is comparable to Anthony

Asquith's *The Way to the Stars*, also scripted by Rattigan, which examined the relations between British and American airmen during the war, while the detailed and lengthy sequences of training, followed by a climax which shows the recruits in action, have the same narrative structure as Carol Reed's Army feature film *The Way Ahead*. As well as being comparable to these studio feature films, *Journey Together* is also closely related to the Crown documentary-features in that there is no romantic interest or domestic drama. As neither Attenborough nor Watling was very well-known at the time, the use of professional actors does not detract from the realism of the film; Robinson's presence was probably intended to sell the film in the American market, but his role is in any case quite small. The film is a genuine narrative-documentary in that it depicts the processes of training and the subsequent operation in an authentic fashion. The tense and tightly-edited sequence of the bombing raid recalls *Target for Tonight*, though *Journey Together* is, if anything, technically more polished.

Although it is now overshadowed in film historiography by the more celebrated Crown features, *Journey Together* was very well received by critics at the time. Richard Winnington thought it was 'one of the most realistic and brilliant films of the war in the air' and considered that it was 'vastly superior to the many fictional films which have claimed the war-time box-office on similar subjects'.[54] Predictably, it appealed to the progressive critics for its combination of documentary authenticity with a human story. 'It belongs to the new type of documentary that has assimilated a dash of fiction,' remarked William Whitebait.[55] Some reviewers did remark, however, that while it was a good film it had come too late in the day to have any effect as propaganda, and this is perhaps one reason why the film is now less well-known than the Crown features which had achieved a more immediate impact.

Journey Together was the RAF Film Unit's most impressive and polished film for public release. However, it was not the only feature-length documentary which the unit made. A film about the clandestine operations of special agents who parachuted into France to help the resistance was begun by the unit in 1944. Directed by Edward Baird, it was closer in technique to the Crown features than *Journey Together* in that it used real secret agents, Harry Rée and Jacqueline Nearne, who re-enacted some of their own experiences in Occupied France. Some location shooting was undertaken in Provence after the liberation, and studio interiors were filmed at Pinewood, but the film remained uncompleted until 1946 when the MOI's successor, the Central Office of Information, decided that it should be released. As the RAF Film Unit had been disbanded at the end of 1945, a commercial contractor had to be brought in to undertake the post-production work.[56] The finished film was entitled *School for Danger* and was released theatrically by United Artists early in 1947; a longer version was made for non-theatrical distribution under the title *Now It Can Be Told*. Now largely overlooked by film historians, it provides a minor coda to the work of the service film units during the war. Although the sequences showing the training of agents are quite well done, the film as a whole lacks the human and dramatic interest of the Crown features and for once the performances of the non-professional actors are unconvincing. *The Times* opined that 'they must have acted magnificently before the enemy, but the camera and sound-track are too much for their natural selves and the dialogue is stilted'. It also suggested that some of the events depicted in the film seemed rather far-fetched: 'If the story were fiction the stupidity of the Germans would seem a little too good to be true.'[57] It was a case, therefore, where the truth did indeed seem stranger than fiction. For propaganda purposes the film came too late to have any impact, and it quickly disappeared among a flood of films on a similar subject which were made in the immediate aftermath of the war, such as Ealing's *Against the Wind* (1947) and, from Hollywood, Fritz Lang's *Cloak and Dagger* (1946). The important work of the service film units had been done mainly between 1943 and 1945, when they had shown the public that Britain was taking the offensive and the tide of the war had turned. But with the war over the public's appetite for films about the war was on the wane. The service units had done their job and were soon to be disbanded.

Part II

Subjects and Themes

7

The People's War

The war film discovered the common denominator of the British people. *Roger Manvell*[1]

I

The idea of 'the people's war' is part of both the myth and the reality of the British experience of the Second World War. The myth owes greatly to the images of the British at war presented in wartime films; if there was one theme which was prominent above all others in film propaganda, it was the part played in the war by ordinary men and women. The ideology of the people's war which emerges from wartime films is one of national unity and social cohesion: class differences have all but disappeared and have been replaced instead by a democratic sense of community and comradeship. Of course, the extent to which the Second World War really did act as a catalyst for social change and class levelling has been a question of much debate among historians. However, the idea of a people's war in which class differences had been erased was encouraged by the government which needed to mobilise popular support for and participation in the war effort.

In the first year or so of the war a sharp contrast can be observed in the way the commercial film industry and the documentary movement presented the British people at war. It was evident even in the difference between the first propaganda feature film of the war and the first wartime documentary. While Korda's *The Lion Has Wings* presented a picture of Britain where a rigid class system still existed, and suggested that the war was being fought to preserve it, the GPO Film Unit's *The First Days* gave the first indication of the class levelling that was often perceived to be taking place during the war. The extent to which the images of the British at war presented in official documentaries were the absolute 'truth', of course, is questionable. They were made as propaganda for the moment rather than as purely objective records for posterity. But the impression of the people's war which they conveyed was one which nevertheless had some basis in reality. In the sense that the British people as a whole were involved in and affected by the war to an extent which far surpassed any previous conflict, it was indeed a people's war. It involved the mass participation of the civilian population on a hitherto unprecedented scale: millions joined the services, both military and civil, while millions more worked in the factories or on the land. Moreover, aerial bombardment meant that civilians were exposed to danger: some 60,000 British people were killed in air raids during the war. The cheerful and phlegmatic spirit of the British people under bombardment depicted in films like *London Can Take It!* has become part of the national consciousness. Although this is partly a myth, many contemporary commentators nevertheless bear witness to how the British people rallied together in the face of adversity. Humphrey Jennings, the documentarist whose films were to reflect so eloquently on the character of the British at war, was deeply affected by what he saw during the Blitz. In October 1940 he wrote to his wife Cicely in America:

> Some of the damage in London is pretty heart-breaking but what an effect it has had on the people! What warmth – what courage! What determination! People sternly encouraging each other by explaining that when you hear a bomb whistle it means it has missed you! People in the north singing in public shelters: 'One man went to mow – went to mow a meadow.' WVS girls serving hot drinks to firefighters during raids explaining that really they were 'terribly afraid all the time!' ... Everybody absolutely determined: secretly delighted with the *privilege* of holding up Hitler. Certain of beating him: a certainty which no amount of bombing can weaken, only strengthen ... Maybe by the time you get this one or two more 18th cent[ury] churches will be smashed up in

London: some civilians killed: some personal loves and treasures wrecked – but it means nothing; a curious kind of unselfishness is developing which can stand all that and more. We have found ourselves on the right side and on the right track at last![2]

The sense of comradeship and stoical courage apparent here was to feature strongly in British films of the war, not least those of Jennings himself. Indeed, it has become the dominant popular image of the British at war.

II

The films which Humphrey Jennings made for the Crown Film Unit during the war represent the most complex and intellectual meditation on the theme of the people's war in British cinema. Lindsay Anderson once famously described Jennings as 'the only real poet the British cinema has yet produced'.[3] Yet Jennings is in many ways a problematic figure in British cinema history. He worked within the documentary movement but was hardly representative of it; indeed his close links with the Surrealist movement and his affinity for the European avant-garde distanced him somewhat from the orthodox British realist discourse. He was a Cambridge-educated intellectual who dabbled as a painter and a poet as well as a film-maker. He directed relatively few films, but his work stands out markedly from that of his contemporaries at Crown. Whereas Harry Watt, Pat Jackson and Jack Holmes all came to specialise in narrative-documentaries, Jennings was always less interested in telling stories than in capturing moods and images. Pat Jackson recalled: 'Humphrey would interpret a situation in disconnected visuals, and he wouldn't quite know why he was shooting them, probably, until he got them together. Then he would create a pattern out of them.' Jackson added that Jennings's approach to film-making was very much that of an artist: 'It was terribly like a painter in a way; it wasn't a story-teller's mind. I don't think the dramatic approach to a subject, in film, really interested him very much. It was an extension of the canvas for him. Patterns, abstractions appealed to him enormously, and those are what people remember most.'[4] Given the very strong pictorial qualities and rich visual texture of his films, it is not surprising that most of the critical writing on Jennings has focused on the formal and aesthetic qualities of his work.[5] However, it is also important to realise that most of the films on which his reputation rests were made as propaganda under official auspices during the war. It is for their unique combination of film art with propaganda that Jennings's films are so memorable.

Jennings had been associated with the GPO Film Unit since the mid-1930s as a set designer, writer and director. His most famous pre-war documentary was *Spare Time* (1939), a description of the leisure activities of the working classes set to popular music. The film was influenced to a large extent by his involvement with Mass-Observation, which he had helped to set up, with Tom Harrisson and Charles Madge, in 1937. It was during the war, however, that his talent as a film-maker was to flourish. After working on collaborative GPO documentaries such as *The First Days* and *London Can Take It!*, Jennings made a series of films which stand out as an *oeuvre* in their own right. *The Heart of Britain* (1941) was a vivid account of the Blitz in the Midlands and the North of England which made imaginative use of music (Beethoven and Handel) as well as commentary. *Words for Battle* (1941) matched images of the nation at war to inspirational extracts from literature (Camden, Milton, Blake, Browning, Kipling) and from history (Churchill and Lincoln), spoken by Laurence Olivier. *Listen to Britain* (1942) dispensed with commentary altogether and instead used music and natural sound to capture the spirit of Britain and its people at war. *Fires Were Started* (1943), Jennings's only feature-length film, was a moving tribute to the London firemen during the Blitz. It adhered more closely to traditional narrative than his other films, but even so it was distinguished by many individual touches and was more poetic in its treatment than the other Crown features. *The Silent Village* (1943) was a re-creation of the Lidice massacre in Czechoslovakia, imagin-atively relocated by Jennings to a Welsh mining village under German occupation. *The True Story of Lili Marlene* (1944) dramatised the story of the famous song which was adopted by British as well as German troops. *The Eighty Days* (1945) was a retrospective account of the V-1 blitz on southern England, narrated by Ed Murrow but again making use of music and natural sound as well as commentary. And *A Diary for Timothy* (1946), narrated by Michael Redgrave, was a moving, im-pressionistic account of the last months of the war, presented in the form of a diary written for a new-born baby. Most (though not all) of these films were made with the film editor Stewart McAllister, who, like Jennings, had a strongly pictorial mind and who was willing to experiment with unconventional editing techniques.[6]

Given that Jennings's most individualistic and memorable work was done during the war, it seems likely that the context was a significant influence on him. Basil Wright later wrote that Jennings 'found in the circumstances of war an inspiration which exactly matched his own personal feelings about his country'.[7] Jennings was an intelligent and highly complex man whose emotional feelings towards his country ran very deep. On the one hand he was a left-wing intellectual who despised the class system and social snobbery and who admired the down-to-earth qualities which he saw in the working classes. On the other hand he was also imbued with a great sense of tradition: he had a deep respect, even love, for English history and heritage. The most instructive assessment of Jennings's outlook is made by Jeffrey Richards, who compares him to George Orwell. Richards shows that what Jennings and Orwell had in common was 'a robust Socialist patriotism, a full-blooded love of England and the English centred on an unashamed admiration for the qualities of the common man'.[8] The war was a revelation for both men in that it brought the essential qualities of the British working classes out into the open. They were both moved by the endurance and fortitude exhibited by ordinary people under the stresses of war, qualities which could be attributed to their historical lineage. For example, when Jennings was living in a South Wales mining community during the filming of *The Silent Village*, he was deeply impressed by the way of life there. 'I never really thought to live to see the honest Christian and Communist principles daily acted on as a matter of course by a large number of British – I won't say English – people,' he wrote to his wife. 'Not merely honesty, culture, manners, practical socialism, but real life: with passion and tenderness and comradeship and heartiness all combined. From these people one can really understand Cromwell's New Model Army and the defenders of many places at the beginning of the Industrial Revolution.'[9] Orwell likewise saw the sturdy working man as the descendant of the soldiers who had fought to defend British liberty in the past. 'The heirs of Nelson and Cromwell are not to be found in the House of Lords,' he wrote in *The Lion and the Unicorn* (1941). 'They are in the fields and streets, in the factories and the armed forces, in the four-ale bar and the suburban back-garden.'[10]

Despite their varied subject matter, Jennings's wartime films are characterised by the strong thematic and stylistic unity which is usually seen as the signature of an *auteur*. The foremost theme of his work is the sense of nationhood and national identity. This was based on his love of the English countryside (pastoral imagery recurs frequently in his films), on a sense of history and culture (exemplified by his frequent references to England's literary and artistic heritage) and on a deep-rooted admiration for the common man (illustrated by his tributes to the working-class firemen in *Fires Were Started* and the Welsh miners in *The Silent Village*). Yet for all Jennings's affection for his country, his films never lapse into jingoism or propagandist speech-making. To quote Furhammar and Isaksson: 'They are patriotic films from a nation at war, but without uniting symbols, fiery slogans or spectacular military feats. Humphrey Jennings's heroes are not the soldiers of the Libyan desert but the firemen of London.'[11] It is significant that Jennings's films focused on civilians and the home front, rather than on the services in action, although one project on which he invested a considerable amount of time was an aborted film about the Royal Marines during the invasion of Sicily.[12] As well as their thematic similarities, Jennings's films also exhibit a characteristic form and style. They are all organised around the device of creative montage, or associative editing, juxtaposing familiar and unfamiliar images and sounds to create new meanings. This was partly due, no doubt, to Jennings's own working methods, but it probably also had much to do with both his and Stewart McAllister's interest in formal experimentation and aspects of the avant-garde.

Jennings's style is so unique that it is tempting to see his influence in films where he was only a co-director. The opening shot of *The First Days*, which shows children playing on German field guns from the First World War outside the Imperial War Museum, is a case in point. This shot seems to have been taken by Jennings and was obviously one of his favourite images in that he later used it again in *The True Story of Lili Marlene*. It is a typical Jennings image in that it illustrates different meanings at the same time: it contrasts the innocence of the children with the horrors of war (instruments of destruction have become playthings), while the past and the future are invoked at the same time through the proximity of the museum (signifying history) and the children (representing the youth of the nation). Jennings was probably aware that the image also recalled the opening of Kipling's novel *Kim* (1902), where the titular hero sits astride a cannon outside the Lahore Museum.[13] Furthermore, the shots of empty streets and of barrage balloons silhouetted against the skyline in *The First Days* are also very suggestive of Jennings, as is the impressionistic use of popular music ('The Music Goes Round and Round', 'It's a Long Way to Tipperary'). *London Can Take It!* also contains numerous images which can be attributed to Jennings. 'The famous last shot of a little Cockney workingman lighting a fag was one of Humphrey Jennings's touches of genius', recalled Harry Watt.[14] The shot of the workman lighting a cigarette and waving a jaunty thankyou is matched to narrator Quentin Reynolds saying that bombing 'cannot kill the unconquerable spirit and courage of the people of London'. In that moment the individual stands for the entire population of the city. It is the sort of marriage between word and image that was to be elevated into an art form in its own right in some of Jennings's later films.

This is not to say that *The First Days* or *London Can Take It!* should be attributed solely or even predominantly to Jennings. They were collaborative efforts in which Jennings was just one of the directors involved. Furthermore, his next project after *London Can Take It!* can be located in the tradition of other GPO/Crown shorts. *The Heart of Britain* was made 'as a companion piece to *The Front Line* and *Britain Can Take It!*' and was intended 'to pay tribute to the Northern and Midland industrial centres and their workers'. It was designed 'primarily for distribution in the Empire and the United States', where it was retitled *This is England*, but it was also shown domestically as a five-minute film and through the non-theatrical programme.[15] It employed the device of on-camera interviews with real people (an ARP warden, a fire-watcher, a woman making tea for relief workers) to show the people at war in a strict documentary sense. But Jennings's individualistic style was becoming evident through the manner in which the rural and industrial faces of Britain are linked by the commentary ('In the shadow of the hills lives a great industrial people, thronging the valleys of power and the rivers of industry') and the visuals (shots of the moors of Yorkshire and Derbyshire are followed by the cathedrals of Durham and Coventry and then by the factories and chimneys of industrial cities such as 'black Sheffield'). Scenes of Coventry devastated by German bombing are accompanied by Beethoven's Fifth Symphony, played by the Halle Orchestra. The combined effect of music and image creates different meanings: the juxtaposition of culture with the devastation of war, and of the civilised Germany of the past with the barbarous Germany of the present. The film ends with a defiant sequence ('And the Nazis will learn, once and for all, that no-one with impunity troubles the heart of Britain') which shows the construction of bombers to the uplifting tune of Handel's 'Hallelujah Chorus', performed by the Huddersfield Choral Society. The tone of the film did not, however, meet with the approval of all critics. 'Even Americans must be tired now of pictures of raid damage, sparing us nothing, not even the ruined churches with crucifixes gaunt against the sky and the usual defensive commentary,' complained *Documentary News Letter*.[16]

The most important of Jennings's short films in the context of the people's war was *Listen to Britain*. This was his most poetic and abstract meditation on the subject of the British at war. Its highly sophisticated intellectual montage has made it the focus of much attention from film theorists.[17] This focus on its aesthetic qualities, however, has tended to obscure its status as a propaganda text. Far from being a timeless portrait of the British people at war, as so many commentators have suggested, it was in fact rooted in a particular historical moment. The film was compiled in the course of 1941–42, during the period after the worst of the Blitz and when the threat of invasion had receded but before there was any prospect of victory in sight. The 'Britain Can Take It' theme of propaganda which had been so effective in 1940 was now consigned to the past. The MOI had come to realise that the British people needed to be mobilised ideologically and economically for what seemed likely to be a long struggle. But the film was made before the two key events towards the end of 1942 which marked an important turning point in the war effort: the victory at El Alamein which Churchill described as 'the end of the beginning', and the publication of the Beveridge Report which focused people's attention more than ever before on the question of post-war reconstruction. The sense of the people's war as it is presented in *Listen to Britain* is therefore historically quite specific: it is a picture of the British people after the Blitz but before Beveridge, during the period which the writer Elizabeth Bowen described as 'the light-less middle of the tunnel'.[18] What the film does is to cast some light on to this period by celebrating different aspects of war culture and the wartime experience. It shows Jennings at his most reflexive, his technique at its most abstract. The creative juxtapositions between shots and even within shots which are his hallmark are again much in evidence, while the absence of a voice-over commentary allows the spectator the freedom to interpret their meaning rather than having one imposed by the film itself. A number of sequences stand out: the opening where the harvest in a quiet cornfield is interrupted by Spitfires flying overhead; the voices of the BBC's overseas broadcasts against images of London in the blackout; Canadian soldiers singing 'Home on the Range'; a convoy of Bren-gun carriers passing noisily through a quiet country village. Like *The Heart of Britain*, it contrasts pastoral and industrial imagery, Arcadian country landscapes on the one hand, Blakean dark satanic mills and factories on the other. The most famous sequence is the juxtaposition of Flanagan and Allen singing 'Underneath the Arches' in a factory canteen with Dame Myra Hess performing a Mozart recital at the National Gallery accompanied by the RAF Central Band. The cut from one location to the next is done on the same chord: one tune segues into the next, implying a fusion of popular and high culture and thus uniting the factory workers and the concert audience. The film therefore constructs a people united across class and cultural differences: music hall songs and Mozart, neither privileged above the other.

How effective was *Listen to Britain* as propaganda? The film's contemporary reception highlights a dichotomy between critical and popular tastes. Jennings's films were not in fact particularly liked among the purists of the documentary movement, who regarded them as too self-consciously artistic. Edgar Anstey in the *Spectator* thought that the propaganda value of *Listen to Britain* was non-existent because it 'will not encourage anyone to do anything at all'. He continued:

> By the time Humphrey Jennings has done with it, it has become the rarest piece of fiddling since the days of Nero. It will be a disaster if this film is sent overseas. One shudders to imagine the effect upon our allies should they learn that an official British film-making unit can find time these days to contemplate the current sights and sounds of Britain as if the country were some curious kind of museum exhibit or a figment of the romantic imagination of Mass-Observation.[19]

In hindsight, Anstey admitted: 'I was often unfair, I think, in my criticism of Humphrey's work in those days because I felt that some of his films were a bit sort of dilettante.' He added that, despite his misgivings, '*Listen to Britain* had enormous influence overseas'.[20] It was also apparently very successful with audiences at home. Lady Helen Forman, who as Miss Helen de Mouilpied was deputy head of the MOI's non-theatrical film programme, later recalled:

One of the NT [non-theatrical] films under the heading 'general' in our jargon which was liked and applauded was Humphrey Jennings's magical *Listen to Britain*. All sorts of audiences felt it to be a distillation and also a magnification of their own experiences of the home front. This was especially true of factory audiences. I remember one show in a factory in the Midlands where about 800 workers clapped and stamped approval. Films got very short shrift if they touched any area of people's experience and did not ring true.[21]

So although it did not meet with the approval of documentarist critics, *Listen to Britain* did win much popular acclaim. Roger Manvell, then a regional films officer for the MOI, also observed that Jennings's films went down well with audiences around the country. 'I can testify personally that they were the ones of all we constantly showed that immediately stirred emotions, not only in the West Country but in the far tougher Northeast of Britain (Tyneside) which I also came to know well at the time,' he later wrote.[22] It was because his films had such widespread popular appeal that Jennings can justly be considered the foremost documentary-poet of the people's war.

III

It would be fair to say that during the first years of the war the commercial film industry had lagged behind somewhat while the documentary movement, in particular the Crown Film Unit, had set the example in the filmic representation of the British people at war. The feature films of the early war years tended to be conventional thriller or romantic narratives which simply used the war as topical background. This was the period of films such as Carol Reed's *Night Train to Munich* (1940), in which gentleman-hero Rex Harrison rescued heroine Margaret Lockwood from pantomime Gestapo villains, and Leslie Howard's *Pimpernel Smith* (1941), where he played a modern-day 'Scarlet Pimpernel' saving political refugees from inside Nazi Germany. While these films were popular at the box-office, they did little to portray the war effort of ordinary people. Indeed, they seemed to imply that fighting the war was an adventure which was best left to the gentlemen of Cambridge University, who could be trusted to stand up for democracy and freedom and run rings around the Nazis every time. Such films were disliked by the progressive critics for their lack of realism. 'Films of this kind are bad propaganda because they present the war in absurdly romantic terms and their entertainment value is impaired by the conflict in the mind of the audience between the hard facts of real war and its glamorous embellishments in the film,' opined *Documentary News Letter*.[23] The popularity of these films at the box-office in the early years of the war, however, requires some explanation. Perhaps they are best understood as 'Boys' Own' fantasies rather than serious war narratives. Assumptions about the natural leadership of the upper classes remain paramount, and in spirit the films still belong the British cinema of the 1930s rather than to the new democratic realism which was to emerge during the war. Indeed, these films are in many ways reminiscent of Alfred Hitchcock's celebrated thrillers, and in particular *Night Train to Munich* bears a strong resemblance to Hitchcock's *The Lady Vanishes* (1938), as both films were written by Frank Launder and Sidney Gilliat and featured those Englishmen abroad, Charters and Caldicott (played as ever by Basil Radford and Naunton Wayne).

It was not until 1941–42 that the emergence of a new type of war narrative could be detected. In retrospect this has been most closely associated with the films of Ealing Studios, and though it would be fair to say that Ealing's war narratives were characteristic of broader developments across the British cinema as a whole rather than unique in themselves, nevertheless it was the Ealing films which most attracted critical plaudits. The key Ealing film in terms of the dramatisation of the people's war was *The Foreman Went to France* (1942). Manvell later wrote that it 'initiated the Ealing "style", the production of relatively low-budget war films derived from actual wartime incidents, reconstructed and dramatized. It also brought to the screen in a creditable way that still rare phenomenon, a British workingman who was a serious and not a comic character.' [24] Its director was Charles Frend, who was later to work on *San Demetrio, London*, while Alberto Cavalcanti acted as associate producer, shortly before his first Ealing directorial assignment with *Went the Day Well?* The story was from an 'original narrative' by J. B. Priestley, which in turn was inspired by a true story (the film's credits state: 'This picture is dedicated to Melbourne Johns. He is the foreman who went to France, and our story is based on his adventures.') 'The importance of this story,' Michael Balcon said in his memoirs, 'was that it showed how the civilian population, particularly those engaged in the manufacture of essentials for wartime purposes, were just as much in the front line as the troops; the works manager (our "foreman") succeeded, in the face of all odds, in bringing back the vital machinery.'[25] It had been planned as early as the summer of 1940 under the title *Portrait of a British Foreman*. It was included in the studio's production programme for 1941, where it was announced that 'a world-famous star will take the title role'.[26] In the event, however, it was made with no big star names (the comedian Tommy Trinder was top-billed), which certainly contributed to its realistic representation of ordinary people.

The Foreman Went to France uses a device which was becoming quite frequent in mid-war films in that the main story is located in the historical past. The film opens in 1942, when it shows Fred Carrick (Clifford Evans) running a factory producing aircraft guns, and then switches back to June 1940 during the German invasion of France. However, the film rejects the popular notion of the summer of 1940 as the time when the British people all rallied together in the common cause and distances itself from the myth of the finest hour. Instead, it suggests that the country was riddled with class divisions which came close to losing the war. Carrick is worried that three special-purpose machines lent by his firm to a French manufacturer will fall into enemy hands, but his bosses are complacent about the German threat and pay little heed to his warning. From the start, therefore, the film takes the side of the ordinary working man against the employers, and throughout it shows the representatives of the governing classes as obstructive and unhelpful. Carrick decides on his own initiative to go over to France to secure the machines, though the urgency of his mission is not realised by the British authorities ('I'm asking for a little common sense and a little collaboration and all I come up against is yards of red tape all the time,' he complains to one bemused official). When he gets to his destination in France, Carrick finds the town has been evacuated, but he enlists the help of an American girl (Constance Cummings) and two British soldiers (Tommy Trinder and Gordon Jackson) who have been cut off from their unit during the retreat. Their journey to the coast brings them into contact with refugees and fifth columnists, but eventually they reach a small fishing village where they are given passage on a French trawler leaving for England. The ending of the film celebrates Anglo-French solidarity: the French people give up their luggage and belongings in order to make room for the machines.

The most significant aspects of the film in terms of the people's war are the narrative and characterisations. The film has a radical edge in that it voices criticisms of the governing classes ('The trouble is the people at the top think they're fighting the last war all over again,' Carrick remarks pointedly). Significantly, the foreman and the two soldiers are all working-class and regional – Welsh (Evans), Cockney (Trinder) and Scots (Jackson) – while the representatives of authority whom they encounter, including a French mayor (Robert Morley) and an upper-class English officer (John Williams) turn out to be, respectively, a quisling and a German spy. The collapse of France is attributed to traitors in the wealthy and privileged classes – people who are shown to be similar to Carrick's bosses at home. The film suggests, irresistibly, that the governing classes are not to be trusted – a theme which would be echoed in *Went the Day Well?* – while it is the initiative and determination of the ordinary man which will finally win the day.

The Foreman Went to France was very well received by both the public and the critics, attracting wide praise for its realism and human qualities. 'Inspiring in its heroism of ordinary people and its emphasis on the best in British character,' was the verdict of one Mass-Observation respondent, who also described it as 'a useful little documentary of the war'.[27] It is interesting that it should be described as a 'documentary', illustrating how the distinction between the feature and documentary modes of film practice had been blurred by the middle of the war. It was for its representation of ordinary people that the film was received warmly by the progressive critical discourse. *Documentary News Letter* nominated it as the best war film made hitherto, rating it above near-contemporary films such as *One of Our Aircraft is Missing* and *The Day Will Dawn* (both 1942) because it 'sticks to its story and tries to stick to its human beings'. It was thought to provide a model for future war narratives:

> This surely is the way to use an entertainment medium to make propaganda for the things we are fighting for. Don't try to tell the whole story of France or Holland or Norway or Britain, but take some people and show what happens to them in a credible war situation – it may be a real situation or an imaginary one – provided it is credible that doesn't matter. The really important thing is that the people you choose should stay human. The public doesn't believe that the war is being fought between an army of

plaster saints on our side and an army of creatures with horns and tails on the other. Outside the cinema they never meet people from either category and it is useless to make propaganda in terms of beings that exist only in the cinema.[28]

This was a typical statement of the views of the documentary-realist discourse on the nature of film propaganda: that it should be based on believable situations and characterisations, and that 'human' considerations should be uppermost rather than old-fashioned melodramatic conventions. It was, in other words, an agenda for the filmic representation of the people's war.

IV

In popular memory the defining experience of the people's war was the Blitz during the winter of 1940–41. By the time that two feature films appeared in 1943 dramatising the work of the Auxiliary Fire Service during the nightly air raids on London, the events which they depicted had already acquired the aura of myth. Those two films were Crown's *Fires Were Started*, directed by Humphrey Jennings, and Ealing's *The Bells Go Down*, directed by Basil Dearden. The pair make an instructive comparison of how the official film unit and a commercial studio interpreted events which had already passed into popular legend.

Fires Were Started was the only one of the five Crown feature films which focused on the home front. The suggestion that Jennings should direct this film came from Harry Watt. 'We must try to get Humphrey to do an action picture, because everything is so static with Humphrey,' he told Dalrymple.[29] As with so many of his films it was a long time in preparation. Jennings began researching the subject in 1941, reading many accounts of fire-fighting in both London and Liverpool, and had a treatment ready by the beginning of 1942.[30] He remained faithful to the Crown tradition of using 'real' people in that all the roles were taken by genuine London firemen. The fire scenes were reconstructed at St Katharine's Dock in London and the shooting was finished by October 1942. The film ran into some resistance from General Film Distributors, who thought it was too slow in the first reels and wanted it cut. But Jennings found an ally in the influential film critic C. A. Lejeune, who after being shown the film described it as 'one of the finest documentaries we have ever made' and remarked that 'I have never known a film as honest and human as this one fail to get its message through'.[31] In the event some cuts were made to the theatrical version, while the longer version was shown non-theatrically under the title *I Was A Fireman*.[32]

Roy Armes describes *Fires Were Started* as 'a perfect fusion of documentary and narrative'.[33] The film may be described as epic in the true sense of the word in that it aspires to a style of narrative poetry which eulogises heroic endeavour and achievement. An opening caption explains that the film is set during the winter of 1940–41, before the formation of the National Fire Service; in other words, the events are already being located in the past. The narrative of *Fires Were Started* displays a highly organised formal structure. There are three sections, covering the build-up to the fire, the fire itself and the aftermath. The first section is a leisurely introduction to the characters. A new recruit, Barrett (William Sansom), arrives at Sub-Station 14Y, where he is assigned to Heavy Unit One and is shown around by a cheerful Cockney taxi-driver, Johnny Daniels (Fred Griffiths). The firemen themselves all have their own distinctive personalities but work together as a team, symbolised by the famous 'One Man Went to Mow' sequence where Barrett plays the piano as the men gather round: while the tune remains the same, for each man there is a slight variation which reflects his individual character. This is also the means by which the new recruit is assimilated into the group, as Barrett is placed at the centre of the frame during the piano sequence.

The second and central part of the film, in which the tempo of editing increases and thus creates a greater sense of urgency, shows the firemen in action and the death of one of their comrades, Jacko (Johnny Houghton). The men are sent to fight a fire in Trinidad Street in the London docks. An ammunition ship moored on the river is threatened; the fire spreads; the sub-officer in charge is injured on the roof of a warehouse. Jacko holds on to a lifeline while the injured man is lowered safely to the ground, but he is left stranded on the rooftop and perishes before he also can be rescued. The fire is depicted as much as a natural disaster than as the result of enemy action (the actual enemy does not feature in the film at all); it is beaten through a combination of teamwork and personal heroism. During the fire sequences there are numerous images which are characteristic of Jennings: an almost surreal shot as a frightened horse is led through the smoke; firemen on the warehouse roof silhouetted against the night sky; a close-up of Jacko's hand as the lifeline slips through his fingers; and Barrett finding Jacko's dented tin hat amidst the rubble.

The third section of the film is a brief coda in which the exhausted firemen return to their station and come to terms with their comrade's death. There is one especially poignant moment where Jacko's wife waits at home while listening to the wireless announce 'it does not appear that casualties are likely to be heavy'. The ending of the film is a bravura example of associative editing: the firemen attend Jacko's funeral, which is intercut with shots of the ammunition ship sailing down the river. The implication is clearly that Jacko's sacrifice has not been in vain. It is moments such as this which make the film stand out from the other Crown features.

Fires Were Started is now widely regarded as the finest film testament to the people's war. Its evocative picture of quiet, undemonstrative, almost casual heroism on the part of ordinary people is undoubtedly one of the greatest achievements of the British cinema. To quote Lindsay Anderson: 'No other British film made during the war, documentary or feature, achieved such a continuous and poignant truthfulness, or treated the subject of men at war with such a sense of its incidental glories and its essential tragedy.'[34] While it is celebrated now for its narrative poetry and its place in film history, the critical discourses of the time constructed it in terms of its honesty and authenticity. The fact that even when it was made it was already looking back at events of the (near) past meant that it was regarded as a historical document. *Documentary News Letter*, usually so averse to Jennings's films, opined: 'It is the great achievement of *Fires Were Started* that you're just as interested and the film means just as much now as if it had been made and shown in the middle of the raids; and it will mean just as much in a few years' time when the war is over.'[35] Audiences also seem to have responded favourably to the film. 'The best wartime documentary yet: never have ordinary people been more convincingly done (Humphrey Jennings's M-O training?) and the film is nevertheless "poetic" in its treatment', wrote one Mass-Observation respondent.[36] Another paid it perhaps the highest compliment: 'Having lived through the London blitz we naturally enjoyed this film. We were impressed with the way things were done and with the lack of heroics.'[37] Even people who had first-hand experience of the events which it depicted found it honest and truthful. It is possible that the perception of realism has as much to do with the role of memory in reconstructing the past as it does with an objective sense of what it was 'really' like during the Blitz; in other words, this was how people liked to remember the Blitz (the humour and camaraderie rather than the danger and fear).

Ealing's *The Bells Go Down* is comparable to Jennings's film in several respects. It tells the story of a group of recruits who join the Auxiliary Fire Service at the outbreak of war, are put through their training by members of the regular London fire brigade, and finally prove their worth during three consecutive nights of air raids in 1940. It was based on a book written (anonymously) by Vic Flint, a former film studio worker who had joined the AFS before the war. Like *Fires Were Started* it brings together a diverse social group, including a newly-wed husband (Philip Friend), a Cockney wideboy (Tommy Trinder), a thief on the run from the police (Mervyn Johns) and a veteran of the International Brigade in the Spanish Civil War (William Hartnell). The scenes showing the training of the firemen, and the climactic fire-fighting sequences, are filmed in the manner of the documentary. However, there is more of an emphasis on broad comedy throughout the film, particularly Tommy Turk's (Trinder's) repeated run-ins with the dour fire chief, MacFarlane (Finlay Currie). The narrative also provides space for the private and romantic lives of its main characters. This was the main difference between Crown's reconstructed documentary account of the Blitz and the version from a commercial studio. The camaraderie as well as the danger of the fire brigade are depicted just as successfully as in *Fires Were Started*, but the film as a whole is less satisfying than Jennings's film and is not as tightly constructed.

The Bells Go Down was promoted as a starring vehicle for Tommy Trinder, the comedian who had previously had considerable success playing a straight role in *The Foreman Went to France*. 'In the part of a Cockney fireman, Tommy Trinder blends laughter and pathos in his own inimitable style,' declared the promotional material.[38] Indeed, one of the weaknesses of *The Bells Go Down* is that it seems unsure as to whether it is a comedy or a drama, and emerges as an uneasy mixture of both. The review of the film by *The Times* made an instructive comparison with the Crown film:

> *The Bells Go Down* is unfortunate in that it so quickly follows the documentary film *Fires Were Started*. It is by no means true that a documentary film must, by the very virtue of its office, be better

than an imaginative reconstruction of events, but here the film which was acted by the men who were actually in the NFS is superior at nearly every point.[39]

The main weakness of *The Bells Go Down*, the reviewer opined, was that the story 'depends too much on unconvincing personal relationships', while Tommy Trinder's performance was 'that of a comedian out on his own' rather than a believable character. Trinder's likeable personality certainly adds a touch of humour to the film, but this makes it all the more surprising that his is one of the characters to be killed at the end. When MacFarlane is trapped under a fallen beam in a burning hospital, Tommy pulls him out, only for the two of them to die moments later when a wall collapses on them. This moment is a shocking and unexpected reversal of the audience's expectations which sits uneasily with the rest of the film, for Tommy has hitherto been the comic relief. In propaganda terms, however, it works as a reminder that civilians were very much in the front line of the people's war.

8

Officers and Men

Popular behaviour in this new war showed little desire for heroics or self-display ... This desire for understatement developed as a regular attitude in the Services, and was faithfully put in the films by screen-writers, directors and actors only too conscious of the emotional implications and the wider national significance of the stories they were representing. *Roger Manvell*[1]

I

It was natural that during the Second World War British feature film-makers should turn to stories of men in battle as a form of propaganda. Patriotic films of the services at war became very prominent in the generic profile of the British cinema, particularly between 1940 and 1943 when the war film was at its most popular with audiences. It was the commercial feature film industry which led the way in the production of war narratives, which producers saw as a way of fulfilling their patriotic duty, though the Crown Film Unit also made an important contribution to the representation of men at war through its feature-length documentaries such as *Target for Tonight*.

Films about the services were important for propaganda in several crucial respects: they gave an impression for people at home of the valour and courage of the men in the armed forces (and in the merchant navy, which was also in the front line); they showed to the world how Britain was fighting; and they were a means for negotiating the significant changes in the nature and composition of the services, particularly the Army, which had been brought about by conscription and recruitment.

The story of the British war film has usually been described in terms of a gradual shift from false heroics and jingoism in the early war years to the emergence of a mature realism in the representation of men in battle by the middle of the war. It was a process which reflected the trend towards realism which characterised the British cinema as a whole during this period. This trend was mirrored by a shift in the narrative interest in service films, from a focus on dashing officers-and-gentlemen in the early war years to a greater emphasis on the ordinary enlisted men in the later years. However, this was not a linear process, and it should not be assumed that all war narratives became gradually more 'documentarised' as the war went on. Furthermore, there was a marked difference between the views of members of the progressive critical discourse and the popular tastes of cinema audiences. In general, the early war films which were dismissed by the critics for their overblown heroics and lack of authenticity were actually more successful with audiences than some of the later films where the realist style had become dominant. Whereas the critics' preference was for the sober realism of *Nine Men* and *San Demetrio, London*, the public's choice was the unabashed patriotism of *Convoy* and *Ships With Wings*.

II

Of the three armed services, it was the Royal Navy which was most frequently represented in serious war films between 1940 and 1943. The concentration on naval subjects by film producers can be explained partly through the traditional affection and respect in which the British held their senior service, and partly through the nature of the war at sea which gave ample scope for action and drama at a time when the British Army had not yet won any major victories. Films such as *For Freedom, Convoy, Ships With Wings, In Which We Serve, We Dive at Dawn* and *San Demetrio, London* (the last focusing specifically on the merchant navy) all illustrated aspects of the war at sea, some based on real events, others entirely fictional. The balance of conventional narrative forms with aspects of the documentary technique in these films was uneven, but they can all be seen as attempts to combine patriotic

17. RIGHT. **Officers and Men (I)**: Judy Campbell and Clive Brook in *Convoy* (Ealing, 1940), a naval drama which was criticised by *Documentary News Letter* for giving 'the impression that the main business of the Navy was resolving triangles involving officers' wives'.

18. BELOW. **Officers and Men (II)**: Basil Sydney and Leslie Banks are the impeccably-attired officers in *Ships With Wings* (Ealing, 1941), which was likewise criticised because 'the propaganda line of the film would be more appropriate to a Ruritanian campaign than to the Second World War'.

19. ABOVE. **Officers and Men (III):** Noël Coward's *In Which We Serve* (Two Cities, 1942) was the definitive film tribute to the Royal Navy, this image of men in the water a powerful metaphor for class levelling.

20. LEFT. **Officers and Men (IV):** *San Demetrio, London* (Ealing, 1943) was a sober, realistic, factually-based narrative of the merchant navy which emphasised unity and teamwork amongst the crew.

21. ABOVE. **Officers and Men (V):** *Nine Men* (Ealing, 1943) was a stark, austere feature which illustrated the fighting spirit of the ordinary British soldier (Jack Lambert, Grant Sutherland, Frederick Piper).

22. RIGHT. **Officers and Men (VI):** Anton Walbrook, Deborah Kerr and Roger Livesey in *The Life and Death of Colonel Blimp* (Rank/The Archers, 1943), the 'foolish production' which Churchill wanted to ban.

23. ABOVE. **Officers and Men (VII):** Civilians are turned into soldiers in *The Way Ahead* (Two Cities, 1944) (John Laurie, Jimmy Hanley, Hugh Burden, James Donald, Stanley Holloway).

24. LEFT. **Officers and Men (VIII):** *The Way to the Stars* (Two Cities, 1945) explored the relations between RAF personnel and civilians (Basil Radford, Stanley Holloway, Bill Owen, John Mills).

25. RIGHT. **Women and War (I):** *The Gentle Sex* (Two Cities, 1943) was a tribute to the ATS in which the women (here represented by Lili Palmer and Joy Shelton) maintained their femininity even in uniform.

26. BELOW. **Women and War (II):** 'You can help your country just as much in an overall as you can in uniform' was the theme of *Millions Like Us* (Gainsborough, 1943), a down-to-earth drama about women working in an aircraft factory (Patricia Roc and Megs Jenkins).

27. LEFT. **Friend and Foe (I):** Wilfrid Lawson as *Pastor Hall* (Charter Films, 1940), who denounces the Nazis as 'the enemies of God'.

28. BELOW. **Friend and Foe (II):** *The Day Will Dawn* (Paul Soskin, 1942) was a somewhat studio-bound tribute to the heroic men and women of Norway who resisted the German occupation.

29. RIGHT. **Friend and Foe (III):** The possibility of a German invasion of England was dramatised in Cavalcanti's *Went the Day Well?* (Ealing, 1942), a powerful film with the vivid quality of a nightmare.

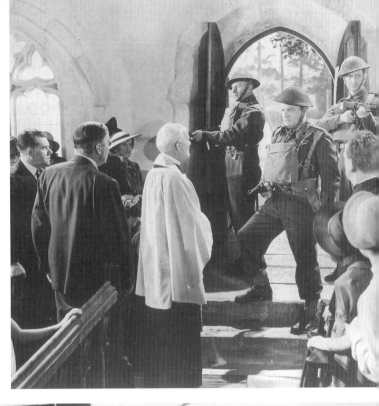

30. BELOW. **Friend and Foe (IV):** Humphrey Jenning's *The Silent Village* (Crown, 1943) was an unusual but effective little film which transposed the Lidice massacre in Czechoslovakia to a Welsh village under imaginary German occupation.

31. ABOVE. **History and Heritage (I):** Robert Donat as *The Young Mr Pitt* (Twentieth Century-Fox, 1942), an inspirational leader of the past portrayed in Churchillian mode.

32. LEFT. **History and Heritage (II):** Laurence Olivier's *Henry V* (Rank/Two Cities, 1944) was a fusion of Shakespeare, propaganda and spectacle on an epic scale.

drama and realism in order to find a formula for the war narrative that would prove acceptable to both audiences and critics.

For Freedom (1940), directed by the veteran Maurice Elvey for Gainsborough Pictures, was the most unusual of the naval films. It bore some relation to *The Lion Has Wings* in that it made use of newsreel and documentary footage within a narrative framework bounded by fictional studio-filmed sequences. It was an account of the Battle of the River Plate (in which the German 'pocket battleship' *Admiral Graf Spee* was engaged by a British cruiser squadron) and its sequel, the *Altmark* incident (the *Graf Spee*'s supply ship was boarded by the Royal Navy in a Norwegian port in order to free British prisoners), seen from the perspective of a British newsreel company. The reconstruction of the action itself was a fairly rudimentary effort using obvious models, though it did include shots of some of the officers of the British cruisers *Ajax* and *Exeter* who played themselves for the film. It now seems, rather like *The Lion Has Wings*, something of a hodgepodge which includes aspects of fictional narrative and documentary reportage but does not succeed in integrating them successfully. At the time, however, there was approval for this technique and the film was generally well received. 'The chief merits of the film lie in its restraint, its sound statement of the British case, an excellent if simple speech on internationalism, and its lack of Blimpish dialogue,' wrote William Whitebait. 'Maurice Elvey, the director, has made a quite solid propaganda brick with comparatively little straw.'[2] The use of 'real' people in the film anticipated the Crown narrative-documentaries, though here they were featured alongside professional actors. The film was promoted as a patriotic tribute to the Royal Navy and did quite well at the box-office in the summer of 1940.

Ealing's *Convoy* (1940), which became the most successful British film of the year, was another naval subject but one which was firmly in the tradition of the conventional film narrative. It was the third and last film directed by the talented Penrose Tennyson, who joined the Navy after completing it and died in a plane crash in 1941. Tennyson's background was upper-class (he was a great-grandson of the Victorian Poet Laureate Alfred, Lord Tennyson), but his previous two films, the boxing drama *There Ain't No Justice* (1939) and the mining drama *The Proud Valley* (1940) had won critical acclaim for their realistic representation of working-class characters and situations. *Convoy*, which was filmed partly at sea by Tennyson and cameraman Roy Kellino, also showed some evidence of the documentary influence in its depiction of the routine of convoy protection. But while the film was realistic in technique, the story and characterisations were imbued with the attitudes towards class reminiscent of mainstream British cinema of the 1930s. It is dedicated 'to the Officers and Men of the Royal and Merchant Navies', but there are pronounced class differences in the film between officers and men – and, indeed, between the Royal Navy and the merchant service.

The film follows a convoy sailing under the protection of the cruiser *Apollo*, commanded by Captain Armytage (Clive Brook). The main sub-plot is straight from the conventions of drawing-room melodrama: the caddish first officer Lieutenant Cranford (John Clements) has previously run off with Armytage's wife. In some ways the film anticipates the more celebrated *In Which We Serve* for the way in which it constructs the warship as a microcosm of the nation at war: personal differences among the crew are put aside in the face of the common enemy. But unlike the later film, it focuses specifically on the officers while other ranks appear briefly and then only as caricatures. Furthermore, while the Royal Navy is represented by traditional officer-types, the merchant navy is represented mainly by a stubborn northerner, Eckersley (Edward Chapman), who scorns the protection of the convoy and sails off on his own, only to be sunk by a German pocket battleship. The climax of the film is a battle between the pocket battleship and the out-gunned *Apollo*: Armytage rams the German ship to allow the convoy to escape, and Cranford dies a hero's death in the action. The critical reception was divided. For the trade and popular press, it was a perfect combination of entertainment and propaganda. 'The film is a worthy tribute to the Senior Service and, at the same time, grand popular entertainment,' said *Kinematograph Weekly*. 'Put another way, patriotism with colossal box-office punch.'[3] But the melodramatic content did not go down well with the documentarist critics, one of whom later complained: '*Convoy* ... for all Pen Tennyson's skill managed to give the impression that the main business of the Navy was resolving triangles involving officers' wives.'[4]

Ealing's *Ships With Wings* (1941) was very similar to *Convoy* in several respects. It again starred John Clements; it was directed by the Russian émigré Sergei Nolbandov, who had been the associate producer on *Convoy* and the other films made by Pen Tennyson; and it again made use of actuality footage taken at sea by Roy Kellino, this time on board the aircraft carrier HMS *Ark Royal* (which was named *Invincible* in the film). It was dedicated 'to the Officers and Men of the Fleet Air Arm', though once again the class distinctions within the service were rigidly observed and the officers were the focus of narrative interest. The senior naval commanders – Leslie Banks as the admiral and Basil Sydney as captain of the aircraft carrier – belonged once again to the upper classes, while the story itself was replete with the sort of 'Boys' Own' style heroics which in retrospect seem false and embarrassing. Dick Stacey (Clements), a dare-devil pilot, is dismissed from the Fleet Air Arm after a reckless stunt goes tragically wrong and kills another man. But in 1941 he contrives to rejoin his old ship in the Mediterranean and redeems himself by dying a heroic death during an aerial attack against a dam on an enemy-held island.

The film is far removed from the sober, understated style of the later, and more celebrated, Ealing war narratives, concluding as it does with the glorification of an individual act of heroic sacrifice. Again there is a tension in the film between the phoney and the authentic, and in particular the actuality footage taken at sea contrasts markedly with the obvious model island which the aircraft attack at the climax. The war is presented in such absurd terms that it prompted a *Documentary News Letter* editorial to declare that 'the propaganda line of the film would be more appropriate to a Ruritanian campaign than to the Second World War'.[5] According to Michael Balcon, it was the reaction of critics who attacked the film as unrealistic which led to a change of policy at Ealing. '*Ships With Wings* was our last film that could attract this particular type of criticism, because from then on we learned to snatch our stories from the headlines and they had the ring of truth,' he wrote in his memoirs.[6] However, Balcon had commissioned Mass-Observation to investigate the reception of the film, and an extensive audience survey found that the overwhelming majority of people who saw it were very impressed, including people from naval towns (Portsmouth and Chatham) as well as provincial cities (Edinburgh, Glasgow, Birmingham, Cardiff) and London. The summative report concluded: 'the film has been a great success among all sections and classes of people.'[7] Although a few remarks were made about the sets, and although there is evidence that audiences were aware of the lack of authenticity, this does not seem on the whole to have been as important to cinema-goers as the patriotic appeal of the film. The assumption that realism alone is the criterion of effective film propaganda is therefore called into question. The popular success of both *Convoy* and *Ships With Wings* suggests that British audiences would accept strong patriotic sentiments and class-bound heroics, particularly in the early years of the war. They should not, therefore, be thought of as inferior films, but rather as examples of a different approach to combining propaganda with popular entertainment.

The definitive film tribute to the Royal Navy, and arguably the finest film about the services made during the war, was Noël Coward's In *Which We Serve* (1942). Written and produced by Coward, who also co-directed with David Lean, this was based on the career of Coward's friend Louis Mountbatten. It is a key film in the representation of the services in that it was the first to give equal importance to other ranks as well as officers. 'I realised from the outset that it was essential to the accuracy of the picture that the lower deck and fo'c'sle should be represented as accurately as the quarterdeck, the bridge and the ward-room,' Coward wrote in his autobiography.[8] The hierarchy of class and rank which had been portrayed in earlier naval dramas is still apparent, but here the narrative links together both officers and men through their shared experiences of service and domestic life. Dilys Powell, writing shortly after the war, opined that 'Noël Coward in *In Which We Serve* took a handful of typically British men and women and made from their stories, ordinary enough in themselves, a distillation of national character'.[9] The production of the film had not been without its problems, for there had been some controversy in the press over the well-known humorist and playboy Coward impersonating a serving naval officer and member of the royal family, while the MOI had not been in favour of the story because it featured one of His Majesty's ships being sunk.[10] It was made for Two Cities, an independent production company set up before the war by the Italian émigré Filippo Del Giudice, and went on to become the most successful British film of 1943, second overall only to Hollywood's *Random Harvest*. It was also very successful in America, where it was voted the best film of 1942 by the National Board of Review of Motion Pictures, while Coward was given a special Academy Award for his 'Outstanding Production Achievement'.

In Which We Serve is more strongly imbued with a sense of Britain's naval tradition than any other film. It begins with a caption which states: 'This film is dedicated to the Royal Navy, "whereon under the good providence of God the wealth, safety and strength of the kingdom chiefly depend".' The Navy as guardian of the nation is represented by the destroyer HMS *Torrin*, while those at home whom it protects are represented by the families of the crew, linked by an imaginative flashback structure which unites both servicemen and civilians within one all-embracing national community. Like so many classic wartime films, it successfully integrates narrative and documentary. The opening sequence is pure documentary. 'This is the story of a ship,' says a commentator (actually the voice of an uncredited Leslie Howard), and there follows a documentary-montage of shipbuilding which, with its crisp images of construction work and close-ups of hot rivets and sweating workers' faces, is reminiscent of pre-war documentaries such as Grierson's *Industrial Britain* (1931). The *Torrin* is then shown in action during the Battle of Crete on 23 May 1941, leading a destroyer flotilla in a successful night attack on an enemy convoy before being hit and sunk the next day by German bombers. A group of survivors swim to a Carley float and, as they cling on, exhausted, wounded, and machine-gunned by German planes, they think about their families at home and other actions in which the ship had been involved.

The flashbacks focus on three principal characters who are drawn from across the spectrum of rank and class: Captain Kinross (Coward), Chief Petty Officer Walter Hardy (Bernard Miles), and Ordinary Seaman Shorty Blake (John Mills). The narrative thus diverges into different lines, providing a space for both the private and the public. Personal storylines are shown against the background of real events (the declaration of war, Dunkirk, the Blitz, the Battle of Crete); the routines of service life and the agonies of separation from loved ones are movingly portrayed; the grief of bereavement (of both shipmates and family members) is played with a beautiful restraint that makes the loss more heart-felt than any dramatic histrionics ever could. Coward's portrayal of Kinross, complete with his distinctive clipped delivery and the mannerisms which are uniquely his, locates him firmly within a class type – he belongs to a world of formal naval dinners and cocktails – but he is no aloof figure like Clive Brook's Armytage in *Convoy*. Rather, he is a paternalistic father-figure who instills loyalty and discipline in his crew but who is also genuinely concerned for the well-being of the men under his command. His policy is to run 'a happy and efficient ship', and the *Torrin* is shown rather like a family united by the common bonds of professionalism and duty. The image of the men clinging to the float becomes a powerful and irresistible metaphor for class levelling: differences in background matter very little when they are up to their necks in seawater and oil. This is not to imply that the class system is swept away, but rather that there is a community of interest and a sense of comradeship between people of different backgrounds. What unites all the men is devotion to their ship and thus, by implication, to the nation. This devotion extends even to their families, exemplified by the scene in which Alex Kinross (Celia Johnson) toasts her husband's ship, which she describes as a permanent and implacable rival for his loyalty and affection. Ship, family, nation: all are symbolically united in the shape of the *Torrin*.

In Which We Serve was a sincere and moving tribute by Coward to the Royal Navy and is deservedly regarded as one of the definitive films of the British at war. It was the most popular choice in Mass-Observation's nationwide survey of favourite films in November 1943. One particularly perceptive and articulate respondent offered a reasoned assessment of the film which corresponds closely with the views of the critics:

> Easily top of the list comes *In Which We Serve*. I liked it because everything was right. The spirit of the Navy was captured excellently and there were so many deft touches in the action and dialogue which revealed how completely and intimately Coward knows the Englishman at war. It was obviously a film of things as they are, and not just a string of hashed-up ideas from the backroom boys of the film world with false heroics and sentiment. Nothing was sacrificed to suit public taste, the language was not emasculated and the love interest was unobtrusively fitted in. The direction was superb and the acting on the part of the whole cast of remarkably high standard, while the production was equally good, not a wrong detail anywhere (I can vouch for this, having talked to a number of Navy men about it) ... Altogether, the finest piece of work to come out of the British Studios for a long time past.[11]

One of the warmest tributes came from the Soviet film-maker Vsevolod Pudovkin. 'This picture is English through and through,' he said. 'You can see the real face of England in it. The scene in which the captain, taking leave, shakes the hand of a whole file of his compatriots, and each conducts himself as though he were like no one but himself, and yet at the same time all are like each other, will remain long in my memory.'[12]

The new realism in the representation of naval officers and men evident in *In Which We Serve* was consolidated by *We Dive at Dawn* (1943), directed by Anthony Asquith for Gainsborough. This is a less well-known film than *In Which We Serve*, but it is worthy of more critical attention than it has received. It was strongly influenced by the documentary technique in telling the story of a submarine sent on a mission to sink a new German battleship. The casting of John Mills as the submarine commander marked the final break from the upper-class officer-types of earlier naval films. The highly-mannered, theatrical acting style of performers such as Clive Brook, Leslie Banks, John Clements and even Coward (who did not act in any more wartime films after *In Which We Serve*) was giving way to the more naturalistic, less affected style of a new generation of actors who came to the fore during the war. Mills, who personified this new generation, is unique as the only British screen actor capable of playing both officers and other ranks with equal conviction. The hierarchy of class and rank has disappeared from *We Dive at Dawn*: Mills's Lieutenant Taylor, wearing a stubbly beard and without any trace of an affected accent, is a more ordinary and down-to-earth character than his cinematic predecessors. The film itself can be located squarely in the 'wartime wedding' of documentary and the feature film. This point was made by *The Times*, which also singled out Mills's performance for particular praise:

> Generally speaking, the best British films have been those which have not concerned themselves with the Gestapo and improbable adventures in occupied countries but have blended the discipline of the documentary with a minimum amount of the story-teller's licence and have gone about the work of showing how normal men react to the normal strains and stresses of war. The camera and the shrewd economic script soon put us on familiar terms with the crew of the 'Sea Tiger' – humour sometimes escapes from the confines of character into the looseness of a music-hall sketch but stays on the right side of caricature – and the voyage, even though it involves the melodramatic torpedoing in the Baltic of a new German battleship, earns the right to be taken seriously. Mr John Mills, as the captain, does much to give an air of authenticity to the adventures in which the submarine is involved. Here is by

no means one of those carelessly heroic captains who can solve
all difficulties with a studied flippancy and an order bellowed down
the speaking-tube. He is a man of nerves, which he can control,
but not altogether conceal, and nothing in the film is better than
the sense of strain which makes itself felt in spite of all that good-
humour, courage and discipline can do while the submarine leads
her intolerably hunted life after the torpedoes have been fired.[13]

We Dive at Dawn is on a smaller scale than *In Which We Serve*: it is spare
and economical in the best documentary style. The confined sets create
a good impression of the claustrophobia of submarine life. Indeed,
the style of the film is comparable to Crown's feature-documentary
Close Quarters. The main difference is that the Crown documentary was
a reconstruction of a routine patrol, culminating in the sinking of a
floating barge, whereas *We Dive at Dawn* told the story of a special
mission to sink a (fictional) German battleship.

Ealing's *San Demetrio, London* (1943), directed by Charles Frend, is
widely regarded as the studio's most mature and realistic war narrative
and shows that by the middle of the war Ealing had come full circle
from the melodramatic heroics of *Convoy* and *Ships With Wings*. It was
based on a real event; there were no star names in the cast; it focused
on a group of working-class merchant seamen who did not depend on
officers for inspiration; and their heroism is so understated as to be
almost matter-of-fact, as if the events in the film were part of a
routine voyage rather than an extraordinary adventure.[14] It was, as
many critics recognised, yet another example of the convergence
between studio narrative and documentary realism. Dedicated 'to the
Officers and Men of the British Merchant Navy', *San Demetrio, London*
was made at a time when the Battle of the Atlantic was at its height
and shipping losses in the merchant fleet were severe. Balcon thought
that 'it was fine propaganda for the Merchant Service and brought
home to the public that thousands of lives were at stake in keeping
the pipelines flowing'.[15] In the autumn of 1940 the *San Demetrio* is
carrying petrol from Texas to the Clyde when the convoy it is sailing
with is shelled by the German pocket battleship *Admiral Scheer*. The
only escort is the armed merchantman *Jervis Bay*, which is quickly sunk.
The *San Demetrio* is hit and set on fire, and the captain gives the order
to abandon ship. The narrative then focuses on one of the lifeboats,
carrying several crewmen including the second officer (Ralph Michael),

the chief engineer (Walter Fitzgerald), the bo'sun (Frederick Piper), a young seaman (Gordon Jackson) and an American (Robert Beatty) who had joined the ship in order to get to Britain and join the RAF. After two days afloat, suffering from the cold and wet, they sight a ship, only to find that it is the *San Demetrio*, burning but still afloat. They reboard her, put the fires out and succeed in sailing her over a thousand miles home to Britain. One of the crew (Mervyn Johns) dies from exposure and is buried at sea. The emphasis is on teamwork: all hands working together in the common cause.

As a tribute to ordinary seamen, the film certainly stands comparison with the Crown documentaries *Merchant Seamen* and *Western Approaches*. The characterisations are believable, the acting naturalistic and, except for the back-projection in the lifeboat scenes, the style is doggedly realistic. The model work and the tanker set itself are impressive, and the film gives a good impression of the dangerous and hostile conditions which the men faced, battling against the sea, the cold, and the ever-present danger of the ship blowing up (they dare not light a fire to make hot food because of the petrol fumes). However, the reception of the film is instructive in that while it was highly praised by the critics, it was only a modest success at the box-office at a time when audience tastes were turning increasingly in favour of costume melodrama. W. J. Speakman, former President of the CEA, told a BFI conference in 1944 that although the earlier war films 'were in most cases completely successful', the most recent ones (of which he cited *San Demetrio, London*) 'were definite failures'. To Speakman, it was 'quite obvious that the public are war-weary, and in reaction from the war itself infinitely prefer to see something escapist'.[16] Thus it was that *San Demetrio, London*, for all its sober realism, was less successful with audiences than some of the earlier, more flamboyantly heroic war films had been.

III

In contrast to the numerous naval dramas made during the early and middle years of the war, military subjects were at first relatively underrepresented in propaganda films. One of the reasons for this was that in the first half of the war there had been no conspicuous victories on land worth dramatising. Another, more profound reason, was probably that the Army had never enjoyed the same affection which the British held for the Royal Navy. 'Well within living memory it was quite common for "the redcoats" to be booed at in the streets and for landlords of respectable public houses to refuse to allow soldiers on the premises,' George Orwell wrote in *The Lion and the Unicorn*. 'In peace time, even when there are two million unemployed, it is difficult to fill the ranks of the tiny standing army, which is officered by the country gentry and a specialised stratum of the middle class, and manned by farm labourers and slum proletarians.'[17] The Army was perceived to be heavily class-ridden. Social differences within the ranks were treated for laughs in a series of 'joining up' comedies such as *Old Mother Riley Joins Up* (1939), *Laugh It Off* (1940) with Tommy Trinder, and *Somewhere in Camp* and *Somewhere on Leave* (both 1942) with Frank Randle. These films made light of the experience of conscription but did little to alter stereotypes about class and rank.

The reception of *The Next of Kin* (1942) suggests that the public held different attitudes towards officers and other ranks in the Army. Made at Ealing for the War Office by Thorold Dickinson, then in the AKS, this was intended originally as a military training film but was also released in the cinemas.[18] A dramatisation of the danger of careless talk, it showed how small pieces of information were leaked by the indiscretion of assorted servicemen and picked up by the German intelligence service. Representatives of all ranks are shown to be guilty of careless talk: soldiers talk too freely in pubs and confide the battalion's movements to their girlfriends, while an RAF officer loses a briefcase containing aerial photographs. The Germans piece together all the clues and deduce, correctly, that the British are planning a raid on submarine pens on the French coast. The raid goes ahead and succeeds in destroying the docks, but the British suffer very heavy casualties because the Germans are waiting for them.

The film was a critical success and evidently made a great impact on the people who saw it. Mass-Observation made a snap survey of audience reaction in London in May 1942 and found that it 'had an overwhelmingly good reception', with some 80 per cent of the sample questioned saying that they liked it. Significantly, when asked about how the film made them feel about the way officers and men behaved, people were more critical of the officers than the ordinary men. Audiences were 'inclined to make excuses for the "tommy", to feel sorry for him, and to treat him as if he were not quite responsible for his actions', but on the other hand 'it seems that the film has to some extent undermined the prestige in which officers are usually held'.[19] Although the War Office had approved it, it was reported in the trade press that the MOI 'are averse to its release in America' because 'they consider it bad propaganda – it doesn't show our Armed Forces in the best possible light'.[20] A print was sent to David O. Selznick, who did not think that it would go down well in America. 'Release in this country of the film in anything like the present version would be a dreadful error from the standpoint of British–American relations,' he told Sidney Bernstein. 'All the English officers are portrayed as stupid, careless and derelict ... [It is] calculated to increase the fears of Americans and mothers especially, that the British are simply muddling along, and that their sons will die because of British incompetence.'[21] In the event, the film was shown in a heavily cut version in America.

Ealing's *Nine Men* (1943), directed by Harry Watt, focused on the fighting capabilities of the ordinary British soldier. The most documentary-like of all Ealing's war narratives, it was stark and spare to the point of austerity. It was Watt's first film for the studio after leaving the Crown Film Unit, and, like *The Next of Kin*, it apparently started as an idea for a training film, written by Gerald Kersh.[22] It told a fictional story of a British patrol which is cut off in the Libyan desert and takes refuge in a small stone hut, defending it against a much larger detachment of Italian troops until relief arrives. It was made cheaply, with Margam Sands in North Wales standing in convincingly for the desert dunes of Libya. Like the Crown documentaries the narrative is economical (the film is barely seventy minutes long) and the characterisations are believable. In propaganda terms, what was most significant about the film was that it showed the Army from the point of view of ordinary soldiers and NCOs; the only officer with the party is killed early on, after which authority is exercised by a tough Scot, Sergeant Watson (Jack Lambert). There are no blood-or-glory false heroics, the soldiers are shown as just doing their job, while the climax gives a realistic and quite brutal impression of close fighting with bayonets. As a tribute to the ordinary British soldier it is just as effective in its simple matter-of-fact way as the more ambitious *The Way Ahead*. 'This film, from the director of *Target for Tonight*, marks yet a further stage in the influence of documentary on the feature film,' wrote Ernest Lindgren in the *Monthly Film Bulletin*. 'The result comes as near to a native style of British film-making as anything which has yet been seen ... One feels that justice has been done in a film to all those qualities in the British character in wartime of which we are most proud.'[23]

The British character in wartime was also the theme of a film which otherwise was the opposite of *Nine Men* in scale and size. Powell and Pressburger's *The Life and Death of Colonel Blimp* (1943) was a lavish Technicolor epic, two-and-a-half hours long and spread over a broad canvas covering a period of forty years of British history. Its subject was the career of an officer in the British Army from the Boer War to the Second World War. It illustrated as well the contrast between the old generation of career officers and the new men who had risen through the ranks during the war. The film was made at a time when there was a considerable body of opinion, both at home and abroad, that the British Army was riddled with 'Blimpery', an old-fashioned and reactionary outlook which resisted change and new ways of doing things (the name came from the character of 'Colonel Blimp' created by cartoonist David Low). Critics attacked the continued existence of a military hierarchy that was class-ridden and backward-looking. 'The higher commanders, drawn from the aristocracy, could never prepare for modern war, because to do so they would have to admit that the world was changing,' George Orwell remarked.[24] The attack on 'Blimpery' was taken up in Parliament by the Labour MP F. W. Pethick-Lawrence, who in February 1942 declared that 'if the Government are to carry the country with them in their war effort, they must set about abolishing "Blimpery" in all fields of life'.[25] In particular, he considered that 'Blimpery' was still rife in the Army, an accusation that was a sore point for the newly-appointed Secretary of State for War, Sir James Grigg. It is against this background of publicly-expressed criticism that Grigg's own opposition to *The Life and Death of Colonel Blimp* must be seen. The film was never likely to appeal to the War Office, and indeed Grigg was of the opinion that it would give a wholly negative impression of the British Army:

> The War Office have refused to give their support to the film in any way on the ground that it would give the Blimp conception of the Army officer a new lease of life at a time when it is already dying from inanition. Whatever the film makes of the spirit of the young soldier of today, the fact remains that it focuses attention on an imaginary type of Army officer which has become an object of ridicule to the general public.[26]

In the event, Grigg withdrew his objections after the finished film had been seen by representatives of the War Office and the MOI, but its controversial subject matter had by then ensured the film much advance publicity. 'Above all, *The Life and Death of Colonel Blimp* dares to be provocative – it is perhaps the first such film of the war – in its handling of the complex British character and its attitudes towards war,' the trade press declared. 'The film's vital theme that we must forget chivalry and sportsmanship to fight the enemy successfully and its dedication to the new aggressive spirit of the Allied Armies is a challenge to those among the democratic peoples who are only just awakening to the meaning of total war.'[27]

The Life and Death of Colonel Blimp is one of the most highly complex of all wartime films. It combines elements of the war narrative, the historical biopic and the romantic drama into a rich Technicolor tapestry of quite remarkable virtuosity. Like *In Which We Serve* it provides a narrative space for both the public and the personal through the use of a lengthy flashback structure which chronicles the career of its 'Blimp' figure, Major-General Clive Wynn-Candy, VC (Roger Livesey), against the background of real events. A framing narrative set in the present (1943) features a clash between Candy and Lieutenant 'Spud' Wilson (James McKechnie), a young officer who has risen through the ranks. Wilson upsets an exercise with the Home Guard, commanded by Candy, by moving before 'war' is supposed to begin, an act which Candy is unable to comprehend ('But war starts at midnight!' he protests, continually, in vain). The clash between Candy and Wilson encapsulates the main theme of the film: the difference between age and youth, between past and present, between the old generation of career officers and the new young men who have risen through the ranks on merit. The film then dissolves into an extended flashback of Candy's life and career over a period of forty years, showing him transform gradually from an impetuous young hot-head to an old-fashioned fuddy-duddy who is out of touch with the reality of modern warfare. Candy is characterised as a sympathetic figure, an honourable man who has become a relic of the past, rather than as the dangerous reactionary lunatic of Low's cartoons. He is a sportsman and a gentle-man who abides by a code of 'clean fighting, honest soldiering' and who would rather fight honourably and lose than win by resorting to dirty and vicious methods. His sentimental attachment to the past is illustrated through his continuing love for the same woman (personified by Deborah Kerr, who plays three different roles) and through his friendship with a German officer (Anton Walbrook) which survives the vicissitudes of two world wars. The film does not condemn Candy for his old-fashioned views, but rather suggests that, although they are admirable in themselves, they are inappropriate to fighting a total war against a ruthless enemy which has no such values or gentlemanly codes. It makes perfectly clear that Candy and his generation are no longer representative of the British Army – they have all been pensioned off into the Home Guard – but at the same time it is a nostalgic and beautifully elegiac film which mourns the passing of a more elegant and graceful world.

Opinion was divided over whether or not *Colonel Blimp* was good propaganda for the British Army. One of the critics who liked the film and its central character was A. J. Cummings of the *News Chronicle*: 'For my part I fell in love with Blimp – a witty and quite sensible soldier, who would lose a war with dignity and might win it with a little luck.'[28] But this view was not shared by the *Daily Mail*. 'To depict British officers as stupid, complacent, self-satisfied and ridiculous may be legitimate comedy in peace-times, but it is disastrously bad propaganda in times of war,' it declared. 'In such times as these, when the respect and confidence of other countries are of vital importance to us, we cannot afford to put out a burlesque figure like this Colonel Blimp to go around the world as a personification of those British officers who gave and are still giving such good service to their country.'[29] The film was popular with cinema-goers, however, and became the second most successful British film of 1943 (after *In Which We Serve*).

It was in the wake of the *Colonel Blimp* controversy that the MOI prompted the production of a feature film which would give the kind of picture of the Army which the government wanted to project to audiences at home and abroad. On 9 October 1942, barely a month after Grigg's memorandum expressing his hostility to *Colonel Blimp*, Brendan Bracken asked Noël Coward to undertake such a film. 'I hope you will consider very carefully my suggestion that you should make a film about the Army,' he wrote. 'I have never seen a really good film about the Army, and I am sure you could make one which would be as rousing a success as *In Which We Serve*.'[30] Coward declined on the grounds that he did not have the same affinity for the Army which he did for the Navy, but the project was taken up by Two Cities, which had produced Coward's naval epic. 'We understand that a feature film, which would be of real entertainment value but treated very carefully and with great sincerity, would be welcome as helping Army "morale" by showing all that the nation owes to the British Army and giving it a rightful place in the minds of the English-speaking peoples,' Filippo Del Giudice wrote to Jack Beddington. He added that Paul Kimberley of the DAK had 'expressed to me his wish to have a film produced by our Company for the Army on a parallel with *In Which We Serve*.'[31] The fact that both the MOI and the War Office offered their fulsome support to this project at this particular moment, so shortly after the furore which *Blimp* had caused in official circles, suggests that the film which eventually became *The Way Ahead* (1944) was seen partly as a response to the Powell–Pressburger film in order to set the record straight about the Army. The War Office released Captain Carol Reed to direct the film, and Lieutenant Eric Ambler and Private Peter Ustinov to write it. All three men had already been involved in making a training film for the AKS entitled *The New Lot* (1943), which was about the induction and training of conscripted men, and it was decided to use this as the model for *The Way Ahead*.[32] But while *The New Lot* had focused solely on conscripted men during their period of basic training, *The Way Ahead* would include officers as well as men and would go on to show the new recruits in action. Major David Niven of the Rifle Brigade, who had temporarily abandoned his Hollywood career to rejoin the Army, was brought in to play the role of the officer and provide a star name for the box-office. The studio interiors were filmed at Denham in the summer of 1943, location work was undertaken in North Africa during the winter of 1943–44, and the film was finished by the summer of 1944.[33]

'Right through our national life,' Orwell remarked, 'we have got to fight against privilege, against the notion that a half-witted public-schoolboy is better for command than an intelligent mechanic.'[34] Lieutenant Jim Perry, David Niven's character in *The Way Ahead*, was a garage mechanic in peacetime who joined the Territorial Army and rose through the ranks when the war came, serving as a sergeant in France in 1940 before being commissioned in the Duke of Glendon's Light Infantry. The film shows how Perry and Sergeant Fletcher (William Hartnell), a tough regular, train a group of new recruits into a fighting team. It starts with an encyclopaedia definition of an army as 'A considerable body of men, armed, organised and disciplined, to

act together for purposes of warfare'. Its main theme is the transformation of civilians into soldiers, and to this end it adopts the familiar
narrative strategy of bringing together a diverse group of individuals
and showing the process by which their personal grudges and complaints are subsumed by the development of team spirit. The men are
reluctant conscripts drawn from all walks of civilian life, while the
Army is a social melting pot in which class differences are levelled.
The men dislike the rigours of training and let themselves down on an
exercise, after which they are given a dressing-down by Perry who
lectures them on the proud history of their regiment. The men begin
to feel a sense of pride, and in the end fulfil Perry's and Fletcher's
view that they will make good soldiers. The value of their training is
amply demonstrated when they are sent to North Africa and they
work efficiently and courageously as a team, first when their troopship
is torpedoed, then in action against the Germans.

The film negotiates the relationship between officers and men in
the new, modern British Army. There are no 'Blimps': Perry has risen
through the ranks and received his commission on merit, and he is
shown to be a fair-minded and humane officer who wins the confidence
and respect of his men without undermining his own authority. The
welding together of diverse characters into a professional team, though
without losing their individuality, exemplifies the sense of unity and
democratic consensus which official propaganda did so much to encourage. Unlike *Colonel Blimp*, which set up an opposition between
military tradition and the new generation, *The Way Ahead* fuses together
tradition and modernity: the regiment to which the men belong has
battle honours going back to the Napoleonic Wars, but its modern
incarnation is part of the citizens' army which has been created through
conscription during the Second World War. Even the old Chelsea
Pensioners, who mourn the fact that the 'Dogs' (as the regiment is
colloquially known) are no longer what they used to be, later read
about their successors with pride.

There was evidently great official satisfaction with the film when it
was completed. 'It is the only picture which I have seen which gives
a true picture of the Army and which keeps the social values right,'
remarked Arthur Calder Marshall of the Films Division.[35] And Ronald
Tritton of the War Office told Carol Reed that '*The Way Ahead* was, I
think, the most effective piece of visual publicity the Army has ever
had – quite apart from its merits as a great film'.[36] It was very well

received by the critics, who predictably admired its realistic style and believable characterisations, but it was not particularly successful at the box-office. Released in mid-1944, it came at a time when the public's taste for war films was on the wane. It was also to some extent overtaken by events and came too late to have the fullest propaganda effect. Its West End release coincided with D-Day, and it was not seen in America until near the end of the war. The need to persuade the British people that conscription was necessary, and the need for showing an image of the modern British Army to the rest of the world, were no longer as pressing as they would have been a year or two earlier.

IV

The last of the three armed services, the Royal Air Force, was the subject of fewer war narratives than either the Army or the Royal Navy. The RAF, of course, had been the subject of Korda's *The Lion Has Wings*, while Bomber Command in particular had been the focus of a more rigorously documentary treatment in Crown's *Target for Tonight*. But while aerial dramas proliferated from Hollywood during the war, there were relatively few from the British studios. The three main feature films involving the RAF were *Dangerous Moonlight*, *The First of the Few* and *The Way to the Stars*, and all were successful with audiences and critics.

Dangerous Moonlight (1941), directed by Brian Desmond Hurst, was produced by RKO British Productions. It was very much a war drama of the early period, comparable to *Convoy* and *Ships With Wings* in that it combined romantic melodrama with a topical war background. Anton Walbrook played a Polish composer and concert pianist who escapes from Warsaw in 1939, settles for a while in America and then returns across the Atlantic to join the RAF during the Battle of Britain. It is a highly romanticised film, now best remembered for its theme, the hauntingly beautiful 'Warsaw Concerto' by Richard Addinsell. The narrative focuses on the conflict between love and duty, between personal desire and patriotism, as the hero leaves his wife (Sally Gray) in order to return and serve his country. Although it includes actuality film of aerial combat, the main focus of the film is on personal relationships rather than documentary reportage. Perhaps surprisingly, *Dangerous Moonlight* appealed to Roger Manvell, who liked the musical

motif which ran throughout: 'The film's emotive force as propaganda
was deepened by the constant resort to music, the rich bravura combination of art and warfare playing on the audience's dual response to
the heroism and the culture of Poland.'[37] It was also successful at the
box-office, and the fact that a romantic and melodramatic film like
Dangerous Moonlight should have been as successful with audiences as
its near contemporary, *Target for Tonight*, once again suggests that realism
and emotional restraint were not necessarily the only criteria of good
propaganda.

Leslie Howard's *The First of the Few* (1942) also combined a personal
storyline with a background of real events, though it did so in a
manner which was closer to the documentary style. It was a biopic of
R. J. Mitchell, the designer of the Spitfire, played with typical sensitivity
by Howard himself. The film adopts the flashback structure which was
becoming familiar in mid-war narratives (and which, indeed, had also
been used in *Dangerous Moonlight*). It begins on 15 September 1940, the
height of the Battle of Britain, with the RAF and the *Luftwaffe* locked
in combat in the skies. Wing-Commander Geoffrey Crisp (David Niven)
then tells his pilots the 'true' story of the Spitfire. In flashback the
film shows how Mitchell designed the Spitfire originally as a racing
plane to compete for the Schneider Trophy (with Crisp as test pilot),
and then dramatises his struggle to have the plane adopted by the Air
Ministry. Mitchell is characterised as a patriotic visionary who battles
against government bureaucracy and commercial pressure to produce
the plane, even though he knows that his health is deteriorating from
over-work and exhaustion. He dies after learning that the Air Ministry
has accepted the Spitfire. The film then switches back to 1940 as Crisp
leads his squadron against the Germans. After a dogfight, Crisp opens
his cockpit hood, looks to the sky and says, 'They can't take the Spitfire,
Mitch, they can't take 'em!' *The First of the Few* combines its personal
and public concerns in that Mitchell's struggle and selflessness in
designing the plane is at one with the national interest: as the ending
makes clear, it is his plane which is held to be Britain's salvation in
1940. It was admired by the critics and was the most successful British
film of 1942, second overall only to *Mrs Miniver*.

The definitive wartime film of the RAF, however, was the Two
Cities production *The Way to the Stars* (1945), directed by Anthony
Asquith and produced by Anatole de Grunwald. The only major feature
to examine the relations between RAF officers and men in any depth,

this film is often seen as the third part of a loose trilogy of service films also consisting of *In Which We Serve* for the Navy and *The Way Ahead* for the Army. The similarities between the three films are instructive, but there are also important points of difference, particularly in the case of *The Way to the Stars*. It is emotionally the most moving of the three, and in a sense is also the most theatrical (not altogether surprising given that it was written by playwright Terence Rattigan). And whereas the other two films both include action sequences, *The Way to the Stars* eschews combat scenes and focuses instead on the emotional impact of war as it affects the lives of the personnel of Halfpenny Field, an airfield in south-eastern England. Once again the events in the narrative take place in the past: the film opens with a celebrated tracking shot around a deserted airfield and then looks back to the events of the war. Jeffrey Richards has suggested that *The Way to the Stars* was 'not only the last war film of the war but also the first war film of the peace'.[38] Made at the very end of the war, and already looking on the war in retrospect, it is indeed a film which is rich in historical resonance. The agony of loss, which is more acute in this film than in any other wartime feature, is made especially poignant by the fact that the war was all but over by the time it was released.

From the opening shot the film switches back to 1940 when Halfpenny Field was a base for British bombers and Peter Penrose (John Mills) arrives straight out of flying school. The commanding officer (Trevor Howard) is killed and Peter's room-mate David Archdale (Michael Redgrave) takes over the squadron. The film switches to 1942, when Archdale too is killed over Germany and Peter has to break the news to his widow 'Toddy' (Rosamund John). When the Americans arrive in Britain the field is taken over by the US Army Air Force. Toddy strikes up a platonic friendship with Johnny Hollis (Douglass Montgomery), one of the American pilots. In 1944, Johnny is killed while attempting a crash-landing with his undercarriage damaged and a bomb stuck on board his plane. The film has two main themes: the adjustments and sacrifices which people have to make during wartime (both servicemen and civilians), and the nature of the Anglo-American relationship. The British and Americans, who at first do not understand one another, come closer together as the war goes on.

The critics again admired *The Way to the Stars* for its realism and sincerity. 'No other film has so subtly and truthfully portrayed the life of the airman in war, its problems, its hazards, its exaggerated casualness towards death, its courage, its humour, its comradeship,' wrote Ernest Lindgren in the *Monthly Film Bulletin*.[39] It was also popular with cinema-goers at a time when the war narrative as such had fallen from favour. Its success seems to have been because it was not a combat film but rather a character study, an elegy for the suffering and losses endured during the war. In this respect, it made a moving and appropriate conclusion to the British cinema's wartime representation of officers and men.

9

Women and War

As this war gradually moves towards its fourth year, more and more does it become, on the Home Front, a war of women. At first, women played the more negative role of keeping the home going, and carrying most of the small worries. Now, every available female body is required in a war factory or uniform. *Tom Harrisson*[1]

I

The conscription of British women during the Second World War posed a thorny problem for the propagandists. On the one hand it was necessary to make women themselves accept the policy of female conscription and to impress upon them that, no matter what job they were doing, they were playing an important part in the national war effort. On the other hand there was the question of having to reassure men that women could perform their new wartime roles perfectly adequately. Propaganda about the role of British women at war was therefore directed at both women and men. As with other aspects of propaganda policy, however, it took the government a while to decide exactly where it stood on the subject of women at war. The early days of the war were characterised by a confused attitude towards the representation of women in propaganda – a confusion which manifested itself in the images of women presented through films and other media. This was partly due to the fact that female conscription had not yet been introduced, and partly due to the legacy of the First World War where the woman's role had often been portrayed as passive and domestic, to look after the home and the family while their menfolk were away fighting. Images of domesticated femininity were also not uncommon during the Second World War, best exemplified by the dutiful wives of *In Which We Serve*. However, the more progressive voices among British women were soon calling for a more rigorous and defined policy from the government as to what their role in wartime was supposed to be. Edith Manvell, for example, admired the Soviet Film Agency's *100 Million Women* (1942), which showed Russian women fighting in the Red Army and working on the land, but lamented that in Britain the government had not addressed the subject of women at war as directly:

> The working-class women in this country are just as efficient and tough, but they are handicapped by two things – on the one hand there are the prejudices of the men who have never employed woman labour, and the men who are unwilling to teach them their own skilled work; and on the other hand there is the failure of the Government to supply that kind of propaganda which makes people believe in the urgency of their job. People are not yet quite sure whether they are working for a victory that will take us back to 1939, or whether victory will bring an opportunity for righting the social and economic evils of the past. This is the problem that makes so much of our propaganda ineffectual.[2]

Thus, the issue of women at war was linked to the question of social and economic progress, a theme that would be explored in the two key feature films about British women during wartime, *Millions Like Us* and *The Gentle Sex*, both released in 1943. Before these films, both made with the close co-operation of the MOI, the wartime work and responsibilities of British women had been presented mainly through short documentaries.

II

Until female conscription was introduced at the end of 1941, the government's attitude towards the wartime role of women was ill-defined. The MOI, for its part, at first had no propaganda policy aimed specifically at women. The official attitude towards the subject of women at war was outlined by Sir Kenneth Clark in a Policy Committee Paper of January 1941:

> The Ministry throughout has been conscious of the important part played by women in maintaining the spirit and resolution of the country. In May, an emergency Committee, formed under the Chairmanship of Mr Harold Nicolson, with the duty of maintaining public feeling, considered the lonely woman as of special importance as the weakest link in the chain. Advice was sought from Lady Reading and Dame Rachel Crowdy. Both emphasised the fact that it would be a mistake to address women directly, but that in all Home propaganda put out by the Ministry the woman's point of view should be kept in mind.[3]

The paper is indicative of the confused nature of the MOI's thinking early in the war. It places reliance upon the views of 'experts' who appear to have been consulted in the most *ad hoc* fashion (Lady Reading was founder of the Women's Royal Voluntary Service, Dame Rachel Crowdy had been Principal Commandant of the Volunteer Ambulance Drivers in France during the First World War and was now a Regions' Adviser to the MOI). The assumption that 'the lonely woman' was 'the weakest link in the chain' seems somewhat patronising and sexist. The paper is also contradictory in that it apparently accepts the experts' view that it would be a 'mistake to address women directly', but then it goes on to enumerate a number of BBC programmes and short films 'which are directed mainly and in most cases exclusively to women'.[4]

There was, however, no consistency in the official propaganda films which were directed mainly or exclusively at women. The five-minute film *Miss Grant Goes to the Door* was a dramatised studio narrative of women being placed in a war situation, but it was criticised for focusing on middle-class and relatively well-to-do characters. Another five-minute film, *A Call to Arms*, told the story of two girls (Jean Gillie and Rene Ray) who volunteer to work in a munitions factory, showing them working so much overtime that one of them collapses from exhaustion. The writer Rodney Ackland testified that although the documentarists disliked the film, it was nevertheless effective in stimulating recruitment:

> All the documentary boys who were working for the MOI derided our munitions-propaganda effort as melodramatic and unreal, which, indeed, it was. But the effect of the picture on the younger

generation of feminine cinema-goers when it was shown – in every Odeon throughout the land – was exactly what Brian [Desmond Hurst] and I had intended and the MOI had hoped for. In point of fact, results exceeded expectation: Labour Exchanges were besieged by young women demanding to be sent to munitions factories.[5]

Even allowing for some exaggeration on Ackland's part, however, this was not the case everywhere. *Documentary News Letter* even reported that 'we hear "another million bullets" from the film *A Call to Arms* has become a term of derision in Glasgow'.[6] Thus it was that opinion about the effect of the film on audiences was divided between the documentarists and the commercial film-makers. Later films about women factory workers would focus on teamwork among women rather than on heroic individual efforts.

Other official films in the early period of the war were more concerned with showing women in their traditional roles as wives and mothers rather than working in factories. Ironically, perhaps, the documentaries which simply showed women in their domestic roles were better received by the critics than those such as *A Call to Arms* which showed them volunteering for war work. A good example was *They Also Serve* (Realist Film Unit, 1940), which was the last film directed by Ruby Grierson before she died escorting evacuee children to Canada on the SS *City of Benares*. The theme of the film was summed up by the opening dedication: 'To the housewives of Britain – every day they are helping to win.' The film centres on a tireless housewife who keeps the home going for her husband and daughter (both shift workers) and who helps out a neighbour when her husband gets leave at short notice. Its realistic and sympathetic picture of an ordinary housewife was the obverse of the intrepid factory girls of *A Call to Arms*. *Documentary News Letter* made an instructive comparison between the two films:

> *A Call to Arms* is frankly theatrical; chorus girls become munition workers, females collapse after twelve-hour shifts, and the climax represents women working what appears to be a sixteen-hour shift in order to meet an urgent order for bullets. Here the melodramatic values must be presumed to be more important than the actual factory facts; but it is difficult to see how one can tell whether the normal audience reaction would be *mépris* at the conditions depicted, or a desire to join the munition workers and

thus ease the shift into more efficient hours. *They Also Serve*, on the other hand, takes the simple story of an ordinary housewife, and makes it dramatic by focusing our attention on the ordinary human kindliness which may be found daily in the millions of semi-detached houses in our cities. Here the film stands or falls purely by whether the audience recognises itself, or its relations, with a humorous and warm delight.[7]

The difference in style between the studio narratives and the documentaries which was detected by critics in relation to other aspects of short film propaganda, therefore, was also evident in films which centred on women at war. The case of *They Also Serve* also illustrates that such films were being aimed specifically at female audiences. Clark explained:

This film was designed for general distribution. It has hitherto been shown in the non-theatrical programme to Women's Unions, etc., where it is very popular. It was made just before the blitz, and for this reason we advised that it might be thought out of date by the general public. e.g. people do not go to shelters, etc. It is therefore being re-made for general distribution, showing blitz conditions, e.g. families sleeping in a shelter, etc.[8]

Although in the event the revised version does not appear to have been made, this does show that the MOI was alive to the need for propaganda aimed at women to be as up-to-date and accurate as possible. It also illustrates that the policy of showing films directly to women through channels such as the Women's Institutes had been adopted fairly early in the war.

Female conscription was not introduced until the end of 1941, and then only reluctantly. The National Service (No 2) Act of December 1941 applied to all single women between nineteen and thirty and enabled them to be conscripted into either the women's auxiliary services or full-time work in essential industries. Furthermore, the Employment of Women Order of February 1942 gave the government the power to direct the movement of female workers between the ages of eighteen and forty. Numerous official films made following the introduction of these measures were intended to illustrate the work which women found themselves doing and to emphasise its importance to the war effort. In general, official films usually concentrated on women in non-military occupations, especially industry, where recruitment was more difficult. There were many problems involved with inducting women into the labour market, particularly as even those women who had worked were unlikely to be experienced in the manufacturing and operating skills required for work in factories.

The role of women in industry was the subject of several official shorts made during 1942–43. *Night Shift* (Paul Rotha Productions, 1942), a non-theatrical two-reeler directed by Jack Chambers from a script by Arthur Calder-Marshall, was the most effective illustration of the working conditions for women in factories. Unlike the melodramatic and personal narrative of *A Call to Arms, Night Shift* opted for a rigorously documentary treatment of a typical ten-hour shift in an ordnance factory in Newport. The routine of work and meal breaks is illustrated well, and the emphasis is on teamwork rather than individual effort. Although one girl is shown to be working flat-out on a machine tool ('Blondie's been on that six months, and she's as good as any man at her job,' the female commentator remarks), it is also pointed out that the women in that work group pool their earnings at the end of the week. There are a few snatches of scripted dialogue, but overall the film gives an authentic picture of factory work. The tensions between men and women on the factory floor, which in real life could become quite acute, are reduced to the level of good-natured banter. When a male co-worker teases one of the women about hammering a gun ('Mind it doesn't go off'), she replies, 'I'd rather be firing 'em than making 'em any day'. The commentator then says: 'But while we can't be firing them, we're putting everything we've got into making them for the men who can.' The women are shown to be a vital part of the war machinery, but the film does not address the resentment which many women felt at being conscripted into factory labour, a problem that was later foregrounded in *Millions Like Us*.

It would seem that female conscription was an uncomfortable issue for official films, given the degree to which even after 1941 they managed to side-step the question. The emphasis continued to be on voluntary war work rather than conscription. *WVS* (Verity, 1942), directed by Louise Birt, was a non-theatrical two-reeler focusing on the work of the Women's Voluntary Service. Edith Manvell was critical of the film: 'It is not enough to be shown well-meaning, kindly and industrious women; we want to feel something of the faith which inspires them and the dynamic will to put every ounce of effort into freeing this country from the threat of defeat and slavery.'9 The five-minute film *Jane Brown Changes Her Job* (Verity, 1942) featured the actress Anne Firth as a secretary who responds to an appeal in a newspaper to produce more aeroplanes. Although her call-up is not due for several months, she volunteers for factory work and retrains as a riveter. Thus the issue of conscription and directed labour is side-stepped. Another highly significant aspect of the film is that Jane Brown is characterised as young, single and middle-class, and the film served an important purpose in appealing to such women to consider a blue-collar occupation. In general, it was thought that the women's auxiliary services were a more fitting and attractive occupation for middle-class women than factory work. Indeed, the perception that the women's services included more middle-class recruits was even reinforced by official films. The AFPU's *ATS* (1941) gave a brief picture of some of the work done by women in the Auxiliary Territorial Service. The anonymous reviewer of *Documentary News Letter* expressed doubts about the film's content and intended audience:

> The film seems to be addressed mainly to middle-class girls, and will, I am sure, be very successful in recruiting them, but it raises quite a number of other thoughts as well. I don't think it, or the ATS for that matter, will appeal to working-class girls much. The accents, in the first place, are all very ladylike, some of them indeed almost unbearable. And then there's the question of the uniform. No one can hope to persuade me that it suits more than a very small percentage of women: the rest look like rather terrifying members of another species. Of course, this, whether designedly or not I am not prepared to say, is an added attraction to middle-class women who, in general, are prone to seek satisfaction for their frustrations in various forms of exhibitionism.[10]

The reviewer's highly opinionated views notwithstanding, this sort of reaction shows that film propaganda about women at war had to negotiate class prejudices as well as sex differences.

The question of sex prejudice directed against women workers by men was addressed in a number of official shorts. The theme is always the same: men are sceptical of women's ability until they see them at work, when they realise that the women can perform their jobs as well as their male counterparts. *They Keep the Wheels Turning* (GB Screen Services, 1942) showed women mechanics working in a repair shop. 'A year ago the women would have caused a sensation, but today things are different,' observes the (male) commentator. 'Joan and Mildred, Mabel and Hilda, took over as if they were born to it. The men soon recognised them as trained and willing workers.' A similar story was told in *Land Girl* (Paul Rotha Productions, 1942), where a girl from the town goes to work on a Scottish farm. She is initially an unwelcome addition for the old farmer and his men, who doubt her ability to work and her 'towny' habits, but their prejudices are overcome when she proves to be a strong and capable labourer. In both these films there is an unspoken assumption that women's war work is a temporary expedient. Official films did not engage directly with the question of what would happen to the new female workforce when the war was over. However, this issue was broached in two important feature films of 1943, which both linked women's wartime experiences with the question of social improvement.

III

The Gentle Sex and *Millions Like Us* are interesting companion pieces in several respects. They were made at approximately the same time in the middle of the war; they both received a significant degree of official support; and they both adopted similar strategies for incorporating the important propaganda theme of women at war into the requirements of the fictional narrative. Both were also examples of the new maturity and realism in the representation of ordinary people and situations which was then being identified in British cinema, though the former was if anything slightly more glamorised in comparison to the latter. While *The Gentle Sex* focused on women in uniform by following seven recruits in the ATS, *Millions Like Us* was about women who are conscripted to work in a factory. The ATS and industry were the two largest catchments for British women during the war, and thus the most important from the viewpoint of propaganda.

The Gentle Sex can be seen in terms of the need to address the problems and resentments caused by conscripting women into the ATS. It is comparable to *The Way Ahead* in that it follows the training and service of a group of conscripts from a range of social backgrounds, the difference being that in this case they are all women. Conscription had been introduced when voluntary appeals failed to provide enough recruits. 'Large sums have been spent in appealing to women to join the ATS,' Tom Harrisson wrote in 1942. 'The response was quite inadequate to meet the need; despite every effort of modern publicity, compulsion eventually had to be introduced on this side, too.' The main problem, he suggested, was that women were put off by the drab uniformity of the ATS which gave little scope for glamour or individuality. He considered that the most effective recruiting poster for the ATS had been one of a blonde in uniform which presented an image of glamorous femininity:

> The Blonde Bombshell was far and away the most 'successful' piece of ATS propaganda. This poster showed a striking woman's head in an idealised and rather Hollywood fashion. It dealt with one of the biggest conscious and unconscious factors against joining the ATS, namely the fear of loss of individuality and of over-uniformity. For every one woman (in a random sample) who criticised the poster, fourteen liked it and disagreed with the decision to withdraw it. The poster which replaced this 'glamour girl' showed a thoroughly uniformed-looking woman marching against the background of a long line of *soldiers*, supported by the caption: You Are Wanted *Too*! However undesirable the blonde bombshell, the brunette martinet who replaced her emphasised the subsidiariness and mass-uniformity, two things which were already putting women off from joining the ATS.[11]

By mid-1942 the MOI had decided that a major feature film about the ATS would be valuable propaganda, but the film had a chequered history before it reached the screen. The MOI 'was anxious for Mr Carol Reed to direct a commercial feature picture dealing with the ATS, which has the approval and active support both of this Ministry and the War Office', but this fell through when Reed joined the Army Kinematograph Service.[12] Adrian Brunel was then assigned to direct the film, which was to be produced jointly by Derrick de Marney's company Concanen and Two Cities. After a few days' shooting at a small studio in Highbury, the film was relocated to Denham and Leslie Howard took over as director with Brunel as associate producer.[13] It seems that this change may have been due to Jack Beddington, who, according to Howard's son Ronald, 'did not want to see such a useful propaganda film permanently immobilised' and who considered that 'quite apart from its recruiting value, with Leslie's name attached to it the film would have greater appeal'.[14] Finally, when Howard became ill towards the end of the production, Maurice Elvey was brought in to complete the shooting and editing.

Feminist historian Antonia Lant considers that *The Gentle Sex* 'clearly manifests the double problem of trying to produce a new cinematic image of women appropriate to the British realist film style and of finding a workable audience address that would not only constitute the nation as unified, but also promote the recruitment of women'.[15] She identifies numerous contradictions within the film, particularly in terms of its mode of address. Its narrative focuses specifically on women, but it also appeals to 'that impossibly ungendered group, the nation'. The film emphasises the woman's point-of-view, and indeed several of the writers were women, but it was produced and directed by men. The opening sequence illustrates these contradictions: the seven women who will be the focus of the narrative are introduced at Victoria Station by a male observer-commentator (Howard himself) who is set apart in the frame, looking down from a balcony over the crowded concourse and picking them out. The scene reflects the male control over the 'look' and the director's control over *mise-en-scène* which are typical of narrative film in general. The women whom Howard picks out repres- ent the usual social mix of wartime feature films: an officer's daughter (Joyce Howard), a 'good-time girl' (Jean Gillie), a Cockney waitress (Joan Gates), a pragmatic Scot (Rosamund John), an unpleasant teacher (Barbara Waring), a sheltered only child (Joan Greenwood) and a Czech refugee (Lili Palmer). The film follows them through training camp, paying particular attention to the uniforming process, though it is careful to show that the women maintain their individuality and femin- inity despite their uniforms. The women include examples of the two types featured on recruiting posters: if Ann, the colonel's daughter, is the 'blonde bombshell', then Joan, the teacher, who for no obvious reason is unpleasant to the others, represents the 'brunette martinet'. Four of the recruits become lorry-drivers, while the others are posted to a mixed ack-ack battery. There is some romantic interest – Ann falls in love with an RAF officer who is killed – but most of the time the emphasis is on the relationships between the women themselves. If the film now seems rather patronising, it was nevertheless a sincere and well-intentioned tribute. Howard's concluding voice-over com- mentary is again indicative of the contradictions within the film in that it acknowledges the debt owed to women during the war but still adopts an old-fashioned and mildly sexist tone:

Well, there they are – the women. Our sweethearts, sisters, mothers, daughters. Let's give in at last and admit that we're really proud of you, you strange, wonderful, incalculable creatures. The world you're helping to shape is going to be a better one because you're helping to shape it. Pray silence, gentlemen, I give you a toast – the gentle sex!

For all the reservations expressed by feminist writers like Lant about the film's 'male' view of womanhood, it was very successful with wartime audiences. It came third equal in Mass-Observation's survey of favourite films in 1943, and, significantly, it was especially popular with women. One Birmingham woman remarked 'that it made even me, over age and ineligible for half a dozen reasons as I am, wish for a few minutes that I could join one of the Women's Services'.[16]

Significantly, *The Gentle Sex* also addresses, albeit in a very general way, the idea that the war has improved the status of British women. It does this through an important scene where some of the women visit the aged Mrs Sheridan (Mary Jerrold), mother of Ann's fiancé, for tea. Ann reflects on the nature of the war. 'Isn't it strange that probably for the first time in English history women are fighting side by side with the men,' she says. 'This is going to make a tremendous difference to the status of women after the war is over.' (The use of 'English' in this scene is itself curious and rather unfortunate, given that the other ATS women with Ann at the time are Maggie, the Scot, and Erna, the Czech.) However, the young women are quite surprised when they learn that their elderly hostess had served in France as an ambulance driver during the First World War and had been wounded in action. Ann apologises for her assumption that her generation were the first women to achieve something worthwhile. But the old lady tells her that she is right to believe that this time the war will bring about improvements for women: 'Oh my dear, you must believe in all those things with all your heart and soul … We didn't really know what we wanted, but I believe you do.' What this scene does is to raise the question of whether the place of women in society will be fundamentally altered by the war. The implication is that British women have twice rallied to the cause in total war, but that whereas the first time had been a measure of expediency which had not resulted in any fundamental social change, this time there was a belief that their involvement would lead to greater opportunities and equality.

The link between women's wartime experiences and the post-war world was made more explicitly in *Millions Like Us*. This film has endured more successfully in the critical historiography of British cinema than *The Gentle Sex* because it is regarded as being more authentic. Even in uniform the actresses of *The Gentle Sex* were more glamorous than the typical ATS recruits, but *Millions Like Us* by contrast is deliberately unglamorous to the point of austerity. This was probably due in large degree to the origin of the film, which was intended in the first place as a documentary about the home front. Frank Launder and Sidney Gilliat, script-writers from the commercial side of the industry, were approached by the MOI to write a script for a film covering the entire civilian war effort. Launder recalled:

> With this object we toured the country, visiting docks, farms and coastal areas, and went to war factories and works all over Britain. We came to the conclusion that the best way to attract a wide public to a subject of this nature, which was what the Ministry wanted, was to cloak it in a simple fictional story.[17]

It was their decision to focus on the story of women working in a factory. The project had now evolved from a pure documentary to a fictional feature film. According to Gilliat:

> We were greatly impressed with the fate – if you like to call it that – of the conscripted woman, the mobile woman. And that's what we would have liked to call the thing if it hadn't been such a silly title! The MOI said they greatly liked the script, but it wasn't the extensive documentary they'd been expecting. However, they strongly recommended Gainsborough to make it with their blessing and co-operation.[18]

The film was therefore made as a commercial venture but with a great deal of official support. It was a first-rate example of how the MOI co-operated with the film industry over the production of a commercial feature with a propaganda message. The ministry, for example, arranged for location shooting to be undertaken in the giant Castle Bromwich aircraft factory near Birmingham, which accounts for much of the documentary-style authenticity of the film.

The feminist critics Christine Gledhill and Gillian Swanson write that *Millions Like Us* 'self-consciously addresses the nation through wartime changes in the role of women, offering "a film covering the whole British war effort at home" through what struck Launder and Gilliat as in some way paradigmatic of wartime experiences, the "mobile woman".[19] In particular, it addresses the anxieties which many women felt about being conscripted for factory labour. Industry was probably the least attractive option for women called up for National Service. Tom Harrisson observed that conscription alone did not solve the problem, but that productivity would be greater if women could be made to feel more enthusiastic about their work. 'Reluctant or apathetic or bored girls working in factories do *produce*,' he wrote, 'but it is not enough that they should produce something – they need to produce (in the interests of the war) *everything they possibly can*.'[20]

The main propaganda theme of *Millions Like Us* is to reassure women about the nature of factory labour, to show them that it is just as vital to the war effort as the services. It does this by personalising the general experience of 'millions like you' into the story of Celia Crowson (Patricia Roc), an ordinary young woman who is sent to work in an aircraft factory. Celia, who is characterised as shy and plain in comparison to her elder sister Phyllis (Joy Shelton), who joins the ATS, is horrified at the idea of working in a factory. When she is called for her interview at the Ministry of Labour and National Service, she sees a poster for the WAAFs on the wall and fantasises about joining one of the women's services. The imagery in the brief 'dream' scenes which follow reinforces the idea that the services represent glamour and romance. Celia is seen in various women's services (the WAAFs, the WRENs, the ATS, as a land girl and as a nurse) where the situations parody the conventions of romance fiction, with Celia always attracting a male suitor, usually an officer. But she is then brought down to earth through her interview with the civil servant Miss Wells (Beatrice Varley) in a drab office. Celia is told that there are no vacancies in the women's services except for cooks and typists. Miss Wells suggests industry, to which Celia replies hysterically that she does not want to work in a factory. 'There's nothing to be afraid of in a factory,' Miss Wells tells her. 'Mr Bevin needs another million women, and I don't think we should disappoint him at a time like this. The men at the front need tanks, guns and planes. You can help your country just as much in an overall as you can in uniform these days.' This is the film's propaganda message, skilfully incorporated into a fictional narrative and presented in personal terms that women audiences would be able to relate to. Celia's fantasy of glamorised, uniformed femininity is rejected in favour of the drab reality of factory overalls. She is sent to live in a government hostel and, with a group of other women, she passes through training school and starts work making aircraft parts. The importance of factory labour (and the fact that it is dirty work) is emphasised again when the new intake are welcomed by the foreman, Charlie Forbes (Eric Portman). 'Now you'd better understand there's not much glamour in a machine shop', he tells them bluntly. 'You'll be working with small component parts you'll never hear of again. But you'll be indispensable, remember that.' Celia soon takes to her new work and finds that the factory does not hold the terrors which she had feared. She even finds romance with a young air-gunner (Gordon Jackson), but he is killed shortly after they get married. Like *The Gentle Sex*, *Millions Like Us* focuses mainly on relations between women, with the community of the factory and the hostel becoming in effect a surrogate family. It is also, once again, an example of the 'wartime wedding' in that it is a fictional narrative which draws heavily on the documentary technique. Indeed, the montage-based sequences which show the factory at work bear a strong similarity to *Night Shift*.[21]

Millions Like Us also engages with the question of social change during the war, in a much more direct way than in *The Gentle Sex*, by means of a romance between the works foreman and one of the women, Jennifer Knowles (Anne Crawford), an upper-class girl who is unaccustomed to hard work and has trouble adapting to wartime changes. There is initially antagonism between Jennifer and Charlie when he thinks she does not pull her weight, but a tentative romance gradually develops between them, until by the end of the film they are discussing marriage. The relationship between the bluff Yorkshire foreman and the West End girl symbolises class levelling and the new-found social consensus of the war years: a coming-together of north and south, working-class and upper-class. But Charlie is reluctant to commit himself to marriage, because he is unsure whether their relationship (and thus by implication the wartime consensus) will survive after the war. 'The world's roughly made up of two kinds of people – you're one sort and I'm the other,' he tells her. 'Oh, we're together now there's a war on, we need to be. But what's going to happen when it's all over? Shall we go on like this or are we going to slide back? That's what I want to know. I'm not marrying you, Jenny, till I'm sure.' Charlie therefore voices the same sort of questions about the future that had been discussed in short films such as *The*

Dawn Guard. Millions Like Us shows that the social concerns of the documentary movement had been taken up by some of the more progressive feature film-makers by the middle of the war: the 'wartime wedding' took place not only at the level of technique but also at the level of ideology.

This concern with class relations in the post-war world was, however, a secondary theme in a film whose main propaganda aim was to show the invaluable work being done in war factories by millions of British women. *The Sunday Times* described it as 'an attempt, largely successful, at giving dramatic form and intensity to the lives of the women drafted into war factories' and considered that it was 'directed with great skill and sensibility to the potentialities of the medium'.[22] It is more realistic but also more humorous than *The Gentle Sex*, and its picture of wartime deprivations, stoically endured, comes as near as any film to capturing the spirit of the British people at war. Even those comic caricatures of English gentlemen Charters and Caldicott, as ever portrayed by Basil Radford and Naunton Wayne, appear in several asides, unconnected to the main line of narrative, which show them adapting to wartime changes, even if it is only sharing their first-class train compartment with a group of evacuee children. It is incidental touches of humour such as this, alongside the very real sense of grief which is felt when Celia loses her husband, that make the film a lasting and memorable testament to the people's war. The reaction of one Mass-Observation respondent, a twenty-five-year-old bombardier, summed up how both critics and audiences felt about *Millions Like Us*: 'Presents Britain and life as it is – we must have truth and integrity in our films.'[23]

10

Friend and Foe

It is not enough to show on the screen the face of the man in the street or behind the lathe and for this man always to be a member of the same single country ... It is not sufficient to show the man in the street in Britain: *you must show the man in the street in Paris, in Prague, in Moscow, in Calcutta ...* The average Briton (and therefore, much more, the Neutral) is fed of course day by day with 'Allied' propaganda. But what does he know of the content of this word or its significance? *Jiri Weiss*[1]

I

It was not only the British war effort that was the subject of film propaganda but also the role of Britain's allies in the war against Nazism. Jiri Weiss, a Czech documentarist exiled in Britain after the German occupation, urged that the documentary coverage of Britain at war which had proved so successful should be extended to cover the Allied nations as well. It was necessary, he argued, to show that Britain was fighting not just to protect herself and to preserve the Empire, but rather to free the people of Europe who had been subjected to the Nazi yoke. He believed this would make effective propaganda both at home and abroad by showing what the war was being fought for:

The enlarging of the line of British film propaganda would certainly have a great effect not only overseas, but also in this country. It would show to the multi-national millions of the Americas that Britain stands for much more than just the British Empire, that the word 'Allies' is not just a common denominator of yesterday's politicians in Sunday dress. British documentary has stirred the world by showing the face of Britain. But why not show also the face of Poland, of Holland, of Czechoslovakia? ... Peoples of this island, of the Dominions, of the USA, would be stirred to greater efforts in the fields of industrial production and elsewhere if they saw true stories of the multitude of nations which have forgotten the enmities of yesterday, and now stand side by side. Have we not seen the British people redoubling their efforts when they were told that they were supplying the needs of our Soviet ally?[2]

Weiss's call for an Allied Film Unit to make the sort of films which he advocated was never realised, but official British documentaries did cover the war efforts of her allies. This was done mainly through short films which showed how people from the occupied countries were continuing the struggle against Nazism, often alongside British forces. Films such as *Guests of Honour* (Ealing, 1941), *Diary of a Polish Airman* (Concanen, 1942), *Free French Navy* (Spectator, 1942), *Fighting Allies* (Movietone, 1942) and *Men of Norway* (March of Time, 1942) provided documentary accounts of the role of fighting units which had escaped from the occupied countries. In addition, a cycle of feature films dramatised stories of resistance to Nazism in Occupied Europe. One of the main themes of British film propaganda was the contrast between democratic, freedom-loving peoples and the aggressive barbarism of Nazi Germany. However, propaganda about Britain's continental allies was to prove problematic. It was subject to political changes and was all too often beset by considerations of foreign policy and the alignment of the warring nations. The entry of the Soviet Union into the war in 1941 was to be the most dramatic of several instances where propaganda had to change in the light of national policy.

II

The case of the Soviet Union represented a fundamental shift in official policy towards the representation of another country. In the period from the Nazi–Soviet Pact of August 1939 to the German invasion of

Russia in June 1941, the Soviet Union had been widely regarded in Britain as just another totalitarian dictatorship, almost on a par with Hitler's regime in Germany. But when Hitler launched 'Operation Barbarossa', the British propaganda services had to adapt almost overnight from their previous policy of staunch anti-Communism to admiration for the heroic war effort of the gallant Russian ally. Churchill had always been a fierce opponent of Communism, but he now publicly declared his solidarity with Soviet Russia in the fight against the common enemy. The MOI not only had to adapt to the change in British foreign policy, but also had to take account of the wave of genuine pro-Russian feeling which swept the country when the heroic resistance of the Russian people to the Germans became known. Perhaps the main channel through which the Russian/Soviet war effort was shown to the British public was the cinema, where Soviet propaganda films were distributed by the MOI. Feature-length documentaries such as *Our Russian Allies* (1941) and *Defeat of the Germans Near Moscow* (1942), made by the Soviet Central Newsreel Studios and shown in Britain with an English commentary, did much to bring home to the British the nature and extent of their new ally's war effort. As the decisive battles of the war in Europe were fought on the Russian Front, Britain's campaigns in North Africa looked in comparison like mere side-shows. For the MOI, however, there was a very real fear that sympathy for the Russian people might translate into admiration for the Soviet system of government.

The MOI therefore had to draw a careful line between praising the efforts of the Russian people while avoiding any possible suggestion that the government endorsed the Communist ideology. Official policy was outlined thus by H. P. Smollett, head of the newly formed Anglo-Soviet Liaison Section:

> While both Russia and Britain fully maintain their very different ideals about future forms of society and remembering clearly that they differ fundamentally over their attitude to religion, among other things, they both realise that neither can pursue their own ideals while Hitler and Germany is unbeaten. They therefore wish to pursue the joint war effort against the enemy most energetically and to let each other's populations draw as much inspiration from their Ally's effort as possible.[3]

The MOI's answer to the problem of popular support for the Soviet

Union was to channel it through official campaigns such as the 'Aid to Russia Week' and the twenty-fifth anniversary celebrations of the Red Army. Prominent members of the British establishment, such as Lord Beaverbrook, were closely involved with this tactic of 'Stealing the Thunder of the Left'.

The most wholehearted support for the Soviet Union naturally came from the left. The most unusual film to come out of this context was the unique *Our Film* (1942), a propaganda short made at the initiative of the studio workers at Denham. It was made by members of the Association of Cine-Technicians and then 'presented' to the MOI. The documentarist Ralph Bond (also a committed Communist) was one of those involved in making the film, which he described as 'the first entirely voluntary and co-operative film to be made by professional workers in this country'.[4] It would be misleading to suggest that *Our Film* was an example of Communist propaganda; rather, it was an expression of the earnest admiration which British workers felt for their Russian counterparts.

The film opens with a Russian family sitting down for a meal and being massacred by a German machine-gunner; it cuts to a British family sitting down to tea, but this time the tap on the window heralds only a neighbour who has come home early from his shift at the factory. He explains that machines are out of action due to a shortage of tools. The film then makes a plea for the British war economy to be run more on the lines of the Soviet model, with joint production committees of management and labour to sort out the problems that hinder maximum production. There is a clear implication that the Russian workers are making greater sacrifices and are suffering far more than their British counterparts in the common cause. It was a sign of the widespread admiration for the Russian war effort that even some critics who did not share the political sentiments of the left were moved by the film. 'This film wages war, using the screen as an armour-piercing bullet against the Hun,' declared Ernest Betts in the *Sunday Express*. 'This film came home with a bang and made me ask what the devil I was doing in this war ... It was Denham's reply to the efforts of the blitzed Russian workers, who put a deadly sting in their war effort and rolled back the enemy.'[5] *Our Film* was a rare example of a short propaganda film conceived outside official policy, and as such it was able to express greater admiration for the Soviet economic system than might otherwise have been possible.

The feature film industry was rather more conservative in its attitude towards the Soviet Union than the workers and documentarists who had made *Our Film*. In fact, there was only one major feature film which explored the relations between the British people and their Russian allies in any depth: Anthony Asquith's *The Demi-Paradise* (1943), which was written and produced by the Russian-born Anatole de Grunwald. It is the complete opposite of the direct, agitational style of *Our Film*, presenting a picture-postcard vision of England seen through the eyes of a visiting Russian engineer, Ivan Kutznetsoff (Laurence Olivier). Most critics have seen the film in terms of a particular construction of English national identity rather than as a serious exploration of Anglo-Russian relations, and it has even been suggested that it was intended more for American audiences.[6] According to Laurence Olivier, however, the aim of the film 'was to win the British public over to the idea of liking the Russians'.[7] Thus there is a difference between the testimony of the film-makers and the interpretation of subsequent critics as to the film's propagandist objective.

Analysing the narrative content of *The Demi-Paradise*, however, it is hard not to see it in the context of the sense of admiration for the Russian people which was widespread at the time. That is not to say that it gives a realistic picture of the man in the street in Moscow, in the way that Jiri Weiss had called for, any more than it gives an authentic picture of Britain in 1943. The film is a light comedy which conceals its propaganda beneath a coating of humour and charm. Ivan is characterised as a bemused innocent who visits the English town of 'Barchester' – an idyllic if unreal and caricatured community populated by amiable eccentrics – both before and during the war. At first he is unable to understand English customs and behaviour and finds the people aloof, but after the outbreak of war he comes to realise that underneath their reserve the British are in fact 'a grand, a great people'. Finally, when Russia is invaded in 1941, the people of Barchester welcome Ivan into the community with open arms.

The 'Englishness' of *The Demi-Paradise* is even more absurd than in *Mrs Miniver*, but rather than being the rose-tinted and backward-looking view of English society that most commentators have suggested, this can actually be seen as a deliberate propaganda device. Criticisms of the film for its sentimentalised, unrealistic depiction of England miss the point in that *The Demi-Paradise* is a fantasy, not a realist narrative. Asquith was, after all, perfectly capable of making a realistic film if he had wanted to, as his direction of *We Dive at Dawn* in the same year proved. The blatant non-realism of the film is intentional, meaning that it is able to avoid having to engage with the problematic political realities of the Anglo-Russian relationship. A more realistic treatment would surely have necessitated some discussion of the Soviet political system, which was the last thing which British propagandists wanted. It is an example, therefore, where realism was not an appropriate mode of representation for film propaganda. Critics admired the film for its charm and quiet sincerity – William Whitebait said that Olivier's performance was 'dazzling', Asquith's direction 'skilful', and alluded to its qualities of whimsical comedy in his observation that it was 'the nearest thing yet to an English René Clair'[8] – but did not, significantly, categorise it as propaganda.

III

While the character of Britain's Soviet ally posed something of a dilemma for propagandists, the representation of the enemy was also not the clear-cut matter that might at first be assumed. Film propaganda was marked by a gradual shift from a distinction between Nazis and 'good' Germans in the early years of the war to a more general equation of Germany with Nazism in the later years. This was broadly in line with the attitude of the British people towards the enemy, which hardened noticeably after the effects of bombing were felt. Surveys by the British Institute of Public Opinion found that while in September 1939 only 6 per cent of those questioned thought that the war was being fought against the German people as a whole rather than their leaders, by the time of the Blitz this had risen to 50 per cent.[9] Although the MOI was careful to distance itself from the type of atrocity propaganda which had proved effective during the First World War, it did nevertheless instigate an 'Anger Campaign' designed to arouse hatred for the enemy. The distinction between Nazis and 'good' Germans was not encouraged by the middle of the war, and in particular Vansittartism – the view expressed in Sir Robert Vansittart's *Black Record* (1941) that the Germans were basically an aggressive and barbarous race and always had been – was embraced.

The most sober and sincere of the anti-Nazi feature films of the war was the Boulting Brothers' *Pastor Hall* (1940), adapted from the play by Ernst Toller which in turn was based on the true story of

Martin Niemoller, a German priest who spoke out against the Nazis. The Boultings had planned to make the film before the war, but their attempt to do so was blocked in July 1939 by the British Board of Film Censors which was opposed to any film which referred directly to internal German affairs.[10]

Pastor Hall dramatises the conflict between Christianity and Nazism, and between the individual and the state. The pastor (played by Wilfrid Lawson) gradually comes to realise that everything which the Nazis stand for is opposed to God's word, and his denunciation of their creed from the pulpit lands him in a concentration camp. The film portrays the horrors of camp life with a brutality that is shocking for the time: the pastor is sentenced to twenty-five lashes a day for calling Hitler the 'architect of evil', and other prisoners are beaten by the SS guards just for their own amusement. Nazism is thus equated with brutality and sadism, but significantly the film makes the distinction between the Nazis and decent Germans. The pastor is helped by one of the guards whose conscience is touched, while the elderly General von Grotjahn (Sir Seymour Hicks) is characterised as a German patriot who dislikes the Nazis. At the end of the film the pastor delivers one last sermon in which he describes the Nazis as 'the enemies of God'. As he leaves the church, a squad of stormtroopers is waiting to shoot him, but the impression given by the film is that decent Germans will heed his words by rejecting the Nazis and all that they stand for.

The MOI was evidently very pleased with the film and its propaganda content. 'I believe that *Pastor Hall* is a great film showing the true nature of our present struggle. I hope it will be widely seen,' said the minister, Duff Cooper.[11] The critics admired the film as a sincere and honest attempt to show the nature of the enemy, but when it was shown in North America there was apparently some scepticism about its content, at least according to a report in *Documentary News Letter*:

> *Pastor Hall*, released in Canada and about to be released – it is said energetically – in the United States, raised another problem of propaganda. Again, the film has been admired for certain intrinsic production qualities, but it is observed that concentration camps and other European cruelties create only a sense of distance in the native mind and a feeling of 'Thank God we emigrated from Europe to a decent country' ... There is also a sneaking feeling that it is the old armless-baby-act of the last war being worked all over again.[12]

The problem for anti-Nazi films, therefore, was that, given the legacy of British atrocity propaganda from the First World War, there was a risk that descriptions of Nazi cruelty would be thought to be exaggerated in neutral America.

The theme of internal German dissent was also the basis of Anthony Asquith's *Freedom Radio* (1941), another film which made the distinction between Nazis and good Germans. It used the fictional story of an underground radio station to suggest that internal German resistance might overthrow Hitler. A Viennese doctor (Clive Brook) and an idealistic young engineer (Derek Farr) run an anti-Nazi radio station which appeals to the German people to 'rise up and make a stand for freedom'. Like other films of the early war period, it was an uneasy combination of thriller and melodrama, with a sub-plot focusing on the estrangement between the doctor and his wife (Diana Wynyard). The film ends with the doctor having been killed, but with the radio station continuing to broadcast, thus implying that there was an underground resistance to Nazism in Germany. But, like the attempts of British propagandists to undermine German morale and feed dissent within Germany, the film was not successful. Its attitude towards the enemy belonged in essence to the phoney war period, but it was released after the Blitz when public attitudes were hardening, and thus its message that there were those in Germany who opposed Hitler did not strike a chord with the British public. The idea of internal dissent – which is also alluded to in Leslie Howard's *Pimpernel Smith* – was not to feature in film propaganda after 1941.

In the middle of the war there was a cycle of feature films which told stories of resistance in occupied Europe. After it had been realised that Hitler would not be overthrown from within Germany, attention switched instead to the people of other nationalities who suffered under the Nazi yoke. At one time or another all the main occupied countries were featured in this cycle of films, which paid tribute to the courage of their people who continued the struggle against Nazism. The many exiled Allied governments in London were only too happy to lend their co-operation to film-makers ready to pay tribute to their homelands, while for the film-makers the resistance narrative provided an ideal means of combining the topical background and romance which they believed audiences wanted. There was little further attempt to differentiate between Nazis and Germans, who had now become stock villains.

The Day Will Dawn (1942), directed by Harold French, was one of the first and more interesting examples of the resistance narrative. 'Terror rules in Europe,' declares an opening commentary. 'The people are chained. Yet their souls do not submit. This film is made in the faith that those who batter down the prison gates from without will find brave allies among the prisoners within.' The film is set in Norway, and follows the adventures of a British journalist, Colin Metcalfe (Hugh Williams), before and after the German occupation. While the film is handicapped by its studio-bound sets and stereotyped characterisations, the narrative does nevertheless have several points of interest. The fictional story is set against the background of real events. There is a reference, for example, to the German propaganda film *Baptism of Fire* having been shown in Oslo ('It's the old Nazi game, terrifying your victim first and then hitting him hard') – a real propaganda event included in a fictional propaganda narrative – while the film contrives to feature the *Altmark* and Dunkirk as well. The fall of the Chamberlain government after the Norway debates is reported by journalists and the film explicitly endorses Churchill. Against this background, the story itself is rather trite, combining a thriller narrative (the British hero teams up with Norwegian patriots to find a secret U-boat base) with a romantic sub-plot (the hero inevitably falls in love with a Norwegian girl, played by Deborah Kerr). The climax is a British Commando raid, inserting some of the AFPU's actuality film of the Vaagso raid. It is evident from the critical reception of *The Day Will Dawn* that it was admired more for its tribute to the Norwegian people than for the originality of its story. *The Times* opined that it was 'a brave expression of faith and its message for the occupied countries is composed in vivid cinematic terms' but lamented that the story 'is not fitted more smoothly into the tribute the film pays to the heroism of a people who are conquered but who persist in calling their souls their own'.[13]

Resistance films proliferated in 1942–43 – *Uncensored* (1942), *Secret Mission* (1942), *The Silver Fleet* (1943), *Escape to Danger* (1943), *The Flemish Farm* (1943) – and the resistance narrative soon took on familiar contours. Secret assignments, underground meetings, the ever-present danger of capture by the Gestapo and betrayal by quislings, and lofty speeches about the inevitable triumph of the subjugated nations over their Nazi oppressors, became the staple ingredients of the genre. *The Times* soon tired of the formulaic plots:

It is surely time that producers should ask themselves whether, if they are determined to set their scenes in one of the occupied countries, they have anything fresh to say or any fresh way of saying what has become distressingly familiar. It is not that the tragedy of the occupied countries or the courage of those who keep up the fight can ever become wearisome – it is simply that heroic themes dragged down to the level of studio commonplaces are themselves degraded.[14]

One of the more original variations on the resistance theme was Powell and Pressburger's *One of Our Aircraft is Missing* (1942), which inverted the basic premise of *49th Parallel* by following the adventures of a British bomber crew shot down over Holland and making their way home with the aid of the Dutch resistance. It benefited from locations in the Fenlands of East Anglia, which resembled the flat Dutch landscape more convincingly than studio interiors. Opening with the spectacular crash of a bomber into a pylon (the crew, it transpires, have already baled out), the film uses its escape story to address several significant issues. First, the heterogeneous bomber crew, drawn from all sections of society, anticipates similar groups in films such as *In Which We Serve* and *The Way Ahead*. And second, the film justifies the British bombing of the occupied countries. As a resistance leader (a woman, played by Googie Withers) tells the men during an air raid: 'Can you hear them running for shelter, can you understand what that means to all the occupied countries, to enslaved people having it drummed into their ears that the Germans are masters of the earth, seeing those masters running to shelter, seeing them crouching under tables and hearing that steady hum, night after night, that noise which is oil for the burning fire in our hearts.'

The resistance films were not immune from the political considerations which sometimes affected relations between the Allies. This was illustrated by the case of *Chetnik*, a feature film about the Yugoslavian resistance made by Ealing Studios. The project was announced to the trade press with that title early in 1942, and Ealing had secured the collaboration of one Dr Sukulic, a 'trusted friend' of Draja Mihailovic, leader of the Chetniks, the Serbian guerrilla fighters.[15] Shortly before the film was released, however, the British government switched its support to Marshal Tito's Communist partisans, a rival faction to the Chetniks. Monja Danischewsky, the Ealing Head of Publicity who was also one of the script-writers on the film, said that the film-makers 'discovered we had backed the wrong horse' and that Mihailovic's name had to be removed from the credits.[16] The film was released in 1943 as *Undercover*. It was to be one of the last films in the resistance cycle, which had all but run its course. However, the film's exterior locations (much of it was shot in the Welsh mountains) and the impressively staged action scenes make it stand out from the more studio-bound resistance films. Set in the spring of 1941, the narrative combines personal interest with an account of the guerrilla movement by focusing on the story of two brothers, one a partisan leader (John Clements), the other a doctor (Stephen Murray) who is reluctant to join them. It was made by Sergei Nolbandov, director of *Ships With Wings*. On this occasion he was more successful in downplaying the 'Boys' Own' heroics and introducing a degree of realism to the style of the film. Although *Undercover* gives a rather confused picture of the Yugoslavian resistance, this was inevitable given the state of misinformation about Yugoslavia and the impossibility of sending film units to the real location.

IV

The British people were fortunate in that, with the exception of the Channel Islands, no part of the British Isles fell under Nazi occupation during the war. While the resistance narratives showed how heroic foreigners stood up to their oppressors, sometimes with the assistance of the British, it was much more difficult to convey what would happen if the British people found themselves in the same position as their French, Belgian, Dutch or Norwegian allies. There were only two films during the war which considered seriously the possibilities of what might happen in Britain under enemy occupation: Ealing's *Went the Day Well?* (1942), directed by Cavalcanti, and the Crown Film Unit's *The Silent Village* (1943), directed by Humphrey Jennings. They make an interesting comparison for the different ways in which they address the idea that 'It might happen here'.

Went the Day Well? is the one Ealing film which does not fit easily into the studio's overall output. Although it bears some comparison with *The Next of Kin* and *The Foreman Went to France* – Charles Barr describes the three films as a 'loose trilogy' in which 'the threat of an enemy which may be all around enforces resource and alertness and

penalises complacency and amateurism'[17] – it has a particularly disturbing quality which distances it from Ealing's other wartime films. It
was based, albeit very loosely, on a short story written by Graham
Greene in 1940 entitled 'The Lieutenant Died Last'.[18]

Opening with a caption – 'Went the day well?/We died and never
knew/But well or ill/Freedom, we died for you' – the film tells the
fictional story of what happened in the village of Bramley End on the
Whitsun weekend of 1942. That the events being unfolded are already
located in the past is established by a prologue in which the church
sexton (Mervyn Johns) points out the German names on a tombstone
in the graveyard and says: 'They wanted England, these Jerries did,
and this is the only bit they got.' England is represented in the film by
the quiet country village of Bramley End (actually Turville in Oxford-
shire). The rural tranquillity is disrupted by the arrival of a detachment
of Royal Engineers who, it turns out, are really the advance guard of
a German invasion force and have come to set up equipment to disrupt
Britain's radiolocation defences. They are assisted by the local squire
Wilsford (Leslie Banks), ostensibly a pillar of the community but in
reality a fifth-columnist. The village is sealed off by barricades and the
villagers are rounded up and imprisoned in the church. The elderly
vicar (C. V. France) is shot dead when he rings the church bells, which
is the warning signal in the event of an invasion. The Home Guard,
who are on an exercise in the woods, pay no heed to the signal, and,
in one of several quite shocking and brutal sequences in the film, they
are ambushed and killed while riding home on their bicycles along a
leafy country lane. It is moments such as this which make the film
stand out: the idyllic country setting juxtaposed with the sudden
eruption of violence. But the villagers are quite capable of fighting
back, and after several attempts to send a warning have been thwarted
by a combination of bad luck and Wilsford's treachery, they succeed
in getting word to the outside world. Led by Tom Sturry (Frank
Lawton), a sailor on leave, the villagers take over the manor house and
hold off the Germans until the regular army arrives, and although a
large number of the villagers are killed in the ensuing battle they
succeed in wiping out the enemy completely.

The main propaganda aim of the film was to warn against complacency, though by the time it was released the danger of invasion
had passed. The most remarkable aspect of the film, however, is the
way in which the villagers match violence with violence. On one level

this is robust self-defence of the kind advocated by Churchill himself – he is said to have favoured the slogan 'You can always take one with you' in the event of an invasion[19] – but the savagery of the film is unusual for the time. The disturbing quality of *Went the Day Well?* lies in the way in which it depicts what is an imaginary event with a degree of brutal realism that is quite shocking. This aspect of the film was emphasised in Ealing's publicity material, which said that 'the realism of the picture is such that even the hard boiled, sceptical cinemagoers should fall under the spell of its convincing power'.[20] The film is realistic in style but is based on a hypothetical event, which the audience of course knows did not happen. Perhaps, therefore, it is best interpreted as a dramatisation of a vivid nightmare rather than as a straightforward realist narrative.

Went the Day Well? presents a harsh view of warfare and an uncompromising picture of what might happen in the event of a German invasion. As a result of this it met with a very mixed reaction from the critics. 'It is a dangerous thing to show your opponents as clowns or bullies, who only get results by treachery, brute force, or the long arm of coincidence,' wrote C. A. Lejeune. 'A director who does this merely cheapens his own countrymen, since victory over such people seems empty and meagre.'[21] The *Monthly Film Bulletin* opined that 'the value of the film could have been increased by a slightly different approach and more convincing dialogue and direction'.[22] Dilys Powell, however, considered that the film was characterised by 'an intensified poignancy and excitement'.[23] In the judgement of posterity, *Went the Day Well?* has come to be regarded as one of the most remarkable propaganda films of the war, not only for its hard-edged realism, but also for its dissection of English society in which the squire, traditionally a figure of social and moral authority, is revealed as an enemy agent. This gives the film a certain degree of radicalism in that it reacts against the consensual ideology of social stability that had characterised British films of the 1930s. Barr suggests, furthermore, that the climax of the film, in which the villagers defend the manor house from the Germans outside and from the traitor within, can be seen as a metaphor for national defence: 'The balance of these two elements is very disturbing, and the whole scene, with the house functioning diagrammatically as a map of "England" under attack, is one of the most intense in all British war films.'[24]

Whereas *Went the Day Well?* used the realist technique to tell an imaginary story, *The Silent Village* was a reconstruction of a true incident told in an abstract way. It was based on a real atrocity in occupied Czechoslovakia – the Lidice massacre of June 1942 when the Germans wiped out an entire village in reprisal for the assassination of Heydrich – but it relocated the events to a Welsh mining village under imaginary German occupation. It is not one of Jennings's better-known films and has been neglected somewhat in critical accounts of his work, but it has an emotive power and force all of its own. The reason for its neglect probably has something to do with the impossibility of classifying it: it is neither documentary in the true sense of the word, nor is it fiction. Dai Vaughan's description of the film as 'both a fictional representation of what has happened and a documentary representation of what has not' illustrates how confusing it is even for film theorists.[25] There appear to have been several influences on the film. The idea of showing a part of Britain under Nazi occupation had been suggested in the Programme for Film Propaganda: 'The value of our institutions could also be brought home to us by showing what it would be like to have them taken away, e.g. a film about a part of the British Isles (e.g. Isle of Man) that the Germans had cut off, showing the effect of the Gestapo on everyday life, breaking up the family, taking away the liberties hitherto unnoticed.'[26] The specific suggestion for the Crown Film Unit to make a film commemorating the people of Lidice came from the exiled Czech government in London, and Jiri Weiss, the Czech documentarist, appears to have been involved in the early stages.[27] But it was Jennings who provided the main creative input, choosing the village of Cwmgiedd in South Wales as the location and contacting the South Wales Miners' Federation for co-operation in making the film. By this time it had been decided that it would not be a straightforward reconstruction of the Lidice massacre but instead would actually be set in Wales. 'Our intention is to stage this in a Welsh mining village with the implication that what happened in Lidice might happen here,' said Eric Hudson, the Crown Film Unit's London Contact Officer.[28]

The Silent Village – which is subtitled 'The story of the men of Lidice who lit in Fascist darkness a lamp that shall never be put out' – begins in the style of a pre-war documentary by establishing the normal tenor of life in the village (which despite the subtitle is Cwmgiedd in Wales rather than Lidice in Czechoslovakia). The congregation sing in church, children are taught in Welsh at school, colliers go to work at the pit, people laugh at a Donald Duck cartoon in the cinema, men drink and play cards in the pub. This apparent documentary record is disturbed by the arrival of the enemy, signified by a black car complete with Nazi insignia and playing martial music over a loudspeaker. This car will be the main visual signifier of the German occupation for the rest of the film. A harsh voice announces: 'Attention! Attention! To the population of Cwmgiedd. As from today, the districts of southern and western Wales stand under the protection of the greater German Reich.' This marks the point at which the film diverges from true documentary realism to become an imaginary account of something which the audience knows is not real (the German occupation of Wales) and yet is based on fact (the Lidice massacre). The film then shows the effects of German occupation: trade unions are banned, strikes are declared illegal, the teaching of the Welsh language is forbidden. The birth of a resistance movement is depicted as a series of fragmented incidents presented in an abstract form: a secret meeting on a hilltop, the sound of machine-guns, a shot of men fleeing, further gunfire, and then several close-ups of people shot dead. The radio car announces an assassination attempt on 'Reichprotektor Heydrich' (which is not shown); later it announces his death from his injuries. Having found 'irrefutable evidence' that the people of Cwmgiedd aided the assassins, the car demands that they are handed over. This is not done, whereupon the women and children of the village are taken away while the men are lined up against the cemetery wall and shot. In a typically audacious Jennings touch, the firing squad themselves are not seen, but the commands in German and then the noise of the rifle volley are heard as the film cuts away from the scene of execution. Images of burning buildings then accompany the announcement in German (a superimposed title provides an English translation) that all the male inhabitants of the village have been shot, the women sent to a concentration camp, and the village itself levelled. An inter-title states: 'That is what the Nazis did to the village – the village of Lidice in Czechoslovakia.' An epilogue shows the people of Cwmgiedd reading the news of the massacre, while Dai Evans, the local agent of the Miners' Federation, asserts that the name of Lidice will be never be forgotten.

The Silent Village now seems a moving and poetic little film which is effective because it focuses not on abstract principles or vague notions of freedom, but rather shows what happened to real men and women (the people of Cwmgiedd played themselves in the film) when they were subjected to Nazi occupation. At the time, rather like *Went the Day Well?*, it met with a mixed reception. *Documentary News Letter*, as usual with Jennings's films, was sceptical of its propaganda value:

> It is impossible to imagine why this film was made. The strangely oblique approach robs the film of any direct impact because it has been translated into 'It might have been like this' not 'It was like this'. It has moments of aesthetic and technical interest but this certainly does not seem the time for the tentative and the semi-obscure.[29]

Jennings's imaginative and impressionistic treatment therefore did not meet with the approval of the documentary purists, but there were others who responded more favourably to the film. *The Times* considered that 'this imaginative record is one of the most powerful exercises in intelligent propaganda yet witnessed on the screen'.[30] And Michael Balcon wrote to Jennings: 'Apart from being wonderful cinema it is one of the most important pictures I have ever seen and incomparably the best anti-Nazi propaganda yet projected.'[31] There is a case to argue that in relocating the events much closer to home, the film would make a greater impact on British audiences than a straightforward reconstruction of an incident in a distant country. There is some evidence of its effect on audiences. 'I saw the film in Sheffield (a city surrounded by coal-mines incidentally) and I felt that it was a success; it was accepted, and it was not dismissed as phoney,' observed the documentarist Donald Alexander.[32] And Roger Manvell testified that it was very well received by refugees from Czechoslovakia: 'The Czechs themselves were deeply touched by this imaginative tribute; I saw the film myself for the first time at a private screening with a Czech army officer, who was unable to restrain his tears.'[33] There could be no greater compliment than that to Jennings's ability to turn propaganda into a form of art.

11

History and Heritage

The keynote is 'our glorious heritage', and as in nearly all patriotic films and literature, the implication all along is that England is an agricultural country, and that its inhabitants derive their patriotism from a passionate love of the English soil. Are such films good for morale in wartime? They may be. It is a fact that many of the things which the jingo history books make the most noise about are things to be proud of. *George Orwell*[1]

I

Orwell's observation on the nature of historical films makes a useful starting point for a consideration of the last major theme of British wartime propaganda. Films about the past were one of the strategies which the British cinema adopted for providing both patriotic propaganda and popular entertainment. Indeed, the tendency to adopt historical and heritage themes in propaganda was even remarked upon by film-makers themselves. There is, for example, a scene in Powell and Pressburger's *The Volunteer* (1943) where Ralph Richardson, playing himself, and his stage 'dresser' Fred (Pat McGrath) are seen at Denham Studios. 'We were making a propaganda film,' Richardson says. 'At the outbreak of war, actors dived into historical costumes and declaimed powerful speeches about the wooden walls of England.' This was an ironic and deprecatory reference to a particular type of historical film which flourished in the early years of the war but which a few years later already appeared crude and simplistic as propaganda. By the end of the war, however, the historical film had reached its artistic maturity in the shape of Laurence Olivier's production of *Henry V*, a film which so transcended its propagandist origins that it is now regarded as one of the masterpieces of British cinema. Charles Barr identifies *Henry V* as 'the culmination of a cycle, almost a genre in itself, of "heritage" films', citing as other examples *This England*, *The Young Mr Pitt*, *A Canterbury Tale*, Humphrey Jennings's short *Words for Battle* and Korda's Hollywood-made *Lady Hamilton*, a historical biopic of Nelson which was Winston Churchill's favourite film.[2] There is an important distinction to be made here between the historical narrative proper (which may be defined as one which is based, however loosely, on real events or real people) and the rather broader category of the 'heritage' film (which derives from literature and the cultural past, most usually represented during the war by Shakespeare and Milton). What most historical and heritage films have in common, however, is that their construction of the past was predominantly in terms of 'England' rather than 'Britain', and, as Orwell remarked, they were characterised by pastoral themes and imagery. Indeed, the most oft-quoted piece of Shakespearean verse during the war was John O'Gaunt's deathbed speech from *Richard II*, which featured regularly on the radio and turned up in numerous anthologies of patriotic literature as well as providing the titles for no fewer than three feature films (*This England, The Demi-Paradise* and *This Happy Breed*).

II

The historical film, unlike the war narrative, had been one of the staple genres of the British cinema during the 1930s. A cycle of historical costume dramas had been produced following the success of Korda's *The Private Life of Henry VIII* (1933). *Fire Over England* (1937) in particular anticipated the films of the war by drawing an allegorical parallel between the time of the Spanish Armada and the European situation in the 1930s in which the Spain of Philip II stood for Hitler's Germany. The Tilbury sequence where Elizabeth I (Flora Robson) rallies her troops with a rousing speech was later included in *The Lion Has Wings*, further reinforcing the propagandist intent and making even more explicit the parallel between past and present.

The first historical film of the war proper was *This England* (1941), directed by David Macdonald for British National. It illustrates perfectly the sort of film described by Ralph Richardson in *The Volunteer*. Leslie Halliwell, who recalled being taken to see the film in Bolton by the school history master, described it as 'an abysmal propaganda film' with 'cardboard sets', while his history teacher 'roared with derisive laughter at the inept and extremely boring goings-on'.[3] Although the film looks to have been cheaply made, with obvious studio interiors and risible sets, it was originally intended to have been a rather more prestigious production. When it was announced as part of the British National production schedule in June 1940, it was described as 'the most ambitious subject the company has undertaken so far'. It was to have been made in Technicolor and 'will be filmed largely out of doors'. The producer, John Corfield, explained the choice of subject thus:

> The swift march of events these days is such that the average film producer has difficulty in keeping abreast of current happenings. For instance, in *Contraband* our neutral Danish skipper in the film became right out of date. Similarly, we had all preparations ready to start on a big Anglo-French subject. Finally, I suggested to our script writers that as the only thing seeming to survive all storms and stresses was the countryside of England, here was something lasting.[4]

This England is an episodic narrative which chronicles English history through the story of one small rural community. If it had been made in colour and on location as originally intended it might have stood the test of time rather better than it has, but production economies took their toll on the film, which ended up being on a much more modest scale. Nevertheless, the rural theme which is at the heart of the film is characteristic of the wartime heritage cycle and thus the film is important as the first, if far from the best, example of this theme of propaganda.

This England begins in the present as an American girl (Constance Cummings) visits the village of Clevely and is impressed by the fortitude of the villagers during an air raid. She is befriended by Rookeby (John Clements) and his friend Appleyard (Emlyn Williams), who proceed to tell her the story of the village. Four episodes from English history are selected which show the people rallying together when danger threatened: 1086, after the Norman Conquest, when the villagers revolt against an oppressive overlord; 1588, during the approach of the Spanish Armada; 1804, during the Napoleonic Wars when threatened with invasion from France; and finally the Great War of 1914–18. The casting of the same actors in each episode, particularly Clements as the yeoman farmer Rookeby and Williams as the farm labourer Appleyard, provides continuity over the centuries, implying a sense of historical destiny in the fortunes of the English country-dwellers. The image of England is that of a feudal society with a hierarchical class system where the landowners accept their responsibilities and the labourers accept their place while occasionally reminding their masters of their duty to the land. Made at a time when invasion was still a possibility, *This England* was an essentially defensive film which showed how the sturdy English people could always be relied upon to pull together when external danger threatened. It was marred, however, by its cliched dialogue and theatrical acting. The film was considered crude even at the time. '*This England* isn't impressive; in fact it is the sort of patriotic film we do worst,' wrote William Whitebait.[5] The title was tactfully changed to *Our Heritage* for the film's release in Scotland.

Although *This England* was a failure, it did not deter other film-makers from tackling historical subjects. Sue Harper has shown that the MOI was very much in favour of using history for propaganda, particularly in the early years of the war, actively encouraging the BBC, for example, to produce historical plays.[6] The MOI encouraged an essentially Whiggish view of history which stressed gradual evolution in terms of both democratic political institutions and social improvement, while Britain's role as a defender of freedom and a bulwark against foreign tyrants should also be stressed. The Programme for Film Propaganda had suggested that 'Ideals such as freedom, and institutions such as parliamentary government, can be made the main subject of a drama or treated historically'. It added that 'we may also consider films of heroic actions, histories of national heroes (Captain Scott) etc., although these may easily become too obvious'.[7] Scott seems an odd example to have mentioned given that his was a story of heroic failure rather than triumph, and indeed it was not until after the war that Ealing Studios tackled the subject in a feature film of 1948, but other national heroes, and in particular inspirational prime ministers, were featured prominently in wartime films.

Harper observes that both *The Prime Minister* and *The Young Mr Pitt* 'displayed an extraordinary consonance with MoI views; there is no firm evidence of their parentage, but they are sufficiently different from straightforward commercial products to encourage us to categorise them as "official" histories'.[8] *The Prime Minister* (1941), directed by Thorold Dickinson, was a biopic starring John Gielgud as Disraeli. It was produced in Britain by Warner Bros as one of the films to fulfil their quota obligations, and it would be fair to say that it is a much less polished film than the studio's Hollywood biopics. Nevertheless, it has some points of interest, and can be seen as a precursor to the altogether more successful *The Young Mr Pitt* for the way in which it uses the historical drama as a vehicle for addressing more contemporary issues. As with most biopics its narrative intertwines the private and public lives of its protagonist, but the patriotic theme is more pronounced than usual. 'I think you can do great things for England,' Lord Melbourne tells the young Disraeli, and the film shows how he matures from a romantic young dandy to a great statesman and tireless servant of his country. It is in the second half of the film that the contemporary parallels come to the fore. The characterisations of Disraeli and his arch rival Gladstone (Stephen Murray) are thinly veiled representations of Churchill and Chamberlain. Disraeli/Churchill is an imperialist patriot and an architect of social reform who is loved by the people but distrusted by the establishment; Gladstone/Chamberlain, by contrast, is a proponent of retrenchment and appeasement. The Congress of Berlin in 1878, in which Disraeli stands firm by defending Turkey (a weak, helpless country) against the territorial ambitions of Germany and Russia, risking war but bringing 'peace with honour', becomes an allegory of the Munich Agreement. The film suggests quite explicitly that Chamberlain should have taken a much firmer stand against Germany in 1938. 'Europe at the moment is at the mercy of the most ruthless band of autocrats the world has yet seen,' Disraeli tells his Cabinet. 'They recognise one argument and one argument alone – force – and that is the argument I beg you to use now for the sake of peace and for the sake of England.' The message was clear: foreign despots had to be opposed, not conciliated. Significantly, given the time of production, both Germany and Russia are seen as enemies (the film was made and released when the Nazi–Soviet Pact was still in force). But the reception of the film from press and public alike was lukewarm.

A rather more successful example of the historical biopic was Carol Reed's *The Young Mr Pitt* (1942), which Jeffrey Richards describes as 'almost a textbook demonstration of the MoI's interpretation of history'.[9] Like *The Prime Minister* it was made in Britain with backing from a major American studio (in this case Twentieth Century-Fox), but it was a much bigger film – the trade press described it as 'the most ambitious British production since the war began'[10] – and benefited from all the production values that a budget of £250,000 could provide, including a highly detailed set of the House of Commons. There is evidence of discreet official input into the film in that Viscount Castlerosse, who wrote a column for the *Sunday Express* and was one of the MOI's favoured journalists, was involved in writing the story (he is credited on the film for 'dramatic narrative and additional dialogue'), though the actual script was the work of Frank Launder and Sidney Gilliat. Historical accuracy, although claimed by the producers, was sacrificed to the needs of propaganda. Launder felt embittered that the character of Pitt was shown without any faults, while his political opponent Charles James Fox was portrayed as an out-and-out rascal. Launder said:

> The battles that Sidney and I fought with Carol Reed, Robert Donat and Ted Black were in the main aimed by us at showing the human imperfections of William Pitt, and giving Charles James Fox a place in the sun. We lost all along the line. Pitt became a paragon of virtue, which he certainly was not, and the part of Fox, by far the most interesting character, was whittled down to give more footage to the heroic Pitt ... I have always taken the view that untainted heroes, unless biblical, are a bore.[11]

Production took place in the latter half of 1941, and the film was released to good reviews and box-office acclaim in June 1942.

The Young Mr Pitt begins with William Pitt the Elder speaking in the House of Commons in favour of ending the war with the American colonists because their cause is just. This would have had obvious contemporary overtones in that America entered the war in December 1941: the film therefore makes a clear bid towards securing American sympathy. Unlike *The Prime Minister*, *The Young Mr Pitt* does not dwell on the early years and romances of its protagonist before he enters politics. Pitt (Robert Donat), a commoner, is appointed Prime Minister by King George III (Raymond Lovell) when the corrupt aristocratic government of Lord North falls. His first speech in the House as Prime Minister is howled down, but he calls a general election and wins a landslide victory by standing on a platform of peace and reform. Pitt's credentials as a social reformer are shown through his friendship with the anti-slavery campaigner William Wilberforce (John Mills). Under his premiership the country enjoys peace and prosperity, and he is shown to be popular with the people. Scenes of rural calm in England are intercut with revolution in France, and when the French revolutionary government invades Holland, England goes to war. The war goes badly and the English army is evacuated from Dunkirk. Although there is a clamour for peace at home, particularly from Fox (Robert Morley), Pitt is adamant that Britain must stand alone against the aggressor. Napoleon (Herbert Lom) seizes power in France – 'a nation of fanatics, led by an arch-fanatic'. When Napoleon promises peace Pitt knows that it is a trick, though the machinations of French diplomats and his own political enemies force him to resign. His successor Addington is tricked into signing the Treaty of Amiens, but the French army mobilises and Pitt is recalled. The threat of invasion is averted by Nelson's victory at Trafalgar, and Pitt declares that 'England has saved herself by her exertions and will, as I trust, save Europe by her example'. The historical parallels are again obvious, with Pitt being cast in Churchillian mode as an advocate of domestic reform and as a staunch opponent of dictatorships. He is a visionary, enjoys popular support, and puts the national interest ahead of his own career (and even his failing health). Britain is shown as the defender of small countries against aggressor powers; appeasement of foreign tyrants is shown as a misguided and futile policy; Britain suffers initial reverses but stands alone and is saved by a famous victory. The film acknowledges that the people sometimes felt war-weary, but Pitt is resolute in his determination that waging war is necessary to secure lasting peace and prosperity. The composition of the film also has a very modern feel: montage sequences show the nation's war production, for example in building a new navy and through increasing industrialisation.

The Young Mr Pitt was well received by most critics and had wide popular appeal. 'Outstanding instance of the British film at its most serious best, the finest form of propaganda on our screens today, and first-class entertainment,' declared *Today's Cinema*. 'Never has any film more perfectly expressed the feeling and temper of the British people in times of stress and trouble such as we are passing through today.'[12] Released at a time when Britain was probably safe from defeat but was still very far from victory, its message that the nation must persevere until that victory was won made it very much a tract for the times.

III

While historical biopics such as *The Prime Minister* and *The Young Mr Pitt* dramatised the events of the past to make an allegorical parallel with the present, there were other films which drew upon Britain's cultural heritage to suggest something of what the war was actually being fought for. Attempts to mobilise the cultural past for propaganda, however, were only partially successful. Humphrey Jennings's five-minute film *Words for Battle* (1941) was the most complex example of the use of cultural themes in official propaganda. It is not one of Jennings's best-known works, though it illustrates his affection for his country and its heritage as perfectly as any of his films. It takes the form of seven extracts from poetry, prose and speech, all eloquently recited by Laurence Olivier. The words of William Camden, John Milton, William Blake, Robert Browning and Rudyard Kipling are followed by extracts from Churchill's 'Finest Hour' speech ('We shall defend our island, whatever the cost may be') and Lincoln's Gettysburg address ('We here highly resolve ... that the government of the people, by the people, for the people, shall not perish from this earth'). These extracts are narrated over images of wartime Britain such as Spitfires, troops and civil defence workers. The marriage of past and present, of literary heritage and the iconography of war, is another example of Jennings's highly sophisticated intellectual montage. The fusion is cemented by the use of Handel's 'Water Music' as a recurring theme. *Documentary News Letter* was doubtful about the value of the film, criticising both the style and the choice of examples:

> *Words for Battle* is an illustrated lantern-slide lecture, with Olivier's curate-like voice reverently intoning various extracts from poetry, verse and topical political speeches. That tough old republican revolutionary, Milton, rubs shoulders with minor Browning ('reeking into Cadiz bay') and lesser Kipling. Winston Churchill with his 'fight on the beaches' is elbowed out of the final pay-off by Lincoln in Gettysburg war-aims vein, and the whole lot is neatly rounded off by long-focus shots of groups of soldiers, sailors, airmen and women in uniform stepping gaily through the civilian

crowds on the pavement. Altogether an extraordinary performance, the effect of which on morale is quite incalculable. The man
who must feel most out of place is poor old Handel. As he stood
on his gaily coloured barge conducting the Water Music that was
to bring him back into royal favour he can hardly have guessed
that it would come to this.[13]

For the documentary purists, therefore, it was another example of
Jennings's self-conscious artistic abstraction rather than the straightforward realism which they prized above all.

The most ambitious of the wartime cycle of heritage films was
Powell and Pressburger's *A Canterbury Tale* (1944), a complex, even
mystical feature which Basil Wright later described as 'the kinkiest film
of the war'.[14] What Humphrey Jennings was to the documentary
movement, Powell and Pressburger were to the commercial cinema:
mavericks who stood out from the rest, whose films were more complex in intellectual and aesthetic terms and could not be accommodated
within the orthodox realist critical discourse. *A Canterbury Tale* was an
attempt to create a modern equivalent of Chaucer's morality tales.
According to Powell it was intended as an examination of what the
war was being fought for. 'That was really the reason for making the
film, because we felt the moral issues of the war were almost as
exciting as the war that was being fought,' Powell said. 'The whole
idea was to examine the values for which we were fighting and to do
it through the eyes of a young American who was training in England.'[15]
A brief prelude shows medieval travellers on the Pilgrims' Way; then,
in a brilliant ellipsis, shots of a falcon launched into the air cut to a
Spitfire. The narrator (Esmond Knight) explains that the countryside
of Kent is still the same six hundred years later but that now 'another
kind of pilgrim walks the way' as Bren-gun carriers thunder across the
fields. The film follows three modern-day pilgrims who meet in a
small Kentish village on the way to Canterbury: an American soldier,
Sergeant Bob Johnson (played by Sergeant John Sweet of the US
Army), a British serviceman Sergeant Peter Gibbs (Dennis Price) and
Alison, an English girl in the Land Army (Sheila Sim). They find the
village of Chillingbourne being terrorised by the 'glueman', a nocturnal
figure who pours glue into the hair of girls consorting with servicemen.
It transpires that the 'glueman' is actually a local magistrate, Thomas
Colpeper (Eric Portman), who has resorted to the attacks partly to

stop local girls having casual affairs with soldiers and partly out of jealousy because the soldiers prefer the attractions of female company to his own lectures on history and the countryside. But Colpeper is not a dangerous villain, and the plot involving the uncovering of the 'glueman's' identity is less important than the pastoral imagery and the mystical attachment to the countryside which pervade the film. It is through Colpeper that the three modern pilgrims come to realise that the values of the countryside and rural customs are constant and still have meaning in the modern world.

The film suggests that the spiritual and moral values for which the war is being fought are to be found in the unchanging spirit of rural England. As Richards observes: 'The England evoked by *A Canterbury Tale* is the England of Chaucer and Shakespeare, a rural England of half-timbered cottages and stately country houses, quiet, leafy church-yards and rich hopfields, an England whose spirit resides in Thomas Colpeper, gentleman farmer, magistrate, historian and archaeologist, a man who understands England's nature and seeks to communicate her values.'[16] It is a conservative idea of national identity which presents 'Englishness' in terms of the traditional ways of life, and thus it is not dissimilar to *This England*, though it is more philosophical and far less obvious in its propaganda. But it is problematic, particularly for a film of the later war years, because of its attachment to the past rather than the future. It is useful to compare the film's idea of 'why we fight' to the Boulting Brothers' short *The Dawn Guard*: whereas the short film had argued that there was much more to the question of war aims than simply preserving the old ways of life, *A Canterbury Tale* does not address the issues of future social reform and reconstruction at all. It was not especially successful and met with a puzzled reception from the critics, though its reputation has improved over the years.

Less ambitious than *A Canterbury Tale*, but on the whole more satisfying, was the delightful *Tawny Pipit* (1944), written and directed by Bernard Miles and Charles Saunders. A whimsical and charming little film, which has been unfairly neglected by most histories of wartime cinema, *Tawny Pipit* tells the story of how the inhabitants of an English village closed ranks to defend a pair of rare nesting birds. It was filmed on location in the Cotswold village of Pinfold which stood in for Lipsbury Lea, an idyllic rural community of quaint cottages, leafy lanes, rustic yokels and children playing in the stream. A convalescing fighter pilot (Niall MacGinnis) and his nurse (Rosamund John) discover a pair of tawny pipits nesting near the village, a species which has bred only once before in England. The defence of the birds against the Army, which wants to use the meadow for manoeuvres, and against egg-stealers becomes a metaphor for the wider conflict. This point is made by the village elder, Colonel Barton-Barrington (Miles), who tells the villagers that 'this love of animals and of nature has always been part and parcel of the British way of life'. He continues:

> Now we've welcomed to our country thousands of foreigners at one time or another – French, Dutch, Poles, Czechs and so on – and a lot of them are jolly decent people, and anyway they can't help being foreigners. Well that's what these little pipits are, you see, and we're jolly well going to see to it that they get fair play or we shall want to know the reason why ... Now we've heard a great deal about the differences between Nazism and democracy, but in my opinion the big difference between ourselves and the Hun is that the Hun doesn't know the meaning of playing the game, he never did and he never will. What we mean to give these little pipits is fair play and a square deal and no hitting below the belt.

A parallel is drawn, therefore, between the British love of animals and the friendship extended to foreign allies and refugees from Nazism. The parallel becomes even more explicit with the visit to Lipsbury Lea of a Russian sniper, Lieutenant Bokolova (Lucie Mannheim), who is welcomed by the schoolchildren singing the *Internationale*. The film also eulogises the countryside, which has a rehabilitating effect on those who embrace its values. Everyone who sees the pipits is enchanted by them and recognises the need to defend them, even the would-be thieves and the tank commander who is persuaded to leave their nesting ground alone. Its subtle propaganda content was recognised by reviewers at the time. 'The eventual hatching of the five fine young pipits comes to embattled Britain as a kind of benison,' said C. A. Lejeune. 'It is just for the right to enjoy such things, the film suggests, that we are fighting; and, although conceivably mad, that is the way we are.'[17]

While *A Canterbury Tale* and *Tawny Pipit* celebrated the rural face of England, showing old communities almost untouched by the modern world, this was not the only aspect of 'Englishness' which came under consideration in the heritage film. *This Happy Breed* (1944), directed by David Lean and based on the play by Noël Coward, was a tribute to the suburban lower middle classes who were regarded as the backbone of English society. The 'happy breed' (the title was another quotation from *Richard II*) are of course the English, and they are personified in the form of the Gibbonses of 17 Sycamore Road, Clapham. Although it is usually described as a family drama, *This Happy Breed* can legitimately be located within the heritage cycle, and not only because of the source of its title. As Andrew Higson writes: '*This Happy Breed*'s narrative of national history situates it at the meeting point of the heritage film and the documentary idea, where the latter is understood as a means of detailing an alternative heritage of the common people.'[18]

The film is a chronicle of the fortunes of the Gibbons family during the interwar years against the background of real events (such as the General Strike, the arrival of talking pictures, the abdication crisis and Munich). Like the same production team's *In Which We Serve*, the narrative provides a space for both the public and the personal. History and documentary are merged as real events which were located firmly in the past for the cinema audiences of 1944 are shown through documentary-montage sequences which are contemporaneous with the lives of the characters in the film. *This Happy Breed* was made in Technicolor, and the production reports in the trade press were at pains to stress its authentic picture of English life: 'Infinite care is being taken to see that the Clapham house and its environment in which most of the action takes place are photographed in colours that will be a truthful portrait of the "Gibbons family".'[19] The film provides a chronicle of recent history which has been carefully distilled by the benefit of hindsight. Frank Gibbons (Robert Newton) is characterised as a staunch patriot, the personification of the English virtues of stability and moderation. He rejects the political extremes of communism and fascism: 'It's up to us ordinary people to keep things steady', he tells his son Reg (John Blythe), who is attracted by radical politics. Significantly, although Frank is a Tory voter, he is critical of the policy of appeasement pursued by Baldwin and Chamberlain. This marked the most obvious reinterpretation of the past, in that appeasement had been a genuinely popular policy during the 1930s. Frank Gibbons is therefore granted a degree of foresight which distances him from a policy which had been discredited by war, and the film was probably intended, in part at least, to ease any feelings of guilt which people may have felt about supporting the National Government during the 1930s. *This Happy Breed* was among the most popular films of 1944 and was well received by the critics as an authentic portrait of an English family which was seen as a distillation of national character.

IV

In most discourses on English heritage, Shakespeare is usually privileged above all other writers and artists as the supreme embodiment of what is best about national culture. It was fitting, therefore, that Laurence Olivier's film of *Henry V* (1944) should have been the culmination of the wartime cycle of heritage films. An innovative, highly cinematic interpretation of the play, made in Technicolor, *Henry V* was a fusion of elite culture, propaganda and popular entertainment on an epic scale.

Sue Harper has argued persuasively that the origins of *Henry V* can be found in the policy of the MOI, that 'although there is no direct evidence of government sponsorship, there are plenty of suggestions that the film enjoyed official support'.[20] The play was a popular one in time of war and lent itself easily to patriotic display. The idea of filming it came from Dallas Bower, who had worked for the MOI Films Division earlier in the war and who was to be the associate producer of the film. Bower had written an adaptation of the play for BBC television before the war, though it had not been performed as it was technically too complicated for the infant medium. When he left the MOI in 1942, he produced a radio programme entitled *Into Battle* which featured Laurence Olivier reciting Henry's 'Harfleur' and 'Crispin's Day' speeches. The film was produced by Two Cities, with further financial backing from the Rank Organisation. Olivier was released from the services to star, and after both William Wyler (then in the US Army Air Force stationed in Britain) and Carol Reed had turned down the offer to direct the film, he assumed that role as well.[21] Substantial portions of Shakespeare's text were cut out in order to make room for a spectacular set piece staging of the Battle of Agincourt. Among the portions of the play to be cut, significantly, were those which featured any internal dissent, including the references to Scotland as a separate kingdom. Further evidence of the MOI's support is that the Agincourt sequence was filmed in Eire, which required official approval. The reason for this location, according to the trade press, was 'the impossibility in this country of utilising suitable backgrounds or to obtain the large numbers of men and horses necessary for the battle sequences'.[22] The irony of filming this patriotic epic of an English monarch in republican Ireland was not lost on 'Sagittarius', the satirical poet of *The New Statesman*:

> Advance, you stout Sinn Feiners, brawny supers
> Whose limbs were made in Eire, show us here
> That you are worth your wages: which I doubt not,
> Are ten times more than those of Harry's bowmen!
> And he that doth enact this scene with me,
> Let him be never so Republican
> He is this day King Harry's follower![23]

The location filming was undertaken during the summer of 1943, with the battle filmed by cameraman Robert Krasker, before the unit returned to Denham for the studio interiors. Made in Technicolor, at a final cost of £475,000, *Henry V* was the most expensive British film of the war, but it was a great popular success and even earned over $1 million when it was belatedly released in the United States after the war.[24] It went on to win numerous awards, including a special Academy Award for Olivier for his 'Outstanding Production Achievement as Actor, Producer and Director in bringing *Henry V* to the Screen'.

As a propaganda text, *Henry V* works in the same allegorical fashion as historical narratives such as *The Young Mr Pitt*. It was released in the autumn of 1944, and its stirring account of an English army crossing the Channel and routing a continental adversary had obvious contemporary parallels in the aftermath of D-Day. This is even inscribed into the filmic text itself through a title caption which declares: 'To the Commandos and Airborne Troops of Great Britain – the spirit of whose ancestors it has been humbly attempted to recapture in some ensuing scenes – this picture is dedicated.' *Henry V*, then, was nothing if not explicit about its propagandist credentials. That the film is more than just an exercise in jingoistic nationalism is due largely to the imaginative way in which the play was adapted for the screen. 'Can this cockpit hold the vasty fields of France?' asks the Chorus (Leslie Banks), and the film ingeniously plays upon the cinema's capacity for illusion and spectacle by gradually breaking free from the confines of the stage. It begins with a reconstruction of a performance of the play at the Globe Theatre in 1600 as Henry receives the French ambassador; when Henry leaves with his army for France the theatre set gives way to background paintings, first quite basic but then becoming increasingly stylised; then it bursts into real exteriors for the battle, before returning to a tapestry background for the peace-making sequence and finally back to the Globe for the closing scene. The composition of the film thus exhibits a symmetry which places the battle at the centre, both structurally and formally. The battle itself is a stunning set piece which exhibits the studied application of the montage techniques of the Soviet cinema, and indeed has often been compared to Eisenstein's *Alexander Nevsky* (1938). The sequence is structured around a juxtaposition of movement and stasis as the mounted French knights break into a charge against the English lines of defence. Shots of the charging French knights are intercut with shots of the English archers waiting with long-bows raised, and close-ups of Olivier himself as Henry in armour and on horseback. These low-angle shots of Henry isolate him, enhancing his status as leader, while one shot in particular, which places him in the frame next to the Flag of St George, is a powerful signifier of 'Englishness'. When Henry's sword falls the archers unleash their volley and the French charge is halted. The abrupt stopping of the enemy in all its massive and flamboyant might by a small, disciplined force has an irresistible symbolism: the defeat of the Nazi war machine by the determined 'Few'. In the *mêlée* which follows, a montage of quick close-ups and rapid movement, the camera follows the English flag, keeping it in centre frame above the heads of the combatants. The English victory is confirmed by Henry's defeat of the Constable of France in single combat, thus emphasising his personal heroism and inspirational leader-ship. The battle sequence presents history as spectacle, with precise accuracy sacrificed in favour of a colourful display of knights, armour and flags, and, accompanied by William Walton's stirring music, it stands out as one of the most memorable sequences in British cinema.

As impressive as it is, Agincourt is not the only important sequence, for *Henry V* also functions as propaganda on other levels. Henry's concern for his men and his ability to speak to them on a personal basis, as demonstrated by his incognito tour of the English camp the night before the battle, illustrates his caring and democratic nature in contrast to the aloof arrogance of the corrupt, aristocratic French leaders. Henry's exhortations to comradeship and unity ('We few, we happy few, we band of brothers/For he today that sheds his blood with me shall be my brother') reflect the wartime consensus between leaders and led. And the lengthy sequence of peace-making which follows the battle, including Henry's courtship of Princess Katharine (Renée Asherson), is a reminder that the war will soon be over and that it will be necessary to come to terms with the vanquished foe.

Henry V was released when an Allied victory was in sight. Its tone is one of patriotic pride and triumphalism, a hymn to the unconquerable spirit and inspired courage of the British nation. The film's promotional material emphasised the parallel between past and present, though this interpretation was resisted by some critics, including C. A. Lejeune:

> There is certain to be an attempt in some quarters to link up Laurence Olivier's film production of *Henry V* with the present war, and to represent the play as an anticipation of the heroic actions that have been fought this summer and autumn so close along the route that Henry Plantagenet followed. This, I think, would be a mistake, diminishing, by unnatural contrast with a different sort of greatness, the stature of the play ... What Shakespeare wrote in *Henry V*, and what Mr Olivier has splendidly caught in his screen adaptation, is a salute to high adventure: a kind of boyish exaltation of man's grim work.[25]

Lejeune was right to suggest there was more to *Henry V* than the obvious contemporary overtones, and this is what sets it apart from other historical films. On one level, of course, it is a historical narrative which used the story of a famous English victory over a larger European enemy to draw a parallel with the present; but on another level it is also a celebration of English culture and heritage, bringing Shakespearean drama to the screen in a vivid and dramatic form. Some of the more theatrically-minded critics objected to the textual changes, but this was probably of less concern to the majority of cinema-goers who thronged to see the film. It made Shakespeare accessible to a mass audience, being the first Shakespearean film to achieve great popular success. There are many probable reasons for this: its spectacle, its stellar cast, its colour (still a rarity in British films), and its status as a prestige film. It may simply have been that it offered a different kind of entertainment for audiences who were becoming weary of war films and documentaries. It seems to have appealed particularly to middle-class audiences, as it enjoyed long runs in the West End of London and, later, on Broadway in New York, suggesting that its status as 'culture' was an attraction in some circles. It was not without its critics abroad. In

France there was some controversy when the Ministry of Foreign Affairs complained that the film 'is extremely painful and almost intolerable' in its depiction of 'the moral faults and weaknesses of the French'.[26] Several American critics focused on its overt propaganda, although they still admired its filmic qualities. 'I have rarely ever seen Shakespeare done with such magnificent success or British propaganda presented with such pushing insistence,' said Elliot Norton of the *Boston Post*, adding that 'the voice is the voice of Shakespeare, but the hand is sometimes the hand of Brendan Bracken'.[27] In general, however, *Henry V* proved to be powerful propaganda for the British cause. Eloquent testimony to its effectiveness was provided by James Agee. 'I am not a Tory, a monarchist, a Catholic, a medievalist, an Englishman, or, despite all the good that it engenders, a lover of war,' he wrote; 'but the beauty and power of this traditional exercise was such that, watching it, I wished I was, thought I was, and was proud of it.'[28]

Conclusion

No doubt about it, the cinema was providing a great morale booster as well as the nation's most effective weapon of propaganda. *Leslie Halliwell*[1]

Many commentators have remarked that during the Second World War the British cinema was used extensively as a medium of propaganda. This was recognised not only in hindsight, but also at the time. 'At the outset of war all concerned with the moulding of opinion expected that the film would play a part of ever increasing importance. That expectation has been realised,' declared a leading article in *The Times* in 1942. 'The screen has served as a medium of propaganda; it has also helped to build up between the allies that understanding which is the only true source of sympathy and confidence.'[2] That is not to say, of course, that all film propaganda had been universally successful, and this survey has shown that the success rate of films made for propaganda purposes was uneven. But there can be no doubt of the scale of the film propaganda effort, or of the extent of the government's involvement with it. By the middle of the war even that most critical and jaundiced of all voices, *Documentary News Letter*, accepted, albeit somewhat grudgingly, that 'the British Government is now making a more widespread use of the film than has ever been attempted by any other public body in the world'.[3]

The extensive use of film propaganda had been made possible by the good relations between cinema and state. Although the MOI attracted much criticism from the different sectors of the film industry in the early period of the war for failing to provide adequate policy or guidance, this situation had been largely remedied by the time that the film propaganda effort really kicked into gear. The MOI developed a policy which found roles for the different modes of film practice. Crucially, the MOI recognised that both the commercial feature film producers and the documentary movement could play a role within the overall scheme of national propaganda. Whereas the feature film was the ideal medium for long-term propaganda by dramatising general stories of the British war effort for audiences both at home and abroad, short films and documentaries were more useful for direct, immediate, short-term information and instruction, particularly on the home front. On the whole the relationship between the MOI and the film-makers themselves was smooth and quite harmonious. There were, of course, some points of friction in the relationship, of which the controversy that raged over *The Life and Death of Colonel Blimp* was the most acute. Inevitably, this friction has attracted much more attention than the many instances where film propaganda can be seen to be operating smoothly and without problem – conflict is always more interesting to historians than consensus – and as a result this has tended to distort perceptions of how effective the official film propaganda policy was. One recent commentator has written that the *Colonel Blimp* episode was really 'a storm in a teacup'.[4] The most important consequence of the incident was not the revelation that the Prime Minister had tried to suppress the film, but rather that he had failed in his attempt to do so. This was in itself very good propaganda in that it reinforced the idea that Britain was a liberal democracy where censorship did not take place.

It would, of course, be absurd to suggest that censorship was not being practised in wartime Britain. Indeed, much of the early criticism of the MOI had been directed at its clumsy, ham-fisted attempts at censorship of the news media. It was the control of the channels of information – the press, the BBC and the film newsreels – that had occupied most attention during the pre-war planning of the MOI but which failed most obviously and dramatically at the outbreak of war. As early as October 1939, Mass-Observation detected 'great public dissatisfaction with present heavily censored news-reels'.[5] This was a matter of particular concern for the Select Committee on National

Expenditure, which was of the view 'that the newsreel is the most important for propaganda purposes of the three principal kinds of film'.[6] This view should perhaps be qualified: the newsreel, like the short documentary, served an immediate and short-term role in the spread of information. Newsreels differed from both features and documentaries, though, in that they did not work in terms of what has been called 'positive propaganda' (the dissemination of a particular theme or idea) but rather as 'negative propaganda' (the control of information). For this reason the newsreels are comparable more to the other news media (newspapers and radio) than to the other modes of film practice.

The role of the news media in wartime, as Nicholas Pronay has observed, is one of information control. 'Its aim is to persuade through affecting the balance of information which reaches the public through omissions,' he writes, 'and the better its work is done the less it is noticed and discussed by contemporaries.'[7] The MOI clearly attached much importance to the newsreels – they were given first priority in the allocation of film stock, for example – but their role needs to be seen in the wider context of the news media generally than just as another type of film propaganda. After the fiascos of 1939, the control mechanisms of censorship were sorted out so that for most of the war the system operated relatively smoothly. All the British news media relied on the news agencies for 'hot' news (the Press Association for home affairs and Reuters for overseas news). The MOI was able to control the supply of information by installing its own censors at the source and then letting journalists and editors do what they wanted with what they were given. In other words, the flow of information was controlled but freedom of interpretation remained, which gave the impression to many that no censorship at all was being imposed. In the case of the newsreels, because of their visual content, they were also subjected to security censorship before they could be sent out to cinemas. The MOI's Press and Censorship Division was responsible for approving over 3000 issues from the five newsreel companies (Gaumont-British News, British Movietone, British Paramount, Universal and Pathe) during the war. The relationship between the MOI and the newsreel companies, like that between the ministry and the press, was based on a large degree of mutual co-operation. The newsreels came to play a vital role in the MOI's policy of providing what it considered 'the truth, nothing but the truth, and as near as possible the whole truth' to the public. News could be withheld and the facts could be interpreted in as favourable a manner as possible, but no outright deliberate falsehoods were allowed. Even news of British military reverses was handled with a frankness that was quite remarkable. This helped to give the impression that the news was uncensored, which, as Philip Taylor writes, 'provided an effective disguise for official propaganda and a clearer conscience for a liberal democracy at war'.[8]

To what extent can British film propaganda be seen in terms of an attempt by those 'above' (the official propagandists of the MOI) to control the opinions and attitudes of those 'below' (the masses)? Given that the cinema-going audience was largely working-class, and given that the MOI was an official state body in a country at war which depended on the co-operation and commitment of its population to the national war effort, it is tempting to see the cinema simply as a channel for presenting the 'official' ideology and point of view to the public. Was it not the MOI's role, after all, to instruct the people how to behave, to instil in them the desire to work for victory, and to persuade them that the government's policy for achieving that victory was the right one? This, however, would be far too simplistic an understanding of the relationship between leaders and led in wartime Britain. It is also an unsatisfactory model for explaining either the role of propaganda in a democracy or the nature of the cinema as a medium of propaganda. The concept of hegemony, much favoured by the Marxist school of writers, has been applied in trying to construct a theoretical basis for film propaganda. The over-simplistic notion that ideas can be imposed from above is rejected in favour of an emphasis on the processes of struggle, resistance and acceptance, whereby a negotiated compromise is reached. As Geoff Hurd has remarked, the British cinema 'was not simply a vehicle for the downward transmission of ideologies which uniformly supported official needs'. Rather, he suggests, it was 'a site of negotiation and transaction: between on the one hand official needs and on the other hand the aspirations of all those groups and classes whose support for the war effort had to be won'.[9] This is a classic statement of Gramscian ideas, but what the film theorists never really get to grips with is precisely what and where the areas of negotiation and transaction were in the relationship between the state and the cinema-going public.

There are several ways in which the historical and empirical approach can identify these points of negotiation. In the first place, of course, the British wartime cinema was not a monolithic institution for the dissemination of official propaganda. There has been a tendency on the part of some writers to assume that because the MOI had (notional) approval of scripts and control over film stock allocation (more correctly, this was in fact exercised by the Board of Trade), therefore all films made in Britain during the war were in some way 'official'.[10] This is misleading in two respects. First, it ignores the fact that the relationship between cinema and state did allow the production of some films which dissented from the official view on what constituted good propaganda (*Colonel Blimp* being the foremost example). Second, it also ignores the fact that by no means all British wartime films can legitimately be described as propaganda. The primary role of the cinema was as a provider of entertainment and escapism, and audience tastes were strongly in favour of films which provided what the trade press described as 'pleasant, harmless relief from the very ugly world in which we are living today'.[11] The different types of war propaganda films were prominent in the generic profile of British cinema, but even so they were still outnumbered by popular comedies and romantic melodramas. While some comedy films can be thought to have a tangential propaganda content – George Formby punching out Hitler in *Let George Do It!* (1940), for instance – it would be stretching the argument to absurd limits to suggest that the costume melodramas such as *The Wicked Lady* (1945), which were the outstanding British popular successes of the 1940s, can be described as propaganda in any real sense. There is no evidence that the MOI ever took a close interest in such mainstream genre cinema. And furthermore, the majority of films shown on British screens still came from Hollywood. The most popular film of the war years was *Gone With the Wind*, and, as Angus Calder suggests, 'the millions of war-weary minds which encountered it were content to be swept away by its colour, costume and glamour'.[12]

There are other, more specific, points of negotiation and transaction which can be identified. Although films could be used to present arguments to the public, there was no guarantee that the public would accept or even recognise those arguments. There is evidence, particularly in regard to short film propaganda, that audiences were left unaffected by appeals and exhortations. Nor, in the last analysis, could films actually compel people to think or behave in a particular way. This was evident, for example, in the reception of the three 'Careless Talk' shorts made by Ealing in 1940. As one trade journalist observed:

Without compulsion, I don't think you will ever stop people gossiping; and certainly the most inveterate characters are those who are unaware of their own shortcomings in this respect. There are none so deaf as those who don't hear – and, as I see it, the message of these shorts is bound to be wasted on the empty air.[13]

There is even some evidence of resistance to film propaganda, such as the woman who made a point of not going to see *The Lion Has Wings* on the grounds that 'I don't go to any British propaganda films, least of all about the war'.[14]

British film propaganda, then, involved much more than simply the downward transmission of an official ideology. Indeed, it could be argued that in adopting as its main theme the idea of a people's war, film propaganda was as much responding to the mood of the country as it was trying to determine it. It has been suggested that film can be either 'witting testimony' (meaning that it conveys an intentional message) or 'unwitting testimony' (whereby film reflects the social and political climate of the times).[15] In the case of Second World War film propaganda, it is both: 'witting' in so far as it set out to encourage a sense of national unity and popular commitment to the war effort, 'unwitting' in the sense that it reflected a national spirit which to a large degree existed already. Of course there is disagreement among historians as to the precise extent of social cohesion in wartime Britain, but most would agree that there was a quite widespread and genuine commitment to the war effort on the part of the British people. The images of the British at war presented through the cinema were a powerful and dramatic means of constructing the people as united in their common struggle, but in the last analysis those images were perhaps just a heightened version of reality.

Notes

For the endnotes books are cited by the date of the edition used. The full publication details of all books referred to are in the bibliography. Where film reviews from newspapers and periodicals are cited without a page number, the source is the British Film Institute's microfiche on the film, which do not usually include page numbers of clippings. All newspapers and periodicals referred to are cited using their full titles used at the time of publication.

Introduction

1. *Report of the Committee on Cinematograph Films*, Cmd 5320 (1936), p 4.
2. Quoted in R. Taylor, *Film Propaganda: Soviet Russia and Nazi Germany* (1979), p 29.
3. *The Times*, 13 April 1926, p 12.
4. J. Grierson, 'Summary and Survey (1935)', in F. Hardy (ed.), *Grierson on Documentary* (1966), p 68.
5. R. Taylor, *Film Propaganda*, p 27.
6. S. Rowson, 'A Statistical Survey of the Cinema Industry in Great Britain in 1934', *Journal of the Royal Statistical Society*, 99 (1936), pp 67–129.
7. *The Cinema Audience* (1943), published in J. P. Mayer, *British Cinemas and their Audiences* (1948), pp 251–75.
8. Ibid, p 252.
9. L. W. Doob, *Propaganda: Its Psychology and Technique* (1935), p 374.
10. R. Taylor, *Film Propaganda*, p 15.
11. F. C. Bartlett, *Political Propaganda* (1940), p 16.
12. The organisation and policies of the BBFC have been well covered by historians. See in particular J. C. Robertson, *The British Board of Film Censors: Film Censorship in Britain, 1896–1950* (1985), and *The Hidden Cinema: British Film Censorship in Action, 1913–1975* (1989). The interwar period is discussed by N. Pronay, 'The First Reality: Film Censorship in Liberal England', in K. R. M. Short (ed.), *Feature Films as History* (1981), pp 113–37, and in two articles by J. Richards in the *Historical Journal of Film, Radio and Television*, 'The British Board of Film Censors and Content Control in the 1930s (1): Images of Britain', 1/2 (1981), pp 95–119, and 'The British Board of Film Censors and Content Control in the 1930s (2): Foreign Affairs', 2/1 (1982), pp 38–48.

13. R. Taylor, *Film Propaganda*, p 230.

14. I. McLaine, *Ministry of Morale: Home Front Morale and the Ministry of Information in World War II* (1979). The only reference to film propaganda in McLaine's book is a single and highly misleading footnote in his conclusion: 'The work of the Crown Film Unit had little impact: "A nice little flash in the cultural pan – kept the documentary film-makers happy, but had almost no effect, as the films had *v. small* audiences." According to Tom Harrisson, Mass-Observation found that audiences did not respond to the films as the makers and the Ministry had intended' (p 279). Charles Barr has since pointed out the 'concentrated wrongness' of this statement: for example, the work of the Crown Film Unit did not keep all the documentary film-makers happy, as some of them were disaffected by the apparent favouritism shown to Crown at the expense of the independent documentary companies; the quotation in the note is not by Tom Harrisson, as it seems to imply, but by Dr Stephen Taylor, who worked for the MOI as Director of Home Intelligence but was not connected with the Films Division; and neither Harrisson, nor Mass-Observation of which he was co-founder, ever dismissed all the MOI's film activities as roundly as McLaine suggests (C. Barr, 'War Record', *Sight and Sound*, 58/4, Autumn 1989, pp 263–4).

15. M. Balfour, *Propaganda in War, 1939–1945: Organisations, Policies and Publics in Britain and Germany* (1979).

16. A. Calder, *The People's War: Britain 1939–1945* (1969). Calder writes: 'Audiences preferred home-made products which reconstructed the boredom and banality, as well as the heroism, of the People's War, to uncomprehendingly romantic American films about life in Britain, Calif. (The infamous *Mrs Miniver*, the saga of middle-class courage set in an olde world utopia, provoked very mixed reactions from British audiences)' (p 369). In fact it was the critics who preferred the home-grown products, whereas popular taste was strongly in favour of the romantic melodramas of Hollywood: *Mrs Miniver* was the most successful film at the British box-office in 1942.

17. There are too many examples of this school of historiography to list them in their entirety. The ones which have most to say about the British cinema of the Second World War are: R. Manvell, *Film* (1946); *The Film and the Public* (1955); *Films and the Second World War* (1974); P. Rotha with R. Griffith, *The Film Till Now: A Survey of World Cinema* (1949), a substantially revised and updated edition of Rotha's original book of 1930 in which the new section, 'The Film Since Then', is largely the work of Griffith); P. Rotha with S. Road and R. Griffith, *Documentary Film* (1952); and B. Wright, *The Long View: A Personal Perspective on World Cinema* (1974).

18. The phrase was apparently first used by the documentarist John Shearman in an article entitled 'Wartime Wedding', *Documentary News Letter*, 6/54 (1946), p 53.

19. R. Murphy, *Realism and Tinsel: Cinema and Society in Britain 1939–1948* (1989) is the most sustained challenge to the critical orthodoxy. In looking at critically neglected genres such as melodramas, costume pictures, comedies and 'morbid thrillers', Murphy's aim is 'to explore the extensive hinterland put out of bounds by this combination of well-intentioned puritanism, snobbery, and timid, derivative aesthetics' (p 233). His own preference is clearly for the 'tinsel' ('I would gladly contend that *The Man in Grey* is a better and more interesting film than *San Demetrio, London*').

20. Preface to P. M. Taylor (ed.), *Britain and the Cinema in the Second World War* (1988), p viii.

21. R. Manvell, *Films and the Second World War*, p 63.

22. J. Richards, 'Wartime Cinema Audiences and the Class System: the case of *Ships With Wings*' (1941), *Historical Journal of Film, Radio and Television*, 7/2 (1987), pp 129–41.

23. J. Richards and A. Aldgate, *Best of British: Cinema and Society 1930–1970* (1983); and

A. Aldgate and J. Richards, *Britain Can Take It: The British Cinema in the Second World War* (1986).

24. M. Dickinson and S. Street, *Cinema and State: The Film Industry and the British Government 1927–84* (1985).

25. S. Harper, *Picturing the Past: The Rise and Fall of the British Costume Film* (1994).

26. S. Neale, 'Propaganda', *Screen*, 18/3 (1977), pp 9–40. Neale starts from the premise that discussion of propaganda in the cinema 'cuts across a number of traditional divisions and demarcations: between art and politics, between documentary and fiction, between text and institution'. He considers that this results in 'a series of insoluble contradictions' and that what is required is 'the replacing of propaganda within a different conceptual space'. He does this by analysing textual systems and modes of address, arguing that propaganda can be seen to be present in films when they break with the conventions of the classical realist narrative to invoke a specific mode of address to the spectator. However, even films which are not in themselves propaganda can nevertheless serve a 'propagandist function' depending upon the context of their exhibition and the 'ideological apparatuses' present. In Neale's analysis, therefore, while the German films *Der Ewige Jude (The Eternal Jew)* and *Jud Süss (Jew Süss)* are both 'closely related in producing an anti-Semitic position', *Der Ewige Jude*, a 'documentary' about the history of European Jews, is propaganda, whereas *Jud Süss*, a narrative feature film, is not propaganda in itself but serves a propagandist function within the anti-Semitic ideological apparatus of Nazi Germany. Similarly, Hollywood's populist films of the 1930s are not propaganda because they conform to the classical narrative and were part of a cinema whose 'ideological conjecture' was escapism and entertainment.

27. A. Kuhn, '*Desert Victory* and the People's War', *Screen*, 22/2 (1981), pp 45–68. Kuhn concludes that the film 'is structured by a complex series of ideological operations whose effect is to position spectators in a particular relationship to World War II, to each other, to nationhood, and finally to history'. What this means is that the film uses words and images to address the spectator beyond the immediate context of the Battle of El Alamein. It does this by using three 'signifiers of Britishness' (Big Ben, the Union Jack and Winston Churchill) to transcend the specific historical moment and construct an eternal, mythic British national identity. 'At this moment,' she writes, 'the subject/ object of the film's address – the People – is effectively dehistoricised ... To this extent, *Desert Victory* is an ideological constitution of the British People as an eternal unity, transcending the vicissitudes of history.' While this sort of textual analysis can be useful in analysing the techniques of film propaganda, it has obvious limitations for the historian who is more concerned with exploring the production and reception of the film. Rather than dehistoricising a film like *Desert Victory*, it seems reasonable to suggest that its success was due in large measure to its historical specificity in that it depicted the first major British victory of the war.

28. Andrew Higson and Steve Neale, 'Afterword', in G. Hurd (ed.), *National Fictions: World War Two in British Films and Television* (1984), p 73.

29. The more recent, post-Thatcher manifestations of the *Screen* school have been less trenchant in their approach. For example, in his book *Waving the Flag: Constructing a National Cinema in Britain* (1995), Andrew Higson undertakes close case studies of selected films from the 1920s to the 1940s in discussing different concepts of national cinema. As well as discussing the textual devices and formal strategies of the films he also adopts (to an extent) the methodology of the empiricists by placing them in relation to contemporary critical discourses. However, the crux of his argument, and his choice of examples, is essentially the same as his essay in G. Hurd (ed.), *National Fictions* ('Five Films', pp 22–6). Moreover, given that he situates wartime features such as *Millions Like*

Us and *This Happy Breed* in the context of the documentary tradition, the book is hardly the major challenge to the critical orthodoxy which it purports to be.

30. C. Barr, *Ealing Studios* (1977), p 13.

31. Barr has been commissioned to write the Second World War volume of the *History of the British Film*, continuing the series started by Rachael Low. Seven volumes were published between 1948 and 1985, all written by Low: *The History of the British Film 1896–1906* (1948), co-written with Roger Manvell; *The History of the British Film 1906–1914* (1949); *The History of the British Film 1914–1918* (1950); *The History of the British Film 1918–1929* (1971); *Documentary and Educational Films of the 1930s* (1979); *Films of Comment and Persuasion in the 1930s* (1979); and *Film Making in 1930s Britain* (1985). Although the early volumes have been overtaken by more recent scholarship, the series as a whole still represents a hugely important contribution to British film history. Barr's volume, provisionally entitled *The Film at War*, has been 'forthcoming' for several years.

32. D. Welch, *Propaganda and the German Cinema 1933–1945* (1983); C. R. Koppes and G. D. Black, *Hollywood Goes to War: How Politics, Profits and Propaganda Shaped World War II Movies* (1988).

33. An example of the caution with which the Mass-Observation material should be treated is the report (File Report 1198) on the film *Arms from Scrap* (British Movietone, 1942), one of the MOI's weekly shorts. 'I thought this a quite particularly bad and uninteresting film,' wrote one observer from a London cinema. The observer complained that the film 'had no logical sequence' and that it was so dull that it 'was rather like looking at some, not very interesting person's holiday snapshots without quite knowing what the snapshots were about'. However, the report on the film found that over 80 per cent of those questioned thought it either 'good' or 'very good' and that two-fifths thought it better than the average MOI film. Thus there was a wide gulf between the audience response and the observer's own views. Len England, Mass-Observation's senior film researcher, was clearly concerned that reports should be unbiased and empirically-based. In June 1941, for example, he told one observer whose report on the feature film *This England* had evidently not matched England's own exacting standards that 'you must be a little bit less subjective. You and I know that *This England* is a complete flop by our standards, but we aren't interested in that as observers. What interests us is (a) the exact as possible story of the film plus such trivia as director, company, cast etc and (b) audience reaction to the film' (quoted in J. Richards and D. Sheridan [eds], *Mass-Observation at the Movies*, 1987, p 9).

1. The MOI Films Division

1. M. Powell, *A Life in Movies: An Autobiography* (1987), p 383.

2. I. McLaine, *Ministry of Morale: Home Front Morale and the Ministry of Information in World War II* (1979), p 3.

3. E. Waugh, *Put Out More Flags* (1942), p 110.

4. K. Clark, *The Other Half: A Self-Portrait* (1986), pp 9–10.

5. A. Duff Cooper, *Old Men Forget* (1957), p 285.

6. PRO FO 371/22839: Memorandum by Lord Halifax, 22 October 1939.

7. *Parliamentary Debates: House of Commons*, 26 September 1939, 5th Series, vol 351, col 1209. In answer to a parliamentary question, Sir Edward Grigg, the MOI's Parliamentary Secretary, said that there were 872 staff employed at Senate House and 127 in the regional offices. When it was realised that the numbers added up to 999, it provided an obvious source of amusement and satire for both MPs and the press.

8. N. Riley, *999 And All That* (1940), p 11.

9. P. Rotha, 'Documentary is Neither Short nor Long' (1946), *Rotha on the Film: A Selection of Writings about the Cinema* (1958), p 234.

10. Quoted in C. Moorehead, *Sidney Bernstein: A Biography* (1984), p 120.

11. *Evening News*, 11 December 1940, p 2.

12. Quoted in I. McLaine, *Ministry of Morale*, p 12.

13. For an account of the work of the Cinema Propaganda Department, see N. Reeves, *Official British Film Propaganda During the First World War* (1986).

14. For a detailed account of the pre-war planning of film censorship and its subsequent operation during the war, see J. C. Robertson, 'British Film Censorship Goes to War', *Historical Journal of Film, Radio and Television*, 2/1 (1982), pp 49–64.

15. Quoted in U. Bialer, *The Shadow of the Bomber: The Fear of Air Attack and British Politics* (1980), p 21.

16. See M. Paris, *From the Wright Brothers to Top Gun: Aviation, Nationalism and Popular Cinema* (1995), pp 105–6; and also C. Frayling's monograph in the BFI's 'Film Classics' series, *Things to Come* (1995).

17. A. Aldgate, *Cinema and History: British Newsreels and the Spanish Civil War* (1979), p 159.

18. 'Introduction' to F. Thorpe and N. Pronay with C. Coultass, *British Official Films in the Second World War: A Descriptive Catalogue* (1980), p 18.

19. N. Riley, *999 And All That*, p 34.

20. PRO INF 1/194: Sir Joseph Ball to Lord Macmillan, 10 October 1939.

21. A. J. P. Taylor, *English History 1914–1945* (1965), p 456.

22. Reith had wanted the job of Minister of Information and had believed that Chamberlain would offer it to him. Both Lord Beaverbrook and Sir Samuel Hoare would apparently have liked him to have been given the post, but he was in America when war was declared. A. Boyle, *Only the Wind Will Listen: Reith of the BBC* (1972), p 300.

23. PRO INF 1/194: Sir Joseph Ball to Lord Macmillan, 10 October 1939.

24. M-O File Report 1: 'Channels of Publicity', 11 October 1939, p 4.

25. F. Thorpe and N. Pronay, *British Official Films*, pp 22 and 23.

26. N. Pronay, '"The Land of Promise": The Projection of Peace Aims in Britain', in K. R. M. Short (ed.), *Film and Radio Propaganda in World War II* (1982), p 56.

27. T. J. Hollins, 'The Conservative Party and Film Propaganda between the Wars', *English Historical Review*, 96/379 (1981), p 366.

28. Quoted in E. Sussex, *The Rise and Fall of British Documentary* (1975), p 119. Sir Kenneth Clark suggested that personal favour was involved in that Ball 'had secured the patronage of Mr Neville Chamberlain because he owned a reach of the River Test, and asked Mr Chamberlain down to fish' (*The Other Half*), p 11.

29. *Parliamentary Debates: House of Commons*, 23 November 1939, 5th Series, vol 353, cols 1438–40. These facts were made known by Sir Edward Grigg in a written answer to a question from the Liberal MP Geoffrey Mander.

30. *Daily Film Renter*, 12 September 1939, p 2.

31. PRO INF 1/194: Ball to Macmillan, 10 October 1939.

32. Ibid. It was decided after the second meeting of the Trade Advisory Committee that the full committee would be 'too unwieldy a body to meet except on rare occasions, and that the best plan would be for me [Ball] to get in touch with the different sections of it whenever necessary'. This does not appear ever to have happened. There was to be no other formal trade body in regular liaison with the MOI until the setting up of the Ideas Committee at the end of 1941.

33. Ibid: 'Ministry of Information Films Division: General Plan of Operations', 25 September 1939.

34. P. Rotha, 'The British Case (2)' (1941), *Rotha on the Film*, p 224. Sir Kenneth Clark also painted a picture of inactivity on Ball's part: 'There was nothing to be learned from my precedecessor in the job ... I paid him a routine call, and found a small, fat man sitting behind an empty desk, with lines of cigarette ash stretched across the folds of his waistcoat. He cannot have moved for a long time. He did not bother to be polite to me, and when I asked him about his staff said that he had never met them' (*The Other Half*), pp 10–11.

35. Arts Enquiry, *The Factual Film* (1947), p 63.

36. *Parliamentary Debates: House of Lords*, 25 October 1939, 5th Series, vol 114, col 1527; *Today's Cinema*, 27 October 1939, p 2.

37. PRO INF 1/30: A. P. Waterfield to D. B. Woodburn, 10 November 1939.

38. Ibid: Forbes to Establishments Division, 1 November 1939.

39. Ibid: Ball to Establishments Division, 30 October 1939.

40. PRO INF 1/196: Undated memorandum by Charles Peake.

41. K. Clark, *The Other Half*, p 10.

42. F. Thorpe and N. Pronay, *British Official Films*, p 34. Film director Thorold Dickinson said that a campaign against Ball was orchestrated behind the scenes by Lady Margot Asquith. Ball supposedly told Dickinson that the cinemas would remain closed and his services would not be needed, whereupon 'I went at once to see Anthony Asquith, and his mother lost no time in inviting a number of Cabinet Ministers and Members of Parliament to 44 Bedford Square. She denounced the Government ... Her attack was devastating: it galvanised the Government into action. Sir Joseph Ball was replaced by Sir Kenneth Clark' (quoted in R. J. Minney, *Puffin Asquith*, 1973, p 103).

43. *Documentary News Letter*, 1 (January 1940), p 1.

44. *Daily Film Renter*, 15 April 1940, p 2.

45. *The Times*, 6 January 1940, p 4.

46. Ibid, p 5.

47. PRO INF 1/867: Co-Ordinating Committee Paper No 1, 'Programme for Film Propaganda'.

48. PRO INF 1/848: Policy Committee Paper No 4, 'The Principles Underlying British Wartime Propaganda'.

49. PRO INF 1/615: Oliver Bell to the Board of Trade, 17 January 1940.

50. Quoted in M. Dickinson and S. Street, *Cinema and State: The Film Industry and the British Government 1927–84* (1985), p 51.

51. PRO INF 1/615: Sir Edward Villiers to Sir Kenneth Clark, 18 March 1940.

52. Ibid: 'Notes on the Services Which the British Film Institute Might Render to the Ministry of Information'. Clark and Brass had met for lunch at the Travellers' Club some time in late March.

53. Ibid: Clark to Brass, 8 April 1940.

54. Ibid: Clark to Lord Hood, 7 May 1940.

55. F. Thorpe and N. Pronay, *British Official Films*, p 21.

56. K. Clark, *The Other Half*, p 15.

57. *Daily Mirror*, 16 April 1940, p 6.

58. M. Powell, *A Life in Movies*, p 383.

59. *Documentary News Letter*, 1/5 (May 1940), p 1.

60. *Daily Film Renter*, 15 April 1940, p 2.

61. Ibid, 17 April 1940, p 2.

62. Ibid, 27 June 1940, p 2.

63. Beddington evidently attached some importance to the criticisms made of the Films Division by the trade press. In July 1940 he asked that 'in order to restore the

reputation of the Films Division ... we should have at least the part time services of a journalist really experienced in Wardour Street technique' whose job would be to 'generally keep the Press sweet'. This request did not meet with the approval of the Director-General Sir Kenneth Lee who was opposed to individual divisions appointing their own press officers when the MOI already had a Press and Public Relations Division (PRO INF 1/30). However, the Films Division did eventually acquire its own press officer in the person of one J. D. Griggs.

64. *Kinematograph Weekly*, 14 May 1940, p 4.

65. *Documentary News Letter*, 1/7 (July 1940), p 3.

66. There is some anecdotal evidence that the MOI took notice of what was said in *Documentary News Letter*. 'It became a very, very influential journal throughout the war,' Basil Wright said. 'It had an enormous influence on government thinking in the information services. This is no joking at all: many the time I went into a government office to see somebody and there would be a file marked "priority", which would be a clipping from *Documentary News Letter* with a notice from the minister asking what was the answer to this question. I believe it was tremendously useful, actually' (quoted in E. Sussex, *The Rise and Fall of British Documentary*, p 121).

67. *Spectator*, 21 June 1940, p 837.

68. F. Thorpe and N. Pronay, *British Official Films*, p 36.

69. Arts Enquiry, *The Factual Film*, p 64. The contents of this memorandum are unknown, as it is not to be found in either the Public Record Office or the Film Centre Collection held by the British Film Institute Library.

70. PRO BW 4/62: M. Neville Kearney to Stuart, 25 April 1941.

71. Quoted in E. Sussex, *The Rise and Fall of British Documentary*, p 122.

72. 'Tatler', for example, wrote: 'Well, thank goodness for one common-sense appointment, because at least Sidney does know what it's all about, which is more than can be said about a lot of people connected with this Department ... it's the first appointment I have been able to chronicle with any real sense of pleasure, and I know the whole trade will endorse it' (*Daily Film Renter*, 26 June 1940, p 2). And *Documentary News Letter* opined: 'His appointment is the most welcome sign of the last few months' (1/7, July 1940, p 2).

73. *Thirteenth Report from the Select Committee on National Expenditure* (1940), p 3.

74. PRO INF 1/59: 'Comments by the Films Division on the Thirteenth Report from the Select Committee on National Expenditure'.

75. *Sight and Sound*, 9/35 (Autumn 1940), p 38.

76. PRO INF 1/615: Beddington to E. L. Mercier, 9 January 1941.

77. Ibid: E. St John Bamford to Beddington, 27 February 1941.

78. K. Clark, *The Other Half*, p 22.

79. *The Times*, 8 July 1942, p 5.

80. *Parliamentary Debates: House of Commons*, 5 August 1943, 5th Series, vol 391, col 2587.

81. Quoted in I. McLaine, *Ministry of Morale*, p 241.

82. *Daily Sketch*, 5 November 1941, p 3.

83. Ibid, 6 November 1941, p 4.

84. *Documentary News Letter*, 2/7 (July 1941), p 121.

85. Ibid, 3/8 (August 1942), p 111.

86. *The Cinema*, 16 September 1942, p 8.

87. *Documentary News Letter*, 5/3 (1944), p 26.

88. Ibid, 5/49 (1945), p 86.

2. A Policy for Film Propaganda

1. PRO INF 1/867: Co-Ordinating Committee Paper No 1, 'Programme for Film Propaganda', p 4 (15).
2. PRO INF 1/196: Memorandum by Charles Peake.
3. PRO FO 371/22839: Lord Lothian to Lord Halifax, 28 September 1939.
4. L. W. Doob, *Propaganda: Its Psychology and Technique* (1935), p 3.
5. J. Richards and D. Sheridan (eds), *Mass-Observation at the Movies* (1987), p 319.
6. A. Duff Cooper, *Old Men Forget* (1957), pp 287–8.
7. Britain's perceived success in propaganda during the First World War was based to a large extent on the views of foreign commentators. In *Mein Kampf* Hitler praised the 'brilliant work' of Crewe House, the British Enemy Propaganda Department under Lord Northcliffe, in undermining German morale. Of course it must be borne in mind that Hitler had a propagandist intention of his own: in attributing Germany's defeat in 1918 to British propaganda he was able to perpetuate the myth that Germany had been 'betrayed' at home and that the German Army had not been defeated on the field of battle. American commentators also believed that Wellington House, the British War Propaganda Bureau under Charles Masterman, had conducted a highly effective campaign to infiltrate the American press and 'trick' America into joining the war. This view was expressed, for example, by H. C. Peterson's *Propaganda for War: The Campaign Against American Neutrality* (1939) which, appearing when it did, was an implicit warning of the possibility that history might repeat itself.
8. C. Barr, 'War Record', *Sight and Sound*, 58/4 (Autumn 1989), p 263.
9. W. J. West (ed.), *Orwell: The War Broadcasts* (1985), p 67. West offers an interesting if not entirely convincing reading of *Nineteen Eighty-Four* as an allegory of Orwell's wartime experiences at the MOI. For example, Winston Smith works for the Ministry of Truth, where his job is the routine falsification of records (i.e. propaganda is all lies). Furthermore, just as Orwell's Ministry of Truth was one of the largest buildings in London, visible from Smith's flat in Victory Mansions, so the Senate House of London University (where the MOI was based) was the tallest building in wartime London and would have been visible from Orwell's flat in St John's Wood. The 'Newspeak' name for the Ministry of Truth is 'Minitrue'; the telegraphic address of the MOI was 'Miniform'. West even suggests that the minister's office at the MOI was the inspiration for Orwell's nightmarish 'Room 101'. Curiously, West misses what seems to be the most obvious parallel, that 'Big Brother' had the same initials as Brendan Bracken, the minister with whom Orwell had experienced difficulties over his broadcasts for the Eastern Section of the BBC.
10. P. M. Taylor, 'Techniques of Persuasion: Basic Ground Rules of British Propaganda During the Second World War', *Historical Journal of Film, Radio and Television*, 1/1 (1981), pp 59–65, provides a verbatim transcript of the original document. The Royal Institute probably had a greater influence on the Foreign Office than on the MOI.
   It should be noted, in the context of the Royal Institute's views on propaganda, that one of its members was the historian A. J. Toynbee who during the First World War had published a supposedly 'authentic' but in fact largely fabricated account of war atrocities, *The German Terror in France* (1917). In *Mein Kampf* Hitler had professed great admiration for this type of propaganda. However, the revelation after the war that atrocity stories had been fabricated to arouse hatred came as a shock to British public opinion and contributed to the negative connotations of propaganda. This was to be a factor in the MOI's very cautious attitude towards hate propaganda during the

Second World War when, with a bitter irony, there was much more truthful evidence of German atrocities.

11. For a discussion of these contemporary discourses, see K. Robins, F. Webster and M. Pickering, 'Propaganda, Information and Social Control', in J. Hawthorn (ed.), *Propaganda, Persuasion and Polemic* (1987), pp 1–17.

12. F. C. Bartlett, *Political Propaganda* (1940), p 153.

13. S. Harper, *Picturing the Past: The Rise and Fall of the British Costume Film* (1994), p 77.

14. F. C. Bartlett, *Political Propaganda*, p 134.

15. Quoted in F. Thorpe and N. Pronay, with C. Coultass, *British Official Films in the Second World War: A Descriptive Catalogue* (1980), p 7. Furthermore, it was during Reith's time as minister that the MOI News Division adopted the policy to 'tell the truth, nothing but the truth, and as near as possible the whole truth' (PRO INF 1/856: Draft policy document, March 1940).

16. Quoted in I. McLaine, *Ministry of Morale: Home Front Morale and the Ministry of Information in World War II* (1979), p 227.

17. Ibid, p 251.

18. F. C. Bartlett, *Political Propaganda*, p 54.

19. M-O File Report 1119: 'Seaman Frank', 28 February 1942, p 1.

20. R. S. Lambert, *Propaganda* (1938), p 61.

21. PRO FO 371/22839: Memorandum by Lord Halifax, 21 October 1939.

22. See H. Mark Glancy, 'Hollywood's British Films, 1935–1945', unpublished PhD thesis, University of East Anglia, 1993.

23. PRO FO 371/24230. A film of *Captain Horatio Hornblower* was suggested by Warner Bros, who employed C. S. Forester to write a script 'with a very strongly pro-British stance'. The Foreign Office told the MOI that 'in our view there could be no better instance than the one under reference in which to relax the dollar remittance for propaganda purposes'. However, the MOI was opposed to such a move. 'I don't think the Ministry of Information could be a party to putting pressure on the Treasury with the object suggested,' said Sir Frederick Whyte, Director of the MOI's American Division. 'The main value of the Hornblower film for us will be in the United States where it has a practically assured market; and I doubt whether Warner Bros would stop production on the film because they were not sure of the original 100% British revenue on it.'

24. *Kinematograph Weekly*, 7 September 1939, p 2.

25. Quoted in M. Dickinson and S. Street, *Cinema and State: The Film Industry and the British Government 1927–84* (1985), p 104.

26. *Kinematograph Weekly*, 28 September 1939, p 19.

27. Ibid, 29 February 1940, p 19.

28. Ibid, 3 October 1940, p 4.

29. P. Swann, *The British Documentary Film Movement, 1926–1946* (1989), p 166.

30. *The Times*, 1 November 1938, p 12.

31. *Documentary News Letter*, 2/4 (April 1941), p 65.

32. Ibid, 1/2 (February 1940), p 2.

33. Ibid, 3/5 (May 1942), p 67.

34. Ibid, 1 (January 1940), p 1.

35. Ibid, 1/3 (March 1940), p 3.

36. A. B. White, *The New Propaganda* (1939), p 304.

37. PRO INF 1/867: 'Programme for Film Propaganda'. This document is published verbatim in I. Christie (ed.), *Powell, Pressburger and Others* (1978), pp 121–4.

38. A. Aldgate and J. Richards, *Britain Can Take It: The British Cinema in the Second World War* (1986), p 27.

39. F. C. Bartlett, *Political Propaganda*, p 143.

40. See, for example, N. Pronay and J. Croft, 'British Film Censorship and Propaganda Policy during the Second World War', in J. Curran and V. Porter (eds), *British Cinema History* (1983), pp 144–63. Pronay and Croft argue, somewhat unconvincingly, that the MOI secretly approved of *The Life and Death of Colonel Blimp* and that the furore surrounding the film was part of an elaborate camouflage to disguise its official status.

41. PRO INF 1/849: Policy Committee Paper, 'Empire Publicity Campaign', 1 October 1940.

42. Although the credits of the film state that the idea 'originated with Leslie Howard and A. G. Macdonell', it is evident that it received official sanction. At a Planning Committee meeting on 9 September 1940 E. L. Mercier asked for immediate sanction for 'a two-reel Empire film to be made by D & P designed to show the underlying motives for the participation of the Dominions in the war effort, primarily for distribution within the Empire' (INF 1/249).

3. The MOI and Feature Film Propaganda

1. *Thirteenth Report from the Select Committee on National Expenditure* (1940), p 5.

2. V. Porter and C. Litewski, '*The Way Ahead*: Case History of a Propaganda Film', *Sight and Sound*, 50/2 (Spring 1981), p 110.

3. A. Aldgate and J. Richards, *Britain Can Take It: The British Cinema in the Second World War* (1986).

4. *The Cine-Technician*, February–March 1940, p 10.

5. *Spectator*, 3 November 1939.

6. C. Coultass, *Images for Battle: British Film and the Second World War, 1939–1945* (1989), p 20.

7. In his annual list of the top box-office attractions in Britain, the trade journalist R. H. 'Josh' Billings placed the film among the top three of 1939 (after *Pygmalion* and *The Citadel*). He added: 'Some may question the decision and put *The Lion Has Wings* on top, but it must be remembered that the UA British opus was given priority. Bars were dropped to give it a clear run. Moreover, its timing was providential' (*Kinematograph Weekly*, 11 January 1940, p E1).

8. I. Dalrymple, 'The Crown Film Unit, 1940–43', in N. Pronay and D. W. Spring (eds), *Propaganda, Politics and Film, 1918–45* (1982), pp 209–10.

9. M. Korda, *Charmed Lives: A Family Romance* (1980), p 137.

10. *Parliamentary Debates: House of Commons*, 20 September 1939, 5th Series, vol 351, col 973.

11. *Daily Film Renter*, 6 November 1939, p 2.

12. *Today's Cinema*, 31 October 1939, p 2.

13. PRO INF 1/199: 'Receipts from Commercial Distribution of Films: Summary of statement 18 prepared for evidence to the Public Accounts Committee in May 1944'.

14. *Kinematograph Weekly*, 2 November 1939, p 4.

15. *Daily Film Renter*, 29 November 1939, p 2.

16. M-O File Report 15: 'The Lion Has Wings', 26 December 1939, published in J. Richards and D. Sheridan (eds), *Mass-Observation at the Movies* (1987), p 330.

17. *Daily Film Renter*, 1 November 1939, p 2.

18. *The Times*, 31 October 1939, p 8.

19. *Documentary News Letter*, 1 (January 1940), p 8.

20. Tom Harrisson, 'Public Response: The Lion Has Wings', *Documentary News Letter*, 1/2 (February 1940), p 5.

21. J. Richards and D. Sheridan, *Mass-Observation at the Movies*, pp 299–330. Some 200 cinema-goers were questioned, of whom 110 had seen the film. Most people (over 70 per cent of those who had seen it) expressed either a 'like' or a 'strong like' for the film. Some described it in superlatives ('Magnificent' and 'A bloody fine picture') though there were a few who disliked it in equally strong measure ('Pretty awful' and 'Utter tripe'). The survey found that of those who had some remark to make about the content, 'by far the largest criticisms were on the propaganda element in the film'. The general impression was that it contained 'too much propaganda', but this did not necessarily mean that people did not like the film. There were a few respondents who actually commented favourably on the propaganda content ('It was an awfully good picture and it acts as a very good piece of propaganda'), though they were in a minority. As for those who had not seen it, reports of the film's strongly patriotic flavour had a mixed effect. Some said they were put off by what they had heard ('I dodged it. It was all flag-waving, wasn't it?') whereas in other cases the patriotism made people want to see it ('I must see that. I don't like aeroplane films but I feel it's my duty'). There is no evidence for Harrisson's assertion that people who had seen the film said they liked it only because they thought it the right thing to say.

22. PRO INF 1/867: Minutes of the Co-Ordination Committee, 19th Meeting, 23 November 1939.

23. PRO FO 371/22840: F. R. Cowell to G. E. G. Forbes, 1 December 1939.

24. Ibid: Sir Frederick Whyte to John Balfour, 3 November 1939.

25. Ibid: Cowell to Balfour, 7 November 1939.

26. *Today's Cinema*, 26 September 1939, p 1.

27. *Parliamentary Debates: House of Lords*, 25 October 1939, 5th Series, vol 114, col 1528.

28. PRO INF 1/196: Sir Edward Villiers to Sir Joseph Ball, 25 September 1939.

29. The debate over the Film Bank is detailed in M. Dickinson and S. Street, *Cinema and State: The Film Industry and the British Government, 1927–84* (1985), pp 129–39.

30. I. Dalrymple, 'The Crown Film Unit', p 210.

31. *Kinematograph Weekly*, 11 January 1940, p E3.

32. Ibid, 9 November 1939, p 19.

33. *Today's Cinema*, 7 June 1940, p 2.

34. *Sunday Express*, 14 July 1940, p 8.

35. PRO INF 1/867: Minutes of the Co-Ordinating Committee, 11th Meeting, 1 April 1940.

36. *Daily Film Renter*, 24 January 1940, p 2.

37. PRO INF 1/196: Undated circular from Sir Kenneth Clark to Regional Information Officers.

38. PRO INF 1/867: Co-Ordinating Committee Paper No 1, 'Programme for Film Propaganda', p 2 (8a).

39. K. Clark, *The Other Half: A Self-Portrait* (1986), p 12.

40. *Kinematograph Weekly*, 10 October 1940, p 18.

41. D. Badder, 'Powell and Pressburger: The War Years', *Sight and Sound*, 48/1 (Winter 1978–79), p 9.

42. A. Aldgate, 'Why We Fight: *49th Parallel*', in A. Aldgate and J. Richards, *Britain Can Take It*, p 37.

43. PRO INF 1/848: Policy Committee Paper, 'Publicity about the British Empire', 20 January 1940. Considerable importance was obviously attached to the depiction on

screen of the Empire, for in April 1940 another Policy Committee Paper (No 35), 'Propaganda about the Empire', suggested two feature films, 'one for Canada on the NW Mounted Police and one for South Africa on the life of General Botha'.

44. K. Clark, *The Other Half*, p 11.

45. 'How *49th Parallel* Was Born', BFI microfiche on *49th Parallel*.

46. K. Gough-Yates, *Michael Powell: In Collaboration with Emeric Pressburger* (1971), p 7.

47. M. Dickinson and S. Street, *Cinema and State*, pp 259–60, note 25.

48. *Parliamentary Debates: House of Commons*, 18 December 1940, 5th Series, vol 367, col 2000.

49. *Today's Cinema*, 2 July 1940, p 2.

50. *Thirteenth Report from the Select Committee*, p 5.

51. *The Times*, 9 October 1941, p 6.

52. *Variety*, 5 November 1941.

53. PRO INF 1/199: 'Receipts from Commercial Distribution of Films'.

54. *The Times*, 13 January 1942, p 5.

55. *Thirteenth Report from the Select Committee*, p 6.

56. PRO INF 1/59: 'Comments by the Films Division on the Thirteenth Report from the Select Committee on National Expenditure'.

57. 'Films and the Problem of the Month', *Documentary News Letter*, 2/12 (December 1941), p 225.

58. PRO INF 1/249: Planning Committee minutes, 16 December 1940.

59. *Evening News*, 11 December 1940, p 2.

60. PRO BT 64/117: Undated memorandum entitled 'Competition from Official Film Units'.

61. M. Balcon, *Michael Balcon Presents ... A Lifetime of Films* (1969), p 132.

62. Quoted in E. Sussex, *The Rise and Fall of British Documentary* (1975), p 140.

63. *Daily Film Renter*, 4 March 1942, p 1.

64. V. Porter and C. Litewksi, '*The Way Ahead*', p 110.

65. Minutes of the British Film Producers' Association, 9 May 1940.

66. Ibid, 29 January 1942.

67. Ibid, 13 February 1942.

68. Ibid, 13 March 1942.

69. Among the ideas which Beddington suggested were 'the story of Mary Kingsley and her life on the Gold Coast, which portrayed past events connected with the foundation of the British Empire' (13 March 1942) and 'True stories of Greek Heroism in Crete and Greece' (7 May 1942). Neither of these suggestions was acted upon. Beddington also used the BFPA to suggest subjects which the MOI did not want included in films. On 7 May he pointed out 'the undesirability of making films showing actual "escapes" as it had been found out that this led to the tightening up of conditions on the Continent by the Axis Powers'.

70. BFPA minutes, 13 March 1942.

71. Ibid, 25 June 1942.

72. Ibid, 27 July 1942.

73. 'Feature Films – MOI Policy, March 1943', BFPA minutes, 23 March 1943.

74. M. Balcon, ... *A Lifetime of Films*, p 148.

75. C. Barr, *Ealing Studios* (1977), p 35.

76. A. Aldgate and J. Richards, *Britain Can Take It*, p 10.

77. D. Badder, 'Powell and Pressburger: The War Years', p 10.

78. Quoted in R. Murphy, 'British Film Production, 1939 to 1945', in G. Hurd (ed.), *National Fictions: World War Two in British Films and Television* (1984), p 15.

79. M. Powell, *A Life in Movies: An Autobiography* (1987), pp 383–4.

80. T. Dickinson, *A Discovery of Cinema* (1971), p 77.

81. PRO BT 64/130. The Cinematograph Film Control Order came into force on 19 March 1943. According to the official documentation the Order was intended to make 'suppliers and commercial users of cinematograph film obtain licences from the Board of Trade ... The allocation to the distributors (for prints for exhibition in the cinemas) will be based on audited returns of each distributor's consumption in 1942. Film production will be dealt with by allotting film to the producers for their individual pictures.'

82. PRO INF 1/947: 'Government Film Production and Distribution', 1946.

83. L. Olivier, *Confessions of an Actor* (1987), p 130.

84. A. Aldgate, 'If the Invader Comes: *Went the Day Well?*', in A. Aldgate and J. Richards, *Britain Can Take It*, p 126.

85. K. Gough-Yates, *Michael Powell*, p 8.

86. Quoted in I. Christie (ed.), *Powell and Pressburger: The Life and Death of Colonel Blimp* (1994), p 29. The letter from Grigg to Powell is dated simply 'June 1942'.

87. Ibid: S. G. Gates to Powell, 25 June 1942.

88. PRO PREM 4 14/5: Churchill to Brendan Bracken, 8 September 1942. This file has been published as 'The Colonel Blimp File', *Sight and Sound*, 48/1 (Winter 1978–79), pp 13–14. It is also included, along with supplementary documentation, in I. Christie, '*Blimp*, Churchill and the State', in I. Christie (ed.), *Powell, Pressburger and Others* (1978), pp 106–11; and again in I. Christie (ed.), *Powell and Pressburger*, pp 42–53.

89. PRO PREM 4 14/5: Bracken to Churchill, 15 September 1942.

90. See, for example, A. Aldgate, 'What a Difference a War Makes: *The Life and Death of Colonel Blimp*', in J. Richards and A. Aldgate, *Best of British: Cinema and Society 1930–1970* (1983), ch 5, pp 61–74; and N. Pronay and J. Croft, 'British Film Censorship and Propaganda Policy during the Second World War', in J. Curran and V. Porter (eds), *British Cinema History* (1983), particularly pp 155–63. The historiographical controversy around the film is discussed in detail in J. Chapman, '*The Life and Death of Colonel Blimp* (1943) Reconsidered', *Historical Journal of Film, Radio and Television*, 15/1 (March 1995), pp 19–54.

91. M. Powell, *A Life in Movies*, pp 455–7.

4. The MOI and Short Film Propaganda

1. A. Buchanan, 'Whither the Short?', *Sight and Sound*, 11/41 (Summer 1942), p 13. Andrew Buchanan was himself a short-film producer.

2. V. Seligman, 'Ministry of Information Films', *Documentary News Letter*, 3/3 (March 1942), p 45.

3. '1943 Directive Replies to Favourite Films', in J. Richards and D. Sheridan (eds), *Mass-Observation at the Movies* (1987), p 255.

4. P. Swann, *The British Documentary Film Movement, 1926–1946* (1989), p 166.

5. N. Pronay, '"The Land of Promise": The Projection of Peace Aims in Britain', in K. R. M. Short (ed.), *Film and Radio Propaganda in World War II* (1983), p 72.

6. PRO INF 1/194: 'Ministry of Information Films Division: General Plan of Operations', 25 September 1939.

7. PRO INF 1/867: Minutes of the Co-Ordination Committee, 21st Meeting, 7 December 1939.

8. PRO INF 1/196: Anonymous paper, franked with an MOI stamp dated 10 March

1940 (suggesting that it was submitted from an outside source). The intitials 'L. B. C.' are written in pencil on the top right-hand corner of the first page.

9. Ibid: Undated circular from Sir Kenneth Clark to Regional Information Officers.

10. *Documentary News Letter*, 1/6 (June 1940), p 1.

11. PRO INF 5/66: Cavalcanti to David Macdonald, 1 March 1940.

12. Ibid: Notes of a meeting held at the Air Ministry on 8 March 1940.

13. Ibid: S. J. Fletcher to A. G. Highet, 9 March 1940.

14. *Kinematograph Weekly*, 15 February 1940, p 24.

15. *The Times*, 21 March 1940, p 6.

16. *Documentary News Letter*, 1/5 (May 1940), p 17.

17. M-O File Report 458: 'Fifteen Ministry of Information Shorts', 16 October 1940, in J. Richards and D. Sheridan (eds), *Mass-Observation at the Movies*, p 425.

18. *The Times*, 3 July 1940, p 6.

19. K. Clark, *The Other Half: A Self-Portrait* (1986), p 12.

20. PRO INF 1/867: Co-Ordinating Committee Paper No 1, 'Programme for Film Propaganda', p 3 (13).

21. PRO INF 1/849: Policy Committee minutes, 13 June 1940.

22. Ibid: Policy Committee minutes, 14 June 1940.

23. *Daily Film Renter*, 27 June 1940, p 2.

24. PRO INF 1/196: Divisional circular by Jack Beddington, 12 July 1940.

25. *Documentary News Letter*, 1/8 (August 1940), p 1.

26. *Kinematograph Weekly*, 12 December 1940, p 1.

27. BBC 'Postscript', 4 October 1940, reprinted in *Documentary News Letter*, 1/11 (November 1940), p 4.

28. J. Richards, *Thorold Dickinson: The Man and His Films* (1986), p 86.

29. *The New Statesman*, 20 July 1940.

30. R. Ackland and E. Grant, *The Celluloid Mistress or the Custard Pie of Dr. Caligari* (1954), p 86.

31. *Documentary News Letter*, 1/9 (September 1940), p 6.

32. *Spectator*, 16 August 1940, p 167.

33. PRO INF 1/208. Howard's treatment was about a retired colonel who thinks the LDV are useless but is persuaded to enlist and finds his experience is useful when a German bomber is shot down and the crew captured. John Betjeman recorded that the War Office 'object to the Leslie Howard script' and so the idea did not progress any further. *Yeomen of the Guard* got a little further, the script having been 'passed by the WO & approved as an interesting and instructional film on how the HG works'. The idea was passed to Ealing, but Michael Balcon considered that 'this script is written on more expensive lines than the standard Ministry of Information five-minute subjects'. The film was thus forestalled because it was unsuitable for the five-minute format. The Films Division were not very keen on the treatment anyway: a script report (unsigned, though presumably by Betjeman) opined that it 'seems to lack a definite objective' and was more like a training film for the Home Guard than a film for showing to the general public. It was finally killed off by Beddington who considered that the script was 'useless'.

34. PRO INF 1/207. In August 1940 Verity submitted a film treatment entitled *A Rill Mill* ('a real meal'), based on the catchphrase of the comedian Jack Warner. It was to be a cookery demonstration on the right-and-wrong principle with Warner preparing his food in a wasteful way and being shown the correct way by his 'littul gel' assistant. The idea was turned down by Beddington. 'The whole subject of the Jack Warner film for the Ministry was discussed, and I am sorry to say that he does not consider it

possible to include the sort of film you have in mind in our 5-minute programme at the moment,' Betjeman told Box on 18 September.

35. *Today's Cinema*, 23 August 1940, p 2.

36. PRO INF 1/206: Dorothy G. Keeling to Dr Stephen Taylor, 7 August 1940.

37. PRO INF 1/249: Planning Committee minutes, 30 September 1940.

38. PRO INF 6/328: Central Office of Information record sheet.

39. 'They [the MOI] explained that they had commissioned a ten-minute film for America on London in the blitz – which by now was at its height – to be made from newsreel material, and thought I could advise on it. I reluctantly agreed to go along and look at the material, and what I saw horrified me. A newsreel cameraman is trained to get maximum impact from his shots, which must tell their story in a minute or so, without any build-up. Thus, in an air crash or an earthquake, master-shots, showing as much chaos or devastation as possible are his principal aim, with perhaps a few details to be used as cut-ins and link shots, added afterwards. When sent out to film the results of the blitz, he continued to shoot in this way, and the more devastation he could show, the better the newsreel shot. This wasn't the cameraman's fault. He wasn't making propaganda, but just showing facts the best way he could. But the two hours of film I saw would have convinced anyone that the whole of London was completely flattened. I rushed back to the Ministry and suggested that the Crown Film Unit should make the film' (H. Watt, *Don't Look at the Camera*, 1974, pp 137–8).

40. PRO INF 6/328: Press handout by Hugh Findlay. On the whole *Britain Can Take It!* seems to have been well received throughout the country as an indication of how the British people (not just Londoners) were withstanding the Blitz. For example, an editorial in the *Eastern Evening News* entitled 'A Triumph of Propaganda' declared that the film was 'one of the best ways of telling those transatlantic millions of the glorious struggle by London and the rest of Britain that can be imagined' (25 October 1940, p 4). However, there is some evidence that in the provincial cities which had also been heavily bombed there was a degree of resentment that the capital should have been chosen to represent the whole nation. Manchester's Co-operative Wholesale Film Company, for example, produced a short film of its own in reply, entitled *Manchester Took It Too* (1941).

41. *Spectator*, 25 October 1940, p 415.

42. M-O File Report 799: 'Preliminary Report on Opinion about Ministry of Information Shorts', 24 July 1941, in J. Richards and D. Sheridan (eds), *Mass-Observation at the Movies*, p 443.

43. *Documentary News Letter*, 2/7 (July 1941), p 129.

44. PRO INF 5/75. Undated notes on 'Xmas Film' by Harry Watt.

45. Ibid: Christian Barman to Sir Kenneth Clark, 3 January 1941.

46. *Documentary News Letter*, 2/4 (April 1941), p 62.

47. *Manchester Guardian*, 14 February 1941, p 6. Letter from George C. Thompson, School of Social Sciences, Liverpool University.

48. *Documentary News Letter*, 2/11 (November 1941), p 207.

49. Ibid, 2/2 (February 1941), p 21.

50. Ibid, 2/7 (July 1941), p 129.

51. *Today's Cinema*, 20 August 1940, p 2.

52. M-O File Report 639: 'You're Telling Me', 5 April 1941, in J. Richards and D. Sheridan (eds), *Mass-Observation at the Movies*, p 437.

53. *Kinematograph Weekly*, 3 October 1940, p 4.

54. *Sight and Sound*, 9/35 (Autumn 1940), p 39.

55. PRO INF 1/627: Undated memorandum entitled 'Objection to an Order for the Compulsory Exhibition of MOI Films'.

56. M-O File Report 458, in J. Richards and D. Sheridan (eds), *Mass-Observation at the Movies*, p 426.

57. M-O File Report 1193: 'Report on Ministry of Information Shorts', 1 April 1942, in J. Richards and D. Sheridan (eds), *Mass-Observation at the Movies*, pp 445–58. This report was a composite of all the survey results. In the report the films are referred to by abbreviated titles which are sometimes misleading. *Newspaper Train* is abbreviated to *Newspaper* and *Rush Hour* is referred to as *Shopping*. *Seaman Frank Goes Back to Sea* is referred to as *Seaman Laskier*, using the broadcaster's surname instead of his first name. The most misleading abbreviation is that used for *War in the East*, which is sometimes referred to as *Pacific*, apparently in the mistaken belief that the film was called *War in the Pacific*. This is particularly confusing, for a film entitled *War in the Pacific* (Shell Film Unit, 1943) was made later for the fifteen-minute film scheme.

58. Quoted in I. McLaine, *Ministry of Morale: Home Front Morale and the Ministry of Information in World War II* (1979), p 257.

59. J. Richards and D. Sheridan (eds), *Mass-Observation at the Movies*, p 457.

60. *Documentary News Letter*, 3/5 (May 1942), p 66.

61. *The Cinema*, 20 May 1942, p 17.

62. *Daily Film Renter*, 11 June 1942, p 1.

63. Ibid, 18 June 1942, p 2.

64. Ibid, 25 June 1942, p 1.

65. Arts Enquiry, *The Factual Film* (1947), p 67.

66. *Documentary News Letter*, 5/48 (1945), p 77.

67. PRO PREM 4 99/5: Churchill to Brendan Bracken, 16 April 1943.

68. John Grierson had reportedly once remarked that 'in Britain there were more seats outside the cinemas than in them' (P. Rotha, *Documentary Diary: An Informal History of the British Documentary Film, 1928–1939*, London, 1973, p 141). Estimates about the size of the non-theatrical audience during the war, however, vary greatly from one source to another. The *Thirteenth Report from the Select Committee on National Expenditure* (1940) had recommended the non-theatrical scheme should be wound up because 'they regard the cost of reaching an audience of one million a week by this method as out of all proportion to the cost of films shown in cinemas which ... are estimated to reach an audience fifteen or twenty times as great' (p 10). William Farr, the Head of the Central Film Library (successor to the GPO Film Library) wrote a survey entitled *The Film in National Life* (1943) in which he estimated that in the year 1942–43 the MOI's travelling film shows reached 2.5 million regular viewers (which he defined as people who attended at least three shows per year). The authors of *The Factual Film* put the size of the non-theatrical audience rather higher, estimating that it rose from 7 million in 1940–41 to 18.5 million in 1943–44 (p 78). Given that this report was the work of the documentarists themselves, who probably wished to maximise the value of the non-theatrical scheme, it is possible that these figures are exaggerated; certainly they are much higher than most other estimates.

69. Tom Harrisson, 'Films and the Home Front – the Evaluation of Their Effectiveness by the Ministry of Information', in N. Pronay and D. W. Spring (eds), *Propaganda, Politics and Film, 1918–45* (1982), p 244.

70. M-O File Report 1119: 'Seaman Frank', 28 February 1942, p 3.

5. The Crown Film Unit

1. PRO BT 64/117: Memorandum 'Competition from Official Film Units'.

2. P. Rotha, *Documentary Diary: An Informal History of the British Documentary Film, 1928–1939* (1973), p 233.

3. PRO INF 1/56: S. G. Tallents to H. V. Rhodes, 13 October 1938.

4. Quoted in P. Swann, *The British Documentary Film Movement, 1926–1946* (1989), p 152.

5. PRO INF 1/56: G. E. G. Forbes to H. V. Rhodes, 24 August 1939.

6. Ibid: 'Outline of suggested arrangements for the control of expenditure by the Post Office Film Unit on behalf of the Ministry of Information' (undated).

7. Quoted in P. Swann, *The British Documentary Film Movement*, p 154.

8. H. Watt, *Don't Look at the Camera* (1974), p 127.

9. Quoted in C. Barr, 'War Record', *Sight and Sound*, 58/4 (Autumn 1989), p 265.

10. Arts Enquiry, *The Factual Film* (1947), p 64.

11. M-O File Report 1: 'Channels of Publicity', 11 October 1939, p 4.

12. H. Watt, *Don't Look at the Camera*, pp 128–9.

13. PRO INF 1/56: Memorandum by G. E. G. Forbes, 9 September 1939.

14. *Observer*, 12 November 1939.

15. By November 1939 the Film Unit had several projects planned, including 'Balloon Barrage', an 'Agricultural film', a 'Pilot training film' and a 'Shoddyness film for the Home Office' (PRO INF 1/56: Note dated 20 November 1939). Only one of these can be identified with any certainty: 'Balloon Barrage' was the working title for *Squadron 992*. The others are too vague to identify, and the reference to a 'Shoddyness film' is cryptic indeed.

16. Ibid: Eric St John Bamford to Sir Kenneth Clark, 21 February 1940.

17. Ibid: 'Notes of a meeting held at the Ministry of Information on Tuesday, 27th February 1940 at 11 a.m. to discuss taking over of GPO Film Unit'. Present at the meeting were Boyd and Wright of the GPO and Bamford, Forbes, Highet and Crossley of the MOI.

18. *Daily Film Renter*, 24 April 1940, p 1.

19. Cavalcanti himself lent some support to this idea. 'They wanted me to get naturalised and I don't want to get naturalised ... I was unhappy ... So I was looking for a job, and Mick (Balcon) had lost lots of his technical people because they had been mobilised ... and my contract with Ealing was very pleasant because I had one film as associate producer and one as director. So that suited me fine, and I felt I was much better remaining a Brazilian at Mick's place.' (Quoted in E. Sussex, 'Cavalcanti in England', *Sight and Sound*, 44/4, Autumn 1975, p 208.)

20. PRO INF 1/56: Bamford to Jack Beddington, 13 July 1940.

21. PRO INF 1/57: Memorandum by Stanley Fletcher, 26 July 1940.

22. Ibid: 'GPO Film Unit Reorganisation', 29 July 1940.

23. Ibid: Michael Balcon to Jack Beddington, 1 August 1940. Balcon suggested three specific films which would be made at Ealing by the GPO Unit: 'Spitfire' (to be made by Walter Forde, a director from the commercial industry), 'ENSA' (Harry Watt) and an unspecified 'Louis Golding story' (Jack Holmes).

24. Ibid: Beddington to Balcon, 2 August 1940.

25. Ibid: Balcon to Beddington, 6 August 1940.

26. *Kinematograph Weekly*, 12 December 1940, p 1.

27. Ibid.

28. I. Dalrymple, 'The Crown Film Unit, 1940–43', in N. Pronay and D. W. Spring (eds), *Propaganda, Politics and Film, 1918–45* (1982), p 212.

29. PRO INF 1/57: Fletcher to Beddington, 5 August 1940.

30. Ibid: D. B. Woodburn to Ian Dalrymple, 13 August 1940.

31. Ibid: Bamford to Beddington, 13 August 1940.

32. PRO INF 1/81: Beddington to H. G. Boxall, 9 August 1940.

33. Ibid: OEPEC Paper No 474 (Minutes of the Meeting of 9 August).

34. Ibid: 'Report on the Re-organisation of the GPO Film Unit' by H. G. Boxall, 26 August 1940.

35. Ibid: Bamford to Woodburn, 25 October 1940.

36. Ibid: Memorandum by Dalrymple, 14 October 1940.

37. Ibid: 'Note of a Meeting held on 11 November 1940 to discuss the future of the GPO Film Unit'.

38. M. Powell, *A Life in Movies: An Autobiography* (1987), p 384.

39. 'Introduction', in F. Thorpe and N. Pronay, with C. Coultass, *British Official Films in the Second World War: A Descriptive Catalogue* (1980), pp 38–9.

40. H. Watt, *Don't Look at the Camera*, p 183.

41. Quoted in E. Sussex, *The Rise and Fall of British Documentary* (1975), p 139.

42. I. Dalrymple, 'The Crown Film Unit', p 212.

43. PRO INF 1/81: Frank Pick to Beddington, 7 November 1940.

44. Ibid: Beddington to Pick, 8 November 1940.

45. C. Barr, 'War Record', p 265.

46. Quoted in P. Swann, *The British Documentary Film Movement*, p 152.

47. Paul Rotha considered that the work of all the official film units had helped to create a new taste for realism among cinema audiences: '*Target for Tonight, Desert Victory, Western Approaches* and other famous feature-length documentaries received a wide commercial distribution in the cinemas earning considerable revenue ... The public wanted to see these films because they were dramatised actuality, with all the physical excitement and dramatic action of raid and battle and shipwreck' (P. Rotha, 'Documentary is Neither Short Nor Long' [1946], in *Rotha on the Film: A Selection of Writings about the Cinema*, 1958, pp 228–9).

48. H. Watt, *Don't Look at the Camera*, p 149.

49. E. Rhode, *A History of the Cinema from its Origins to 1970* (1978), p 372.

50. Dai Vaughan argues that, far from being 'mistakes', the jump-cuts were a deliberate device on the part of the editor Stewart McAllister to differentiate the film from the seamless continuity editing of the classical film. He writes: 'The sequence indicates a commitment on McAllister's part to the documentary imperative. By abandoning the fictive narrative device of the dissolve, he is able, with no sacrifice of narrative coherence, to insist upon the individuality of each shot, and hence to the aircraft as a material prerequisite for that shot rather than to the purely notional aircraft entailed in its construction as fiction' (D. Vaughan, *Portrait of an Invisible Man: The Working Life of Stewart McAllister, Film Editor*, 1983, p 78).

51. PRO INF 1/210: Undated memorandum 'Bomber Command Film'.

52. Ibid: Minutes of the Home Planning Committee, 30 November 1940.

53. PRO INF 5/78: Harry Watt to Wing-Commander Williams, 7 February 1941.

54. PRO INF 1/210: Minutes of the Home Planning Committee, 24 April 1941.

55. PRO INF 6/335: Central Office of Information record sheet.

56. *The Times*, 24 July 1941, p 6.

57. *Daily Express*, 24 July 1941, p 1.

58. PRO INF 1/199: 'Receipts from Commercial Distribution of Films', May 1944.

59. F. Hardy, 'The British Documentary Film', in M. Balcon et al., *Twenty Years of British Film 1925–1945* (1947), p 57.

60. PRO INF 1/210: Lord Beaverbrook to Sidney Bernstein, 31 July 1941.

61. *Variety*, 15 October 1941.

62. *New York Times*, 21 September 1941.

63. PRO INF 1/210. *Ferry Pilot* was included by Dalrymple on a production schedule of 8 November 1940 (the same schedule included the two-reel *Bomber Command*) and was originally to have been a five-minute film.

64. *The Times*, 16 January 1942, p 6.

65. PRO INF 6/24: Central Office of Information record sheet.

66. PRO INF 1/199: 'Receipts from Commercial Distribution of Films'.

67. *The Times*, 15 October 1942, p 6.

68. Ibid, 23 June 1943, p 6.

69. Quoted in E. Sussex, *The Rise and Fall of British Documentary*, p 137.

70. PRO BT 64/116: 'Competition from Official Film Units'.

71. PRO INF 1/81: Bamford to J. P. Harvey, 22 September 1941.

72. Ibid: Beddington to Bamford, 13 September 1941.

73. I. Dalrymple, 'The Crown Film Unit', p 216.

74. PRO BT 64/117: Minutes of the 40th Meeting of the Cinematograph Films Council of the Board of Trade, 3 December 1941.

75. Quoted in E. Sussex, *The Rise and Fall of British Documentary*, p 151.

76. PRO INF 1/58: Crown Film Unit Board of Management Paper No 1, March 1943.

77. In his resignation letter Dalrymple said that 'the present constitution and functions of the Board of Management or Control seem to me to be unsatisfactory. In the first place, it does not manage; secondly, it is not permitted to control; thirdly, the representation of the Administrative Departments is limited to points of information and is not on a level of responsibility; and fourthly, although we have on the Board an eminent representative of the Trade [J. Arthur Rank], we are not using him either as an adviser, on the one hand, or as an advocate, on the other' (quoted in E. Sussex, *The Rise and Fall of British Documentary*, p 151).

78. Quoted in ibid, pp 151–2.

79. PRO INF 1/56: Cyril Radcliffe to Brendan Bracken, 9 April 1945.

80. Ibid: Ralph Nunn May to Beddington, 24 April 1945.

81. The production history of the film is detailed in A. Aldgate, 'The War the Documentarists Won: *Western Approaches*', in A. Aldgate and J. Richards, *Britain Can Take It: The British Cinema in the Second World War* (1986), ch 11, pp 246–76.

82. PRO INF 1/213: Bamford to S. G. Gates, 7 September 1942.

83. Ibid: Lord Beaverbrook to Beddington, 6 November 1944.

84. J. Shearman, 'Wartime Wedding', *Documentary News Letter*, 6/54 (November–December 1946), p 53.

85. I. McLaine, *Ministry of Morale: Home Front Morale and the Ministry of Information in World War II* (1979), p 279.

6. The Service Film Units

1. Quoted in E. Sussex, *The Rise and Fall of British Documentary* (1975), pp 174–5.

2. PRO INF 1/947: 'Government Film Production and Distribution', 1946.

3. Arts Enquiry, *The Factual Film* (1947), p 99.

4. R. Manvell, *Film* (1946), p 113.

5. *Documentary News Letter*, 2/3 (March 1941), p 47.

6. Ibid, 2/4 (April 1941), p 67.

7. *Daily Sketch*, 5 November 1941, p 3.

8. H. Watt, 'Notes on Vaagso', *Documentary News Letter*, 3/2 (February 1942), p 23.

9. I. Dalrymple, 'The Crown Film Unit, 1940–43', in N. Pronay and D. W. Spring (eds), *Propaganda, Politics and Film, 1918–45* (1982), p 215.

10. PRO INF 1/627: Ralph Nunn May to Jack Beddington, 27 February 1942.

11. PRO INF 6/342: Central Office of Information record sheet.

12. This is transcribed from the version of the film currently available in the United Kingdom on DD Video, which is the British release version, taken from the print held by the Film Archive of the Imperial War Museum. On the American release version (previously available in the 'After the Battle' video series) the dedication is worded slightly differently. There are also screen credits for Hodson and Alwyn on the American version which are not on the British version.

13. INF 1/221: R. E. Tritton to Jack Beddington, 25 November 1942.

14. See A. Aldgate, 'Creative Tensions: *Desert Victory*, the Army Film Unit and Anglo-American Rivalry, 1943–5', in P. M. Taylor (ed.), *Britain and the Cinema in the Second World War* (1988), pp 144–67, for a detailed account of the film's production history.

15. Documentation in the Public Record Office (PREM 4 12/2) establishes that Churchill did not record the speech until after the film's first public exhibition. On 5 March, T. L. Rowan, one of Churchill's private secretaries, sent a memorandum to the Prime Minister: 'If it was convenient to you, the War Office could send the van down tomorrow and you could record the extract just before luncheon. It would only take a moment or two, and there would be no need for you to go outside the house. May I arrange accordingly?' A handwritten note on the same document says 'Recording was taken today at Chequers'. The addendum is dated 6 March, which was the day after the film's premiere at the Odeon, Leicester Square. It is evident, therefore, that the first version of the film shown in Britain cannot have included Churchill's own voice. The fact that an actor recorded Churchill's speech is confirmed by Rowan's memorandum to Churchill of 16 March: 'I have spoken to the Ministry of Information about the new last reel for *Victory in the Desert* [sic] and I am informed that the one which is now ready is only different from the original by the substitution of your voice on the soundtrack for that of the original reader of your speech.' The 'original reader' was Lieutenant-Colonel Leo Genn.

16. PRO INF 1/221: Lord Beaverbrook to Sidney Bernstein, 16 March 1943.

17. Ibid: Beddington to J. L. Hodson, 10 March 1943.

18. W. S. Churchill, *The Second World War. Volume IV: The Hinge of Fate* (1985), p 661.

19. PRO PREM 4 12/2: Churchill to Roosevelt, 5 March 1943.

20. Ibid: B. C. Sendall to T. L. Rowan, 5 March 1943.

21. Ibid: Stalin to Churchill, 29 March 1943.

22. PRO INF 1/199: 'Receipts from Commercial Distribution of Films', May 1944.

23. *The Times*, 4 March 1943, p 6.

24. '1943 Directive Replies on Favourite Films', in J. Richards and D. Sheridan (eds), *Mass-Observation at the Movies* (1987), pp 220–91. Two hundred and twenty people replied to a questionnaire asking which films they had liked in the past year and why. The most popular films with the respondents were *In Which We Serve* (mentioned by fifty-four people) and *The Life and Death of Colonel Blimp* (mentioned by fifty-two people). *Desert Victory* came in equal third with *Mrs Miniver* and *The Gentle Sex*, each being mentioned twenty-six times.

25. PRO INF 1/627: H. T. W. Gaitskell to Jack Beddington, 5 June 1943.

26. Ibid: Beddington to Gaitskell, 21 June 1943.

27. *Kinematograph Weekly*, 19 August 1943, p 3.

28. PRO INF 1/221: George Archibald to Thomas Baird, 18 April 1944.

29. Ibid: Baird to Archibald, 27 April 1944.

30. I. Dalrymple, 'The Crown Film Unit', p 218.

31. See A. Aldgate, 'Mr Capra Goes to War: Frank Capra, the British Army Film Unit, and Anglo-American travails in the production of *Tunisian Victory*', *Historical Journal of Film, Radio and Television*, 11/1 (March 1991), pp 21–39. This article is reprinted as 'National Pride and Prejudices: *Tunisian Victory*' in the second edition of A. Aldgate and J. Richards, *Britain Can Take It: The British Cinema in the Second World War* (1994), ch 13, pp 299–325. See also C. Coultass, '*Tunisian Victory* – a Film Too Late?', *Imperial War Museum Review*, 1 (1986), pp 64–73.

32. F. Capra, *The Name Above the Title: An Autobiography* (1972), p 352.

33. J. L. Hodson, *The Sea and the Land* (1945), p 117.

34. *Daily Telegraph*, 20 March 1944.

35. *Documentary News Letter*, 5/2 (1944), p 20.

36. R. Manvell, *Films and the Second World War* (1974), p 156.

37. See J. Chapman, '"The Yanks are Shown to Such Advantage": Anglo-American Rivalry in the Production of *The True Glory* (1945)', *Historical Journal of Film, Radio and Television*, 16/4 (October 1996), pp 533–54.

38. Quoted in N. Wapshott, *The Man Between: A Biography of Carol Reed* (1990), p 169.

39. D. Bull, 'Filming the European Campaign', *Documentary News Letter*, 6/2 (1945), p 90.

40. I. Grant, *Cameramen at War* (1980), p 191.

41. Although the individual commentators are supposedly real servicemen and women, the voices of numerous actors can be identified among them. For example, the voice of the Admiralty Wren ('Of course, we only saw it happening on the wall map, and yet it was ... well, quite real') is unmistakably Celia Johnson's, and one of the British soldiers at Caen ('We didn't think that we'd spend fifteen days in the same field outside Caen') is Richard Attenborough. Other voices in the film sound like those of John Mills, James Donald, Geoffrey Keen, Jimmy Hanley, Leslie Dwyer, Robert Beatty, Burgess Meredith and Bonar Colleano.

42. *Evening Standard*, 4 August 1945.

43. *The Listener*, 8 August 1945.

44. *New York Times*, 7 September 1945.

45. See I. C. Jarvie, 'The Burma Campaign on Film: *Objective Burma* (1945), *The Stilwell Road* (1945) and *Burma Victory* (1945)', *Historical Journal of Film, Radio and Television*, 8/1 (1988), pp 55–73.

46. PRO WO 203/5165: Admiral Lord Louis Mountbatten to General George C. Marshall, 3 June 1944.

47. Ibid: Brendan Bracken to Air Chief Marshal Sir Philip Joubert, 27 July 1944.

48. Ibid: Field Marshal Wilson to Minister of Information, 9 May 1945.

49. See I. C. Jarvie, 'Fanning the Flames: Anti-American Reaction to *Operation Burma* (1945)', *Historical Journal of Film, Radio and Television*, 1/2 (1981), pp 117–37. The title of the film is cited incorrectly in the article heading but correctly in the main text.

50. *The New Statesman*, 3 November 1945.

51. See K. Buckman, 'The Royal Air Force Film Production Unit, 1941–45', *Historical Journal of Film, Radio and Television*, 17/2 (June 1997), pp 219–44.

52. This information is from a set of typed notes on the BFI microfiche for *Journey Together*.

53. M. Paris, *From the Wright Brothers to Top Gun: Aviation, Nationalism and Popular Cinema* (1995), p 145.

54. *News Chronicle*, 2 October 1945.

55. *The New Statesman*, 20 November 1945.

56. For further details of the production of the film, see C. Coultass, *Images for Battle: British Film and the Second World War, 1939–45* (1989), pp 166–7.

57. *The Times*, 7 February 1947, p 7.

7. The People's War

1. R. Manvell, 'The British Feature Film from 1940 to 1945', in M. Balcon et al., *Twenty Years of British Film 1925–1945* (1947), p 85.

2. Quoted in M.-L. Jennings (ed.), *Humphrey Jennings: Film-Maker, Painter, Poet* (1982), p 25.

3. L. Anderson, 'Only Connect: Some Aspects of the Work of Humphrey Jennings', in M.-L. Jennings (ed.), *Humphrey Jennings*, p 53. The article was originally published in *Sight and Sound*, 23/4 (April–June 1954).

4. Quoted in E. Sussex, *The Rise and Fall of British Documentary* (1975), p 144.

5. See, for example, J. Hillier, 'Humphrey Jennings', in A. Lovell and J. Hillier, *Studies in Documentary* (1971), pp 62–120; and A. W. Hodgkinson and R. E. Sheratsky, *Humphrey Jennings: More Than a Maker of Films* (1982).

6. McAllister's work, and particularly his collaboration with Jennings, is the subject of an important book by D. Vaughan, *Portrait of an Invisible Man: The Working Life of Stewart McAllister, Film Editor* (1983). Vaughan was himself a film editor and the book should perhaps be seen partly as an attempt to retrieve the role of the editor against the continued prevalence of the *auteur* theory which assigns the prime creative role to the director.

7. B. Wright, *The Long View: A Personal Perspective on World Cinema* (1974), p 200.

8. J. Richards, 'England, Their England: *Fires Were Started*', in A. Aldgate and J. Richards, *Britain Can Take It: The British Cinema in the Second World War* (1986), p 225.

9. Quoted in M.-L. Jennings (ed.), *Humphrey Jennings*, p 33.

10. G. Orwell, *The Lion and the Unicorn: Socialism and the English Genius* (1941), in S. Orwell and I. Angus (eds), *The Collected Essays, Journalism and Letters of George Orwell. Volume 2: My Country Right or Left, 1940–1943* (1970), p 133.

11. L. Furhammar and F. Isaksson, *Politics and Film* (1971), p 85.

12. Jennings was working on this film during the summer of 1943. He and cameraman Jonah Jones had covered the landings in Sicily and had come back with several thousand feet of actuality footage. The project was abandoned due to 'Difficulty in getting facilities, and subject would be long and costly' (PRO INF 1/199: 'Film projects commenced since 1st April 1942, but abandoned, up to 30th November 1944').

Jennings's papers deposited with the British Film Institute reveal some of his plans for this film, which were clearly very ambitious. 'My idea is to avoid at all costs making another ruddy documentary service picture; but at the same time not to fall back on a fictional story with action as the only alternative – because it isn't,' he wrote in September 1943. 'As I see it parts of this tremendous story are documentary – parts fictional – but all of it basically fact – history – *already* dramatic, thrilling, human, box-office and so on.' Jennings intended to show the history of the Royal Marines as well as their role in the Sicilian campaign, and to this end he envisaged a highly complex structure: 'I therefore propose to disregard the usual unities of space and time and use flashbacks – historical and even in costume – to illustrate the central theme. This is that in a global war of combined ops the Royal Marines have been the original commandos' (BFI: Humphrey Jennings Collection, File 13).

13. W. Hodgkinson and E. Sheratsky, *Humphrey Jennings*, p 67.

14. Quoted in E. Sussex, *The Rise and Fall of British Documentary*, p 126.

15. PRO INF 6/331: Central Office of Information record sheet.

16. *Documentary News Letter*, 2/3 (March 1941), p 48.

17. See, for example, A. Lovell and J. Hillier, *Studies in Documentary*, pp 86–9; D. Vaughan, *Portrait of an Invisible Man*, pp 83–100; and A. Higson, 'Five Films', in G. Hurd (ed.), *National Fictions: World War Two in British Films and Television* (1984), pp 22–6. The most useful discussion of *Listen to Britain*, in that it combines textual analysis with historical context, is M. Smith, 'Narrative and Ideology in *Listen to Britain*', in J. Hawthorn (ed.), *Narrative: From Malory to Motion Pictures* (1985), pp 145–57.

18. Quoted in A. Calder, *The People's War: Britain 1939–1945* (1969), p 228.

19. *Spectator*, 13 March 1942.

20. Quoted in E. Sussex, *The Rise of British Documentary*, pp 144–5.

21. H. Forman, 'The Non-theatrical Distribution of Films by the Ministry of Information', in N. Pronay and D. W. Spring (eds), *Propaganda, Politics and Film, 1918–45* (1982), p 230.

22. R. Manvell, *Films and the Second World War* (1974), p 149.

23. 'Feature Film Propaganda', *Documentary News Letter*, 3/5 (May 1942), p 67.

24. Manvell, *Films and the Second World War*, p 102.

25. M. Balcon, *Michael Balcon Presents ... A Lifetime of Films* (1969), p 137.

26. *Daily Film Renter*, 1 January 1941, p 30.

27. J. Richards and D. Sheridan (eds), *Mass-Observation at the Movies* (1987), p 240.

28. 'Feature Film Propaganda', *Documentary News Letter*, 3/5 (May 1942), p 67.

29. Quoted in E. Sussex, *The Rise and Fall of British Documentary*, p 145.

30. BFI Humphrey Jennings Collection File 6 contains various drafts and treatments. The first outline, dated 25 October 1941, is entitled *NFS*, which was the first of several titles by which the project was known, including *The Bells Went Down*, *Heavy One Rides Again* and *I Was A Fireman*.

31. PRO INF 6/985: C. A. Lejeune to Jack Beddington, no date.

32. The theatrical version, *Fires Were Started*, ran for 63 minutes while the non-theatrical version, *I Was A Fireman*, ran for 75 minutes. The title of the theatrical version, generally thought to be more evocative, is now generally used even when the longer version of the film is being referred to. However, the longer version is currently available in the UK on DD Video as *I Was a Fireman*.

33. Roy Armes, *A Critical History of the British Cinema* (1978), p 154.

34. L. Anderson, 'Only Connect', in M.-L. Jennings (ed.), *Humphrey Jennings*, p 57.

35. *Documentary News Letter*, 4/4 (1943), p 200.

36. J. Richards and D. Sheridan, *Mass-Observation at the Movies*, p 225.

37. Ibid, p 249.

38. Exhibitors' campaign booklet on BFI microfiche for *The Bells Go Down*.

39. *The Times*, 15 April 1943, p 6.

8. Officers and Men

1. R. Manvell, 'The British Feature Film from 1940 to 1945', in M. Balcon et al., *Twenty Years of British Film 1925–1945* (1947), p 84.

2. *The New Statesman*, 20 April 1940.

3. *Kinematograph Weekly*, 13 June 1940, p 14.

4. 'Films and the Problem of the Month', *Documentary News Letter*, 2/12 (December 1941), p 225.

5. *Documentary News Letter*, 2/12 (December 1941), p 221.

6. M. Balcon, *Michael Balcon Presents ... A Lifetime of Films* (1969), p 134.

7. M-O File Report 1218: 'Ships With Wings', 21 April 1942, published in J. Richards and D. Sheridan (eds), *Mass-Observation at the Movies* (1987), p 377. For a case study of the critical and popular reception of the film, drawing on the Mass-Observation survey and other sources, see J. Richards, 'Wartime Cinema Audiences and the Class System: the Case of *Ships with Wings* (1941)', *Historical Journal of Film, Radio and Television*, 7/2 (1987), pp 129–41. This article is reprinted as 'Class and Nation: *Ships With Wings*' in the second edition of A. Aldgate and J. Richards, *Britain Can Take It: The British Cinema in the Second World War* (1994), ch 14, pp 326–45.

8. N. Coward, *Future Indefinite* (1954), p 229.

9. C. Cook (ed.), *The Dilys Powell Film Reader* (1991), p 6.

10. See J. Richards, 'Naval Cavalcade: *In Which We Serve*', in A. Aldgate and J. Richards, *Britain Can Take It*, ch 9, pp 187–217. Coward's own account of the production is in *Future Indefinite*, pp 210–31.

11. '1943 Directive Replies on Favourite Films', in J. Richards and D Sheridan (eds), *Mass-Observation at the Movies*, p 223.

12. *Documentary News Letter*, 5/1 (1944), p 2.

13. *The Times*, 20 May 1943, p 6.

14. For an interesting account of how the film compares to the real incident, see C. Coultass, 'Film and Reality: the *San Demetrio* Episode', *Imperial War Museum Review*, 5 (1990), pp 79–85.

15. M. Balcon, *... A Lifetime of Films*, p 148.

16. Quoted in J. Richards, 'Class and Nation', p 340.

17. G. Orwell, *The Lion and the Unicorn: Socialism and the English Genius* (1941), in S. Orwell and I. Angus (eds), *The Collected Essays, Journalism and Letters of George Orwell. Volume 2: My Country Right or Left 1940–1943* (1970), p 79.

18. See J. Richards, 'Careless Talk Costs Lives: *The Next of Kin*', in A. Aldgate and J. Richards, *Britain Can Take It*, ch 5, pp 96–114.

19. M-O File Report 1342: 'Next of Kin', pp 2–4.

20. *Daily Film Renter*, 2 July 1942, p 2.

21. Quoted in C. Moorehead, *Sidney Bernstein: A Biography* (1984), p 147.

22. '*Nine Men* arose from a rather sketchy synopsis for an Army training film written by Gerald Kersh. I was never sure how it got to Ealing, as they were not geared for that kind of thing, but all studios were anxious to keep in with the Services and the Ministries, as they needed so much official help to function, so it may have come through the old boy network.' This is taken from notes by Harry Watt for a National Film Theatre screening on the BFI microfiche for *Nine Men*.

23. *Monthly Film Bulletin*, 10/110 (February 1943), p 13.

24. G. Orwell, *My Country Right or Left*, pp 90–1.

25. *Parliamentary Debates: House of Commons*, 28 February 1942, 5th Series, vol 378, col 304. Pethick-Lawrence's attack on 'Blimpery' is discussed by A. Aldgate, 'What a Difference a War Makes: *The Life and Death of Colonel Blimp*', in J. Richards and A. Aldgate, *Best of British: Cinema and Society 1930–1970* (1983), ch 5, pp 61–74.

26. PRO PREM 4 14/15: Sir James Grigg to Churchill, 8 September 1942.

27. *Kinematograph Weekly*, 1 April 1943.

28. *News Chronicle*, 11 June 1943.

29. *Daily Mail*, 11 June 1943.

30. PRO INF 1/224: Brendan Bracken to Noël Coward, 9 October 1942.

31. Ibid: Filippo Del Giudice to Jack Beddington, 7 November 1942.

32. *The New Lot*, which was long thought to be a 'lost' film, has now been preserved by the Imperial War Museum after a print was discovered by the National Film Archive of India.

33. See V. Porter and C. Litewski, '*The Way Ahead*: Case History of a Propaganda Film', *Sight and Sound*, 50/2 (Spring 1981), pp 110–16.

34. G. Orwell, *My Country Right or Left*, p 108.

35. PRO INF 1/224: Arthur Calder Marshall to Carol Reed, 5 June 1944.

36. BFI Carol Reed Collection File 33: R. E. Tritton to Reed, 12 September 1945.

37. R. Manvell, *Films and the Second World War* (1974), p 65.

38. J. Richards, 'Our American Cousins: *The Way to the Stars*', in A. Aldgate and J. Richards, *Britain Can Take It*, ch 12, pp 277–98.

39. *Monthly Film Bulletin*, 12/138 (June 1945), p 70.

9. Women and War

1. T. Harrisson, 'Appeals to Women', *Political Quarterly*, 13/3 (July–September 1942), p 265.

2. E. Manvell, 'Women and Propaganda', *Documentary News Letter*, 3/4 (April 1942), p 59.

3. PRO INF 1/849: Policy Committee Paper 'Propaganda Directed Exclusively to Women', 23 January 1941.

4. The films which Clark cited were *They Also Serve*, *Call to Arms* [sic], *Neighbours Under Fire*, *Miss Grant Goes to the Door*, *Channel Incident*, *Her Father's Daughter*, *Miss Knowall*, *Women in Wartime*, *Home Front*, *Health in War*, *Nurse*, *Welfare of the Workers*, *Village School*, *Salvage With A Smile* and *From Family to Farm*.

5. R. Ackland and E. Grant, *The Celluloid Mistress, or the Custard Pie of Dr. Caligari* (1954), p 88.

6. *Documentary News Letter*, 1/9 (September 1940), p 2.

7. 'Five Minutes', *Documentary News Letter*, 1/8 (August 1940), p 5.

8. PRO INF 1/849: 'Propaganda Directed Exclusively to Women'.

9. E. Manvell, 'Women and Propaganda', p 59.

10. *Documentary News Letter*, 2/7 (July 1941), p 128.

11. T. Harrisson, 'Appeals to Women', pp 277–8.

12. PRO BT 64/117: Sylvester Gates to Sir Walter Venning, 13 July 1942.

13. Brunel's account of the film is given in his autobiography, *Nice Work: The Story of Thirty Years in British Film Production* (1949), pp 192–4.

14. R. Howard, *In Search of My Father: A Portrait of Leslie Howard* (1981), p 125.

15. A. Lant, *Blackout: Reinventing Women for Wartime British Cinema* (1991), pp 89–90.

16. '1943 Directive Replies on Favourite Films', in J. Richards and D. Sheridan (eds), *Mass-Observation at the Movies* (1987), p 267.

17. Quoted in G. Brown, *Launder and Gilliat* (1977), p 108.

18. Ibid.

19. C. Gledhill and G. Swanson, 'Gender and Sexuality in Second World War Films – A Feminist Approach', in G. Hurd (ed.), *National Fictions: World War Two in British Films and Television* (1984), p 59.

20. T. Harrisson, 'Appeals to Women', p 276.

21. Paul Rotha, whose company made *Night Shift*, later said that it 'was shown one night after the ideas committee meeting, and Frank Launder and Sidney Gilliat saw it, and it gave them the idea to make a feature film called *Millions Like Us*, which was

highly successful and completely based on the documentary *Night Shift*' (quoted in E. Sussex, *The Rise and Fall of British Documentary* (1975, p 141). However, according to an anonymous programme note for a National Film Theatre screening of *Millions Like Us*, 'Launder and Gilliat deny ever having seen *Night Shift*' (from the BFI microfiche on *Millions Like Us*). The relationship of *Millions Like Us* to the British documentary movement in terms of style and mode of address is analysed in depth in A. Higson, *Waving the Flag: Constructing a National Cinema in Britain* (1995), pp 220–43.

22. *The Sunday Times*, 10 October 1943.

23. J. Richards and D. Sheridan, *Mass-Observation at the Movies*, p 238.

10. Friend and Foe

1. J. Weiss, 'An Allied Film Unit', *Documentary News Letter*, 2/12 (December 1941), p 233.

2. Ibid.

3. Quoted in I. McLaine, *Ministry of Morale: Home Front Morale and the Ministry of Information in World War II* (1979), pp 201–2.

4. R. Bond, 'Our Film', *Documentary News Letter*, 2/4 (April 1942), p 113. This article is the main source of information on the film.

5. *Sunday Express*, 29 March 1942, p 6.

6. N. Rattigan, '*The Demi-Paradise* and Images of Class in British Wartime Films', in W. W. Dixon (ed.), *Re-Viewing British Cinema, 1900–1992: Essays and Interviews* (1994), pp 83–93.

7. L. Olivier, *Confessions of an Actor* (1987), p 130. Further evidence that the pro-Russian theme was the aim of the film is that the script was sent to the Russian Embassy for approval, according to R. J. Minney, *Puffin Asquith* (1973), p 107.

8. *The New Statesman*, 27 November 1943.

9. I. McLaine, *Ministry of Morale*, p 169.

10. See J. C. Robertson, *The Hidden Cinema: British Film Censorship in Action, 1913–1975* (1993), pp 74–8.

11. Telegram from Duff Cooper to the production company Grand National, quoted on the press booklet for the film, on the BFI microfiche for *Pastor Hall*.

12. 'The Other Side of the Atlantic', *Documentary News Letter*, 1/9 (September 1940), p 3.

13. *The Times*, 6 May 1942, p 6.

14. *The Times*, 10 September 1942, p 6.

15. *Daily Film Renter*, 11 February 1942, p 1.

16. M. Danischewsky, *White Russian – Red Face* (1966), p 151.

17. C. Barr, *Ealing Studios* (1977), p 33.

18. See A. Aldgate, 'If the Invader Comes: *Went the Day Well?*', in A. Aldgate and J. Richards, *Britain Can Take It: The British Cinema in the Second World War* (1986), ch 6, pp 115–37. Some of Aldgate's conclusions are questioned by Penelope Huston in her monograph on the film for the BFI's 'Film Classics' series. See P. Huston, *Went the Day Well?* (1992).

19. A. J. P. Taylor, *English History 1914–1945* (1965), p 492.

20. Press notes by Hugh Findlay, on the BFI microfiche for *Went the Day Well?* They continue: 'What makes this film stand out among the propaganda and semi-propaganda films of this war is the utter sincerity with which every type and character is put over. The people of Bramley End are living human beings and not fictional figures. Their

fate may be our fate to-morrow. They show us how to stand up to the trial of invasion if this nightmare were to become reality, and be able to emerge proud of ourselves.'

21. *Observer*, 1 November 1942.

22. *Monthly Film Bulletin*, 9/107 (November 1942), p 142.

23. *The Sunday Times*, 1 November 1942.

24. Barr, *Ealing Studios*, pp 32–3.

25. D. Vaughan, *Portrait of an Invisible Man: The Working Life of Stewart McAllister, Film Editor* (1983), p 113.

26. PRO INF 1/867: Co-Ordinating Committee Paper No 1, 'Programme for Film Propaganda', p 1 (4).

27. BFI Humphrey Jennings Collection, File 8 contains a long transcript of a radio interview which Jennings gave by telephone on 26 May 1943 and which is the main source of information on the production. Jennings said that a treatment entitled *A Village in Bohemia* was submitted to the Crown Film Unit in July 1942 by a Mr Fischel of the Czech Ministry of Information. The idea of comparing Lidice with a Welsh village was already in the treatment. Jennings thought that 'it was one of the most brilliant ideas for a short film that we'd ever come across'.

Evidence of Weiss's involvement is to be found in a letter from Eric Hudson (PRO INF 5/90) to Captain Josef Tichy at the Czech government's residence in Piccadilly to ask for a large-scale map of Czechoslovakia, which he said 'is for use in a Ministry of Information film production as I believe Mr Jiri Weiss has already explained to you'.

28. PRO INF 5/90: Hudson to Ibbotson James (Ministry of Fuel and Power), 20 August 1942.

29. *Documentary News Letter*, 4/5 (1943), p 216.

30. *The Times*, 10 June 1943, p 6.

31. BFI Humphrey Jennings Collection File 8: Michael Balcon to Humphrey Jennings, 22 May 1943.

32. *Documentary News Letter*, 4/6 (1943), p 232.

33. R. Manvell, *Films and the Second World War* (1974), p 161.

11. History and Heritage

1. *Time and Tide*, 31 May 1941, quoted in J. Richards, 'Mobilizing the Past: *The Young Mr Pitt*', in A. Aldgate and J. Richards, *Britain Can Take It: The British Cinema in the Second World War* (1986), p 140. Orwell was reviewing the film *This England*.

2. C. Barr, 'Introduction: Amnesia and Schizophrenia', in C. Barr (ed.), *All Our Yesterdays: 90 Years of British Cinema* (1986), p 12.

3. L. Halliwell, *Seats in All Parts: Half a Lifetime at the Movies* (1985), p 93.

4. *Today's Cinema*, 25 June 1940, p 1.

5. *The New Statesman*, 24 May 1941.

6. S. Harper, *Picturing the Past: The Rise and Fall of the British Costume Film* (1994), ch 6, pp 77–94.

7. PRO INF 1/867: Co-Ordinating Committee Paper No 1, 'Programme for Film Propaganda', p 1 (4).

8. S. Harper, *Picturing the Past*, p 88.

9. J. Richards, 'Mobilizing the Past', p 151.

10. *Kinematograph Weekly*, 20 November 1941, p 1.

11. Quoted in G. Brown, *Launder and Gilliat* (1978), p 104.

12. *Today's Cinema*, 17 June 1942.

13. *Documentary News Letter*, 2/5 (May 1941), p 89.

14. B. Wright, *The Long View: A Personal Perspective on World Cinema* (1974), p 197.

15. D. Badder, 'Powell and Pressburger: The War Years', *Sight and Sound*, 48/1 (Winter 1978–79), p 11.

16. J. Richards, 'Why We Fight: *A Canterbury Tale*', in J. Richards and A. Aldgate, *Best of British: Cinema and Society 1930–1970* (1983), p 46.

17. C. A. Lejeune, *Chestnuts in Her Lap, 1939–1946* (1947), p 122.

18. A. Higson, *Waving the Flag: Constructing a National Cinema in Britain* (1995), p 261.

19. *Kinematograph Weekly*, 27 May 1943.

20. S. Harper, *Picturing the Past*, p 86.

21. The background of the film, along with some useful textual analysis, is in H. M. Geduld, *Filmguide to Henry V* (1973).

22. *Kinematograph Weekly*, 22 April 1943.

23. *The New Statesman*, 5 June 1943.

24. According to notes written to accompany a screening of the film for the Sittingbourne Film Society in 1965, its final cost was £475,708. These notes, on the BFI microfiche for *Henry V*, include a break-down of the production costs, though the source is uncredited. Quotations for the film's revenues vary from one source to another, though it was undoubtedly very successful in America.

25. *Observer*, 29 November 1944.

26. J. W. Young, '*Henry V*, the Quai D'Orsai, and the Well-Being of the Franco-British Alliance', *Historical Journal of Film, Radio and Television*, 7/3 (1987), p 320.

27. *Boston Post*, 7 April 1946.

28. *The Nation*, 20 July 1946.

Conclusion

1. L. Halliwell, *Seats in All Parts: Half a Lifetime at the Movies* (1985), p 86.

2. *The Times*, 28 August 1942, p 5.

3. *Documentary News Letter*, 3/1 (January 1942), p 1.

4. P. M. Taylor, *Munitions of the Mind: A History of Propaganda from the Ancient World to the Present Day* (1995), p 215.

5. M-O File Report 1: 'Channels of Publicity', 11 October 1939, p 4.

6. *Thirteenth Report from the Select Committee on National Expenditure* (1940), p 8.

7. N. Pronay, 'The News Media at War', in N. Pronay and D. W. Spring (eds), *Propaganda, Politics and Film, 1918–45* (1982), p 173.

8. P. M. Taylor, *Munitions of the Mind*, p 213.

9. G. Hurd, 'Notes on Hegemony, the War and Cinema', in G. Hurd (ed.), *National Fictions: World War Two in British Films and Television* (1984), p 18.

10. Neil Rattigan, for example, writes that 'all British films were, to some degree, "official" inasmuch as the Ministry of Information had a whole network of statutory and bureaucratic controls that amounted to approval, direction, and supervision of all filmmaking activity' (N. Rattigan, '*The Demi-Paradise* and Images of Class in British Wartime Films', in W. W. Dixon [ed.], *Re-Viewing British Cinema, 1900–1992: Essays and Interviews*, 1994, p 83).

11. *Kinematograph Weekly*, 7 September 1939, p 2.

12. Angus Calder, *The People's War: Britain 1939–1945* (1969), p 370.

13. *Daily Film Renter*, 27 March 1940, p 2.

14. J. Richards and D. Sheridan (eds), *Mass-Observation at the Movies* (1987), p 322.

15. A. Marwick, *The Nature of History* (1989), p 216.

Filmography

The Filmography is divided into three sections: commercial feature films; official feature and short-feature documentaries (including all Crown and service film unit long productions); and official shorts made for the MOI. Films running between 30 and 50 minutes are classed as short features. Only those films discussed in the main text are included here. Further details of official films can be found in Frances Thorpe and Nicholas Pronay with Clive Coultass, *British Official Films in the Second World War: A Descriptive Catalogue* (Oxford: Clio Press, 1980).

The format for entries is as follows:

Title: year; production company; *prod*–producer; *dir*–director; *sc*–screenplay *st*–story/scenario; *comm*–commentator (where applicable); principal cast; running time (in minutes).

Commercial feature films

The Bells Go Down: 1943; Ealing Studios; *prod*–Michael Balcon; *dir*–Basil Dearden; *sc*–Roger MacDougall, Stephen Black; *cast*: Tommy Trinder, James Mason, Philip Friend, Finlay Currie, Mervyn Johns, Billy Hartnell; 80 mins.

A Canterbury Tale: 1944; Rank/The Archers; *prod/dir/sc*–Michael Powell and Emeric Pressburger; *cast*: Eric Portman, Sheila Sim, Sgt John Sweet, Dennis Price, Hay Petrie, Edward Rigby, George Merritt; 124 mins.

Convoy: 1940; Ealing Studios; *prod*–Michael Balcon; *dir*–Penrose Tennyson; *sc*–Penrose Tennyson, Patrick Kirwan; *cast*: Clive Brook, John Clements, Judy Campbell, Penelope Dudley Ward, Edward Chapman, Stewart Granger; 90 mins.

Dangerous Moonlight (US: *Suicide Squadron*): 1941; RKO Radio British Productions; *prod*–William Sistrom; *dir*–Brian Desmond Hurst; *sc*–Terence Young, Rodney Ackland, Brian Desmond Hurst; *cast*: Anton Walbrook, Sally Grey, Cecil Parker, Derrick de Marney, Percy Parsons; 98 mins.

The Day Will Dawn (US: *The Avengers*); 1942; GFD/Paul Soskin; *prod*–Paul Soskin; *dir*–Harold French; *sc*–Terence Rattigan, Anatole de Grunwald, Patrick Kirwan; *cast*: Hugh Williams, Griffith Jones, Deborah Kerr, Ralph Richardson, Finlay Currie, Francis L. Sullivan, Roland Pertwee; 98 mins.

The Demi-Paradise (US: *Adventure for Two*): 1943; Two Cities; *prod/sc*–Anatole de Grunwald; *dir*–Anthony Asquith; *cast*: Laurence Olivier, Penelope Dudley Ward, Marjorie Fielding, Margaret Rutherford, Felix Aylmer; 114 mins.

The First of the Few: 1942; British Aviation Pictures; *prod/dir*–Leslie Howard; *sc*–Miles Malleson, Anatole de Grunwald; *st*–Henry C. James, Kay Strueby; *cast*: Leslie Howard, David Niven, Rosamund John, Roland Culver, Derrick de Marney, Filippo Del Giudice; 124 mins.

For Freedom: 1940; Gainsborough Pictures; *prod*–Edward Black; *dir*–Maurice Elvey, Castleton Knight; *sc*–Leslie Arliss, Miles Malleson; *comm*–E. V. H. Emmett, Vice-Admiral J. E. T. Harper; *cast*: Will Fyffe, Anthony Hulme, E. V. H. Emmett, Guy Middleton, Albert Lieven, Hugh McDermott; 80 mins.

The Foreman Went to France (US: *Somewhere in France*): 1942; Ealing Studios; *prod*–Michael Balcon; *dir*–Charles Frend; *sc*–John Dighton, Angus MacPhail, Leslie Arliss; *st*–J. B. Priestley; *cast*: Clifford Evans, Tommy Trinder, Constance Cummings, Gordon Jackson, Robert Morley, John Williams; 87 mins.

49th Parallel (US: *The Invaders*): 1941; GFD/Ortus Films; *prod*–John Sutro, Michael Powell; *dir*–Michael Powell; *sc*–Emeric Pressburger, Rodney Ackland; *cast*: Leslie Howard, Laurence Olivier, Anton Walbrook, Raymond Massey, Eric Portman, Glynis Johns, Finlay Currie, Niall MacGinnis; 123 mins.

Freedom Radio (US: *A Voice in the Night*): 1941; Two Cities; *prod*–Mario Zampi; *dir*–Anthony Asquith; *sc*–Anatole de Grunwald, Jeffrey Dell, Basil Wood, *st*–Louis Golding, Gordon Wellesley, Roland Pertwee, Bridget Boland; *cast*: Clive Brook, Diana Wynyard, Raymond Huntley, Derek Farr; 95 mins.

The Gentle Sex: 1943; Two Cities/Concanen; *prod*–Derrick de Marney; *dir*–Leslie Howard, Maurice Elvey (uncredited); *sc*–Moie Charles, Aimee Stuart, Roland Pertwee; *cast*: Joan Gates, Jean Gillie, Joan Greenwood, Lili Palmer, Joyce Howard, Rosamund John, Barbara Waring, Mary Jerrold; 93 mins.

Henry V: 1944; Rank/Two Cities; *prod/dir*–Laurence Olivier; *sc*–Laurence Olivier, Alan Dent, from the play by William Shakespeare; *cast*: Laurence Olivier, Leslie Banks, Felix Aylmer, Griffith Jones, Ernest Thesiger, Robert Newton, George Robey, Renée Asherson, Harcourt Williams, Leo Genn, Esmond Knight, Jimmy Hanley, John Laurie, Niall MacGinnis; 137 mins.

In Which We Serve: 1942; Two Cities; *prod*–Noël Coward; *dir*–Noël Coward, David Lean; *sc*–Noël Coward; *cast*: Noël Coward, Bernard Miles, John Mills, Celia Johnson, Joyce Carey, Kay Walsh, Richard Attenborough; 115 mins.

The Life and Death of Colonel Blimp: 1943; Rank/The Archers; *prod/dir/sc*–Michael Powell and Emeric Pressburger; *cast*: Anton Walbrook, Deborah Kerr, Roger Livesey, James McKechnie, Roland Culver, Arthur Wontner, John Laurie, A.E. Matthews; 163 mins.

The Lion Has Wings: 1939; London Film Productions; *prod*–Alexander Korda; *dir*–Michael Powell, Adrian Brunel, Brian Desmond Hurst; *sc*–Ian Dalrymple, Adrian Brunel,

E. V. H. Emmett; *comm*–E. V. H. Emmett (British version), Lowell Thomas (US version); *cast*: Merle Oberon, Ralph Richardson, June Duprez, Derrick de Marney, John Longden, Miles Malleson; 76 mins.

Millions Like Us: 1943; Gainsborough Pictures; *prod*–Edward Black; *dir/sc*–Frank Launder and Sidney Gilliat; *cast*: Patricia Roc, Eric Portman, Gordon Jackson, Anne Crawford, Moore Marriott, Basil Radford, Naunton Wayne; 103 mins.

The Next of Kin: 1942; Ealing Studios; *prod*–Michael Balcon; *dir*–Thorold Dickinson; *sc*–Thorold Dickinson, Angus MacPhail, John Dighton, Basil Bartlett; *cast*: Mervyn Johns, John Chandos, David Hutcheson, Stephen Murray, Nova Pilbeam, Geoffrey Hibbert, Jack Hawkins, Mary Clare; 102 mins.

Nine Men: 1943; Ealing Studios; *prod*–Michael Balcon; *dir/sc*–Harry Watt; *st*–Gerald Kersh; *cast*: Jack Lambert, Gordon Jackson, Frederick Piper, Grant Sutherland, Bill Blewett, Eric Micklewood; 68 mins.

One of Our Aircraft is Missing: 1942; British National; *prod*–John Corfield; *dir*–Michael Powell; *sc*–Emeric Pressburger; *cast*: Godfrey Tearle, Eric Portman, Hugh Williams, Bernard Miles, Hugh Burden, Emrys Jones; 102 mins.

Pastor Hall: 1940; Charter Films; *prod*–John Boulting; *dir*–Roy Boulting; *sc*–Leslie Arliss, Haworth Bromley, Anna Reiner, from the play by Ernst Toller; *cast*: Wilfrid Lawson, Nova Pilbeam, Seymour Hicks, Marius Goring; 97 mins.

Pimpernel Smith (US: *Mister V*): 1941; British National; *prod/dir*–Leslie Howard; *sc*–Anatole de Grunwald, Roland Pertwee; *st*–A. G. Macdonell, Wolfgang Wilhelm; *cast*: Leslie Howard, Mary Morris, Francis L. Sullivan, Hugh McDermott, Raymond Huntley, David Tomlinson; 121 mins.

The Prime Minister: 1941; Warner Bros. British Productions; *prod*–Max Milder; *dir*–Thorold Dickinson; *sc*–Michael Hogan, Brock Williams; *cast*: John Gielgud, Diana Wynyard, Stephen Murray, Glynis Johns; 109 mins.

San Demetrio, London: 1943; Ealing Studios; *prod*–Michael Balcon; *dir*–Charles Frend; *sc*–Charles Frend, Robert Hamer; *cast*: Walter Fitzgerald, Ralph Michael, Robert Beatty, Mervyn Johns, Gordon Jackson, Frederick Piper; 104 mins.

Ships With Wings: 1941; Ealing Studios; *prod*–Michael Balcon; *dir*–Sergei Nolbandov; *sc*–Sergei Nolbandov, Patrick Kirwan, Austin Melford, Diana Morgan; *cast*: John Clements, Leslie Banks, Michael Rennie, Michael Wilding, Ann Todd, Basil Sydney; 103 mins.

Tawny Pipit: 1944; Two Cities; *prod*–Bernard Miles; *dir/sc*–Bernard Miles, Charles Saunders; *cast*: Bernard Miles, Rosamund John, Niall MacGinnis, Christopher Steele, Lucie Mannheim; 85 mins.

This England (*Our Heritage*): 1941; British National; *prod*–John Corfield; *dir*–David Macdonald; *sc*–A. R. Rawlinson, Bridget Boland, Emlyn Williams; *cast*: John Clements, Emlyn Williams, Constance Cummings; 84 mins.

This Happy Breed: 1944; Two Cities/Cineguild; *prod*–Anthony Havelock-Allan, Noël Coward; *dir*–David Lean; *sc*–Anthony Havelock-Allan, Ronald Neame, David Lean, from the play by Noël Coward; *cast*: Celia Johnson, Robert Newton, John Mills, Kay Walsh, Stanley Holloway, John Blythe; 111 mins.

Undercover: 1943; Ealing Studios; *prod*–Michael Balcon; *dir*–Sergei Nolbandov; sc–John Dighton, Monja Danischewsky; *st*–George Slocombe; *cast*: John Clements, Tom Walls, Stephen Murray, Mary Morris; 80 mins.

The Way Ahead: 1944; Two Cities; *prod*–John Sutro, Norman Walker; *dir*–Carol Reed; *sc*–Eric Ambler, Peter Ustinov; *cast*: David Niven, Billy Hartnell, Stanley Holloway,

Raymond Huntley, Hugh Burden, Leslie Dwyer, James Donald, Jimmy Hanley, John Laurie, Penelope Dudley Ward, Peter Ustinov; 115 mins.

The Way to the Stars (US: *Johnny in the Clouds*): 1945; Two Cities; *prod*–Anatole de Grunwald; *dir*–Anthony Asquith; *sc*–Terence Rattigan; *cast*: Michael Redgrave, John Mills, Rosamund John, Douglass Montgomery, Basil Radford, Bonar Colleano, Bill Owen, Trevor Howard, Jean Simmons; 109 mins.

We Dive at Dawn: 1943; Gainsborough Pictures; *prod*–Edward Black; *dir*–Anthony Asquith; *sc*–J. B Williams, Val Valentine; *cast*: John Mills, Eric Portman, Reginald Purdell, Niall MacGinnis, Cavan Watson; 98 mins.

Went the Day Well? (US: *48 Hours*): 1942; Ealing Studios; *prod*–Michael Balcon; *dir*–Alberto Cavalcanti; *sc*–John Dighton, Diana Morgan, Angus MacPhail; *st*–Graham Greene; *cast*: Leslie Banks, Frank Lawton, Elizabeth Allan, Valerie Taylor, Marie Lohr, C. V. France, Muriel George, Mervyn Johns, Thora Hird, Basil Sydney, Harry Fowler, Edward Rigby; 92 mins.

The Young Mr Pitt: 1942; Gainsborough/20th Century-Fox British Productions; *prod*–Edward Black; *dir*–Carol Reed; *sc*–Frank Launder, Sidney Gilliat; *cast*: Robert Donat, Robert Morley, Phyllis Calvert, John Mills, Herbert Lom; 118 mins.

Official feature and short-feature documentaries

The Big Pack: 1945; RAF Film Production Unit; *prod*–Derek Twist; *dir*–John Shearman; *sc*–Hugh Gray; 35 mins.

Burma Victory: 1945; Army Film and Photographic Unit; *prod*–David Macdonald; *dir*–Roy Boulting; *comm*–Frank Harvey; 62 mins.

Close Quarters: 1943; Crown Film Unit; *prod*–Ian Dalrymple; *dir/sc*–Jack Lee; *cast*: Officers and men of the Royal Navy; 75 mins.

Coastal Command: 1942; Crown Film Unit; *prod*–Ian Dalrymple; *dir/sc*–J. B. Holmes; *cast*: Officers and men of the RAF Coastal Command; 73 mins.

Desert Victory: 1943; Army Film and Photographic Unit and RAF Film Production Unit; *prod*–David Macdonald; *dir*–Roy Boulting; *sc/comm*–James Lansdale Hodson; 60 mins.

A Diary for Timothy: 1946; Crown Film Unit; *prod*–Basil Wright; *dir*–Humphrey Jennings; *sc*–Humphrey Jennings, E. M. Forster; *comm*–Michael Redgrave; 40 mins.

Ferry Pilot: 1941; Crown Film Unit; *prod*–Ian Dalrymple; *dir*–Pat Jackson; 35 mins.

Fires Were Started (*I Was A Fireman*): 1943; Crown Film Unit; *prod*–Ian Dalrymple; *dir/sc*–Humphrey Jennings; *cast*: George Gravett, Fred Griffiths, William Sansom, Johnny Houghton, Philip Wilson-Dickson, T. P. Smith, Joe Barker, Loris Rey (all members of the National Fire Service); 63 mins (theatrical version), 75 mins (nontheatrical version).

Journey Together: 1945; RAF Film Production Unit; *prod/dir*–John Boulting; *sc*–Terence Rattigan; *cast*: Richard Attenborough, Jack Watling, Edward G. Robinson, Bessie Love; 80 mins.

The New Lot: 1943; Army Kinematograph Service; *dir*–Carol Reed; *sc*–Eric Ambler, Peter Ustinov; *cast*: Raymond Huntley, Bernard Miles, Peter Ustinov, John Laurie, Geoffrey Keen, Robert Donat; 42 mins; training film.

Operational Height: 1943; RAF Film Production Unit; *prod*–Derek Twist; *dir/sc*–Arthur Taylor; 32 mins.

School for Danger (*Now It Can Be Told*): 1946; RAF Film Production Unit; *prod/dir*–Edward Baird; *cast*: Captain Harry Rée, Jacqueline Nearne; 86 mins.

The Silent Village: 1943; Crown Film Unit; *prod/dir/sc*–Humphrey Jennings; *cast*: Members of the South Wales Miners' Federation and people of Cwmgiedd; 36 mins.

Target for Tonight: 1941; Crown Film Unit; *prod*–Ian Dalrymple; *dir/sc*–Harry Watt; *cast*: Officers and men of the RAF Bomber Command; 50 mins.

The True Glory: 1945; British Army Film and Photographic Unit and American and Allied Film Services; *prod/dir*–Carol Reed, Garson Kanin; *sc*–Eric Maschwitz, Arthur Macrae, Jenny Nicholson, Gerald Kersh, Guy Trosper; *comm*–Robert Harris; 87 mins.

Tunisian Victory: 1944; Army Film and Photographic Unit and US Service Film Units; *prod/dir*–Hugh Stewart, Frank Capra; *sc*–James Lansdale Hodson, Anthony Veiller; *comm*–Leo Genn, Anthony Veiller, Bernard Miles, Burgess Meredith; 78 mins.

Wavell's 30,000: 1942; Crown Film Unit and Army Film and Photographic Unit; *prod*–Ian Dalrymple; *dir*–John Monck; *comm*–Colin Wills; 50 mins.

Western Approaches (US: *The Raider*): 1944; Crown Film Unit; *prod*–Ian Dalrymple; *dir/sc*–Pat Jackson; *cast*: Officers and men of the Allied Navies and the Merchant Navy; 82 mins.

Official shorts

ABCA: 1943; Army Film and Photographic Unit; *prod/dir*–Ronald Riley; *sc*–Jack Saward; *comm*–Geoffrey Sumner; 15 mins; non-theatrical.

All Hands: 1940; Ealing Studios; *prod*–Michael Balcon; *dir*–John Paddy Carstairs; *cast*: John Mills et al; 12 mins.

Arms From Scrap: 1942; British Movietone; *prod*–Gerald Sanger; *comm*–Leslie Mitchell; 9 mins.

ATS: 1941; Army Film Unit; *dir*–Hugh Stewart; 7 mins.

The Biter Bit: 1943; Coombe Productions; *prod*–Alexander Korda; *sc*–Michael Foot; *comm*–Ralph Richardson; 14 mins.

Britain at Bay: 1940; GPO Film Unit; *sc/comm*–J. B. Priestley; 8 mins.

Britain Can Take It!: see *London Can Take It!*

A Call to Arms: 1940; Denham and Pinewood; *prod/dir*–Brian Desmond Hurst; *sc*–Rodney Ackland; *cast*: Jean Gillie, Rene Ray; 5 mins.

Christmas Under Fire: 1941; Crown Film Unit; *dir*–Harry Watt; *sc/comm*–Quentin Reynolds; 7 mins.

Citizens' Advice Bureau: 1941; GB Screen Services; *prod*–Leslie Arliss; *dir*–Francis Searle; 8 mins.

Dai Jones Lends a Hand: 1941; Verity; *prod*–Jay Gardner Lewis; *dir*–Dan Birt; 5 mins.

Dangerous Comment: 1940; Ealing Studios; *prod*–Michael Balcon; *dir*–John Paddy Carstairs; 13 mins.

Dangers in the Dark: 1941; Public Relations Films; *dir*–Richard Massingham; 7 mins.

The Dawn Guard: 1941; Charter Films; *prod*–John Boulting; *dir*–Roy Boulting; *st*–Anna Reiner; *cast*: Percy Walsh, Bernard Miles; 7 mins.

Diary of a Polish Airman: 1942; Concanen; *prod*–Derrick de Marney; *dir*–Eugene Cekalski; 8 mins.

Eating Out with Tommy Trinder: 1941; Strand; *prod*–Donald Taylor; *dir*–Desmond Dickinson; *cast*: Tommy Trinder; 5 mins.

The Eighty Days: 1945; Crown Film Unit; *dir*–Humphrey Jennings; *sc/comm*–Ed Murrow; 14 mins.

A Few Ounces a Day: 1941; Paul Rotha Productions; *prod*–Paul Rotha; *dir*–Donald Alexander; *sc*–Henry Hallatt; 7 mins.

The First Days: 1939; GPO Film Unit; *prod*–Alberto Cavalcanti; *dir*–Humphrey Jennings, Harry Watt, Pat Jackson; *comm*–Robert Sinclair; 23 mins.

Food for Thought: 1940; Ealing Studios; *prod*–John Croydon; *dir*–Adrian Brunel; *cast*: Mabel Constanduros, Muriel George; 5 mins.

Free French Navy: 1942; Spectator; *prod*–Michael Hankinson; *dir*–Robin Carruthers; 7 mins.

From the Four Corners: 1941; Denham and Pinewood; *prod/dir*–Anthony Havelock-Allan; *sc*–Sidney Gilliat; *cast*: Private J. Johnston, Corporal W. Atkinson, Private R. Gilbert, Leslie Howard; 15 mins.

Go to Blazes: 1942; Ealing Studios; *prod*–Michael Balcon; *dir*–Walter Forde; *sc*–Diana Morgan, Angus MacPhail; *cast*: Will Hay; 5 mins.

Guests of Honour: 1941; Ealing Studios; *prod*–Alberto Cavalcanti; *dir*–Ray Pitt; 25 mins.

The Heart of Britain (US: *This Is England*): 1941; Crown Film Unit; *dir*–Humphrey Jennings; *comm*–Jack Holmes (domestic), Ed Murrow (American); 9 mins.

Jane Brown Changes Her Job: 1942; Verity; *prod*–Sydney Box, James Carr; *dir*–Harold Cooper; *cast*: Anne Firth; 9 mins.

Land Girl: 1942; Paul Rotha Productions; *prod*–Donald Alexander; *dir*–John Page; 7 mins.

Lift Your Head, Comrade: 1942; Spectator; *prod*–Basil Wright; *dir*–Michael Hankinson; *sc*–Arthur Koestler; 15 mins.

Listen to Britain: 1942; Crown Film Unit; *prod*–Ian Dalrymple; *dir*–Humphrey Jennings, Stewart McAllister; introduced by Leonard Brockington; 19 mins.

Lofoten: 1941; Crown Film Unit and Army Film Unit; *prod*–David Macdonald; *dir*–Walter Tennyson d'Eyncourt; *comm*–Anthony Kimmins; 7 mins.

London Can Take It!: 1940; GPO Film Unit; *dir*–Harry Watt, Humphrey Jennings; *sc/comm*–Quentin Reynolds; 10 mins. Shorter domestic version entitled *Britain Can Take It!*; 5 mins.

Men of the Lightship: 1940; GPO Film Unit; *prod*–Alberto Cavalcanti; *dir*–David Macdonald; *sc*–Hugh Grant; *cast*: Officers and men of the Royal Navy and Trinity House; 25 mins.

Miss Grant Goes to the Door: 1940; Denham and Pinewood; *prod/dir*–Brian Desmond Hurst; *sc*–Rodney Ackland; *st*–Thorold Dickinson, Donald Bull; *cast*: Mary Clare, Martita Hunt, Manning Whiley, Ivan Brandt; 7 mins.

Mr Proudfoot Shows a Light: 1941; 20th Century-Fox; *prod*–Edward Black; *dir*–Herbert Mason; *sc*–Sidney Gilliat; *cast*: Sydney Howard, Muriel George, Percy Walsh; 7 mins.

Newspaper Train: 1941; Realist Film Unit; *prod*–John Taylor; *dir*–Len Lye; *sc*–Merril Mueller; 6 mins.

Night Shift: 1942; Paul Rotha Productions; *prod*–Paul Rotha; *dir*–Jack Chambers; *sc*–Arthur Calder-Marshall; 15 mins; non-theatrical.

Northern Outpost: 1941; Army Film Unit; *prod*–David Macdonald; *dir*–Walter Tennyson d'Eyncourt; 9 mins.

The Nose Has It: 1942; Gainsborough; *prod*–Edward Black; *dir*–Val Guest; *cast*: Arthur Askey; 8 mins.

Now You're Talking: 1940; Ealing Studios; *prod*–Michael Balcon; *dir*–John Paddy Carstairs; *cast*: Sebastian Shaw, Dorothy Hyson; 12 mins.

Our Film: 1942; Denham Film Studios; *prod*–Ralph Bond; *cast*: John Slater et al; 10 mins.

Partners in Crime: 1942; Gainsborough Pictures; *prod*–Edward Black; *dir/sc*–Frank Launder, Sidney Gilliat; *cast*: Irene Handl, Robert Morley; 8 mins.

Rush Hour: 1942; 20th Century-Fox; *prod*–Edward Black; *dir*–Anthony Asquith; *cast*: Muriel George; 6 mins.

Salvage With A Smile: 1940; Ealing Studios; *prod*–Alberto Cavalcanti; *dir*–Adrian Brunel; 7 mins.

Seaman Frank Goes Back to Sea: 1942; Concanen; *prod*–Derrick de Marney; *dir*–Eugene Cekalski; *sc*–Terence de Marney; *cast*: Frank Laskier; 7 mins.

Shunter Black's Night Off: 1941; Verity; *prod*–Sydney Box, James Carr; *dir*–Maxwell Munden; *comm*–John Slater; 8 mins.

Squadron 992: 1940; GPO Film Unit; *prod*–Alberto Cavalcanti; *dir*–Harry Watt; *sc*–W. D. H. McCullough; *comm*–Lionel Gamlin; 25 mins.

Stricken Peninsula: 1944; Army Film and Photographic Unit and Seven League Productions; *dir*–Paul Fletcher; 15 mins.

They Also Serve: 1940; Realist Film Unit; *prod*–John Taylor; *dir*–R. I. Grierson; 8 mins.

They Keep the Wheels Turning: 1942; GB Screen Services; *dir*–Francis Searle; *sc*–Harold B. Goodwin; 9 mins.

The True Story of Lili Marlene: 1944; Crown Film Unit; *prod*–J. B. Holmes; *dir/sc*–Humphrey Jennings; *cast*: Marius Goring, Lucie Mannheim; 29 mins.

War in the East: 1942; Shell Film Unit; *prod*–Edgar Anstey; *dir*–R. K. Neilson Baxter; 6 mins.

Westward Ho! 1940: 1940; Denham and Pinewood; *dir*–Thorold Dickinson; *comm*–Donald Bull; 5 mins.

Words for Battle: 1941; Crown Film Unit; *prod*–Ian Dalrymple; *dir/sc*–Humphrey Jennings; 8 mins.

WVS: 1942; Verity; *prod*–Sydney Box; *dir*–Louise Birt; 22 mins; non-theatrical.

You're Telling Me: 1941; Paul Rotha Productions; *dir*–Bladon Peake; 7 mins.

Bibliography

Archival and unpublished document sources

Public Record Office, Kew, London

BT 64: The Board of Trade Manufactures Department, including records of the Cinematograph Films Council and general policy towards the film industry.
BW 4: British Council film production records.
FO 371: Correspondence files on British publicity abroad.
INF 1: General memoranda, correspondence and records of the Ministry of Information, including the Films Division.
INF 5: Records of film production by the GPO/Crown Film Unit.
INF 6: Records of film production for the Films Division, including the GPO/Crown Film Unit and other producers.
PREM 4: Churchill's wartime prime-ministerial correspondence, including files on propaganda and films.
WO 165: Records of the War Office Directorates, including the Directorate of Army Kinematography.

British Film Institute, London

Thorold Dickinson Collection; Humphrey Jennings Collection; Carol Reed Collection; Film Centre Collection.

Imperial War Museum, London

Ronald Tritton diary.

Other Sources

The Tom Harrisson-Mass Observation Archive (London: Harvester Press, microfilm, 1983).
Minutes of the British Film Producers' Association.

Published document sources

Parliamentary Debates: House of Commons, 5th Series (Hansard).
Parliamentary Debates: House of Lords, 5th Series (Hansard).
Report of the Committee on Cinematograph Films, Cmd 5320 (London: HMSO, 1936).
Thirteenth Report from the Select Committee on National Expenditure (London: HMSO, 1940).

Newspapers and periodicals

Daily Express; *Daily Mail*; *Daily Mirror*; *Daily Sketch*; *The Daily Telegraph*; *Evening News*; *The Listener*; *Manchester Guardian*; *The New Statesman and Nation*; *New York Times* (US); *Observer*; *Political Quarterly*; *Spectator*; *Sunday Express*; *The Sunday Times*; *The Times*

Film journals and trade papers

The Cinema; *The Cine-Technician*; *Daily Film Renter*; *Documentary News Letter*; *Kinematograph Weekly*; *Monthly Film Bulletin*; *Motion Picture Herald* (US); *Sight and Sound*; *Today's Cinema*; *Variety* (US)

Memoirs, diaries and letters

Ackland, Rodney and Elspeth Grant, *The Celluloid Mistress, or The Custard Pie of Dr. Caligari* (London: Allan Wingate, 1954).

Ambler, Eric, *Here Lies: An Autobiography* (London: Weidenfeld and Nicolson, 1985).

Balcon, Michael, *Michael Balcon Presents ... A Lifetime of Films* (London: Hutchinson, 1969).

Brunel, Adrian, *Nice Work: The Story of Thirty Years in British Film Production* (London: Forbes Robertson, 1949).

Capra, Frank, *The Name Above the Title: An Autobiography* (London: W. H. Allen, 1972).

Churchill, Winston S., *The Second World War. Volume IV: The Hinge of Fate* (London: Cassell, 1951; Penguin, 1985).

Clark, Kenneth, *The Other Half: A Self-Portrait* (London: John Murray, 1977; Hamish Hamilton, 1986).

Coward, Noël, *Future Indefinite* (London: William Heinemann, 1954).

Danischewsky, Monja, *White Russian – Red Face* (London: Victor Gollancz, 1966).

Duff Cooper, Alfred, *Old Men Forget* (London: Rupert Hart-Davis, 1957).

Halliwell, Leslie, *Seats in All Parts: Half a Lifetime at the Movies* (London: Granada, 1985).

Hodson, James Lansdale, *The Home Front* (London: Victor Gollancz, 1944).

— *The Sea and the Land* (London: Victor Gollancz, 1945).

Korda, Michael, *Charmed Lives: A Family Romance* (London: Allen Lane, 1980).

Nicolson, Nigel (ed.), *Harold Nicolson: Diaries and Letters, 1939–45* (London: Weidenfeld and Nicolson, 1970).

Olivier, Laurence, *Confessions of an Actor* (London: Weidenfeld and Nicolson, 1982; Sceptre, 1987).

Orwell, Sonia, and Ian Angus (eds), *The Collected Essays, Journalism and Letters of George Orwell. Volume 2: My Country Right or Left, 1940–1943* (London, 1968; Harmondsworth: Penguin, 1970).

— (eds), *The Collected Essays, Journalism and Letters of George Orwell. Volume 3: As I Please, 1943–1945* (London, 1968; Harmondsworth: Penguin, 1970).

Powell, Michael, *A Life in Movies: An Autobiography* (London: William Heinemann, 1986; Methuen, 1987).

Ustinov, Peter, *Dear Me* (London: William Heinemann, 1977).

Watt, Harry, *Don't Look at the Camera* (London: Paul Elek, 1974).

Biographies

Boyle, Andrew, *Only the Wind Will Listen: Reith of the BBC* (London: Hutchinson, 1972).

— *Poor, Dear Brendan: The Quest for Brendan Bracken* (London: Hutchinson, 1974).

Brownlow, Kevin, *David Lean* (London: Richard Cohen, 1996).

Howard, Ronald, *In Search of My Father: A Portrait of Leslie Howard* (London: William Kimber, 1981).

Kulik, Karol, *Alexander Korda: The Man Who Could Work Miracles* (London: W. H. Allen, 1975).

Macdonald, Kevin, *Emeric Pressburger: The Life and Death of a Screenwriter* (London: Faber and Faber, 1994).

Minney, R. J., *Puffin Asquith* (London: Leslie Frewin, 1973).

Moorehead, Caroline, *Sidney Bernstein: A Biography* (London: Jonathan Cape, 1984).

Wapshott, Nicholas, *The Man Between: A Biography of Carol Reed* (London: Chatto and Windus, 1990).

Books and monographs

Addison, Paul, *The Road to 1945: British Politics and the Second World War* (London: Jonathan Cape, 1975).

Aitken, Ian, *Film and Reform: John Grierson and the Documentary Film Movement* (London: Routledge, 1990).

Aldgate, Anthony, *Cinema and History: British Newsreels and the Spanish Civil War* (London: Scolar Press, 1979).

Aldgate, Anthony, and Jeffrey Richards, *Britain Can Take It: The British Cinema in the Second World War* (Oxford: Basil Blackwell, 1986; 2nd edn, Edinburgh: Edinburgh University Press, 1994).

Armes, Roy, *A Critical History of the British Cinema* (London: Secker & Warburg, 1978).

Arts Enquiry, *The Factual Film* (London: Political and Economic Planning/Oxford University Press, 1947).

Balcon, Michael, Ernest Lindgren, Forsyth Hardy, and Roger Manvell, *Twenty Years of British Film 1925–1945* (London: Falcon Press, 1947).

Balfour, Michael, *Propaganda in War, 1939–1945: Organisations, Policies and Publics in Britain and Germany* (London: Routledge and Kegan Paul, 1979).

Barr, Charles, *Ealing Studios* (Newton Abbot and London: Cameron & Tayleur/David & Charles, 1977; rev. edn, London: Studio Vista, 1993).

— (ed.), *All Our Yesterdays: 90 Years of British Cinema* (London: British Film Institute, 1986).

Bartlett, F. C., *Political Propaganda* (Cambridge: Cambridge University Press, 1940).

Bialer, Uri, *The Shadow of the Bomber: The Fear of Air Attack and British Politics* (London: Royal Historical Society, 1980).

Brown, Geoff, *Launder and Gilliat* (London: British Film Institute, 1977).

— *Walter Forde* (London: British Film Institute, 1977).

Brown, Geoff with Tony Aldgate, *The Common Touch: The Films of John Baxter* (London: British Film Institute, 1989).

Calder, Angus, *The People's War: Britain 1939–1945* (London: Jonathan Cape, 1969).

Christie, Ian, *Arrows of Desire: The Films of Michael Powell and Emeric Pressburger* (London: Waterstone, 1985; 2nd edn, London: Faber and Faber, 1994).

— (ed.), *Powell, Pressburger and Others* (London: British Film Institute, 1978).

— (ed.), *Powell and Pressburger: The Life and Death of Colonel Blimp* (London: Faber and Faber, 1994).

Cook, Christopher (ed.), *The Dilys Powell Film Reader* (Manchester: Carcanet, 1991).

Coultass, Clive, *Images for Battle: British Film and the Second World War, 1939–1945* (London and Toronto: Associated University Presses, 1989).

Cull, Nicholas John, *Selling War: The British Propaganda Campaign Against American 'Neutrality' in World War II* (Oxford: Oxford University Press, 1995).

Dickinson, Margaret and Sarah Street, *Cinema and State: The Film Industry and the British Government 1927–84* (London: British Film Institute, 1985).

Dickinson, Thorold, *A Discovery of Cinema* (London: Oxford University Press, 1971).

Doob, L. W., *Propaganda: Its Psychology and Technique* (New York: Henry Holt, 1935).

Fraser, Lindley, *Propaganda* (London: Oxford University Press, 1957).

Frayling, Christopher, *Things to Come* (London: British Film Institute, 1995).

Furhammar, Leif, and Folke Isaksson, *Politics and Film*, trans. Kersti French (London: Studio Vista, 1971).

Geduld, Harry M., *Filmguide to Henry V* (Bloomington: Indiana University Press, 1973).

Gifford, Denis, *The British Film Catalogue 1895–1970: A Guide to Entertainment Films* (Newton Abbot: David and Charles, 1973).

Gledhill, Christine and Gillian Swanson, (eds), *Nationalising Femininity: Culture, Sexuality and British Cinema in the Second World War* (Manchester: Manchester University Press, 1996).

Gough-Yates, Kevin, *Michael Powell: In Collaboration with Emeric Pressburger* (London: Faber and Faber, 1971).

Grant, Ian, *Cameramen at War* (Cambridge: Patrick Stephens, 1980).

Hardy, Forsyth (ed.) *Grierson on Documentary*, (London: 1946; rev. edn, London: Faber and Faber, 1966).

Harper, Sue, *Picturing the Past: The Rise and Fall of the British Costume Film* (London: British Film Institute, 1994).

Higson, Andrew, *Waving the Flag: Constructing a National Cinema in Britain* (Oxford: Clarendon Press, 1995).

Hillier, Jim and Alan Lovell, *Studies in Documentary* (London: Secker and Warburg, 1972).

Hodgkinson, Anthony W. and Rodney E. Sherastsky, *Humphrey Jennings: More Than a Maker of Films* (Hanover: University of New England Press, 1982).

Houston, Penelope, *Went the Day Well?* (London: British Film Institute, 1992).

Hurd, Geoff (ed.), *National Fictions: World War Two in British Films and Television* (London: British Film Institute, 1984).

Jackson, Kevin (ed.), *The Humphrey Jennings Film Reader* (Manchester: Carcanet, 1993).

Jennings, Mary-Lou (ed.), *Humphrey Jennings: Film-Maker, Painter, Poet* (London: British Film Institute/Riverside Studios, 1982).

Kardish, Lawrence (ed.), *Michael Balcon: The Pursuit of British Cinema* (New York: Museum of Modern Art, 1984).

Koppes, Clayton R., and Gregory D. Black, *Hollywood Goes to War: How Politics, Profits and Propaganda Shaped World War II Movies* (London: I.B.Tauris, 1988).

Lambert, R. S., *Propaganda* (London: Nelson and Sons, 1938).

Lant, Antonia, *Blackout: Reinventing Women for Wartime British Cinema* (Princeton: Princeton University Press, 1991).

Lejeune, Anthony (ed.), *The C. A. Lejeune Film Reader* (Manchester: Carcanet, 1991).

Lejeune, C. A., *Chestnuts in Her Lap, 1936–1946* (London: Phoenix House, 1947).

MacKenzie, A. J., *Propaganda Boom* (London: John Clifford, 1938).

MacKenzie, John M., *Propaganda and Empire: The Manipulation of British Public Opinion 1880–1960* (Manchester: Manchester University Press, 1984).

McLaine, Ian, *Ministry of Morale: Home Front Morale and the Ministry of Information in World War II* (London: George Allen and Unwin, 1979).

MacNab, Geoffrey, *J. Arthur Rank and the British Film Industry* (London: Routledge, 1993).

Manvell, Roger, *Film* (Harmondsworth: Penguin, 1944; rev. edn, 1946).

— *The Film and the Public* (Harmondsworth: Penguin, 1955).

— *Films and the Second World War* (London: J. M. Dent, 1974).

Marris, Paul (ed.), *BFI Dossier Number 16: Paul Rotha* (London: British Film Institute, 1982).

Marwick, Arthur, *The Nature of History* (London: Macmillan, 1970; 3rd edn, 1989).

— *The Home Front: The British and the Second World War* (London: Thames and Hudson, 1976).

Mayer, J. P., *Sociology of Film: Studies and Documents* (London: Faber and Faber, 1946).

— *British Cinemas and their Audiences* (London: Denis Dobson, 1948).

Morgan, Guy, *Red Roses Every Night* (London: Quality Press, 1948).

Murphy, Robert, *Realism and Tinsel: Cinema and Society in Britain 1939–1948* (London: Routledge, 1989).

Paris, Michael, *From the Wright Brothers to Top Gun: Aviation, Nationalism and Popular Cinema* (Manchester: Manchester University Press, 1995).

Parkinson, David (ed.), *Mornings in the Dark: The Graham Greene Film Reader* (Manchester: Carcanet, 1993).

Powell, Dilys, *Films Since 1939* (London: Longmans Green, 1947).

Priestley, J. B., *Postscripts* (London: William Heinemann, 1940).

Pronay, Nicholas and D. W. Spring (eds), *Propaganda, Politics and Film, 1918–45* (London: Macmillan, 1982).

Reeves, Nicholas, *Official British Film Propaganda During the First World War* (London: Croom Helm, 1986).

Rhode, Eric, *A History of the Cinema from its Origins to 1970* (London: Allen Lane, 1976).

Richards, Jeffrey, *The Age of the Dream Palace: Cinema and Society in Britain 1930–1939* (London: Routledge and Kegan Paul, 1984).

— *Thorold Dickinson: The Man and His Films* (London: Croom Helm, 1986).

— *Films and British National Identity: From Dickens to Dad's Army* (Manchester: Manchester University Press, 1997).

Richards, Jeffrey and Anthony Aldgate, *Best of British: Cinema and Society 1930–1970* (Oxford: Basil Blackwell, 1983).

Richards, Jeffrey, and Dorothy Sheridan (eds), *Mass-Observation at the Movies* (London: Routledge and Kegan Paul, 1987).

Riley, Norman, *999 And All That* (London: Victor Gollancz, 1940).

Robertson, James C., *The British Board of Film Censors: Film Censorship in Britain, 1896–1950* (London: Croom Helm, 1985).

— *The Hidden Cinema: British Film Censorship in Action, 1913–1975* (London: Routledge, 1989).

Robson, E. W. and M. M., *The Shame and Disgrace of Colonel Blimp: The True Story of the Film* (London: The Sidneyan Society, 1944).

Rotha, Paul, *Rotha on the Film: A Selection of Writings About the Cinema* (London: Faber and Faber, 1958).

— *Documentary Diary: An Informal History of the British Documentary Film, 1928–1939* (London: Secker and Warburg, 1973).

Rotha, Paul with Richard Griffith, *The Film Till Now: A Survey of World Cinema* (London: Jonathan Cape, 1930; rev. edn, London: Vision Press, 1949).

Rotha, Paul, with Sinclair Road and Richard Griffith, *Documentary Film* (London: Faber and Faber, 1936; 3rd edn, 1952).

Short, K. R. M. (ed.), *Feature Films as History* (London: Croom Helm, 1981).

— (ed.), *Film and Radio Propaganda in World War II* (London: Croom Helm, 1983).

Sussex, Elizabeth, *The Rise and Fall of British Documentary* (Berkeley and London: University of California Press, 1975).

Swann, Paul, *The British Documentary Film Movement, 1926–1946* (Cambridge: Cambridge University Press, 1989).

Taylor, A. J. P., *English History 1914–1945* (Oxford: Clarendon Press, 1965).

Taylor, Philip M., *Munitions of the Mind: A History of Propaganda from the Ancient World to the Present Day* (Manchester: Manchester University Press, 1995).

— (ed.), *Britain and the Cinema in the Second World War* (London: Macmillan, 1988).

Taylor, Richard, *Film Propaganda: Soviet Russia and Nazi Germany* (London: Croom Helm, 1979).

Thorpe, Frances, and Nicholas Pronay with Clive Coultass, *British Official Films in the Second World War: A Descriptive Catalogue* (Oxford: Clio Press, 1980).

Vaughan, Dai, *Portrait of an Invisible Man: The Working Life of Stewart McAllister, Film Editor* (London: British Film Institute, 1983).

Virilio, Paul, *War and Cinema: The Logistics of Perception*, trans. Patrick Camiller (London: Verso, 1989).

Welch, David, *Propaganda and the German Cinema, 1933–1945* (Oxford: Clarendon Press, 1983).

West, W. J. (ed.), *Orwell: The War Broadcasts* (London: Gerald Duckworth, 1985).

White, Amber Blanco, *The New Propaganda* (London: Victor Gollancz, 1939).

Wood, Linda, *The Commercial Imperative in the British Film Industry: Maurice Elvey, A Case Study* (London: British Film Institute, 1987).

Wright, Basil, *The Long View: A Personal Perspective on World Cinema* (London: Secker and Warburg, 1974).

Articles and chapters

Aldgate, Tony, 'Ideological Consensus in British Feature Films, 1935–1947', in K. R. M. Short (ed.), *Feature Films as History* (London: Croom Helm, 1981), pp 94–112.

— 'Mr Capra Goes to War: Frank Capra, the British Army Film Unit, and Anglo-American Travails in the Production of *Tunisian Victory*', *Historical Journal of Film, Radio and Television*, 11/1, March 1991, pp 21–39.

Badder, David, 'Powell and Pressburger: The War Years', *Sight and Sound*, 48/1, Winter 1978–79, pp 8–12.

Balcon, Michael, 'The British Feature Film during the War', *The Penguin Film Review*, 1/1, August 1946, pp 66–73.

Barr, Charles, 'War Record', *Sight and Sound*, 58/4, Autumn 1989, pp 260–5.

Buckman, Keith, 'The Royal Air Force Film Production Unit, 1941–45', *Historical Journal of Film, Radio and Television*, 17/2, June 1997, pp 219–44.

Chapman, James, '*The Life and Death of Colonel Blimp* (1943) Reconsidered', *Historical Journal of Film, Radio and Television*, 15/1, March 1995, pp 19–54.

— '"The Yanks Are Shown to Such Advantage": Anglo-American Rivalry in the Production of *The True Glory* (1945)', *Historical Journal of Film, Radio and Television*, 16/4, October 1996, pp 533–54.

Christie, Ian, 'The Colonel Blimp File', *Sight and Sound*, 48/1, Winter 1978–79, pp 94–112.

Colls, Robert and Philip Dodd, 'Representing the Nation: British Documentary Film, 1930–45', *Screen*, 26/1, Spring 1985, pp 21–33.

Coultass, Clive, 'British Feature Films and the Second World War', *Journal of Contemporary History*, 19/1, 1984, pp 7–22.

— '*Tunisian Victory* – a Film Too Late?', *Imperial War Museum Review*, 1, 1986, pp 64–73.

— 'The Ministry of Information and Documentary Film, 1939–45', *Imperial War Museum Review*, 4, 1989, pp 103–11.

— 'Film and Reality: the *San Demetrio* Episode', *Imperial War Museum Review*, 5, 1990, pp 79–85.

Ellis, John, 'Art, Culture, Quality: Terms for a Cinema in the Forties and Seventies', *Screen*, 19/3, Autumn 1978, pp 9–49.

— 'Victory of the Voice?', *Screen*, 22/2, Summer 1981, pp 69–72.

Hollins, T.J., 'The Conservative Party and Film Propaganda between the Wars', *English Historical Review*, 96/379, 1981, pp 359–69.

Jarvie, I. C., 'Fanning the Flames: anti-American Reaction to *Objective Burma* (1945)', *Historical Journal of Film, Radio and Television*, 1/2, 1981, pp 117–37.

— 'The Burma Campaign on Film: *Objective Burma* (1945), *The Stillwell Road* (1945) and *Burma Victory* (1945)', *Historical Journal of Film, Radio and Television*, 8/1, 1988, pp 55–73.

Kuhn, Annette, '*Desert Victory* and the People's War', *Screen*, 22/2, Summer 1981, pp 45–68.

Neale, Steve, 'Propaganda', *Screen*, 18/3, Autumn 1977, pp 9–40.

Poole, Julian, 'British Wartime Cinema Audiences: Audience Preference at the Majestic, Macclesfield', *Historical Journal of Film, Radio and Television*, 7/1, 1987, pp 15–34.

Porter, Vincent and Chaim Litewski, '*The Way Ahead*: Case History of a Propaganda Film', *Sight and Sound*, 50/2, Spring 1981, pp 110–16.

Pronay, Nicholas, and Jeremy Croft, 'British Film Censorship and Propaganda Policy during the Second World War', in James Curran and Vincent Porter (eds), *British Cinema History* (London: Weidenfeld and Nicolson, 1983, pp 144–63.

Rattigan, Neil, '*The Demi-Paradise* and Images of Class in British Wartime Films', in Wheeler Winston Dixon (ed.), *Re-Viewing British Cinema, 1900–1992: Essays and Interviews* (Albany: State University of New York Press, 1994, pp 83–93.

Richards, Jeffrey, 'Wartime Cinema Audiences and the Class System: the Case of *Ships With Wings* (1941)', *Historical Journal of Film, Radio and Television*, 7/2, 1987, pp 129–41.

Robertson, James C., 'British Film Censorship Goes to War', *Historical Journal of Film, Radio and Television*, 2/1, 1982, pp 49–64.

Robins, Kevin, Frank Webster and Michael Pickering, 'Propaganda, Information and Social Control', in Jeremy Hawthorn (ed.), *Propaganda, Persuasion and Polemic* (London: Edward Arnold, 1987, pp 1–17.

Rowson, Simon, 'A Statistical Survey of the Cinema Industry in Great Britain in 1934', *Journal of the Royal Statistical Society*, 99, 1936, pp 67–129.

Short, K. R. M., 'RAF Bomber Command's *Target for Tonight*', *Historical Journal of Film, Radio and Television*, 17/2, June 1997, pp 181–218.

Smith, Malcolm, 'Narrative and Ideology in *Listen to Britain*', in Jeremy Hawthorn (ed.), *Narrative: From Malory to Motion Pictures* (London: Edward Arnold, 1985, pp 145–57.

Sussex, Elizabeth, 'Cavalcanti in England', *Sight and Sound*, 44/4, Autumn 1975, pp 206–9.

— 'The Fate of Film F3080', *Sight and Sound*, 53/2, Spring 1984, pp 92–7.

Taylor, Philip M., 'Techniques of Persuasion: Basic Ground Rules of British Propaganda During the Second World War', *Historical Journal of Film, Radio and Television*, 1/1, 1981, pp 59–65.

Wenden, D. J. and K. R. M. Short, 'Winston S. Churchill: Film Fan', *Historical Journal of Film, Radio and Television*, 11/3, 1991, pp 197–214.

Young, John W., '*Henry V*, the Quai d'Orsay and the Well-Being of the Franco-British Alliance', *Historical Journal of Film, Radio and Television*, 7/3, 1987, pp 319–21.

Film Index

General Index